The CANOE

A LIVING TRADITION

Conceived by John Jennings

With contributions from
Eugene Arima
Hallie E. Bond
Steven C. Brown
David Finch
Don Gardner
Gwyneth Hoyle
C. Fred Johnston
Kenneth R. Lister
Ted Moores
Rick Nash
James Raffan

FIREFLY BOOKS

A FIREFLY BOOK

Published by Firefly Books Ltd., 2002

First Printing

National Library of Canada Cataloguing in Publication Data

Main entry under title:

    The canoe : a living tradition

Includes bibliographical references and index.
ISBN 1-55209-509-6
    1. Canoes and canoeing—Canada—History. I. Arima, E. Y.
(Eugene Yuji), 1938- II. Jennings, John, 1941-
VM353.C343 2002   386'.229   C2002-900755-0

Publisher Cataloging-in-Publication Data (U.S.)

Jennings, John.
    The canoe : a living tradition / conceived by John Jennings ;
with contributions from Eugene Arima, Hallie E. Bond, Steven C. Brown,
David Finch, Don Gardner, Gwyneth Hoyle, C. Fred Johnston,
Kenneth R. Lister, Rick Nash, Ted Moores, James Raffan.—1st ed.
Published in cooperation with the Canadian Canoe Museum.
[272] p. : ill. (some col.) , photos., maps ; cm.
Includes bibliographical references and index.
Summary: A comprehensive history of North American canoe traditions.
Includes contributions from eleven experts, photographs, maps and
step-by-step photographs showing the building process.
ISBN 1-55209-509-6
1. Canoes and canoeing. I. Canadian Canoe Museum. II. Title.
623.8/29 21   CIP   E98.J46 2002

Published in Canada in 2002 by
Firefly Books Ltd.
3680 Victoria Park Avenue
Toronto, Ontario M2H 3K1

Published in the United States in 2002 by
Firefly Books (U.S.) Inc.
P.O. Box 1338, Ellicott Station
Buffalo, New York 14205

Design: Bob Wilcox
Managing Editor: Charis Cotter
Photo Research: Vivien Leong, Anna Filippone

Printed and bound in Canada by
Friesens
Altona, Manitoba

*The Publisher acknowledges the financial support of the Government of Canada
through the Book Publishing Industry Development Program for its publishing activities.*

Produced in collaboration with the Canadian Canoe Museum.

ACKNOWLEDGMENTS

This book grew out of a collaboration between Firefly Books and the Canadian Canoe Museum. Michael Worek of Firefly initially approached me with the idea for the book. Since then, as the scope and complexity of the book increased enormously, he has remained supportive, encouraging and cajoling in exactly the right proportions. The authors represent the foremost experts in the respective fields of canoe and kayak scholarship and canoe culture. They enthusiastically contributed their expertise to the book in the interests of the Canoe Museum, and as the project developed and grew more complicated, they generously gave much more of their time than originally promised. I thank them for their patience and understanding.

With over four hundred images and twelve authors, the logistics involved in bringing this book to print were staggering. It took the combined skills of the outstanding production team from Firefly and the goodwill of many individuals, museums, archives and other institutions. Charis Cotter, the editor, presided over this increasingly complex project with a most impressive combination of determination, superb organization and tact. The other members of the Firefly team were equally delightful to work with. Vivien Leong and Anna Filippone, the photo researchers, were critical to the success of the book. Vivien's incredible thoroughness and relentless pursuit of photos was amazing. Bob Wilcox, the book's designer, needs very special recognition. At all times cheerful and unflappable, he transformed a huge mass of material into something visually coherent and stunning.

It was both exciting and illuminating to work with a photographer of the caliber of Michael Cullen, whose photographs of the craft of the Canadian Canoe Museum provide the visual anchor for the book. The early shaping and direction of the book owes much to Ramsay Derry. I especially want to thank him for his steady, exacting and wise advice.

The following people were particularly helpful: Tom Andrews, Chuck Arnold, Jim Bowman, Louis Campeau, Doug Cass, Bill Cogar, Grete Dalum-Tilds, David Désy, Heather Friedle, Andrea Gordon, Keld Hansen, Toni Harting, Valerie Hatten, Brenda Hobbs, Vickie Jensen, Mark Katzman, Tim Kent, Bill McLennan, Jim Meehan, Debra Moore, Antony Pacey, Tracy Paulhus, John Pemberton, Stéphanie Poisson, Ken Powell, Tanya Richard, Lynanne Rollins, Dan Savard, Virginia Smith, Vicky Turner, Thomas Vennum Jr., Alan Wilkinson, Richard A. Wood and Nicola Woods. Some artists and photographers were very generous with their donation of pictures: Stephen R. Braund, Joe David, Jun Hoshikawa, H.C. Petersen and Hilary Stewart.

Without the cooperation of museums and institutions around the world, we could not have completed the book. Special thanks go to: Adirondack Museum, American Museum of Natural History, Canadian Museum of Civilization, Glenbow Museum, Hudson's Bay Company, Mariners' Museum, McCord Museum, Museum of Anthropology at the University of British Columbia, National Archives of Canada, National Gallery of Canada, National Museum of Science and Technology, Old Fort William Historical Park, Ontario Science Centre, Prince of Wales Northern Heritage Centre, Provincial Archives of Manitoba, Rothmans, Benson & Hedges Inc., Royal British Columbia Museum, Royal Ontario Museum, Saffron Walden Museum in England, Sitka National Historical Park, the Viking Ship Museum in Roskilde, Denmark, and the Smithsonian Institution, in particular the National Anthropological Archives, the Department of Anthropology and the National Museum of American History.

The generous support from a very special anonymous patron of the Canoe Museum was crucial. This freed me from my teaching duties at Trent University so that I could work on the book. Those at the Canoe Museum that I would especially like to thank are Dawn McColl and Burke Penny, who were crucial in gathering archival images, and Rick Beaver, Neil Broadfoot, Ken Brown, Bill Byrick, Cathy Hooke, Nicola Jennings, Dale Standen, Jeremy Ward and Christie Wooh.

INTRODUCTION 8

The NATIVE CRAFT

BARK CANOES
    The Realm of the Birchbark Canoe *John Jennings* 14
    The Canoe Frontier *John Jennings* 26
    Building Birchbark Canoes *Rick Nash* 46
    Light Craft from the Great Northwest *David Finch and Don Gardner* 64
DUGOUTS
    Vessels of Life: Northwest Coast Dugouts *Steven C. Brown* 74
    Building Dugouts *Eugene Arima* 96
KAYAKS
    The Kayak and the Walrus *Kenneth R. Lister* 120
UMIAKS
    Building Umiaks *Eugene Arima* 138

The RECREATIONAL CANOE

    From Forest to Factory: Innovations and Mass Production *Ted Moores* 162
    Paddling for Pleasure in the Northeastern States *Hallie E. Bond* 194
    Fast Paddles and Fast Boats: The Origins of Canoe Racing *C. Fred Johnston* 212

PRESERVING the HISTORY of the CANOE

    The Scholar: Tappan Adney *John Jennings* 240
    The Collector: Kirk Wipper *Gwyneth Hoyle* 242

The CANOE: A LIVING TRADITION *James Raffan* 250

    GLOSSARY 252
    SOURCES AND FURTHER READING 254
    CONTRIBUTORS 258
    PICTURE SOURCES 261
    INDEX 264

MAPS

    Native Peoples 12
    Growing Area of the Birch Tree in North America 14
    Territory of the Hunter-Gatherer Peoples 17
    The Fur Trade Frontier 24
    Peterborough, Ontario and Surrounding Area 160
    Northeastern United States and Canada 161

INTRODUCTION

The canoe is an enduring symbol of wilderness and freedom throughout North America. Hand-made vessels moved people and goods for centuries before Europeans arrived, providing an excellent and practical mode of transportation that developed regionally to serve the needs of the Native peoples. Canoes were used by hunters, travelers, traders and warriors. The canoes of various regions went through many transformations after the Europeans came. In the eighteenth century birchbark canoes grew larger and wider to carry big loads of furs in the exploding fur trade market. Then in 1865 the canoe was made smaller and fitted with decks to become the *Rob Roy*, a little canoe designed by John MacGregor to carry him on long trips across Europe. In the 1850s the wooden building form was invented, using an overturned dugout as a mold, to create a method of building wooden canoes in quantity to satisfy the growing market of recreational paddlers. Factories sprang up in Peterborough, Ontario, in Maine and in New Brunswick, supplying cedar-strip canoes for surveyors, missionaries, hunters, Mounties and campers. The canoe was made lighter and longer for racing and was sometimes fitted out with a sail. In the latter half of the twentieth century aluminum, Kevlar and fiberglass were used to make canoes and kayaks, and the designs changed once again to accommodate the new materials.

But the North American Native canoe went through many transformations long before Samuel de Champlain decided it was the best way to get around in the immense new continent he was exploring. Across North America different Native groups developed the canoe to suit their needs and environment, making their boats from the materials at hand. Birchbark was used in the wide path across the central and northern half of the continent where the tree grew in huge forests that covered the landscape. The inferior elm bark was awkwardly wrapped around a frame further south where birch trees weren't available. In the cold, unforested regions of the Arctic, driftwood, stunted trees and sealskin were used to build kayaks, with the distinctive characteristic of covered decks. Huge red cedars and gigantic spruce were felled to carve dugouts on the wet and rainy west coast.

The shape and size of Native watercraft varied according to their environment and purpose. The Mi'kmaqs on the east coast built carefully designed long birchbark canoes with inward sloping upper sides (tumblehome) to maneuver through the swells of the Atlantic Ocean on their fishing expeditions. The Algonquin, Montagnais, Cree and Ojibwa crafted beautiful, featherlight birchbark canoes that were easy to portage over the rough terrain between the rivers of the northeastern and central regions of the birchbark belt. Northwest of Hudson Bay, where trees were stunted, the Dogrib people built small, light canoes, often patching the bark together from birch or spruce trees, because the trees were too small to provide the large sections of bark used in canoe making further south. The Inuit hunted seals in the icy waters of the Arctic in sleek kayaks, boats that were easy to negotiate through the ocean, sturdy enough to carry home heavy loads, but light enough to transport over the ice. Another, lesser-known cousin of the canoe in the north, was the umiak, called the "women's boat": a large, wide boat built on a wooden frame lashed together and covered with sealskin or walrus hide. These were used for whale and big game hunting, war parties and transporting people and their goods over long distances. On the west coast the Native peoples designed their own forms of the ocean-going dugout for whale hunting, fishing and warfare.

When the French arrived in the early seventeenth century, they quickly adapted Native canoes to their own use. Soon huge, thirty-six-foot Montreal canoes were being paddled by teams of voyageurs across hundreds of miles, laden with beaver pelts to be made into hats and other products, bound for the European markets. With white settlement the canoe began to have a new role as a recreational vessel, and builders experimented with various methods to produce canoes in quantity. Canoe races were held at local regattas and the American Canoe Association, then the Canadian Canoe Association, were founded, and the classification of boats in races became a science. Many refinements and design innovations were developed to make the boats lighter and faster. The international sport of canoe and kayak racing was born.

Anthropologists and historians study canoes to understand the cultures that used them. The materials and building methods and the design of the boats can reveal valuable information about how the Native peoples survived in what was often a very harsh environment. In this book, twelve authors, each an expert in his or her field, write about different canoes, kayaks and umiaks in North America: how they were built, how they were used and how they affected the history of this continent. The design of these boats is described in detail in terms of their function, with the traditional methods of building the craft carefully explained.

By their very nature, canoes are transitory. Birchbark and animal skins deteriorate quickly when exposed to the elements. For a long time people did not consider them worthy of preserving, but in the twentieth century a movement began to conserve our history as embodied in the canoe. Two of the contributors to that history are Tappan Adney and Kirk Wipper. Tappan Adney was a scholar who singlehandedly recorded and saved hundreds of canoe designs. Working with decaying specimens, drawings and oral accounts, he built perfect models. Kirk Wipper, who ran a children's camp in central Ontario, began to rescue canoes from across the continent, and over nearly forty years he built up one of the largest collections of canoes in the world. When it outgrew the log building it was housed in at his camp, the Canadian Canoe Museum was created and a permanent home was found for the collection in Peterborough, Ontario.

Many of the vintage canoes from the Canoe Museum grace the pages of this book. Northern birchbarks, Naskapi crooked canoes, Salish dugouts, Greenland kayaks, Peterborough cedar strips and Old Town wood-canvas canoes drift through the chapters, perfect unto themselves, highly functional, energy efficient, lovingly crafted boats that all have a story to tell. Throughout the centuries and its many transformations in North America, the canoe has evolved and endured, a living tradition that continues to serve and delight the people who take it on the water.

The NATIVE CRAFT

For thousands of years the lives of the Native peoples in what was to become Canada and the United States were largely defined by water. In a land of rivers, the canoe developed as the most practical vehicle for transportation, hunting and communication. Made from the most appropriate materials that were available, the design and construction of vessels changed from region to region with the climate and geography.

Birchbark was one of the most sought-after building materials, prized for its strength and flexibility. From the east coast and throughout the northern central region, Native peoples shaped their birchbark canoes according to their need, whether it be ocean fishing or negotiating the turbulent rapids on a river. On the west coast huge cedar trees were transformed into majestic dugout ocean canoes, used for hunting whales, fishing and carrying travelers and freight. In the far north, the Inuit perfected the kayak: a swift hunter's boat made from sealskin stretched and sewn over a light wood frame. A much larger skin boat, the umiak, transported hunting parties or their families and possessions over long distances.

Whatever the material, the canoe was a triumph of uniting form and function: a vehicle of great beauty and rugged serviceability. Inevitably, it played a vital role in European exploration and settlement. When the French came to North America, they adopted it as their vehicle of transportation, forging war and trade alliances with various Native groups to further their interests. The huge Montreal canoe and the North canoe were created to carry furs over vast distances on their way to the European market.

Ever adaptable, the canoe has undergone many transformations, but in several Native communities there have been revivals of the traditional building methods, with groups coming together to build canoes the way their ancestors did. Sometimes modern tools and materials are used to hasten the process, but the spirit of craftsmanship and community effort have been preserved. While the canoe remains a universal and enduring symbol of wilderness and independence, it continues in its importance to the Native world, as a living tradition to be respected and conserved.

BARK CANOES

The Realm of the Birchbark Canoe 14
JOHN JENNINGS

The Canoe Frontier 26
JOHN JENNINGS

Building Birchbark Canoes 46
RICK NASH

Light Craft from the Great Northwest 64
DAVID FINCH AND DON GARDNER

DUGOUTS

Vessels of Life: Northwest Coast Dugouts 74
STEVEN C. BROWN

Building Dugouts 96
EUGENE ARIMA

KAYAKS

The Kayak and the Walrus 120
KENNETH R. LISTER

UMIAKS

Building Umiaks 138
EUGENE ARIMA

NATIVE PEOPLES

Native peoples whose canoes, kayaks, umiaks and dugouts are referred to in the text. These locations are approximate, circa 2000.

Polar Inuit

West Greenlanders

East Greenlanders

glulingmiut

Iglulingmiut

Nunatsiarmiut

Labrador Inuit

Nunavimiut

Innu

East Cree

Montagnais

Mi'kmaq

Passamaquoddy

Northern Ojibwa

Algonquin

Maliseet

Southeastern Ojibwa

Abenaki

Iroquois

GROWING AREA OF
THE BIRCH TREE IN
NORTH AMERICA

The REALM of the BIRCHBARK CANOE

JOHN JENNINGS

FACING PAGE: Growing area of the birch tree in North America. A map of the range of the birch tree is essentially a map of Canada. The birchbark canoe was used universally from the Atlantic to the Pacific and from the Arctic to the northern United States. Trade bark was one of the important trading articles of northern peoples, so the birchbark canoe was found well beyond the limits of the birch tree. During the fur trade era, birchbark canoes were used to the mouth of the Mississippi River and, in the west, as far south as the tributaries of the Columbia River.

ABOVE: 1850 Chippewa Long-nose birchbark canoe, fifteen feet, ten inches long and forty-two inches wide, from Leech Lake, Minnesota, circa 1850. The canoe is typical of the Lake of the Woods Ojibwa people and may have been traded from them. The five thwarts in this craft are unusual.

The northern half of the continent of North America is a land of forest and water. This region contains far more than its fair share of the fresh water of the world and has the world's longest coastline. For thousands of years the lives of the Native peoples in this region were largely defined by water. In no other part of the world have water and the canoe had such a huge influence on both the original indigenous culture and the development of its history after European contact. Canoes and water are found around the world, but only in upper North America have indigenous craft been used by later European migrants to create a nation. The unique geography of this area and its special connection to the canoe define the boundaries of this book.

Without doubt, the most important invention of early North America, and one essentially unique to the continent, was the bark canoe—but not just any bark canoe. Canoes fashioned from bark were used around the world: elm, chestnut, hickory, beech, spruce, cottonwood, bass-wood, eucalyptus, purpleheart and, of course, birch. But only in North America was the bark canoe developed to such perfection that, after European contact, it continued, unaltered except in size, to be the central element in the development of what is now Canada. All this was only possible with one kind of bark—the bark of the birch tree.

Of all the different kinds of bark in the world, only the bark of the birch is capable of sophisticated shaping into elegant and subtle forms. The reason is deceptively simple. All canoe building bark is longitudinally grained, or "long-grained," and thus cannot be cut transversely and shaped—except for the birch. The white, or canoe, birch has a grain that is transverse, running around the tree rather than along the line of vertical growth. Unlike many other barks, birchbark does not shrink or stretch and is remarkably strong. It can be manipulated in different ways and a canoe can be fashioned from many separate sheets. When stitched and gummed, these

15

sheets are as strong and watertight as a single sheet.

When combined with ribs and sheathing of cedar and binding of spruce root, the Native birchbark canoe became a triumph of design and engineering, tough enough to cope with the turbulent waterways of the Canadian Shield and easily repaired from the surrounding forests. So successful was this basic design that when the European "carpentered" canoe was developed in the 1850s, it was essentially the same shape. Only the materials and method of construction differed.

A map of the range of the white birch is essentially the map of Canada. The white birch is found from coast to coast and from the Canadian Arctic to slightly below the American border. Its range dips down into American territory as far south as Long Island in New York State on the east, and in a line to the west through central Michigan, Wisconsin and Minnesota. Then it skirts north of the Great Plains and drops down again west of the Rocky Mountains into Idaho and Washington.

The geography of this area, largely determined by the Ice Ages, also has a unique connection with water. The predominant feature of the region, the Canadian Shield, comprises almost three-quarters of Canada, from Labrador to the Rocky Mountains. It is a land of elemental and brooding beauty. The receding glaciers left a series of vast lakes and connecting rivers—dubbed the "Necklace"—which stretch from the St. Lawrence on the Atlantic to the mouth of the Mackenzie River in the Arctic. Three vast drainage systems, the St. Lawrence–Great Lakes system, the Hudson and James Bay system and the Mackenzie River system made this an ideal region for the canoe. These river systems defined much of the communication and history of the area.

Water dictated the patterns of life. The vast arterial system of rivers and lakes and the unlimited presence of birchbark for canoes created an ideal setting for hunting, trapping and communication by water and canoe. This landscape, and the limited possibilities for agriculture in

A group of Montagnais building a canoe on the north shore of the St. Lawrence River. This is one of the earliest photos of Native canoe building. The Montagnais were intermediaries in the fur trade between the French and the Cree of northern Quebec.

much of the region were to create a very different set of dynamics for the French colonizers than was the case in most of the hemisphere. In the St. Lawrence Valley, as historian Donald Creighton pointed out, agriculture "struggled with an ineffectual persistence against the lures of the fur trade." Initially, instead of coveting the land, the French quickly accommodated themselves to the existing Native patterns of hunting and trade and soon exploited the region's foremost economic opportunity—the trade in furs.

For at least twenty thousand years, this had been a region of hunters. Agriculture did exist here and there below the southern limit of the Shield, but usually it augmented hunting, trapping and fishing. Certainly the Huron, Petun, Neutral and Odawa (Ottawa) of southern Ontario practiced extensive agriculture, as did the Iroquois of the Great Lakes region, growing corn, beans, squash and tobacco, but they were in the minority in a vast land of dense forests and waterways that determined that commerce and communication were mostly by water.

Because of this geography, which covered most of the region except for the northern extension of the Great Plains, travel was mostly by soft water in summer and by hard water in winter. In the open season, the bark canoe was the principal means of communication and trade across the continent. In winter, the same river routes were used with snowshoe and toboggan.

Archeological evidence shows that articles such as obsidian, used for making tools, traveled over great distances, probably by canoe, and was traded from one people to another. There were, for instance, very elaborate canoe trading systems in the eastern part of the continent, ranging from the Mi'kmaq and Maliseet on the east coast to the land beyond the Great Lakes and from Hudson Bay to the Mississippi River.

When Europeans arrived in the northern part of the continent, they found ancient routes linking well established trade patterns across the continent and soon realized that in this region, the canoe was the defining element in Native life. It was clear to the early French explorers that the birchbark canoe was the ideal craft for the waterways of the continent. First Jacques Cartier in the 1530s and later Samuel de Champlain in the early 1600s found that heavy and awkward rowing craft were useless on the interior waterways of North America. It was essential to survival in the heart-stopping rapids of America's rivers to have a craft that faced in the direction of travel and could maneuver easily. The lightness of birchbark was also a necessity on the frequent portages.

LEFT: A Mi'kmaq petroglyph (rock carving) from Fairy Bay, Kejimkujik National Park, Nova Scotia. Native petroglyphs and pictographs (rock paintings) are found across the continent and usually depict the culture and legends of the Native peoples. Those in Canada are often found along river routes.

BELOW: Today the territory of the hunter-gatherer peoples has shrunk, in most cases, to tiny sanctuaries. Only in Canada and Alaska, interior Australia and the Amazon rain forest of Brazil are there still significant hunting areas. Canada, with only five percent of its territory arable, and Alaska, with virtually no arable land, possess more hunting territory than all the rest of the world put together.

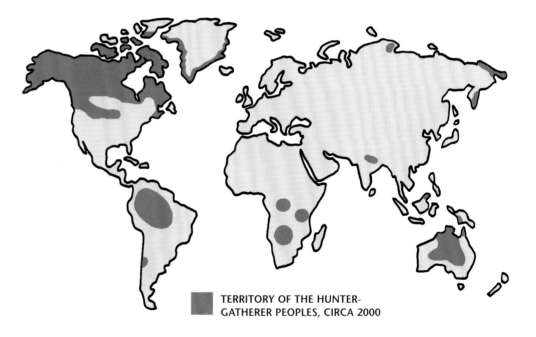

TERRITORY OF THE HUNTER-GATHERER PEOPLES, CIRCA 2000

ABOVE: *Ojibwa Encampment* by T. Mower Martin, 1880. The canoes are larger than the average Native canoe and the lack of curve in the bow and the stern would indicate that they are eastern Ojibwa canoes. The wigwams are also constructed of birchbark.

RIGHT: This photograph of a Cree paddler was taken by Edward S. Curtis at the end of the nineteenth century. Many of Curtis' photographs are posed, but they still depict Native life very accurately and are invaluable for giving us a detailed knowledge of Native peoples and the artifacts of the time.

The Hunting Cultures of North America

Europeans came to North America to establish frontiers of agriculture and commerce. As Hugh Brody has shown in his book *The Other Side of Eden*, this influx was a rather belated part of a global movement of agricultural migrants, "perhaps the most profound of all changes in human history," which, he claims, began in Greece at least ten thousand years ago. Europeans arrived in the New World to settle the land or to exploit its riches. Over the next several centuries, the original hunter-gatherer cultures of the western hemisphere in most cases disappeared, either dispossessed or absorbed into colonial society as cheap labor. The justification for these actions by the Christian peoples of Europe was that hunters were not using the land as God ordained. The God of the European was keen on efficient land use and the canoeing peoples of North America fell well short of the mark. They were accused of being nomads who wandered the land and thus had no right to it; it was God's will that the Garden be made to flower. But as Brody has shown so compellingly, these newcomers were really the nomads, not the hunting peoples of America who, as a matter of survival, knew every geographic feature of their land and had a deep respect for the natural world and an intimate relationship with the other creatures who shared their homeland. Unlike Europeans, who saw man at the center of the universe, the hunting peoples believed in a cosmological order with humans as only one of the reciprocal forces in a harmonious universe. The Europeans conveniently forgot that when Adam and Eve were expelled from the Garden, their punishment was to become agriculturists.

In most parts of the world, except in upper North America, hunters have been pushed aside by this agricultural frontier and have largely disappeared. But a map of where hunting cultures continue to exist today shows that these cultures, which probably dominated upper North America for at least a few thousand years before the arrival of Europeans, still persist in a vast region, twenty-five hundred miles across, from the eastern shores of Canada to Alaska, north of the limits of agriculture. Thus the geography that created this special place of the canoe has continued to keep agriculture at bay and has allowed hunting cultures to survive. Only in the interior of Australia and in the rapidly receding rain forests of the Amazon are other significant hunting areas still to be found. The hunting territory of Canada and Alaska today, according to Brody, is larger than all others in the world put together.

These hunting cultures, from the Atlantic to the Rockies above the line of agriculture, were organized socially, politically and economically into small units, based on kinship, egalitarianism and a division of labor between the sexes. Larger units could not function in hunting cultures. Gatherings of related groups usually took place in the summer at some traditional canoe stopping place for trading and socializing.

The map of North American hunting societies mirrors the map of the range of the birch tree and again emphasizes why this one area of the world has a special relationship with the canoe. It was not happenstance that when the Native craft was transformed into its European counterpart in the mid-nineteenth century, it developed in Peterborough, where the European farming frontier met the country of the Canadian Shield, and in the rugged country at the lower limits of the hunters' world in Maine and New Brunswick, and in a band below the Great Lakes from the Adirondacks of New York State to Minnesota.

The Birchbark Canoe

We owe most of our knowledge of the bark canoes of this region to one definitive book, Tappan Adney's *The Bark Canoes and Skin Boats of North America,* the result of a lifetime of research. Adney's voluminous notes and a preliminary partial draft were turned into the bible of the bark canoe after his death by Howard Chapelle, Curator of Transportation at the Smithsonian Institution.

Adney's papers contain a fascinating discussion of bark canoe types around the world. He found archeological evidence that birchbark craft had existed in western and northern Europe during the Stone Age. He claimed that bark canoes were found in only five other areas in the world: the land of the Ainu in Japan, the Amur Valley of Manchuria, the Orinoco River of Venezuela, Tierra del Fuego in Chile and Argentina, and Australia. He also mentioned a bark canoe that the explorer David Livingstone had seen in the Congo.

A Cree camp at Fort George, District of Ungava, 1902. Fort George, at the mouth of the Fort George River, is about halfway up the east side of James Bay. The teepee here is made of canvas, but birchbark continues to be used for building canoes. The canoe in the background is a "crooked canoe," very similar to the extreme modern "playboats" used for shooting rapids that most sane people would portage around. The crooked canoe was used in rivers with many rapids and also in the open water of James Bay, where the high ends could deflect waves. They were horrible to maneuver in wind.

This model of a canoe from the Amur Valley of Asia is virtually identical in shape to the Kutenai canoe of the interior region of British Columbia (see page 245). Nowhere else in the world are bark canoes of this shape found. It is, of course, tempting to speculate on the possibilities of the Amur and Kutenai people being related, via the land bridge between Siberia and Alaska during ancient times. This type of canoe was fast, though rather unstable, and was used in rivers and lakes where rapids were not an issue.

But this was an isolated sighting, so he did not include it as a type.

It would seem, however, that most of these craft were not very sophisticated. The Congolese craft described by Livingstone was a "crude affair"; the Australian eucalyptus bark canoe took several forms, from a saucer-shaped sheet to a well built sea-going canoe; the Orinoco River craft was a very primitive one formed from a sheet of purple-heart tree bark; the beech bark craft of Tierra del Fuego was similar to the reed boat of Peru and disappeared when European tools came to the area. The Ainu canoes of Japan, shaped somewhat like Chinese junks, did not have an enduring influence. Only the birchbark canoes of the Amur Valley of Manchuria were refined, and Adney was clearly fascinated by their striking similarity to the sturgeon-nosed craft of the lower British Columbia mainland. He was convinced that there must be a connection between them.

All these bark craft, according to Adney, had no continuing historical importance. Only in North America did the bark canoe reach near perfection and play an important role in the development of later European craft. It shared this distinction with the Inuit kayak.

Most of Adney's research involved the Native bark craft of the continent. These he divided into three basic categories: the eastern woodland craft, stretching from the Mi'kmaq and Maliseet of the east coast to the western Cree in Manitoba; the Athapaskan craft of the Mackenzie-Yukon region of the northwest, and the sturgeon-nosed craft of the Kutenai in the British Columbia interior.

The bark canoes of the eastern seaboard, ranging from the Maritime provinces to Maine, came in two forms: ocean-going canoes and canoes for river travel. The Mi'kmaq and Maliseet of this area are generally considered to have been the finest bark canoe builders on the continent. When Europeans arrived, the Mi'kmaq occupied territory from the Gaspé Peninsula in Quebec to part of New Brunswick, including Prince Edward Island and Nova Scotia. They and their Maliseet neighbors were hunting and fishing peoples who spent much of their time on the ocean, hunting seals, porpoises, walruses, swordfish, small whales, sturgeon, salmon, cod and eels in large canoes up to twenty-four feet long. Inland they hunted in smaller canoes for moose, bear and caribou.

The Maliseet occupied most of New Brunswick, with tribal offshoots as far south as the Penobscot and Kennebec rivers in Maine. Their settlements were centered on the St. John River in New Brunswick, where later the Chestnut Canoe Company would become famous for adapting the Native canoe shape to the modern era. They had originally ranged further south but were pushed north during colonial times by the Penobscot and Kennebec, later known as the Abenaki, who in turn had been displaced by American settlers. The Maliseet, like the Mi'kmaq, spent much time on the ocean and developed large canoes capable of maneuvering on heavy seas. They were closely related to their southern neighbors, the Passamaquoddy of Maine, who built almost identical canoes.

The Abenakis, from the region of Maine and New Hampshire, were the most southerly of the birchbark

builders. Those from the area around the Penobscot and Kennebec rivers were to have an important influence on American canoe building traditions. Many of the western Abenaki drifted north to finally settle on the St. François River in Quebec, just east of Montreal, and became known as the "St. Francis" people. They held a strong animosity for Americans and became staunch allies of the French in their raids on New England. The canoes of the Abenaki were fairly similar to those of the Maliseet.

Little is known of the other people of this region, since they were exterminated and left few traces of their canoes. When Europeans arrived, the Beothuk of Newfoundland retreated into the interior, but they had the bad luck to inhabit an island where escape was impossible. They were completely wiped out; the last Beothuk died in 1839. They are thought to have built canoes that were quite distinctive, but no one really knows because none has survived. Somewhat vague descriptions have been left to us and toy canoes were found in the mid-nineteenth century in a boy's grave at Pilley's Tickle, Notre Dame Bay, appropriately by a man named Samuel Coffin. But the contemporary descriptions and the toy canoes do not give accurate details of what would appear to be a very distinctive canoe, with high pointed ends and a hump amidships, almost like a suspension bridge. There seems to be agreement that the canoe was V-bottomed and designed to take ballast on the open seas.

The canoes of the eastern subarctic constituted a type, differing from each other in bow and stern profiles but otherwise quite similar. This group of canoes was found from northeastern Quebec and Labrador to northeastern Alberta and south from the St. Lawrence Valley to the Sioux and Assiniboine of the western Plains. They were built for portaging and maneuvering in rapids. Thus they were light and all had a degree of rocker (curved bottom) for easy handling. The main Native groups of this vast area included the Naskapi of northern Quebec and Labrador and the Montagnais of the north shore of the St. Lawrence (collectively known as the Innu); the eastern Cree of Hudson Bay; the Algonquins and Tête de Boule of the northern tributaries of the upper St. Lawrence Valley and Ottawa River; the Odawa (Ottawa) and Nipissing of Ontario; the Ojibwa (called Chippewa in the United States and Saulteaux in the region of Lake Winnipeg), who occupied territory from Ontario to Lake Winnipeg and south of the Great Lakes; and the western Cree, who were found in the area stretching from the western side of James Bay to Lake Athabasca in northeastern Alberta. The line of division between the eastern and western Cree was roughly the Moose-Missinaibi river system, which joins James Bay to Lake Superior at Michipicoten. In fur trade days this route from Moose Factory on James Bay to Michipicoten became a major artery.

All these peoples lived above the line of agriculture and existed mainly by hunting, fishing and trapping. Throughout this region the birchbark canoe was universal, but to the north, as the birch tree became smaller, spruce bark was often substituted. Spruce bark was quite adaptable to the building of canoes and was actually preferred to birchbark at the extreme range of the birch, where birchbark became thin or the trees so small that many sheets of bark were necessary for one canoe.

For some people in this region no record of their canoes has survived. The Huron, who were almost obliterated by the Iroquois, and the Sioux and Assiniboine, who increasingly became horse people, certainly built canoes but have left no trace of their design. The Huron, in particular, were known as canoe traders. They were exterminated largely because the Iroquois wanted to replace them as middlemen in the fur trade with the French. The land of the Huron in southern Ontario had been at the crossroads of the canoe trade and the Huron language was the *lingua franca* of Native trade in the Great Lakes region. The Iroquois raided their settlements for their canoes, leaving behind their distinctly inferior elm bark canoes.

The Iroquois, some of whom had been in the St. Lawrence Valley when Cartier visited, had consolidated their territory by the time of Champlain in the early seventeenth century in the area of the Mohawk River and the Finger Lakes region of New York State. Being

below the range of the birch tree, they were not originally known as canoe people. When many of them migrated to Canada, pushed out of American territory by the settlement frontier, they settled in Catholic missions around Montreal or on land grants given to them by the British Government after the American Revolution on the Bay of Quinte and on the Grand River in southern Ontario. Those near Montreal became expert birchbark canoe builders and elite voyageurs. As many as three hundred went west with the fur trade as contract trappers and eventually settled there among other Native groups.

The divide between the eastern woodland peoples and those of the northwest followed the watershed between the Arctic and Hudson Bay. In the northwest, there were essentially three types of bark canoe. The first bore some resemblance to that of the eastern woodlands. A second type was closer to the Inuit kayak both in shape and construction, often having some form of decking. The third type, the sturgeon-nosed canoe of lower British Columbia and Washington, was found only in a small area and differed significantly from all other canoes on the continent in the shape of its ends.

The canoeing peoples of the northwest were mostly Athapaskan speaking peoples—Chipewyan, Slavey, Dogrib, Beaver, Yellowknife, Gwich'in (Kutchin, Loucheux), Hare, Tanana, Han, Tuchone, Kaska, Secani, Tahltan and Wet'suwet'en (Carrier)—who lived by hunting caribou, moose, bison and migratory birds and also fished extensively. Since the birchbark of the northwest near the tree line was somewhat inferior, canoes in this region were often built of spruce bark. Near the coast, the Inuit built some bark canoes for use on rivers or covered their canoes with skin.

The first type of canoe, the cargo or family canoe that was built extensively by the Chipewyan, Dogrib and Slavey, was usually from sixteen to twenty-two feet long and bore a similarity to eastern canoes—and may indeed have been influenced by them. It is known that in the pre-contact era, trade goods traveled over very long distances, so it is only logical that there would be outside influences on canoe building as well.

The second kayak-type canoe was essentially a hunting craft and was usually lighter and shorter. It often had decking at one or both ends and, unlike most other canoes, was not symmetrical. Like the Inuit kayak, it was usually broadest in the rear. Unlike the sea-going kayak, it was shorter and more maneuvrable for chasing down zigzagging caribou as they crossed rivers.

TOP: A Montagnais/Cree canoe from the Lac St.-Jean region, which is part of the Saguenay River area of eastern Quebec, circa 1900.

BOTTOM: Ojibwa women, in northern Manitoba circa 1900. Women usually sat in the bottom of canoes and used very short paddles.

The sturgeon-nosed canoes of lower British Columbia and Washington were confined to the Kutenai and interior Salish. Since western birchbark beyond the Rocky Mountains was distinctly inferior, these canoes were sometimes constructed from other bark: spruce, fir, white pine or balsam. These were fast but unstable canoes and are now considered more a curiosity than an important type. The primary interest of these canoes to the historian and anthropologist is their striking similarity to the Manchurian birchbark canoe of the Amur Valley (just north of Japan), one of the few bark canoes found outside North America. The similarities both in shape and in construction do provide rather compelling evidence of a migration at some time between Asia and North America.

On the west coast, where good birchbark was scarce but where huge cedars grew in the coastal rain forests, dugouts replaced bark canoes. Like the sea-going birchbark canoes of the Mi'kmaq and Maliseet, they were used for hunting. But the great canoes of the Pacific were built for whaling, which was beyond the capacity of a bark canoe.

The Legacy of the Birchbark Canoe

The birchbark canoe has largely disappeared from the North American continent, except as a very expensive novelty. But its legacy lives on in the modern canoe. The shapes of the Peterborough, Chestnut and Old Town canoes owe much to their birchbark forerunners. Ironically, many Native people still live as hunters in the Canadian north, but they now have southern canoes, usually with an engine on the back.

Northrop Frye, one of Canada's leading thinkers of the twentieth century, wrote in *The Bush Garden* that white North Americans have come a long way in a hundred years in their attitude toward the land. In the nineteenth century it was a religious imperative that the land be tilled and not left to shiftless wanderers. This imperative served as a most convenient justification for dispossessing most of North America's Native people. Now, a century later, it is beginning to be considered next to original sin to despoil nature. It has taken a while, but we are finally absorbing the wisdom of the hunters toward their homeland. The canoe enters the twenty-first century as a powerful reminder of that connection to the land.

Algonquin canoe, fourteen feet, two inches long and thirty-six inches wide, from the Gatineau region in Quebec, north of Ottawa. This area was an important source for trade bark in the fur trade era and continues to be one of the best sources for good bark and one of the last remaining areas of Native birchbark canoe building. This is probably a Rapid Lake canoe, perhaps built by Patrick Maranda or Noel Jerome in the 1950s. It is build from one piece of bark and has very meticulous lashing.

Foxe Channel

Great Bear Lake

A

Great Slave Lake

Fort Rae
(Yellowknife)

Fort Simpson

Fort Halkett

Liard River

South Nahanni R.

nzie River

River

Fort Liard

Fort Nelson

Dease Lake Post

Fort Nelson R.

Hay River

Fort Vermillion

Fort Fitzgerald

Fort Smith

Fort Resolution

Fort Smith

Fort Chipewyan

Fond du Lac R.

Lake Athabasca

Wollaston Lake

HUDSON

Bay

Prince Of Wales Fort

Churchill R.

Churchill

Finlay River

Fort Dunvegan

River

Peace River

Clearwater R.

Fort McMurray

Methye Portage

Reindeer Lake

Churchill River

Burntwood R.

Nelson River

York Factory

Oxford House

Hayes River

Fort McLeod

Athabasca River

Beaver R.

Fort Ile-a-la-Crosse

Fort George

Boat Encampment

Fraser River

Fort Alexandria

Jasper House

Fort Assiniboine

Athabasca Landing

Fort Pitt

Fort la Montée (Fort Carlton)

Saskatchewan R.

Cumberland House

Norway House

Lake Winnipegosis

Lake Winnipeg

Fort Edmonton

North Saskatchewan R.

Rocky Mountain House

Red Deer River

Fort à la Corne

Kootenay House

Piegan Post

Fort La Jonquière (Calgary)

Bow River

South Saskatchewan River

Fort Pelly

Lake Manitoba

Albany

Fort Hope

River

Fraser River

Fort Langley

Fort Okanagan

Fort Colville

Spokane House

Kootenay River

Chesterfield House

Qu'Appelle River

Fort Qu'Appelle

Assiniboine R.

Fort Maurepas

Lake of the Woods

Lake Nipigon

Fort William

Astoria (Fort George)

Columbia

Columbia River

Walla Walla

Fort Vancouver

Fort la Jonquière

Souris R.

Fort la Reine

Fort Garry

Red River

Grand Portage

Lake Superior

Fort Daer

Yellowstone River

Missouri

James River

Fort De Buc

Wiscon

Fort La Pointe

Prairie du Chien

Fort La Baye

Fox River

Lake Michigan

Fort Boise

Snake River

Regis Loisels Post (Cedar Post)

Truteau's Post

Missouri River

Fort St. Antoine

Fort Beauharnois

Fort Vaudreuil

Chicago Portage

River

Fort Pimitoui

Fort Crèvecoeur

Illinois River

St. Louis

Fort Orleans

Wabash

Fort St. Louis

Fort de Chartres

Kaskaskia

B

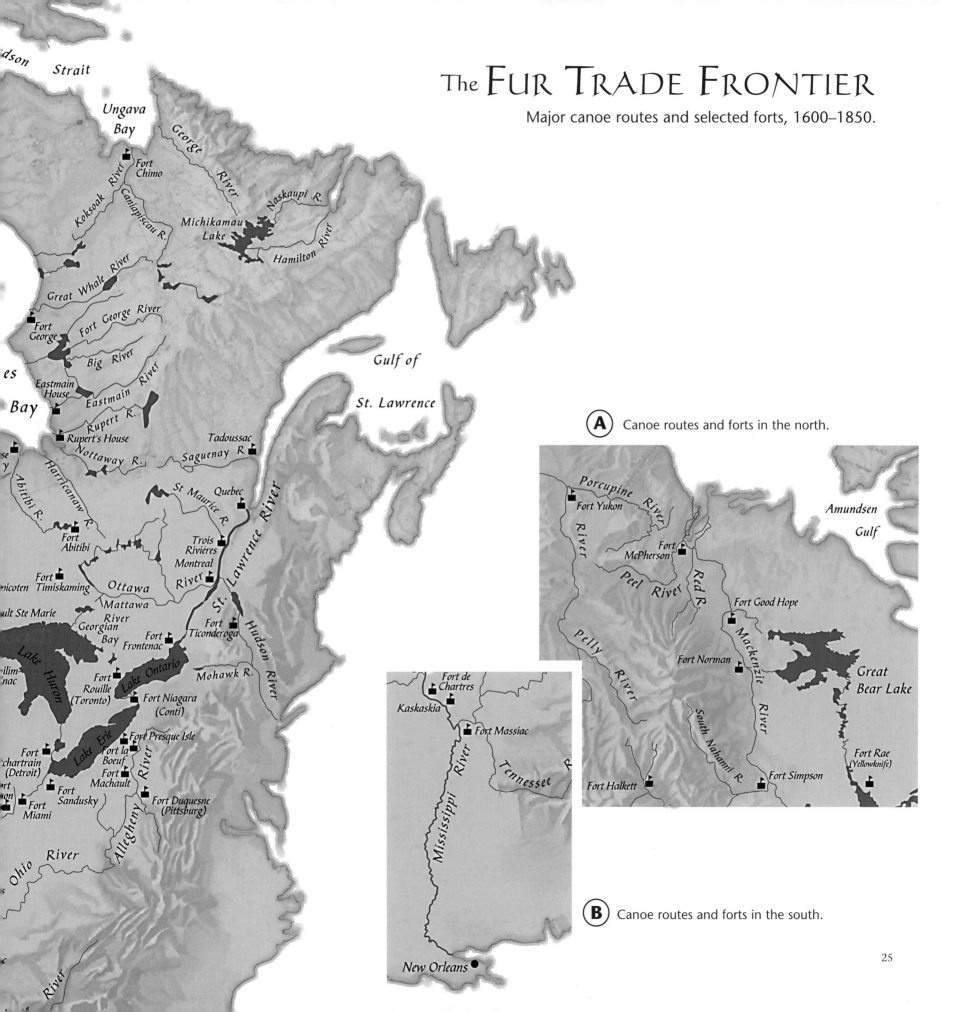

The FUR TRADE FRONTIER

Major canoe routes and selected forts, 1600–1850.

Hudson Strait

Ungava Bay

George River

Koksoak River

Fort Chimo

Caniapiscau R.

Naskaupi R.

Michikamau Lake

Hamilton River

Great Whale River

Fort George River

Fort George

Big River

Eastmain River

Eastmain House

Eastmain

es Bay

Rupert R.

Rupert's House

Nottaway R.

Saguenay R.

Tadoussac

se y

Abitibi R.

Harricanaw R.

St Maurice R.

Quebec

Fort Abitibi

Trois Riviéres

Montreal

nicoten

Fort Timiskaming

Ottawa River

St. Lawrence River

ault Ste Marie

Mattawa

River

Georgian Bay

Fort Frontenac

Fort Ticonderoga

Hudson River

Lake Huron

ilim-nac

Lake Ontario

Fort Rouille (Toronto)

Mohawk R.

Fort Niagara (Conti)

Lake Erie

Fort Presque Isle

Fort la Boeuf

chartrain (Detroit)

Fort Machault

Allegheny River

ort on

Fort Sandusky

Fort Duquesne (Pittsburg)

Fort Miami

Ohio River

River

Gulf of

St. Lawrence

Ⓐ Canoe routes and forts in the north.

Porcupine River

Fort Yukon

River

Amundsen Gulf

Fort McPherson

Peel River

Red R.

Fort Good Hope

Pelly River

Mackenzie River

Fort Norman

Great Bear Lake

South Nahanni R.

Fort Rae (Yellowknife)

Fort Halkett

Fort Simpson

Fort de Chartres

Kaskaskia

Fort Massiac

Mississippi River

Tennessee R.

Ⓑ Canoe routes and forts in the south.

New Orleans

25

The CANOE FRONTIER

JOHN JENNINGS

I cried out to God and began to pull my canoe toward me ... As for our Frenchmen, they did not fare any better, and several times were nearly lost.

Samuel de Champlain

Samuel de Champlain's entreaty to his deity was prompted by his first attempt, in 1613, to travel inland in the bark craft of the Native peoples. Specifically, he was asking for a bit of help in lining a canoe (pulling it on a rope) up a rather difficult rapid on the Ottawa River. His Algonquin allies had made it look easy, but his canoe had spun broadside in a whirlpool and "had I not luckily fallen between two rocks, the canoe would have dragged me in, since I could not quickly enough loosen the rope that was twisted around my hand, which hurt me very much, and nearly cut it off ... Having escaped I gave praise to God, beseeching Him to preserve us." Actually Champlain's bemused Algonquin allies did the preserving, especially after Champlain next lost his astrolabe on a mosquito-infested portage a short time later. Fortunately, the Algonquins were patient tutors as the French bumbled their way into the interior. The French, on their part, quickly realized that they had much to learn if they were to venture west in a country where travel was only possible by water.

The canoe frontier of North America began with the French. As the European powers (the Spanish, Portuguese, English, Dutch and French) turned their attention to the New World after Columbus, the French

FACING PAGE: The Main Channel on the French River, used by fur traders to travel between Lake Nipissing and Georgian Bay.

ABOVE: Algonquin birchbark, fourteen feet, eight inches long, thirty-four inches wide, built in the 1970s by William Commanda and his wife Mary at Maniwaki, Quebec. Maniwaki continues to be an important canoe building center. William Commanda is considered to be one of the greatest living canoe builders. In 1995 he was inducted into the Canadian Canoe Museum's Hall of Honour.

by pure luck stumbled onto the only river on the eastern seaboard that led to the heart of the continent. When the French laid claim to the St. Lawrence Valley in the early seventeenth century, they had no idea that their history in the next century and a half would be unlike that of all the other colonizing nations in the western hemisphere.

Much of the greatness of New France was based on her command of the complex network of rivers, lakes and natural portages—the legacy of the Ice Ages—which was linked to the St. Lawrence River. This river, where Jacques Cartier first ventured in 1535, was North America's one avenue to the interior from the eastern seaboard, via the Ottawa and Mattawa rivers to Lake Nipissing and then down the French River to Georgian Bay on Lake Huron. From there it was clear paddling to Michilimacinac at the narrows between Lake Huron and Lake Michigan and the Mississippi Valley or Grand Portage at the head of Lake Superior. By happening on this river in the sixteenth century and then laying claim to it, the French determined their destiny for the next two centuries as traders and explorers of the inland waterways of the continent.

The St. Lawrence was also the key to the vast network of rivers and lakes above the Great Lakes. Here there emerged a "dominion of the North," as historian Donald Creighton called it, a geographic dominion of rivers and lakes upon which the bark canoe of the original peoples reigned supreme. This geography, and the adoption of the Native craft to go with it, defined a very significant part of the early history of European expansion in the northern half of the continent. The vast St. Lawrence River system formed the basis of a great transportation system on which the commodities of the old world were traded for the products of the new.

The North American frontier of the canoe, which the French initiated, was unlike all other frontiers of the western hemisphere. While it lasted, it was the meeting place of cultures who each found mutual benefit in a trading relationship that was undertaken on relatively equal terms. For the French, it was a frontier of discovery and commerce; for Native peoples, of course, it was not a frontier at all. It was home.

In broad terms, there were three North American frontiers; the frontier of the canoe, the settler frontier of the axe and plow, and the frontier of the horse, which began with the Spanish in Mexico and the southern United States and was later incorporated by Americans. A vast expanse of the frontier of the horse, the part that is so imbedded in the American psyche, was given its character by the absence of water. The Great Plains, roughly the

ABOVE: *The Fur Traders at Montreal.* George Agnew Reid, 1916. At first Native traders came to French settlements in the St. Lawrence Valley; later the French began to venture into the interior. The trading rendezvous was the most important venue for the meeting of cultures: a mixture of Native trade gathering and European trade fair, with roots in the Middle Ages.

RIGHT: Drawing of Iroquois canoes by Baron de Lahontan in *New Voyages to North America, 1703.* The canoe sketch at the bottom has nine thwarts: a very large canoe. Some of the Iroquois war canoes were thirty feet long, constructed from one sheet of bark.

middle third of America, was, at one time, referred to as the Great American Desert and was considered too arid for civilized use.

The canoe frontier was based on the fact that the northern half of the continent contains a large portion of the fresh water of the world. Whoever controlled these water routes, starting with the St. Lawrence–Great Lakes axis, controlled the early trade of half a continent. This canoe frontier was not an agricultural frontier of land acquisition and settlement involving the dispossession of Native peoples. While it lasted, the canoe frontier set itself apart from all the others in the western world. Unlike the frontiers of the settler and the horse, the frontier of the canoe did not covet the land, only its bounty. Native peoples were not pushed aside; they were wooed as partners in a very lucrative trade.

At first, the French were content to let Native traders come to them, and in the first half of the seventeenth century flotillas of trading canoes, sometimes in the hundreds, descended on Montreal for the annual trade fair. These fairs were an intriguing mix of the traditional Native trading rendezvous and the French fairs that reached back to medieval times. Here cultures met on

equal footing and began to forge the bonds that would extend later to the interior. From the beginning it was the intention of the French to incorporate the Native peoples into French culture. Intermarriage was encouraged and the Catholic Church played a major role, both in the colony of New France and in canoe country, in attempting to convert Native people. As Champlain said, "Our young men will marry your daughters, and we shall be one people." Wishful thinking, perhaps, but it did point

LEFT: *Hudson's Bay Store, Fort William*. William Armstrong, circa 1860–70. After the amalgamation of the HBC and the NWC in 1821, Fort William declined in importance as a fur trade post, but it was still a significant Metis community.

BELOW: *Indian Encampment, Fort William*. William Armstrong, 1912. Fort William, situated at the western end of Lake Superior, became one of the most important inland trade centers of the North West Company. It was the midpoint between Montreal and the rich fur territory of the Athabasca country. Goods from Montreal were brought to Fort William in Montreal canoes and exchanged for furs brought in North canoes from the western interior.

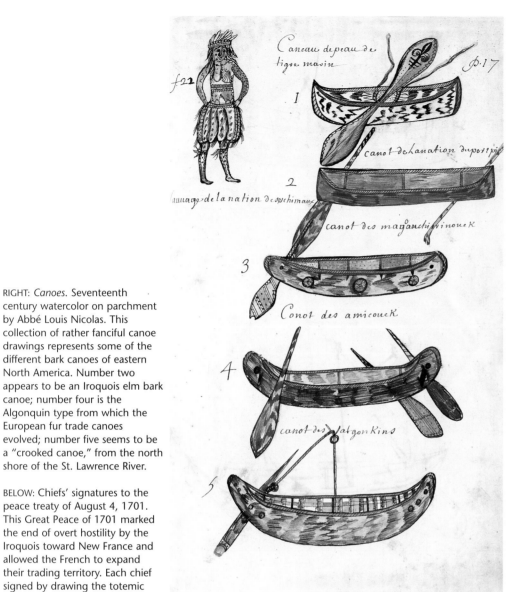

Caneau de peau de tigre marin

f.22

p.17

1

canot de la nation du possipi

sauuage de la nation des esquimaux

2

canot des maganchi kinouek

3

Conot des amicouek

4

canot des algonkins

5

RIGHT: *Canoes*. Seventeenth century watercolor on parchment by Abbé Louis Nicolas. This collection of rather fanciful canoe drawings represents some of the different bark canoes of eastern North America. Number two appears to be an Iroquois elm bark canoe; number four is the Algonquin type from which the European fur trade canoes evolved; number five seems to be a "crooked canoe," from the north shore of the St. Lawrence River.

BELOW: Chiefs' signatures to the peace treaty of August 4, 1701. This Great Peace of 1701 marked the end of overt hostility by the Iroquois toward New France and allowed the French to expand their trading territory. Each chief signed by drawing the totemic animal representing his tribe.

to a very different relationship which was developing on the canoe trading frontier.

Unlike all other colonizers in the western hemisphere, the French initiated relations with the Native peoples that were based on respect and partnership and, of course, on a desire to acquire souls for the Catholic Church. The French—to use Richard White's now famous phrase—sought a "middle ground" of mutual benefit and understanding.

But what needs to be much better recognized is the huge importance of the French style in their relations with Native peoples, a style quite at odds with that of the other colonizers of the western world. The French style had partly to do with an acceptance of Native culture. It was also based on the unique social dynamics of the canoe. On all other European frontiers, relations were distant and often confrontational, leading Robert Utley, a leading historian of the American West, to sum up the relationship between Americans and Native peoples as "mutual incomprehension" in *The Indian Frontier of the American West, 1846–1890*. Not so in the forced intimacy of the canoe. Here cultural barriers broke down, especially when Native women accompanied white traders and voyageurs as wives or companions.

This French canoe empire was built, not by force—which the French did not possess—but on diplomacy, a willingness to learn Native ways of survival in the wilderness, and by treating the Native people with a respect accorded to equals. One of the central features of this French system was the authority of the monarchy. In stark contrast to the freewheeling license of the American frontiersmen, French officials and priests were able to dictate a code of conduct in relations with their Native allies that was the key to the relationship. In effect, the

mechayon chef de la montagne

Kiledis Kingie pr. les Kiskakon

Elaisesse pr. la fourche

marque des missisagues

marque des amikoü chef mahingan

marque des sauteurs chef sabanque

ABOVE: *Iroquois Defeat at Lake Champlain,* 1613 sketch by Samuel de Champlain depicting the 1609 battle he won with his Native allies against the Iroquois. The canoes on the left are the birch-bark canoes of the Algonquins, Hurons and Montagnais; those on the right are the elm bark canoes of the Iroquois.

LEFT: Model of an Iroquois elm bark canoe made by Tappan Adney, scale 5:1. The inside bark of the tree is used on the outside of the canoe. Elm bark can only be crudely shaped, with the two ends crimped together. Compare the shape of the bow and stern with the elegant profiles of birchbark canoes.

officials of New France established policies of racial tolerance and respect on this frontier that were later adopted by the English and Scottish traders of the Hudson's Bay and North West companies and eventually by the North West Mounted Police, when they brought law and order to the Plains region of the new Canadian state.

Beginning with Champlain, but gaining considerable momentum in the era of La Salle and Frontenac at the end of the seventeenth century, France's small outpost in the New World wilderness mounted expeditions of discovery and her small group of explorers exerted an immense influence on the vast territories they paddled through. At the peak of its power and influence, the population of New France never exceeded 70,000. Yet at a time when the American colonies, with a population of 1,500,000 in 1760, were just beginning to poke their noses over the first serious hill—the Appalachians— French explorers, with their French and Native crews and Native guides, had already descended the Mississippi to its mouth and journeyed to the shadow of the Rockies to establish a vast fur empire that was one of the determining factors in the development of what was to become Canada.

As military historian John Keegan has noted in *Warpaths*:

> Theirs is a history of discovery as dramatic and certainly as gallant and enterprising as any in the record of the European exploration of the world; their encounter with harsh climate, natural dangers and often hostile peoples has few parallels. The America of the French explorations, even more than the Africa of the Victorians, was the dark continent, hiding its secrets from all but the most persistent, and instantaneous in its punishment of the foolhardy and the unprepared. The distances covered by those whose base rested at Québec or Montréal—500 miles to Sault Ste Marie, 1000 miles to Lake of the Woods, 1500 miles to the Saskatchewan River—were unprecedented for journeys into unrecorded territory and were scarcely equaled later by the explorers of Australia or rainforest Africa.

During the French regime, the French colonists and their Native allies were at war variously with Britain, the American colonies and the powerful Iroquois confederacy. Until the British fleet tipped the balance in 1759 and General Wolfe and his men managed to scramble up a seemingly impossible cliff to rout the French forces in one devastating volley, the French and their Native allies consistently prevailed over vastly superior forces, largely because of the strategic use of the canoe and the extended lines of communication and the network of fortified posts that they were able to establish, using flotillas of large voyaging canoes. The mobility and carrying capacity of the birchbark canoe gave the French and their allies an enormous advantage over their adversaries. To date, no account has done justice to the importance of the canoe in this frontier warfare. Without it, the French and Native coalition could not possibly have sustained its military dominance during the colonial period. During the seventeenth century New France was often threatened by the Iroquois and owed its very existence to the Native trading alliances that finally managed to subdue them.

By 1701, the Iroquois, who for a century had blocked French expansion into the interior and had exterminated the Huron in their attempt to become middlemen in the canoe trade, had been thoroughly humbled by the French–Native alliance and they sued for peace. The Iroquois were not canoe peoples, being south of the range of the birch tree, and were thus at a great disadvantage in wars with an enemy who could strike quickly and in force from a great distance without losing touch with its commissary. The Iroquois did build canoes of elm bark, but they were rather nasty craft, since elm bark cannot be properly shaped.

The Great Peace of 1701 represented a triumph for French diplomacy. Forty Nations signed a treaty of peace in Montreal, representing in part an acknowledgment of the success of French trading practices. For the next half century the French canoe frontier would expand its trading and military presence in the Ohio Valley and down the Mississippi as far as the Ohio River. As well, French policy and trading alliances had the effect of inducing far greater loyalty among Native peoples of the region than was the case on the other side. Perhaps the foremost example of French diplomatic genius was the order and stability that they brought to the *pays d'en haut* (the far country of the Great Lakes and beyond)—a Babylon of dialects and feuding tribes. The French acted as a catalyst in the formation of a confederacy of tribes, brought together in trading alliances.

When the end came for New France on the Plains of Abraham, it was not because of defeats in canoe country and it was certainly not because of fickle Native allies. Pontiac, the Ottawa chief who organized an armed Native resistance in 1763, paid the French regime one of its greatest compliments shortly after its demise. In justifying the mass revolt of former French Native allies south of the Great Lakes against the new British and American presence, he made this testament to the French:

[We] tell you now the French never conquered us neither did they purchase a foot of our Country, nor have they a right to give it to you, we gave them liberty to settle for which they always rewarded us and treated us with great Civility while they had it in their power, but as they are become now your people, if you expect to keep these Posts, we will expect to have proper returns from you.

from *Warpaths* by Ian K. Steele

Pontiac's rebellion at its most fundamental level represented a lashing out by hunting societies, the trading allies of the French, against the encroachment of the American settlement frontier. These Native trading allies had been fundamental to the survival of New France when it was threatened by the Iroquois. Twice more, during the American Revolution and the War of 1812, they were crucial in saving Canada from American invasion. The irony in both cases was that many of the Mohawk, former implacable enemies of New France, now became Canada's ranking Native allies.

The French in the American West

By the fall of New France in the middle of the eighteenth century, the trading territory that the French had incorporated in their canoe frontier included more than half the continent, based on the St. Lawrence and extending twenty-five hundred miles to the mouth of the Mississippi. By 1760, French traders had established a network of posts and religious missions below the Great Lakes, beyond Lake Winnipeg to the Rockies and down the

Mississippi to the Missouri River. At the same time, the French colony of Louisiana, established in the early eighteenth century, reinforced France's hold on all territory west of the Appalachian Mountains, from above the Great Lakes to the Gulf of Mexico.

After Louisiana was established, the French managed to contain the English behind the Appalachians by building posts throughout the Ohio and Illinois country. The English had only one easy route to this country, the Hudson-Mohawk system, and it was jealously guarded by the Iroquois. The region today is full of the legacy of the French canoe frontier—Kingston (Fort Frontenac), Toronto

ABOVE: *Shooting the Rapids*, by Frances Anne Hopkins, 1879. This accurate painting records an actual descent of the Lachine Rapid west of Montreal in 1863 in a Montreal canoe manned by sixteen voyageurs. This forty-foot canoe is thought to be one of the largest fur trade canoes ever built. Frances Hopkins can be seen in the middle of the canoe with her husband Edward (with the beard).

Algonquin canoe, twenty-six feet, ten inches long, sixty-one inches wide, 1972. Built by Cesar Nawashish, one of the great bark canoe builders of the twentieth century. The North canoe was from twenty-four to twenty-eight feet in length and could carry thirty-five packs of trade goods, supplies or furs weighing as much as three thousand pounds. Weighing about 280 pounds, it was paddled by four to six men and was portaged upright by two men.

(Fort Rouille), Niagara, Detroit, Chicago, Michilimacinac, Peoria on the Illinois, Prairie du Chien on the Wisconsin, Pittsburgh (Fort Duquesne) at the junction of the Monongahela and the Allegheny, Vincennes and Lafayette (Fort Ouiatenon) on the Wabash, Green Bay on Lake Michigan, and Cahokia, Kaskaskia and finally, Fort de Chartres on the Mississippi just above the Missouri, which was the meeting point of the canoe frontier of the St. Lawrence and the French colony of Louisiana at the mouth of the Mississippi.

It was because of this French presence in the Ohio Valley that the British Government gave this territory to Canada, rather than the American colonies, in the Quebec Act of 1774. This act gave the new colony of Canada all the territory from the Alleghenies to the Mississippi and south to the Ohio River. The Americans, of course, were enraged to see their western destiny thwarted, but the American claim to this area was very slight compared to that of the French canoe frontier. This issue was central to the outbreak of the American Revolution and, even though the British during the Revolution triumphed over the Americans in the Ohio Valley—thanks largely to the Native alliances that the British inherited from the French

TOP: Montreal canoe on Lake Chibougamau, Quebec, 1892. By the late nineteenth century, the Geological Survey of Canada was continuing the fur traders' exploration and mapping of the north, sending canoe expeditions to survey vast territory. Some of this area, most notably the Barren Lands between Great Slave Lake and Hudson Bay, had never yet been visited by Europeans.

BOTTOM: The Montreal canoe (*canot du maître*). Tappan Adney model, scale 5:1. These canoes, built mostly at Trois Rivières at the junction of the St. Maurice and St. Lawrence rivers, midway between Montreal and Quebec City, were usually between thirty-five and forty feet in length. They were capable of carrying up to eight thousand pounds of cargo, plus eight to twelve paddlers.

canoe frontier—the British were not willing to stand by their Native allies and callously ceded much of the old French canoe frontier to the Americans in the peace treaty of 1783, even though the Native peoples of this region had not been defeated.

Despite the official loss of this trading frontier below the Great Lakes after the Revolution, the French influence persisted. Many of the French and Metis communities that had grown up around the canoe trade continued to exert an influence. Many Canadian voyageurs stayed in American territory and found employment as guides, interpreters and boatmen as the Americans poured into the Ohio Valley after the Revolution and continued across the Mississippi after 1803.

It is the popular perception that after 1760 French influence withered away beyond the borders of Quebec. Certainly the official French presence did, but a significant legacy of the French canoe trade remained in the form of numerous French communities south of the Great Lakes and at former posts. Even in the opening of the American West there was a large French element. Before the era of the cowboy and the prospector in the American West, there were first Lewis and Clark and then the fabled Mountain Men, who explored the territory west of the Mississippi and established the fur trade there. Kit Carson, Jim Bridger and Bill Williams are legendary. Yet three-quarters of these Mountain Men were actually of French origin, former canoemen who drifted west through the Canadian fur trade, to follow in the footsteps of men like Etienne de Véniard, sieur de Bourgmont, who had established a post on the Missouri River in 1724, almost a century before Lewis and Clark came west.

And in 1803, when Lewis and Clark's "Corps of Discovery" set off to discover the American West, it did so with much crucial advice from the French fur traders of St. Louis, with French scouts and interpreters (George Drouillard, René Jusseaume, Touissaint Charbonneau and Jean Baptiste Lepage) and with a rather large number of French canoemen at the sweeps of their river boats.

Subsequently, these same St. Louis traders were fundamental to the development of the American fur trade and the expansion of American knowledge of the west. The first great name of the American fur trade, Manuel Lisa, was essentially financed by the French of St. Louis: Pierre Menard, Sylvestre Labbadie, Pierre and Auguste Chouteau. John Jacob Astor of American Fur Company fame came to prominence in the West through his financial links with the powerful Chouteau family of St. Louis. With Chouteau's backing, Astor turned the American Fur Company into

America's largest monopoly. So the legacy of the French canoe frontier remained strong in the American West until at least the middle of the nineteenth century.

The Canadian Fur Trade

After 1760, when New France became the British province of Quebec, most of the leading French fur traders left and were replaced by an ever-increasing swarm of Scots traders. However, a bond developed between the Scots and the remaining French fur traders. A reflection of this bond can be found in the charter membership of Canada's oldest club, the Beaver Club, chartered in 1785. Of the original members, six were Scots and eight were French. In a significant way, the Scots became an extension of the French fur trade.

One reason for the strength of this bond was the aftermath of the Battle of Culloden in 1746 at which English forces decisively defeated the Highland Scots rallying around Bonnie Prince Charlie and the Catholic Stuart

ABOVE: Crest of the North West Company, drawing by Neil Broadfoot. The crest's offical name is "The Perserverence Coat of Arms."

LEFT: *The Spring Brigade leaves Montreal for the West* by Franklin Arbuckle. Canoes leaving the Hudson's Bay Company warehouse at Lachine (Montreal) for the voyage west. Lachine was the starting point for western voyages from the time of Champlain until the nineteenth century. This is where Champlain looked up the Lachine Rapids in the early 1600s and realized that the boats of Europe were unsuited to the waterways of America.

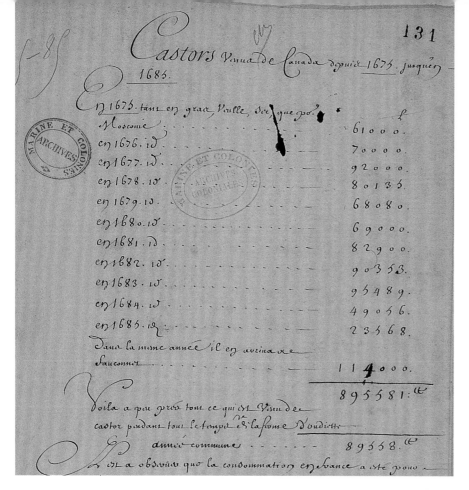

ABOVE: Beaver skins exported from Canada between 1675 and 1685. In just one decade, almost one million beaver skins were exported to France, traded by Native hunters for French manufactured goods. The cured beaver skins, known as "made beaver," were used mainly for making hats throughout Europe. Beaver skins became the monetary system of the fur trade, with all items given a value in made beaver.

RIGHT: This popular postage stamp, designed by Sanford Fleming, was first issued on April 23, 1851 by the Province of Canada. The beaver later became Canada's national emblem.

FACING PAGE: Trader at Fort Chipewyan in 1890s. Furs are being compressed into ninety-pound bales for shipping. After Canadian fur traders were driven out of American territory, the Athabasca region became the most important in the northwestern fur trade, with Fort Chipewyan on Lake Athabasca as the central trading post.

monarchy. After Culloden, Prince Charles sought sanctuary in France as the English attempted to destroy the Scottish clans. Thus Scots traders who later settled in Montreal had an affinity for both the Catholic culture of New France and for the plight of a conquered people. French and Scots could happily agree on disliking the English. Culloden marked the dispersal of the clans and the era of the enclosures, which drove so many Highlanders off the land. Many of the dispossessed and the disillusioned found their way to North America and took naturally to the challenges of the wilderness. By the late eighteenth century, both north and south of the American border, the influx of Scottish fur traders became the predominant element in advancing the frontier.

After the fall of New France the tight control on the northern canoe frontier that had been exerted by the agents of the French monarchy was replaced by the fierce loyalty of the Scottish clans and the Scots aggressive business ethic. So the tight cohesion of the French fur trade persisted, as did the large pool of expert canoemen, who still signed on annually at Lachine and pledged to abide by the ancient understandings of the fur trade. Despite the distinct drop in civilized leadership, with cultured French aristocrats being replaced by hard, direct and roistering Scots, the canoe frontier of the St. Lawrence retained its essential character after 1760.

In 1779 the North West Company (NWC) began as a loose coalition of traders based in Montreal. By 1783, the same year that the British treaty with the United States effectively drew the boundary between British North America and the United States, these Scottish traders had organized themselves into Canada's first joint stock company. At first they concentrated their energies on the vast trading area below the Great Lakes. But after being pushed out of this area in the 1790s by American settlement, they put their emphasis on the far northwest country beyond the Methye Portage and into the Arctic drainage of the Mackenzie River, centered on Lake Athabasca and Fort Chipewyan. By the 1790s, after extending their reach to the Athabasca country, they controlled two-thirds of the Canadian fur trade. For a brief period, from 1798 to 1804, a group of disgruntled Nor'Westers broke away to form the New North West Company (or XY Company, as they were usually called), but differences were reconciled and from 1804 to 1821 the NWC and the Hudson's Bay Company (HBC) battled it out for dominance in the fur trade.

In the realm of exploration, the Scots continued where the French had been forced to stop. The diplomatic relations with Native groups, steeped in ritual, remained

essentially unaltered. The Scots in the half century after the fall of New France filled in the rest of the map of northern North America. By 1793, Alexander Mackenzie, traveling by canoe, had completed European knowledge of the water routes to both the Arctic and the Pacific, thus extending the canoe frontier of North America from sea to sea to sea. He was followed shortly by Simon Fraser and by the extraordinary wanderings of David Thompson, the Englishman who changed loyalties and joined the Scots of the North West Company. His explorations and surveys of North America surpassed all others in the field.

However, none of this would have been possible without the French, Metis and Native voyageurs and guides who should be acknowledged for their enormous contribution. The exploration and mapping of Canada, from the era of New France to the Geological Survey of Canada in the late nineteenth century, would not have been possible without them. After all, the ones who are remembered today (Mackenzie, Thompson and Fraser) sat in the middle of the canoe, rarely lifted a paddle or carried a pack and were lifted in and out of the canoes at portages so as not to get their feet wet.

The figure of the voyageur has been passed down to us through generations of folklore. Behind the image was a life of unrelenting work: fifty strokes a minute, thirty thousand strokes a day in the height of bug season, hernias at thirty and the ultimate in boring food. Yet there was another side. Father Pierre-François-Xavier Charlevoix's description in the 1740s could just as easily describe the voyageurs of the Geological Survey canoe explorations in the twentieth century.

The journeys they undertake; the fatigues they undergo; the dangers to which they expose themselves; and the efforts they make surpass all imagination…. They love to breathe a free air, they are early accustomed to a wandering life; it has charms for them, which make them forget past dangers and fatigues, and they place their glory in encountering them often…. I know not whether I ought to reckon amongst the defects of our Canadians the good opinion they entertain of themselves. It is at least certain that it inspires them with a confidence, which leads them to undertake and execute what would appear impossible to many others…. It is alleged they make bad servants.

The Hudson's Bay Company was very much a latecomer on the canoe frontier. Although it was inaugurated in 1670 and claimed a vast exclusive trading territory, for more than a century the Honourable Company of Adventurers, as they called themselves, remained huddled on the frozen shores of Hudson and James Bay. It took aggressive competition from the Scots of the St. Lawrence fur trade in the late eighteenth century to budge them from their complacency. In theory the HBC had exclusive trading rights over all territory that drained into Hudson and James Bay, a vast territory which included much of northern Quebec and Ontario, most of the Canadian Plains to the Rocky Mountains and much of northern Manitoba, Saskatchewan and Alberta. But for over a century the Honourable Company was content to build posts on the Bay and wait for clients. Why should they venture inland when Native traders came to them, often from great distances?

This situation changed only when the Montreal traders were forced out of their traditional territory south of the Great Lakes after the American Revolution. Only then did the Nor'Westers stake their future on the far

Poling a voyaging canoe up the Abitibi River, 1905. Very few canoeists today travel up rivers, against the current. Voyageurs had no such luxury. They spent many exhausting days, dawn to dusk, traveling upstream, either zigzagging from one eddy to another, lining the craft from shore (pulling it upstream with a rope) or poling where the water was shallow enough to gain purchase with an iron-tipped pole. This can only be done standing and requires either a stable canoe or acrobatic ability.

LEFT: *Voyageurs at Dawn*, by Frances Anne Hopkins, 1871. Voyageurs were up with the sun, before the wind came up, and paddled till dusk. They slept under their overturned canoes, frequently using a large canvas as both groundsheet and makeshift tent. During the day this canvas was often used as a sail on lakes. The voyageurs had no protection from the millions of blackflies and mosquitoes except wood smoke and dirt.

BELOW: Coat of Arms of the Hudson's Bay Company. Watercolor by Neil Broadfoot.

northwest and pose an increasing threat to the HBC monopoly. By the 1780s the HBC reacted strongly to this challenge and began to match the NWC post for post in the northwest.

Thus began a period of intense competition, accompanied by alarming levels of violence. Liquor became the chief commodity of trade and unprecedented amounts of rotgut entered the western regions. As a result, for the first time it could be said that Native society was in serious danger of disintegration. Finally, the situation was bad enough that the British Government stepped in and forced the HBC and the NWC to amalgamate under the name of the Hudson's Bay Company, thus imposing a return to centralized authority and commercial monopoly.

As soon as the strict authority of the HBC was reimposed in 1821, with policies shaped by the formidably able Governor George Simpson, the violence evaporated and the natural inclinations of the "servants" of the Company were stifled in the interests of trading harmony. At the same time, as an inducement to the HBC and the NWC to join forces, the British Government gave the new company a trading monopoly to the territory beyond the original HBC charter—the territory of the lower Columbia River (present-day Washington, Oregon and part of Idaho), New Caledonia (the interior of British Columbia), Athabasca and the Mackenzie Basin. Thus, the vast majority of what was to become Canada was now included in the HBC canoe empire, including a tentative claim to the drainage of the Columbia and Snake rivers—an area that included all or part of present-day Oregon, Washington, Idaho, Wyoming and Montana. The HBC canoe territory included all of Quebec above the St. Lawrence watershed, which France had relinquished to Britain in the Treaty of Utrecht in 1713. This new canoe empire comprised one-twelfth of the earth's surface.

Governor Simpson administered the HBC from his offices at Lachine, traveling west and north by canoe every year to review progress at the Company's numerous trading posts. Some of the most famous images of canoes of the fur trade, the paintings of Frances Hopkins, originated from these tours, when the artist accompanied her husband, Edward Hopkins, who was Governor Simpson's secretary. The focus of the trade was now on the Mackenzie drainage, especially the Athabasca country. As much as possible, the Montreal route was abandoned for the much shorter one from Hudson Bay via the Hayes River to Lake Winnipeg and then west on the Saskatchewan River.

With a strong endorsement from Governor Simpson, a series of canoe expeditions were sent after 1821 to probe the watersheds of the Mackenzie and Yukon rivers, with the express purpose of cutting off both the Russians and the Americans in the Pacific fur trade by blocking their way to the interior of the continent. Simpson was

Canoe Manned by Voyageurs Passing a Waterfall, by Frances Anne Hopkins, 1869. This canoe represents a third type of voyaging canoe, the *bâtard* canoe (Bastard), which could be anywhere from twenty-seven to thirty-four feet long. Many think that this canoe has the most aesthetic proportions of all voyaging canoes.

motivated by his obsession to monopolize the fur trade but, in a larger sense, he clearly saw himself as an agent of imperial policy. What was at stake was the destiny of the northern half of the continent.

In the 1830s and '40s, the headwaters of the Yukon River were determined and posts established on the Peel River at Fort McPherson and on the Yukon River at Fort Yukon in what is now Alaska. At the time this probing into the extreme northwest did not appear to profit the Company but, in retrospect, it can be seen that the HBC was leading the way for the Geological Survey of Canada in the next generation to lay the groundwork for a solid knowledge of the area. And when this region suddenly became the focus of the world during the Klondike gold rush of 1898, a Canadian presence through the canoes of the fur traders and the Geological Survey guaranteed that the area would not be contested by the flood of Americans entering the region.

The southern Canadian canoe frontier ended with Confederation in 1867. In 1870 the HBC ceded its canoe empire to the new nation. The first priority of the new federation was to connect the country by steel, thus replacing the continental canoe routes that had served so

long to bind the west to British North America. This year also marked the first of two revolts by those of mixed blood in the west against the coming of the new order and the end of the fur trade and the buffalo hunt. It is significant that the Metis under Louis Riel chose this moment of transition, just as Pontiac has lashed out against the demise of the French canoe frontier. The Metis identity was shaped by the canoe frontier, in their roles as canoemen and guides and as buffalo hunters who provisioned the fur trade. It is important to realize that the Metis were reacting to the end of the Canadian canoe frontier and to the beginning of the new settler frontier, which shared many similarities with the American frontier.

With the transfer of Rupert's Land to Canada in 1870, the old canoe frontier ended, especially after the coming of the railway across the Canadian Plains in 1885. But the fur trade itself did not die; it merely shifted north to country that was not coveted for agriculture. For a while the canoe was still used extensively in the north by fur traders, the Geological Survey of Canada, the Mounted Police and trappers, prospectors and missionaries. Finally, the coming of the airplane to the north in the 1930s marked the ultimate passing of the canoe frontier.

Thirty-foot HBC *bâtard* (Bastard) canoe being portaged. Canoes between twenty-nine and thirty-three feet in length were called *bâtard* canoes. Voyaging canoes ranged in size from the small twenty-four-foot North canoe to the huge forty-foot *canot du maître*. The *bâtard* was paddled by six to eight men with a capacity of thirty-five to fifty packs (three thousand to five thousand pounds). These canoes were typically used by the HBC on the route from Hudson Bay to Fort Chipewyan in northern Alberta.

Canoemen for a survey crew portaging from Great Slave Lake to the Salt River, Alberta, 1920. The role of the voyageur continued into the twentieth century, when the Geological Survey of Canada ventured into far north by canoe. Portaging canoes and cargo was a standard part of a voyageur's job. The usual load weighed about 180 pounds and the portages were often treacherous. The voyageur routes were marked with the crosses of those who unwisely decided to shoot a rapid to avoid a hard portage. Many voyageurs were crippled with arthritis and hernias by the time they reached their thirties.

VOYAGING CANOES of the FUR TRADE

As the French began to venture into the interior, especially after the Iroquois threat started to subside in the middle of the seventeenth century, canoe building became a priority. The French established their own building centers, using Native labor and, of course, the basic Algonquin craft of the region. Gradually the craft were enlarged in the interests of trade.

Although "fur trade canoe" is the most common term to describe the birchbark canoes of the European fur trade, the term is rather misleading. "Voyaging canoe," perhaps gives a better sense of the multiple roles performed by these canoes. Certainly Europeans were intent, above all, on the pursuit of anything covered in fur. But in the process of discovering possible sources of wealth and developing them, the uses of the canoe were diversified. The fur trade canoe was, initially, a vehicle of exploration, but it soon assumed all the roles of the relationship between Europeans and North Americans: trade, diplomacy, religious conversion and warfare.

In the early days of contact in New France, Native groups came to the French along the St. Lawrence River to trade. Gradually, as the French went further into the interior, the need to have their own canoes grew, and in the middle of the seventeenth century, the first great European canoe building center became established midway between Quebec City and Montreal at Trois Rivières. By then, French trading posts had been established: at Tadoussac, at the mouth of the Saguenay River in 1599, at Quebec City in 1608, at Trois Rivières in 1634 and, finally, at Montreal in 1642.

Trois Rivières, situated on the north side of the St. Lawrence at the mouth of the St. Maurice River, soon became the canoe building center of North America. Here the de Maître dynasty built voyaging canoes for two hundred years and gave their name to the great six-fathom (thirty-six-foot) fur trade canoes. This dynasty, including the Auger, Lottinville, Leclerc, du Guay and Jutras families, built voyaging canoes at Trois Rivières and at St. François du Lac, Rivière du Loup, Louiseville and St. Pierre. Louis de Maître was the patriarch and the most famous member of the family. The last of this great family, Antoine du Guay, was building canoes into the

This is either a HBC North canoe or a *bâtard* at the company's Bear Island post, Lake Temagami, Ontario, 1896. This photograph would have been very delicately set up. Canoemen always got out of bark canoes before reaching shore to avoid punctures from rocks. Important passengers were piggybacked in and out of the canoe by the canoemen to keep their feet dry.

middle of the nineteenth century. After that, some Native canoe building for sportsmen persisted in the region, based on the Algonquin "Wabanaki Chimen" style, but the great days were over after 1821.

Though the canoe yards were managed by the de Maître clan, most of the actual building of birchbark canoes continued to be done by the Algonquin builders of the region in their traditional style. The men determined the shape of the craft and the women and children did the laborious work of sewing with spruce root and caulking with an ancient concoction of gum, charcoal and animal fat. It appears that the voyaging canoes of the St. Lawrence Valley were based originally on the "old style" Algonquin craft of the Native group closest to the initial French canoe building industry. The great canoe scholar, Tappan Adney, gives credit to the Tête de Boule, but it has been convincingly argued by Tim Kent that the Tête de Boule did not migrate from the upper St. Maurice, Gatineau, Lièvre and Dumoine rivers to Trois Rivières and other canoe building centers along the St. Lawrence until the fur trade was in decline.

According to Kent, other birchbark canoe building centers for the fur trade began to flourish further west, first at Grand Portage (and Fort William when Grand Portage was abandoned in 1803) with Ojibwa builders and, then, progressively across the country: at Rainy River, where the Montreal and inland brigades met, at Michilimacinac, at the narrows between Lake Huron and Lake Michigan, and then at lesser points to the west.

At Trois Rivières and Fort William, the two preeminent building centers, at least five sizes of canoes were built. In general fur trade literature the impression is left that European influence resulted in two distinct voyaging canoes: the thirty-six-foot Montreal canoe (*canot du maître*), which traveled the route from Lachine to the head of Lake Superior, and the twenty-six-foot North canoe (*canot du nord*), which was used on the smaller and more obstreperous waters further west. In fact, voyaging canoes came in a variety of sizes, depending on their use and the waters they were to traverse.

Indeed, there was a third standard size, the *bâtard* (bastard) canoe, twenty-eight to thirty-two feet long, which filled the gap between the Montreal and North canoes and was often fashioned for speed rather than carrying capacity. Frances Hopkins' famous painting of a fur trade canoe passing a rock face is a *bâtard* canoe. The proportions are the most aesthetic of voyaging canoes, graceful and majestic, but not ungainly, as some Montreal canoes can appear.

Most of these inland canoe building centers were

LEFT: Hudson's Bay Company canoe at Lake Kippewa, Quebec, 1902. Kippewa was situated in an area where furs were taken by the HBC north to Hudson Bay or down the Ottawa River to Montreal. By 1902 the railway had reached nearby Lake Timiskaming, so these furs would probably have gone out by rail.

BELOW: *York Boats on Lake Winnipeg,* by Walter Phillips, 1930. York boats replaced voyaging canoes on the main fur trade routes in the nineteenth century. They could carry larger loads than a Montreal canoe and were rowed, not paddled, by fewer men. Because they required less skill in handling, men could be hired for lower wages. They could only be portaged by rolling them over logs on groomed portages.

established by the North West Company, such as Fort William and Michipicoten (present-day Wawa) on the north shore of Lake Superior, at the junction of the canoe route south from the bottom of James Bay via the Moose and Missinaibi rivers, and the main east-west artery of the fur trade from Montreal. But several important locations originated with the Hudson's Bay Company. Cumberland House on the North Saskatchewan River, HBC's first inland post, became a major building center, as did Rupert Fort at the bottom of James Bay. At both locations Cree builders, working under HBC direction, produced voyaging canoes. At Rupert Fort trade bark probably had to be acquired from further south because James Bay is effectively beyond the range of good bark. This lack of good bark accounts both for the slowness with which the HBC left the Bay and moved by canoe into the interior and also for the policy of using York boats wherever possible. Native builders at Rupert Fort were still producing traditional canoes into the 1960s, though after 1902 they made increasing use

Indians and specially their women excel in the art of making canoes, but few Frenchmen succeed in it" (*Birchbark Canoes of the Fur Trade* by Timothy Kent). As late as 1796, Isaac Weld, in his *Travels through the States of North America*, remarked, "Nearly all the birch bark canoes in use on the St. Lawrence and Ottawa rivers … are manufactured at Trois Rivières … by Indians." Canoe building was begun, and continues to this day, at Loretteville, a community on the outskirts of Quebec City that was established by the remnants of the Wendat (Huron) Nation after its destruction at the hands of the Iroquois.

The Iroquois were an unlikely group to become central to the Montreal fur trade both as builders and as elite voyageurs, since they did not have a canoe building tradition of any distinction. They had come from a region south of good birchbark and were known for their rather crude and nasty elm bark canoes, which they often used for raids on more northerly tribes, with the intent of ditching their own canoes and returning with their birchbark trophies. But in 1667 and 1676 two mission settlements were established, first at Kahnawake (Lachine) and then at Kanesatake (Oka) for Iroquois who embraced the Catholic religion and migrated north from the colony of New York to New France. By the end of the eighteenth century, mission Iroquois of the St. Lawrence had become renowned both as canoe builders and as canoemen, considered by many to be the most daring and skilled of all voyageurs. In the quarter century between 1790 and 1815, approximately 350 Iroquois voyageurs signed with the NWC and the XY Company. And in 1860, when Sir George Simpson, Governor of the HBC, choreographed the official visit of the Prince of Wales, one hundred picked Iroquois, resplendent in their traditional finery, were the focus of the event.

Sir George Simpson's royal event could perhaps serve to mark the climax of the voyaging canoe. By this time, the great era of the Montreal canoe was over. Instead of the voyaging canoes, the distinctly inelegant but utilitarian York boat came into ever greater prominence on established routes because it could carry greater loads with fewer and less skilled men at the sweeps. The great canoe building tradition of the St. Lawrence Valley withered, as did the annual voyageur brigades setting off from Lachine. However, off the major routes, the canoe remained the only mode of transport. The smaller North canoe still held sway from Labrador to the Pacific on rivers unsuitable for York boats, as long as the fur trade lasted. After the railway came in the 1870s and 1880s, the voyaging canoe was relegated to the margins.

of canvas rather than bark, probably due to the difficulty of finding good bark.

Though the building of voyaging canoes spread across the continent in the range of the birch tree and in adjacent regions where trade bark was available, the St. Lawrence Valley—and especially Trois Rivières—remained the mecca of canoe building. Here canoe building centers were established near Native communities, where steady supplies of labor were available. Denis Riverin, a merchant close to the fur trade, observed in 1705: "The

FACING PAGE: *Canoes in a Fog, Lake Superior,* by Frances Anne Hopkins, 1869. Frances Hopkins is generally acknowledged as the foremost painter of the fur trade. Her canoes are extremely accurate and she carefully recorded all the trappings of the fur trade. Married to Edward Hopkins, who was the private secretary to the Governor of the Hudson's Bay Company, Sir George Simpson, Hopkins was one of the few English women who traveled by canoe with a fur trade husband.

BUILDING

BIRCHBARK CANOES

RICK NASH

In the eyes of the first European explorers to record their experiences, the birchbark canoe was perhaps the most distinctive and desirable artifact of Native culture. From the Atlantic coast across the northern half of the continent, different tribal groups built birchbark canoes using a shared basic technology of rib-and-plank construction, with marked regional differences. Light, elegant, easily repaired and built of accessible local materials, the birchbark canoe was essential in the day-to-day life and seasonal migrations of most Native groups. For Europeans, it became the only way to explore the vast network of waterways across North America that was accessible mainly through the St. Lawrence River.

The Native birchbark canoe was first of all a practical craft, and the variations that could be found from one region to another reflect not only traditional building skills, but local needs, varying water conditions (from ocean to small lakes and rivers) and the availability of materials. Not surprisingly, the range of the birchbark canoe matches the range of the white birch tree (*Betula papyrifera*—the paper birch, or canoe birch), a broad sweep of land covering much of present-day Canada and extending into the northeastern United States as far south as Boston. When Native groups moved into white birch territory, joining, supplanting or driving out earlier inhabitants, they soon learned the technique of building birchbark canoes. However, few Europeans ever mastered the complex communal skills that the Native peoples used to build these craft, and building birchbark canoes remained a Native skill throughout the succeeding four centuries of European settlement in North America.

Because the birchbark canoe is comparatively fragile, and because any Native canoe would be used until it disintegrated, no craft survive today that predate European contact. Consequently, it is possible only to surmise the origins and evolution of the craft. It remains an open argument whether this type of canoe was brought from elsewhere in the world (for example from Asia), or whether it originated or largely evolved in the regions where it was first recorded by Europeans.

Nevertheless, it is possible to understand the natural resources and tools that the Native peoples had available to them in the millennia preceding the arrival of Europeans. Woodland Native bands can be grouped into northern and southern regions, according to the differing traditions of hunting and gathering methods. The technology in the manufacture of necessary tools, however, varied little in most of these regions. The people in the pre-history period learned to use raw materials such as stone and bone, and present-day Native bands still use bone in conjunction with steel tools.

The advancement of building skills depended on the ease with which the necessary materials could be gathered. Pine, spruce, fir, white cedar and bark were easily worked materials that did not require sophisticated tools. It is quite probable, for example, that the axe wasn't used significantly in the felling or working of timber. The simple method by which stone axes were fastened to their handles would not, in all probability, have held together upon repeated impact. The only

FACING PAGE: One of the channels of the French River, used by fur traders to gain access to Georgian Bay and Lake Huron.

BELOW: In this romanticized oil painting done in the nineteenth century by an unknown artist, Mi'kmaqs are shown hunting in their canoes for geese. The canoes are clearly sea-going ones; the raised gunwales amidships did not appear on river canoes. The gunwales were raised both to deflect waves and to allow the craft to lean over without taking on water as a heavy sea mammal was pulled aboard at the quarter. The sail is a European adaptation. Two quilled birchbark boxes sit in front of the women in the tent.

Mi'kmaq birchbark, fourteen feet, three inches long and thirty-one inches wide, from Yarmouth, Nova Scotia, circa 1900. This cigar-shaped canoe with a low profile and rounded ends was quite unlike other bark canoes.

suitable tool for chopping was the adze. The stone blade was fastened to its handle by means of a notched backing that prevented the lashings from loosening upon impact.

The unique characteristics of the forests in these regions also had an impact on the ease with which timber was obtained. The soft terrain of the swamps and marshes that had been formed by glacial movement and extensive beaver activity, gave standing timber little anchorage and support. Similarly, the shallow layer of topsoil covering the bedrock crust in the northern regions did not protect trees from toppling over in wind storms, or falling under the weight of heavy snows or

being downed by the natural felling of neighboring trees.

As trees were uprooted, the trunks splintered into usable lengths. Early Native peoples were able to obtain necessary materials from these splintered trees by using wedges. These were made with ground or shoreline stones with workable edges, which were placed in an open split. The stone wedge would have been pounded through by blows with a heavy stone.

The northern white cedar was the timber of choice for the Native inhabitants in the lake regions. It was used to build toboggans, cradleboards, plank snowshoes and canoes. In the northern regions where white cedar

Passamaquoddy birchbark, eighteen feet, seven inches long and thirty-four inches wide, from the Passamaquoddy River, Maine, circa 1890. The canoes of the Maliseet and Passamaquoddy were considered to be the finest of all bark canoes.

was widely used in almost all aspects of Native life: for shelter, kindling and fuel; for fashioning containers and creating artwork; and in the making of canoes. Birchbark was a major trade item for early peoples and during the European fur trade era it retained its value.

Mi'kmaq and Maliseet

It is now difficult to identify accurately the different tribal groupings of the Algonquian people who originally lived in the Maritime regions north and south of the mouth of the St. Lawrence River, in present-day Nova Scotia, New Brunswick, Prince Edward Island, Maine and New Hampshire. European settlement and the French and English struggles for control of the region throughout the seventeenth and eighteenth centuries all drove the Native populations into new federations and tribal combinations and often forced them to occupy different territory.

became scarce, species of spruce trees were used. They were felled and split using the same wood gathering techniques as in the more southerly regions, but with greater difficulty due to the "string-type" grain of the spruce tree and the large number of knots. Wood fibers were scraped, cleaned and finished using small chippings of flint or other sharp-edged stones. Smooth stones or fallen hardwood were used for rubbing the wood to finish it off. Cedar, given its softer, more workable nature, required less labor and fewer tools.

The bark of the white birch was a valuable commodity. Easily removed from the tree and easily worked, it

Thus the canoes of these two major tribal groups, known in English as Mi'kmaq and Maliseet (including the Passamaquoddy and Penobscot), are best dealt with together, since not only do their territories overlap, but their canoes also share the same general form and design. These people depended on both coastal and inland resources and they built canoes for use on the rivers (such as the St. John, the St. Croix and the Penobscot)

Model made by Tappan Adney of a Mi'kmaq sea-going birchbark canoe from the Restigouche River area of northern New Brunswick. Scale is 5:1. The canoe has raised gunwales amidships and a pronounced tumblehome, both of which would give it added stability in rough seas. The decoration on the side is typical of Mi'kmaq and Maliseet craft.

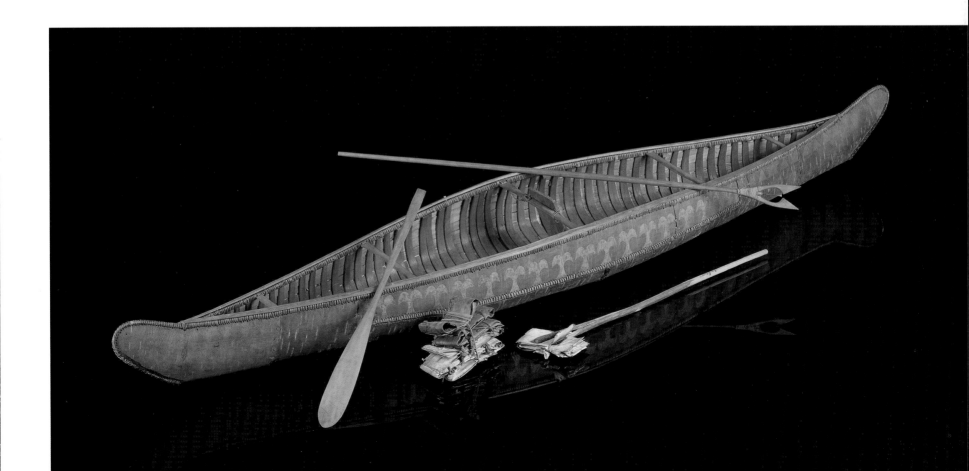

and on the ocean. The Mi'kmaq, for example, spent at least half of the year living on or near the coast and the greater proportion of their diet came from the sea, including not only shellfish but coastal ocean fish such as cod, as well as porpoises, small whales and seals.

Mi'kmaq and Maliseet canoes displayed finer workmanship than any others in the canoe building regions of North America. This is particularly evident in the Maliseet examples. This high quality of workmanship was noted early on by European observers. It is also true that the Native builders of these regions had been in contact with Europeans for a longer period of time and had learned how to use their tools and woodworking skills, resulting in a refinement of an already high level of traditional canoe building.

Both the Mi'kmaq and Maliseet canoes have pronounced characteristics, such as the tumblehome shaping of the hulls (the inward slope of the upper sides of the canoe) and a considerable length, generally between eighteen and twenty feet. The average beam across the gunwale structures is relatively narrow, from thirty-two to thirty-four inches, with maximum beams depending on the hull's tumblehome breadth, extending

at times over one inch beyond the gunwale structure. The long hull lengths combined with the tumblehome shaping are typical characteristics of canoes designed for stability and tracking in rough open water. The twenty-foot long Inuit kayaks of Baffin Island are similar in this respect. Some Mi'kmaq canoes were built with a pronounced rise midship in the gunwale line, another design refinement for ocean travel. This also provided greater stability when navigating with loads.

Poling upriver was a common practice of the Mi'kmaq and Maliseet when their canoes were used on inland waterways. Again, the canoe design contributed to stable handling. However, these canoes were not easy to portage. The Mi'kmaq and Maliseet sometimes used a carryboard in union with a tumpline to ease the weight of the canoe. Henry David Thoreau, in *The Maine Woods*, written in the 1850s, described the method used by his Indian guide.

He prepared his canoe for carry in this wise. He took a cedar shingle or splint eighteen inches long and four or five wide, rounded at one end, that the corners might not be in the way, and tied it with cedar-bark by two

A large (eighteen- to twenty-foot) Chippewa canoe under construction, 1895. This was a family undertaking: women can be seen in the background and a young boy is standing second from the right. It appears that the canoe is being constructed from one piece of bark.

holes made midway, near edge on each side, to the middle cross-bar of the canoe. When the canoe was lifted upon his head bottom up, this shingle, with its rounded end uppermost, distributed the weight over shoulders and head, while a band of cedar-bark, tied to the cross-bar on each side of the shingle, passed round his breast, and another longer one, outside of the last, round his forehead; also a hand on each rail served to steer the canoe and keep it from rocking. He thus carried it with his shoulders, head, breast, forehead, and both hands, as if the upper part of his body were all one hand to clasp and hold it. If you know of a better way, I should like to hear it.

Thoreau also mentions the preference for long-hulled canoes:

When I was there four years before we had a rather small canoe for three persons, and I had thought that this time I would get a larger one, but the present one was even smaller than that. It was 18 feet 3 inches long, by 2 feet 6 1/2 inches wide in middle, and one foot deep within.

The Mi'kmaq and Maliseet canoes were sometimes built in shorter lengths of fourteen to sixteen feet, but these were fairly uncommon in these regions, and usually built for specific purposes. Size was also determined by the length of available bark.

The canoes of the Mi'kmaqs and Maliseets were characteristically of the eastern rib-and-plank form of construction. Distinct features of these canoes were the shaping and placement of the sheathing, or planks. These were neatly shaped long splints, measuring approximately half the hull's length. In Maliseet examples (Passamaquoddy and Penobscot), planks were shaped in tapering lengths, which measured from two to two-and-a-half inches in width at the butt ends, to about one-and-a-half inches at the tapered ends, where they were fitted into the stem ends. They were roughly one-eighth of an inch in thickness, and were assembled in the hull edge to edge. In some old Maliseet examples, planks tapered from three to four inches at the butts to one or one-and-a-half inches at the ends, or stems. This method of edge-to-edge plank fitting created a hinging effect of the canoe's hull at midship, resulting in the development of a hog (rise) in the hull. This is more evident in longer canoes. To counteract this effect, the canoe's ribs (or frame members) were shaped in wide widths, giving the canoe more strength and restricting the working (movement) of the planks at the center

point. Planks were shaved thin at the butt ends and overlapped where they met, at approximately two to three ribs midship.

The ribs of these canoes were, on average, three to four inches in width, with very little tapering at the rib ends where they are received by the gunwale structure. The ribs were bent with an almost returning hard bend, shaping the hull's tumblehome when driven in under pressure. The shaping and bending of ribs for Maliseet canoes was executed with great precision. The hulls have a gradual V-shaping towards the ends, resulting in a kind of keel in the canoe bottom. This was achieved by bending the ribs increasingly sharply at their center point; the ribs were pulled back against the builder's knee. The rib member was gradually worked into a hard bend to form the bilge. This form of tumblehoming canoe construction puts a heavy strain on the gunwale structure, and the gunwales tend to develop a cant (slope) from the rib pressure pushing up. Gunwale assemblies fastened with pegs would in time blow apart due to warping and the shearing of pegs from the rib action. The later use of nails for fastening the gunwale member helped preserve gunwales but did not solve the

A Montagnais/Cree crooked canoe under construction about 1900. The builder in the middle is holding his crooked knife in his teeth. In order to achieve the extreme rocker in this canoe, the ends of the building frame have been blocked up to a great height by building up the earth bed at each end with piles of packed earth or sod patches.

problem of gunwale canting from the stress and strain of the ribs.

Planking at the canoe's prow or projection was fitted between the inner stem fixture and bark cover, or hull. Shavings were then packed in to stiffen the ends. A bent headboard was fitted to pressure the planks against the hull and to act as an extended last rib. The extending of the canoe's bow was common practice among both Mi'kmaq and Maliseet, where the projection from the point of the inwale or the main gunwale extends from twelve to sixteen inches in some craft.

Mi'kmaq canoes were likewise constructed by the eastern rib-and-plank method, although the shaping and fitting of planks differs somewhat from the Maliseet style. Planks were shaped like boards, three to four inches wide and without tapering at the end. The thickness was a standard one-eighth of an inch. Again, the planks were fitted edge to edge, but only the center plank, placed first, measured half the canoe's hull length. Adjoining planks were fitted with acute angles shaped as they were needed to fit the plank lining in the bark shell. In this form of planking (also known as sheathing layout), gaps occur at random while the planking progresses. These are then filled in with wedge-shaped plank pieces or fillers. Neatly fitted edge to edge, Mi'kmaq planking at midship joins butt to butt, much like the Maliseet planks, overlapping two to three ribs in length.

In Mi'kmaq canoes, plank fittings at the prows were set loose, held fast against the bark cover by the packing of shavings and pressure from the headboards, like the canoes of the Maliseets. Mi'kmaq canoes, however, were fitted with outer stems, or batten stems. The bark here was pinched. A pair of these outer battens were bent into a compass curvature (a sideways U) and fastened together on each side of the bark, sandwiching the cover between the batten members with root lashing or nails. White and black ash are generally used, but birch would occasionally be employed in Mi'kmaq stems. Maliseet canoe stems were manufactured from white cedar splints, which were split into a series of laminations and bent to the desired shape for the prow ends of the canoe. To hold their shape, these laminates were bound together with the inner bark of either cedar or basswood, and then these stems were inserted between the bark folds. After trimming bark to stem, fastening was accomplished by sewing through with spruce roots.

The bark hulls of Mi'kmaq and Maliseet canoes were most often made from one full length of bark. If needed,

Maliseet old form birchbark canoe, eighteen feet long, thirty-four inches wide, built by Rick Nash, 1980. The old form Maliseet canoe has a gradual upward curve of the bow. Nash has built between fifteen and twenty Maliseet-type canoes. The paddles, also made by Nash, are the type used by the Maliseet. Across the center of the canoe is a reinforcement thwart lashed to the crossbar. This is a common device used to make portaging easier by distributing the weight more evenly along the gunwales.

A freight canoe on the Mackenzie River. Although the general style of this canoe is eastern, borrowed from the fur trade canoes that traveled into this region, this canoe was definitely built in the northwest, with several features common to canoes from that area. The rib-and-batten construction, the plank stem and bark decks are all typical of northwest canoes, as well as the narrow ribs, which are similar to that of a kayak.

bark panels of varying lengths were sewn to the main sheet to extend the hull to gunwale depth. The root-and-batten form of fastening, or sewing, was the common method employed in eastern rib-and-plank construction. The bark was joined where maximum strength was needed, as in tumblehome canoe construction. Bark at the gunwale was folded over and held in place first by lashing at intervals or by using nails or tacks. It was further secured by fitting the gunwale with a cap or top rail. Mi'kmaq canoe construction omits the use of the outwale member, but in the boundary regions of New Brunswick (and according to the builder's preference) outwales were sometimes fitted to the main gunwale assembly, much like those of the bordering Maliseets. Mi'kmaq canoes displayed the method of continuous lashing across the gunwales to secure the bark cover, unlike the Maliseet method of lashing at intervals.

Algonquin, Attikamek, Abenaki

The Algonquin bands primarily inhabited the regions surrounding the Upper St. Lawrence and the Ottawa river systems, adjacent to the territories of the Maliseet, Iroquois, Cree and Ojibwa. The Algonquins were centralized along the Ottawa river region where random communities developed in the tributary river systems of the Coulonge and Gatineau river basins. In the course of migration into nearby tribal hunting boundaries, these bands would eventually mix with the Cree in the lower St. Lawrence River system or along the St. Maurice, forming the federation band of the Attikamek. It can be speculated that due to the nomadic movements of the Cree and Montagnais/Naskapi, these groups gradually merged with the Algonquins in these regions.

As a consequence of the intermingling between Native groups in the regions of the Gatineau, the Ottawa, the St. Maurice and the St. Francis rivers, the canoe hybrids of these regions varied little in most aspects of form and construction. The canoes were Algonquin in form, with pointed or pitched prows. They also exhibited hard-ribbed or slightly flared hulls with average lengths between fourteen and sixteen feet, while the beams across the gunwales were thirty-four inches. In the dense lake and river systems, these canoes could be carried or portaged with a degree of ease by one canoeist.

These river regions experienced a marked degree of white influence during the heyday of the fur trade, with many of the surrounding bands employed as builders at the fur trade building posts. There may have been significant mixing and sharing of various building skills

An eastern Cree encampment at Oxford House, Manitoba, 1890. This photograph demonstrates in a striking way that Native peoples built very different canoes for different uses. The canoe with the extreme rocker (curve of the bottom line) was very responsive in rapids but would have been unstable on windy lakes. The canoes with long, flat bottoms performed well in rough open water, but were much harder to negotiate through rapids.

and techniques, as well as the selective use of steel tools, all of which would contribute to the hybrid canoe forms attributed to these bands and tribes.

Canoes built in the St. Francis region were generally the best examples of the hybrid forms in this area. Maliseet influence was somewhat evident in these craft (most likely related to the Penobscot), in that the canoe ends tapered sharply with neat pinching of the outwale and cap members, giving the craft a fine cutwater edge at the stems. The existence of finely molded hulls from uniform rib shaping, similar to most eastern birchbark canoes, was also apparent in the St. Francis canoes.

Canoes of the St. Francis River region were constructed using the western rib-and-plank system. This was the predominant construction form of the rib-and-plank birchbark canoe, with the sheathing and planks made in an overlap pattern set in the hull shell in three sections; ends first, then midship. Planks were thin splints of white cedar no more than one-sixteenth of an inch thick, with their ends either rounded or pointed in shape. They were of short lengths, reaching roughly from crossbar to crossbar (thwarts pairs) on each

position past the center, and from these to the inside stems. When set in place, the planking edges, which were shaved or planed to a paper edge, overlapped the adjoining plank by approximately one-half to one inch. The rib shaping was narrow, similar to that of the rib and frame components of the eastern canoe builders. Canoe ribs manufactured in these regions were about two to two-and-a-half inches in width and tapered at the ends, or shoulders, to receive the gunwales. Neatly shaped and planed, the ribs were either bent with a hard bend or straight sided, depending on the builder's preference and what kind of canoe was needed, and gradually bent into a perfect U progressing up the hull.

The center crossbars or thwarts were shaped with a pronounced tumpline notch carved approximately three to four inches in from the gunwale tension to prevent the tumpline from slipping during carry. The tumpline notching of the center crossbars was a common practice in eastern canoe construction. In the St. Francis River area, this method of tumpline use may have been of white origin, since it was not otherwise used much beyond the eastern regions, or it might have

Cree/Naskapi birchbark, fifteen feet, six inches long and thirty-five inches wide, from Lac St.-Jean, Quebec, circa 1880.

come about as need arose during the fur trade period.

The majority of the surviving birchbark canoes in existence today are from the Gatineau Algonquins. The Algonquin birchbark canoes of the Gatineau and the Coulonge river basins were similar in construction to the St. Francis canoes and may have represented a hybrid type of canoe influenced by, or originating from, the St. Francis River region. The Algonquin canoes constructed in the Gatineau were built to an average length of fourteen to sixteen feet, with the beams across the gunwales approximately thirty-four inches wide, and with perpendicular shaping of the stem ends. On average, these canoes had a gradual or soft rise of the gunwale sheer at the prows and had less, or minimal, pinching of the outwale and cap members. Various canoe examples built in the Coulonge river system demonstrate tight pinching of these members, but this varied depending on the builder's preferred manner of construction. The rib and

planking were also typical of western rib and plank, with the rib shaping and planking roughly two to two-and-a-half inches in width and uniform in shape through the rib members' length, and the rib-ends' shoulders shaped to receive the gunwales. The shaping of the canoe's hull by the ribs was generally hard-ribbed to slightly flared, similar to the shaping of the St. Francis canoe type. The planking was finished throughout in the three sectional pattern and overlapped at the edges. Most commonly the bark used for the hulls of these canoes was always of one piece, a full length of birchbark. The Algonquin canoes built along the Ottawa river systems displayed high-quality bark used in the hulls, with suitable girth. It was gathered mostly from the Gatineau and Coulonge river basins and either used locally or shipped to fur trade outposts.

In later periods, canoes of these regions began to be less refined in construction when the Gatineau vicinity became popular with white sportsmen. With increasing demand for canoes to facilitate travel on rivers and lakes, canoes were constructed more hastily and workmanship deteriorated.

Eastern Cree canoes arriving at the fort at the mouth of Great Whale River on the eastern side of Hudson Bay in 1903. Here is a dramatic example of people using very different canoes for different purposes. The canoe in the foreground, a crooked canoe, would not have been of much use for carrying heavy loads, but would turn on a dime in rapids. The canoe in the background, with the flatter bottom, could carry substantial loads safely across a windy lake.

Cree

Native inhabitants of the northern boreal forest regions have been designated by complex documentation under such groups as the Eastern Cree (Naskapi/Montagnais in eastern James Bay and Hudson Bay) and Western Cree/Ojibwa (western James Bay and Hudson Bay). These bands were nomadic, governed by the seasons and settling wherever the food sources were suitable. Territorial boundaries for these groups were generally fluid, due to their constant movement. These bands would later be categorized under different tribal names by whites.

Whatever their designation, the Cree groups inhabited the northern shores of the Gulf of the St. Lawrence and Labrador and the Hudson Bay regions of the Little and Great Whale river systems. Cree bands in the boreal forest climate migrated from season to season, leaving their summer encampments for winter settlements, which were generally re-used annually by family groups. These hunting grounds neighbored the hunting areas of other Native groups or families likewise moving to winter grounds.

The surviving Cree canoes that exist in museum storage or in private collections were primarily constructed in these river regions and almost all display fine qualities of workmanship. Those canoes built by the Cree bands of the Saguenay River region or Lake St. John, designated as Montagnais Cree, are noted for their excellent craftsmanship.

Canoes throughout these regions were between fourteen and fifteen feet in length, with beams of approximately thirty-two to thirty-four inches, yet some canoes were observed as large as eighteen feet in length with beams of thirty-four inches. The hull designs were commonly U-shaped to slightly flared, with a hull rise or rocker of about six to eight inches at ends from the hull plane, similar to those built in the Lake St. John region and the lower St. Lawrence. Another feature of these canoes was a complete rocker, where the canoe hull rises as much as one foot from midship to the ends, like those canoes classified as "crooked canoes" built by the Cree bands from the Great Whale and Little

Whale rivers of Hudson Bay to Fort Chimo at Ungava Bay.

Canoes from the St. Lawrence regions and Hudson Bay had constructed depths of approximately fifteen to twenty inches, sometimes presenting a misconception of a V-shaped hull design. Birchbark canoes built at or near Lake St. John by those bands designated as the Montagnais were built in lengths averaging fourteen to fifteen feet and were, as mentioned previously, the best built canoes of the Cree bands. This may have been the result of either early contact with whites or influence from neighboring Mi'kmaq or Algonquins, as well as their location within range of good quality building materials such as white birch and northern white cedar. White cedar, the most sought-out wood source for Native canoe manufacturing, had an extended range including the regions from Lake St. John to the southern tip of James Bay, and around the Moose Factory area. These Cree bands or Montagnais also extended their boundaries into the neighboring Gatineau Valley, where the best stands of white birch on the North American continent grew in abundance.

The canoe construction was of rib-and-plank form and the typical method of bark layout was employed. In Cree construction, blocks, or round log debris, were placed under the bark and building frame at the ends, fastened by building stones. The Montagnais and various Naskapi builders practiced this method, with the bed carefully leveled for the building process. The Cree bands to the north, or those designated as Eastern Cree/Naskapi, often constructed a hybrid canoe form with an extreme rocker, called a "crooked canoe." This canoe type was built by carefully forming a sloped or depressed building bed. In these regions, as well as along the St. Lawrence Valley, sand-based soil made up much of the terrain, making the bed easy to dig. However, the sand beds were less stable than a more packed ground soil, which provided a more solid building ground with less shifting of the building frame during canoe construction. If the desired rocker was not maintained to the builders' standard, blocking was employed on the slope bed to further shape the desired sheer or rocker at the canoe's ends.

Observation of canoes built by the Montagnais of these regions demonstrates that the bark used for the hull covers was of excellent quality, with one sheet used for the bottom. The Montagnais bands most likely built their canoes at or near the trading posts at Lake St. John or Roberval, where suitable materials of white cedar and birchbark were available from the Gatineau Valley regions or the St. Maurice River Valley.

Narrow building frames, or molds, with beams no wider than twenty to twenty-two inches, were used

TOP: This is the same crooked canoe seen in the foreground of the picture on the facing page.

BOTTOM: Model made by Tappan Adney of a Naskapi (Innu) birchbark crooked canoe from northern Quebec. This craft is very similar to the one above, though lacking the extreme rocker.

when laying out and staking the bark hull. In length, the building frame measured about the same as that of the main gunwales. The gunwale structures were constructed in advance and set aside, then when needed they were set in the bark hull and fastened. This was a standard practice with eastern and Maritime rib-and-plank methods of construction.

The sewing of the hulls' bark panels was also done using the eastern or Maritime method, used in conjunction with the root-and-batten method of stitching. Most often caribou hide was used for sewing the batten for the main hull seam, as well as for closing or sewing in the stems.

Gunwale members, ribs, planking and sheathing were constructed of white cedar by the Lake St. John bands. Crossbars or thwarts were constructed of either cedar or spruce and were generally heavily shaped at their midsection, measuring approximately one to one-and-a-half inches thick. All crossbars were fastened to the main gunwale with the above-noted notch method demonstrated in most Mi'kmaq canoe construction. The bark cover was secured to the gunwale structure through a method whereby it was folded over, trimmed and held fast by tacking or the use of continual lashing with spruce roots along the gunwale. Caribou hide may have been employed at times in this process, depending on the builder, but this was uncommon since that degree of strength was not required for this process and the caribou hide strand was more crucial for the construction of artifacts used on a daily basis. The addition of the gunwale cap would further secure the bark cover to the gunwale assembly. As in Mi'kmaq canoe building, the Montagnais Cree of this region also omitted the use of an outwale member.

The canoe ends were finished with outer stems that were made from either birch or black ash, and fastened by small nails or lashed together by caribou hide, or both. As in Mi'kmaq canoes, the bark ends were fastened between the outer stem members, while the stems ends were shaved thin and tucked or fitted in slits made in the bark hull, then secured by lashings or with nails.

The planking and sheathing was made of white cedar splints, board shaped and fitted with typical Maritime edge-to-edge patterns, with the plank ends butted together at midship in the hull, similar to the construction in Mi'kmaq canoes. Planks were also fitted with varying lengths of wedge pieces, or fillers, when gaps occurred during the process of fitting the planks to the hull lining.

The canoe ribs were also manufactured of spruce or white cedar and were board-shaped without tapering at the end, with average widths of two-and-a-quarter to two-and-a-half inches, with no more than a quarter-inch in thickness. These ribs were neatly formed into a soft bend, giving shape to the hull's bilge section, where gradually ribs were flared into a V-shape to the canoe's end.

The seams and gores were pitched (or gummed) with either black or white spruce gum, and on several of these canoes red ocher pigment was mixed with the pitch. This was accomplished by adding the pigment powder to the gum while it was being boiled into liquid form. The red pigment powder was also used to add color to the canoe's crossbar ends, as well as to highlight the outer batten stems.

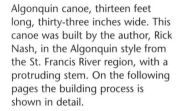

Algonquin canoe, thirteen feet long, thirty-three inches wide. This canoe was built by the author, Rick Nash, in the Algonquin style from the St. Francis River region, with a protruding stem. On the following pages the building process is shown in detail.

CONSTRUCTION OF A BIRCHBARK CANOE

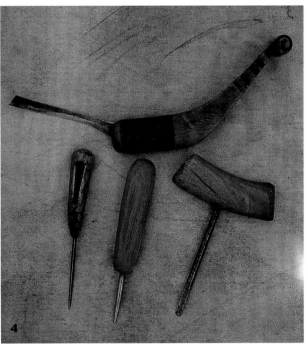

Rick Nash built this canoe during June and July of 1982. He chose the site because of the ample supply of all the materials in the surrounding area. A large, clean cedar was felled for making gunwale stock, main gunwales, outwales, caps and for the construction of the building frame (1). The cedar was about eighteen feet long. The top end of the tree was opened up first with an axe, and then with wedges (2). It was split evenly in half, then into quarters, then sixteenths (3). Gunwale members were hewn into rough shapes (4). Tools used in construction, clockwise from top: triangular awl mounted on shaped moose antler (used for goring holes in bark); T-shaped twist drill for boring holes in wood and for gouging out wood;

crooked knife (one-hand drawknife); rounded steel awl for rounding out holes in bark for lashing to gunwales. Gunwale members were shaped to dimensions with the crooked knife, then marked off with the spacing gauge for placement of ribs and lashing in between, with notches at the end for the crossbars. The gunwale members were put in position to check the evenness of the shape, then hot water was poured on the ends to soften them for bending. The gunwales were spread to shape using notched crossbars to hold them in place. Twine or heavy cord was tied from the ends and strung with struts to hold sheer. At this point the gunwales were left for a few days to dry. A building frame was constructed, about three inches shorter than the length of the main gunwale, and a few inches narrower in the beam. It was marked off using the spacing gauge. Maple splits were shaped into crossbars with the crooked knife and hung to dry. The gunwale members were unassembled from their drying position and fitted with crossbars.

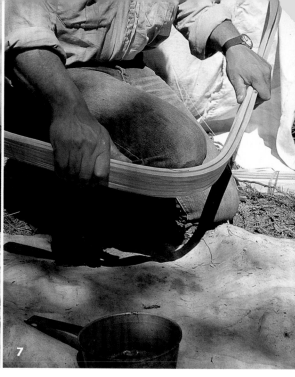

Finished gunwale assembly with outwale tied to main gunwales for dry shaping (5).

Sheer struts assembled back to maintain shape. Cedar was split for ribs and canoe planking, then shaped and planed (6).

The ribs were laid out along the building frame and marked at edges for bending. Hot water was poured over them and then they were bent over the knee at the building frame mark (7).

Selected white birch trees were cut down and peeling was started with one continuous cut along the length of the trunk (11). In June and July bark separates from the trunk with little resistance. The loose outer layer of the bark was

scraped off, then laid out on a flat prepared site. The building frame was centered on the bark and weighed down with stones resting on boards across the building frame (12). The bark was folded around the frame by cutting slots or gores.

Then the bark was staked out around the building frame from one end to center, then from the opposite end to the center. Long wooden splints or battens are used between the stakes and the bark to help fold bark evenly and to keep the bark from cracking (13).

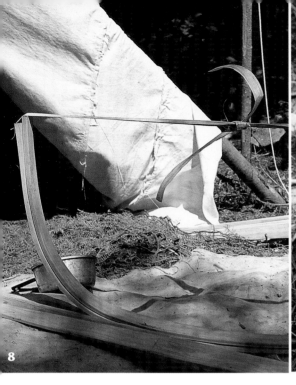

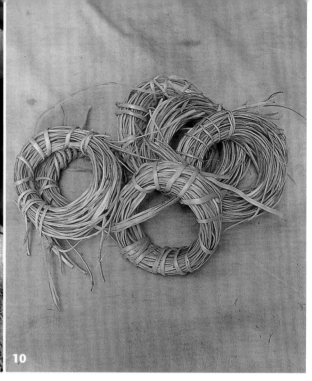

Ribs were dried to shape using cedar bark ties. Sometimes amp wick is used for this (8).

Spruce roots were boiled until the bark loosened and could be pulled off (9).

The roots were then split, resembling caning and rolled into bundles, then soaked in water to keep them pliable until they were needed (10).

Where the bark was not wide enough to reach full depth, extra panels were set in to add to bark hull (14). These were held tightly in place by inner stakes that were

wedged between the bark and the building frame and tied to main stakes with basswood bark, cedar bark or twine. They acted as clamps. The panels were sewn to the main hull with spruce roots (15). The sewing was done by shaping both ends

of a length of root to a point, then passing the end through holes made by a triangular awl, using a blanket stitch. Inner stakes were temporarily taken out and main gunwales were set in on depth, or sheer posts and inner stakes were used again to clamp gunwales in place (16).

Outwales were then placed between bark and main outer stakes and held in position for assembly (17).

They were fastened by pegs placed in holes that were bored with the twist drill. The main gunwale assembly was lashed together with spruce root (18).

The canoe stem piece, made from a cedar split, piece was set to dry to shape (19).

Cedar splints were split to use for sheathing (planking) inside the hull (23).

The sheathing lay across the thwarts, ready for assembly (24).

The canoe planking was fitted into the hull, held fast by temporary ribs, which were removed as the permanent ribs were set (25).

The stem pieces were then set into the bark ends of the canoe and held in place with makeshift "clothespin" clamps. The excess bark was trimmed for shape (20).

Sewing holes were drilled with a triangular awl and then the stem was sewn in place, using spruce root (21).

Spruce gum was collected and then boiled and strained. Animal fat or lard was added to temper the mixture, then it was used to seal the seams of the canoe (22).

The permanent ribs were set in position and marked for trimming of excess length (26).

Once trimmed, the rib ends were shaped to a wedge shape and fixed to the canoe by being forced under and between the outwale and the main gunwale, then driven forward (27).

After the ribs were in place, the canoe was left to set for five days, then the ribs were driven completely home. The canoe was finished with a decorative cutback cap, gunwale caps and gum pitching (28).

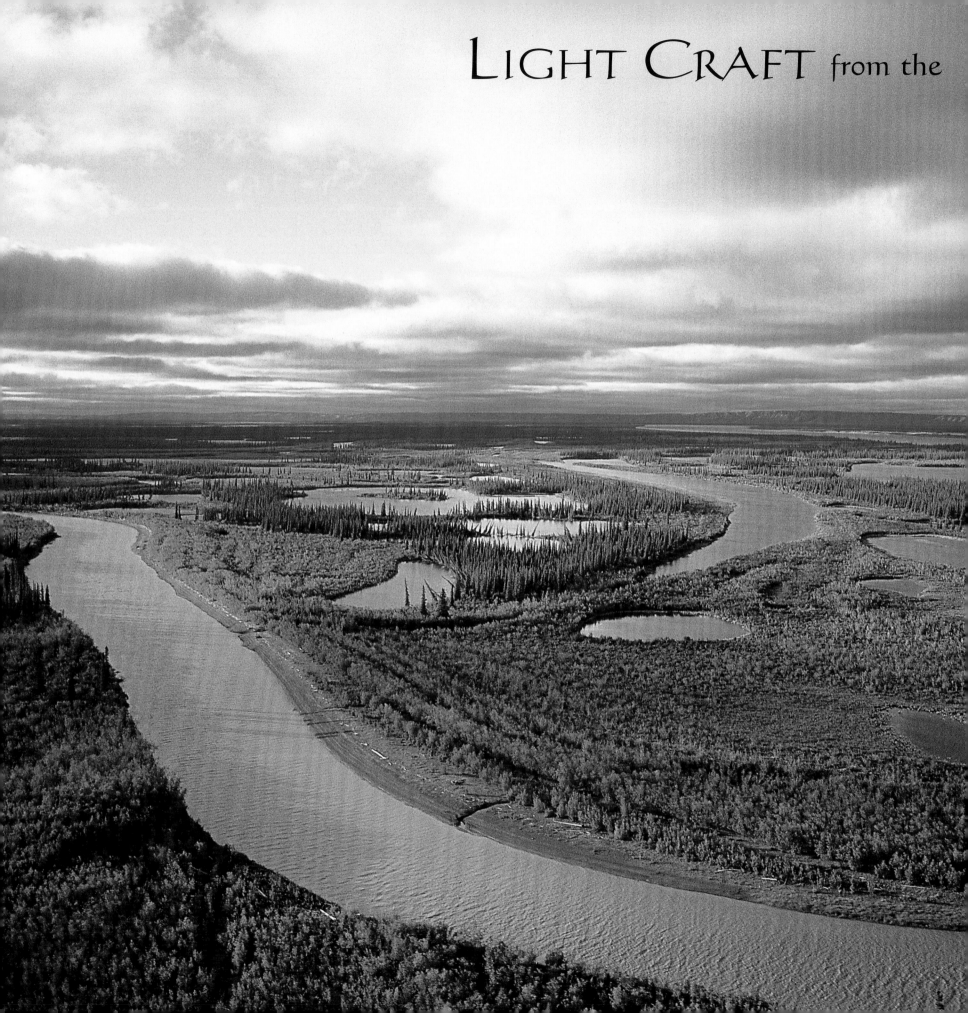

GREAT NORTHWEST

DAVID FINCH AND **DON GARDNER**

FACING PAGE: The Mackenzie River delta, where the river flows into the Arctic Ocean.

TOP: Slavey birchbark, thirteen feet, four inches long, twenty-seven inches wide. From Fort Norman, Northwest Territories. In the far northwest birch trees are very small; it often took a large number to build a canoe.

BOTTOM: These Athapaskan birchbark canoes from the region of the Yukon River in Alaska are very similar in shape to the Inuit kayak.

The great Canadian west is prairies. Images from the past of buffalo, Indians, cowboys, settlers and oil wells spring to mind. Further north, however, lies another Canadian west where the waters flow to the Arctic Ocean, not to the Pacific or Hudson Bay.

This remotest of Canadian watersheds offers a window into the past, to a time before contact with European commerce and culture. From downtown Yellowknife or Fort Simpson, it is hard to see into the past. But a short walk takes you into a time before pavement and gravel, jets and bush planes, outboard motors or awkward York boats; to a time when seasons and survival, not commerce or the calendar, directed society.

Even the long arms of the fur trade did not reach into this remote area until the early 1800s—over a century after furs began flowing to England from Hudson Bay. Commerce from this distant corner of the Canadian northwest was unreliable and costly. The Hudson's Bay Company and the North West Company struggled in competition, expending most of their energy fighting each other from their meager outposts on Lake Athabasca. Though the furs were of superior quality, the high cost of moving them to market left little profit.

TOP: Fort Rae, Northwest Territories, 1913. Here a Dogrib man is seated in the bottom of his canoe in the characteristic position used by his people. They never knelt, and the thwarts were not strong enough to support their weight. At the edge of the front deck, nearest the paddler, a curl of bark is visible. This served as a splash guard.

BOTTOM:
Gwich'in birch-bark, eighteen feet, five inches long, twenty-five inches wide, circa 1850. The beads at the stern are Chinese trade beads from the period of the Russian fur trade on the Northwest Coast before 1850. The sea otter trade was part of a global trade system that included England, Spain, Russia and the United States. Trade goods were traded with Northwest Coast peoples for furs, but especially the highly prized sea otter skins. Traders would then sail to the tightly controlled port city of Canton, where the Chinese aristocracy and rich merchants traded the otter skins for tea, silk and porcelain. Then the ships proceeded westward around Africa. It was recently discovered that the lashing around the gunwales of this craft is not root, as would be expected, but Chinese rattan.

And so the old ways survived longer in this remote corner of Canada. Trade did not change the northwest as quickly as it did along the fur trade routes in southern Canada. The far northwest still offers us a chance to look back into history and to understand the creation story of skin boats and bark canoes.

Here, timeless fundamentals still affect everyday life and pragmatism rules the north. Northern people have always existed in a land that most of us would consider a frigid wasteland, but they thrived and prospered. In the 1770s, the early European explorer Samuel Hearne found the north anything but empty. In spite of feeling superior to his native guides and their primitive tools, he wrote, "... every thing they make is executed with a neatness not to be excelled by the most expert mechanic, assisted with every tool he could wish." Explorer Alexander Mackenzie and mapmaker Peter Fidler also marveled at their ingenuity.

Like pre-contact people in the south, northerners lived in a symbiotic relationship with the land. They were part of the chain of life. They harvested caribou, deer, rabbits, moose, fish and birds. In the winter, they crossed the snow-covered expanses with dog teams and sleds. In warmer months, traveling on foot, they moved through the land with speed, grace and safety, until they reached lakes or rivers, where they created craft to move them over the water. Where trees grew, they used bark to build canoes and kayaks. Elsewhere they used skins for kayaks and umiaks. Sometimes they even pieced together several moose hides to make a massive canoe big enough to transport several families and their winter catch of fur.

Perfectly suited to the land, their watercraft also reflected the land. Their boats were usually very small and sparse, making wise use of precious materials. Though the craft seem perilously small to us now and are

sometimes considered only hunting canoes, they were large enough to float entire families and all their possessions. Small size and light weight made sense in a landscape where portages were frequent—a family often had to carry their canoes and gear across dozens or even hundreds of portages each year.

Besides, building material was scarce in the north. In the subarctic, large spruce or birch trees sacrificed their bark to make canoes. Birchbark was the material of choice, and a trade in the more pliable, light bark sprang up. People even carried rolls of birchbark along on their migrations, building canoes as necessary. These canoes were built to be light in every aspect, including interior framing and sheathing. Though sheathing or planking was common between the ribs and the birchbark in central Canadian canoes, it was almost unknown in the North, where small poles acted as stringers and the bark itself served as both sheathing and waterproof cover. The emphasis was always on utility: lightness, ease of repair, use of readily available local materials and functionality.

In areas where large pieces of bark were hard to find, builders used smaller sections, sometimes fitting together twenty or more pieces of bark to build a small canoe. In the far north, skins from moose, seals, caribou and walrus covered frames. Sparse and spare, these light craft reflected the reality of life in Canada's last frontier.

Northern people quickly adapted to new materials when Europeans arrived, forgetting old ways quickly. Utility being paramount, they enthusiastically embraced outboard motors, bush planes, chainsaws, snow machines, automobiles and jet planes. In the process, they lost part of their culture.

Today northerners are rediscovering their love for the old ways. More than recapturing lost skills, they realize they can balance some of the negative effects of industrial society by connecting with the past. Canoe building was recently reborn near Yellowknife in the Northwest Territories where a local yearning to rediscover long-forgotten trails fostered the desire to rebuild the Dogrib canoe. Tom Andrews of the Prince of Wales Northern Heritage Centre researched the history of the Dogrib canoes along with John B. Zoe. They entertained a proposal from Don Gardner of Calgary to hold a canoe-building workshop to craft a light, simple Dogrib hunter's canoe. Weighing about thirty pounds—light for portaging—the Dogrib is thirteen feet long, has a twenty-eight-inch beam and a depth of ten inches. Bark covers both decks. Due to the small size of birch trees in the area, it took twenty-two pieces to make this canoe, but, historically it sometimes took twenty-five or thirty small pieces of bark to build a canoe. A rushed effort could create a serviceable craft in a few days, but construction

Moosehide boat, Northwest Territories, 1981. This boat was built in 1981 by Dene elder and master builder Gabe Etchinelle, pictured here holding the steering oar, and his understudy, George Pellissey, who is in the bow. Sadly both are now dead and with them goes much of the knowledge of the building of these craft. However, a videotape was made of the construction process and the boat itself is in the Prince of Wales Northern Heritage Centre in Yellowknife.

usually took ten days or more. Though modern tools helped speed up the construction of this canoe, the only tools necessary were an axe, an awl and a crooked knife.

Another canoe from the far northwest is the kayak-form canoe. Adney and Chapelle termed them "kayak model." These canoes were also pieced together from many panels of bark. Instead of interior sheathing or planks, they used a simple lattice-like rigid bottom frame to give shape to the flat-bottomed hull. Neither woven together nor tied in any way, this latticework of stringers and ribs provided all the structure necessary to give form and strength to these light craft. They appear quite fragile, but they were never subjected to the heavy use and brutal conditions under which the fur trade canoes functioned. Elders recalled these little canoes being treated with the care and attention that precious and fragile craft deserved. On the exterior, the stems were exposed wood, with the bark attached well back of the leading edge. Slightly hogged during construction, the canoe flattened out when loaded for travel.

When Gardner showed the elders the building frame around which most birchbark canoes are constructed, they could recall no such equipment from their childhoods. Instead of building on a soft bed in the ground, where stakes could hold the frame in place while the bark was molded around its pattern, the elders remembered building the canoes on rocky slabs using hundreds of little pegs. Perhaps, given the lack of materials with which to create a form, the old way was to simply drill holes with an awl along the edges of the numerous pieces of bark and then peg them together into the

approximate shape of the desired canoe. Then, removing the pegs as they worked their way around the canoe, the builders stitched up the craft with spruce roots. Only after the envelope of bark was completed did these canoes receive the interior structure of a simple and flimsy latticework of stringers and ribs, which gave a final form to these light craft.

Other features distinguished these canoes from their central Canadian cousins. For example, their stems were almost always highly raked, sometimes extremely raked. Headboards were missing from these craft too, perhaps because they were usually heavily decked in the bow—sometimes as much as a full third of the length of the craft—hence the comparison to the kayak. Headboards were not structurally necessary. These utilitarian boats sometimes included protection against waves in the form of an additional splash guard: a roll of bark, half curled, stitched to the back of the front deck in order to deflect the water that tried to spill back into the canoe.

These kayak-type canoes were commonly constructed by the Chipewyan, Slavey, Beaver, Hare, Dogrib, Tanana and Gwich'in peoples. Built without much adornment, most were wider and deeper in the stern, reflecting their use and the heavy loads they carried. Especially in the Dogrib canoes, the stern stem was higher than the bow, in keeping with the other larger features of the stern of the boat.

The Athabaskan Gwich'in canoe, formerly known as Loucheux, is a special subgroup of the kayak-form canoes and some of its unique features deserve additional

A moosehide boat made by the Gravel River people (Deh-cho) at Fort Norman in the Northwest Territories, in 1921. The moosehide boat, modeled on the York boat, was first built in the 1880s to transport dried meat for the Hudson's Bay Company. These craft were usually about forty feet long and could carry two tons of cargo. They were assembled in the spring in the mountain hunting camps of the Dene, paddled down to the trading posts on the Mackenzie River, and there dismantled. The moosehides were either sold or fashioned into a variety of items. Because of this cycle, there are very few moosehide boats in existence, although it seems they were used quite extensively until the 1920s.

attention. More finely crafted and built with great adornment, they were the grandest canoes of this area. The elegant craft boasted a rigid floor frame of strong but light construction. Stems were typically twice the height of the depth in the middle of the canoe and made of much heavier material than in most canoes of this type, protruding from the bark and sharpened. Decks covered both ends of these craft and adornment was often very complex, sometimes including painted gunwales and even imported trade beads. Of all the canoes, the Gwich'in most resembled the kayak, a similarity not unexpected due to their proximity to the Alaskan and Inuit influences.

When the peoples of this area needed larger canoes, some authors speculate that they turned to a narrow-bottomed cargo or family craft. It is unclear why these skilled builders of the kayak-form craft did not simply builder larger versions of the canoes that already served them very well, and perhaps they did. However, many of the larger canoes seem to point to the influences of central Canadian canoe building, most likely from the fur trade as it spread throughout the North.

These cargo canoes resemble fur trade craft so clearly that it is hard to consider them indigenous to the far north. For example, their ends boasted laminated and bent stem-pieces, almost identical to Algonquin-Ojibwa fur trade canoes. Bows with plank stems were higher than sterns, lashing patterns resembled those on fur trade craft, as did sheathing and conventional split ribs. These canoes could be up to twenty-three feet long and four feet wide. Although the Natives of the northwest applied their individual signatures to certain aspects of the crafting of these canoes, these larger boats appear to show a direct link to their economic links with the central Canadian trade in furs.

A more puzzling craft in the Canadian west, and one that shows possible influences from far afield, is the "sturgeon nose" canoe that appears to have been built with its bow and stern upside down. Common in only a relatively small area of British Columbia and part of today's Washington State, this craft was usually built of spruce or pine bark. Canoes built along the Amur River in Russia resemble these unusual craft, often called Kutenai (or Kootenay) canoes due to the fact that Natives built them along the Kootenay River. Some hogging was common in these canoes, a feature that probably flattened once the lightly crafted canoe was loaded. The ram-shaped ends made the craft quite fast to paddle, though they were not known for their stability and were hard to turn.

Speculation persists as to the reason for the unusual shape of the Kutenai canoe, and the link to similar craft far away may be more apparent than real. Though birchbark was available in historic times in this area, most canoes in this region of British Columbia were made of spruce or pine bark. Although built with inferior materials, they generally stood up better to the canoe-building process than the paper-thin birchbark of the British Columbia interior. Even though large birch trees were found in this region, birchbark usually only found its way into side panels of the Kutenai craft.

Function rather than design probably forced the Kutenai to build their canoes with the unusual sturgeon nose. Although birchbark resists cracking along its grain, both spruce and pine bark are notorious for failing longitudinally. Therefore, if the canoe builder was forced to use the inferior but thicker bark from the coniferous trees, he probably chose to use as long a piece of spruce or pine bark as possible along the bottom of the end of the canoe in order to prevent splitting. The only way to bind the end of the canoe was to taper it back and up from the end of the canoe, creating the unusual shape for which these craft are best known. As with the other craft of the Canadian northwest, it appears as though these unique canoes also reflected the landscape and took advantage of the best the natural world had to offer.

Fort Rae, Northwest Territories, approximately 125 miles north of Yellowknife, 1913. A Dogrib man braces his paddle on the ground as he steps into his canoe. It is interesting to note the uniformity of these canoes, with their almost identical construction. It was important for each individual to identify strongly with the Dogrib people as a group and there was seldom any variation in building techniques. They built their canoes together and exactly the same. The beautiful latticework of the ribs and stringers is evident in all these canoes, with the bark deck characteristic of the Dogrib and the Dene canoes.

CONSTRUCTION OF A
DOGRIB
CANOE

During two weeks in June 1996 at a spring hunting camp near Rae-Edzo, about two hours drive north from Yellowknife, Northwest Territories, Dogrib elders, students and helpers collected materials and built a canoe. About twelve hundred students and other visitors came to the camp to watch and learn. The hope was that the students would embrace the old skills, claim them as their own and become skilled canoe builders. The tradition of creating fine watercraft could then become an important economic force in this part of the north, allowing Natives to once again build canoes of high quality, destined for museums and other collections around the world.

The canoe-building workshop was planned by The Dogrib Divisional Board of Education in Rae-Edzo, Dogrib Treaty 11 Council in Rae and the Prince of Wales Northern Heritage Centre in Yellowknife.

Most important to the workshop were six elders—three couples—Joe and Julie Mackenzie, Paul and Elizabeth Rabesca and Nick and Annie Black. All were at least seventy years old, and remembered helping their parents building canoes, though none had built any of their own as adults. A translator was needed because most of the elders spoke only Dogrib.

The project sought to pass on the canoe-building tradition from the elders to a generation that had never seen their parents build canoes. One of the goals was to connect their children and the generations to come with their ancestors' way of life and thus preserve some of the values of the past. Some techniques came back quickly. The elders had good eyes for detail and they seemed to see into the grain of the wood. Splitting the roots came easily and stitching the bark was second nature. But more complex techniques were lost and can only be coaxed back with great effort and time.

From the ancient traditions the people of the 1990s built a new canoe. Cameras and video recorders collected information about the project and an artist recorded the event with drawings. As a result of this community effort, there has been a regeneration of interest in traditional canoe building in the area and the elders built two more canoes in 1997.

1. **Collecting bark**
The search for bark begins the process of building a birchbark canoe. In June and early July the sap runs, making it easy to remove the bark from the standing trees. Six elders and twenty-five students spent half a day in the bush gathering bark. Elder Joe Mackenzie and his son George, a schoolteacher, worked together. The elders seemed to have a map in their heads; they knew the landscape intimately, almost every tree. They harvested bark from smallish trees, but the best the area had to offer. Joe showed the students the technique and the film crew recorded the process.

4. **Building the frame**
Stitching together the main panels came next, while a temporary framework provided the shape. Nick Black, his wife Annie Black and a student worked together. As people milled about and discussed the project, elders and students worked together, slowly at first, recreating the ancient ways of building a boat from the land itself. The importance of the collaboration can not be overemphasized: men and women, elders and students, fathers and sons, mothers and daughters all came together in a new way as they knelt by the canoe and formed it from the earth.

2. Collecting black spruce

The elders can tell what the tree will do when split, but they sometimes check by taking off a piece of bark and examining the wood. It is important that the tree has as few branches as possible and a grain that doesn't curl, so that it can be split lengthwise and not twist. Small chainsaws made the job go fast, even the splitting. As skilled as the elders are with an axe, they have become even more skilful with the chainsaw. After another half day the group had all the materials necessary for the canoe.

3. Choosing the best bark

The elders, Joe and Nick, chose and matched the pieces of bark that went into the canoe. The bark was of good thickness even though the pieces were relatively small. Setting aside those with the most serious blemishes, the elders fashioned the skin of the bark canoe.

5. Stitching with roots

The spruce root had been collected from the same area as the black spruce trees used in the canoe. The women spent many days preparing the roots by stripping off the bark, splitting them along the fine fibers and creating the material that holds the craft together. Holes to receive the lashing were made by hand with a nail, but in historic times a sharpened bone served as an awl. The bone is actually better because it does not tear the fiber of the birchbark as does a steel tool. Instead, the softer bone spreads the fiber as it pushes its way through, and causes less tearing.

6. Carving the stem

Women did most of the repetitive work, splitting the roots and sewing the panels together. The men were involved in a wider array of activities. They did the planning and talking, running off into the bush and getting materials, carving all the woodwork and bending. Joe Mackenzie carved the stem from a carefully selected tree in the bush. Seasoned, bent wood is best, because green wood bends as it dries. The crooked knife, a one-handed drawknife, was the instrument of choice. With it they carved almost anything. Working with wood was very natural to all of them.

7. Work huddle

The historic photos show groups of women, usually, working on the canoes. Here elders and students worked together to recreate the old way of building a canoe. The awning protected against the hot sun and prevented the bark from drying out, curling and becoming hard to work. The greatest danger was that the bark would dry out.

8. Working together

This demonstrates one of the processes that was so hoped for—and worked out very well— where the elders worked with, and taught, the young people the old skills. Joe Mackenzie watched as a student lashed the bark to the inwale of the canoe. Elders had prepared the gunwales by splitting the black spruce with a small chainsaw. Hand planes then came into use, a fast and efficient system for working wood.

11. Fitting the ribs

With the stringers all in place and a few temporary ribs installed too, Nick began the process of crafting each permanent rib to fit its final location. Paul had split the rib stock with a chainsaw and then prepared each of the thin little ribs by hand. The fact that they were taken from green wood helped make them pliable, but they kept them wet with hot water.

12. Rest and inspection

A temporary brace was necessary to give stability to the canoe until all the permanent ribs were installed. The final product looks quite different from canoes from other areas, where the ribs are wider and the sheathing completely covers the bottom. The canoes from this area show more of the building process, with the ribs and sheathing forming a latticework.

9. Pegging the stems
The students were very involved in pegging and sewing the bark onto the stems. Pegging was probably a very old technique common in this part of the north. These temporary long pegs go right through the bark, the stem and the bark on the other side. All the drilling was done with an awl. The green spruce was so soft that one twisting motion would go through easily, without splitting the wood.

10. Placing stringers
Paul Rabesca, who had been planing black spruce into gunwales, stringers and ribs, joined Nick Black as the group began installing stringers. As Paul's daughter said, "I've never seen him work so hard or be so happy." The stringers were different from the sheathing used in central Canadian canoes. They were just poles, really, planed down to flat sides. No cedar is available in this area so they made the stringers from the trees in their landscape. Thwarts were already in place, made of very light spruce, mortised and tenoned into the inwale. No sitting on these thwarts.

13. Pitching the seams
Using school chairs to support the nearly completed craft, students and elders worked together to seal the seams and the holes that were made in the bark while stitching. They used amber-colored spruce gum taken from damaged trees, mixed it with some lard to make it a little less brittle, and then heated it.

14. Blessing the canoe
The elders gave prayers, in Dogrib, over the final canoe. They thanked all who participated in the creation of the canoe. But most of all they gave thanks for the canoe: in a spirit of cooperation and hard work, remembering the old ways and passing on traditions to the students, they had once again built a Dogrib canoe in the north. Thanks for the canoe.

VESSELS of LIFE

STEVEN C. BROWN

NORTHWEST COAST DUGOUTS

The **Northwest Coast** is an area that sustained numerous water-oriented Aboriginal cultures, from the lower Columbia River (on the border between Oregon and Washington states), to Yakutat Bay on the Gulf of Alaska. Throughout this region, the dugout canoe was synonymous with life—a way of life that enfolded the canoe into nearly every aspect of daily living. From the outer barrier islands of this coast, such as the Alexander Archipelago (in southeast Alaska), the Queen Charlotte Islands and Vancouver Island, along the web of seaways and fjord-like inlets that slice the region into myriad separate islands and peninsulas, and up the larger mainland rivers that cut through the coastal mountain range, the first inhabitants of the Northwest Coast made their homes and food gathering camps. In a wide range of regional environments, the existence of sea-going canoes enabled the Aboriginal Northwest Coast peoples to become the masters of their worlds, living in a seasonal round of camp and village locations that were advantageous for the harvesting of varied and plentiful food resources. Without the development of sea-going watercraft, the peoples of the Northwest Coast would have lived a marginal existence devoid of many of the characteristics that we associate with the wealth and artistry of their

world. Food gathering, trade, cultural expansion and warfare all depended on seaworthy, capable vessels.

The major tribes or First Nations of the Northwest Coast each have occupied their traditional territories for many millennia, and these lands are for the most part reflected in their historical geographic locations. Though these lands today in most areas are greatly reduced in size, many historic village sites are no longer occupied and Native populations are only just returning to prehistoric levels, the Northwest Coast First Nations continue to survive in their traditional homelands. The territories of the Chinook and Chinookan language family are found on the lower Columbia River. The Coast Salish, which is the largest language division, with numerous subdivisions (including Puget Sound Salish, Straits Salish, Central Coast Salish, Northern Coast Salish and others) live in western Washington State and southern British Columbia. The Makah dwell on the northwest tip of Washington State and the Nuu-chah-nulth (formerly referred to as

FACING PAGE: A beach in British Columbia near the Queen Charlotte Islands.

ABOVE LEFT: Rain hat woven from spruce root by Isabella Edenshaw and painted by her husband Charles, a renowned Haida carver and painter.

ABOVE RIGHT: Salish water bucket. This handled bucket has a carefully fitted bottom to make it watertight, and was used as a water container for household use or perhaps when traveling in canoes.

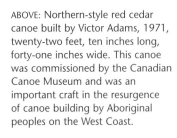

ABOVE: Northern-style red cedar canoe built by Victor Adams, 1971, twenty-two feet, ten inches long, forty-one inches wide. This canoe was commissioned by the Canadian Canoe Museum and was an important craft in the resurgence of canoe building by Aboriginal peoples on the West Coast.

Nootka or Nootkan) are found between the mountains and the sea on the west coast of Vancouver Island in British Columbia. The Kwakwaka'wakw (formerly referred to as Kwakiutl) occupy the north end and northeast side of Vancouver Island, the adjacent mainland inlets and the myriad islands in between. The Heiltsuk (also called Bella Bella), a language family that also includes several subdialects (Oowekeno, Haihais, and Haisla) are centered in Milbanke Sound and the surrounding islands on the central British Columbia coast. The Nuxalk (Bella Coola) village sites are at the head of Burke and Dean channels and at the mouth of the Bella Coola River east of the Heiltsuk territory. The territories of the Coast Tsimshian, Nishga'a, and Gitk'san (all speakers of dialects of the S'malgyixw language) are on the northern British Columbia coast and extend up the Nass and Skeena rivers as much as two hundred miles. The Haida occupy the Queen Charlotte Islands and their relatives the Kaigani Haida are found on the southwestern islands of southeast Alaska. The lands and villages of the Tlingit are distributed over the many islands and inlets of the southeastern Alaska panhandle.

Each of these coastal First Nations developed watercraft with unique forms and capabilities, expertly adapted to the specialized environments in which they were deployed—fishing and seafood gathering, sea mammal hunting and traveling with loads of passengers or freight. Northwest Coast canoes were (and still are) made from the solid trunks of certain species of old-growth trees: millions of them grew in the rain forests that once blanketed the westernmost slopes of the North American continent. The western red cedar was clearly preferred by canoe builders within its native habitat range, while Sitka spruce and even cottonwood were used in the area

north of the red cedar's limited climactic zone. The trees would be felled, shaped on the outside, hollowed out and precisely thinned, steamed (by boiling water inside to limber the wood) and opened out to a dimension wider than that of the original log. Though commonly known as a dugout canoe, this term does not accurately convey the care and precision evident in the design and construction that characterize the sculptured wooden vessels of the Northwest Coast.

Some of the Northwest Coast canoe types have evolved in form over recent historic time, while other now-traditional types were newly developed in the last two hundred years. Other canoe forms went out of traditional use quite suddenly in response to changing developments within the canoe cultures. Several Northwest Coast First Nations used similar widespread canoe types, while other canoe forms were limited in manufacture and use to single language groups or nations.

No one knows exactly when the first Northwest Coast canoes were developed, or precisely what they looked like. From the surviving oral histories of the families and clans, we know that the original First Peoples were waterborne, traveling in canoes down the mainland rivers after the retreat of the Great Glaciers or exploring the shorelines of channels and inlets in search of a fruitful home after the waters of the Great Flood receded. Both of these geophysical events are recorded in the oral histories of Northwest Coast peoples. Little from these great woodworking cultures has survived from the very distant past to be recovered archaeologically: the material was too perishable, the conditions too prone to decay. More durable bone and stone evidence, however, from the northern Northwest Coast (in southeast Alaska) shows that there have been coastal peoples who harvested sea

The Kaigani Haida village of Klinkwan, circa 1895. The clan houses of this village show the incorporation of milled lumber and glass windows into the traditional Native architecture that took place in the late nineteenth century. Oriented to the sea, the fronts of the houses overlook the foreshore, where many canoes have been drawn up or anchored in the intertidal zone. Most of these canoes are of the classic Northern type, though others of related design can be seen as well, indicating how canoe makers appeared to experiment with a variety of forms for a range of uses. None of these vessels exhibit a painted design on the hull, which is typical of the region and time period.

resources at least as far back as nine thousand years ago. The most recent work and thought in this field suggests that the first people migrated into this area long before that time (possibly as much as twenty thousand years ago), traveling from Asia around the northern Pacific Rim by skin boat or wooden canoe from landfall to landfall. Perhaps the forms of these vessels survive in some measure in the historic vessels of the Northwest Coast, as other remnants of Asian origins survive in certain bowl and tool forms, painted and carved design structures and characteristics, and of course in the appearance of the people themselves.

Basketry fragments found in waterlogged archaeological sites in Washington State and Alaska demonstrate a clear continuity of form, weaving techniques and materials that reaches back from three thousand to fifty-five hundred years ago. Regarding the antiquity of canoe forms, one important village location has provided evidence of continuity over half a millennium. At the Ozette village site on the southern Northwest Coast in Washington State, an archaeological site dubbed the "Pompeii of the Northwest Coast" has been excavated. In it were parts of five ancient houses of the Makah people, which had been inundated by a catastrophic mudslide between three hundred and five hundred years ago. The systematic excavation of this unique site yielded examples of all kinds of household objects: tools, weaving materials and equipment, bowls, boxes, carved house screens and even canoe models. All were damaged by the impact of the slide, but nonetheless serve as invaluable ties to the past. Even though only fragments survive, the parts of canoe models that have been recovered show us that Makah canoes of nearly five hundred years ago were of the same design and appearance as those recorded by the earliest Euro-American explorers at the end of the eighteenth century. The full-sized canoes, unfortunately for posterity, were down on the beach at the time of the slide, washed out to sea by the force of the mud torrent. Only a few scattered pieces of these vessels survived under the mud and rock of the landslide.

Visual documentation of Native canoes by Euro-American artists who accompanied the Spanish, English, American and Russian explorers and traders on the Northwest Coast in the late eighteenth century shows fully developed, familiar canoe types, most of which remained the same into the nineteenth and even the twentieth century. One could readily presume that most of these vessels shared at least a similar antiquity with those of the Makah at Ozette, and probably underwent their initial development more than a thousand years

ABOVE: *Return of the War Party*. In this 1847 painting by Canadian artist Paul Kane, he has depicted highly decorated war canoes returning to what is now Victoria Harbour with their war trophies: the heads of slain enemies. Kane fabricated the scene from stories related to him by local Native historians, using model canoes as subjects for the picture. He was not aware of which end was the bow on the lead canoe (a Head canoe type) and illustrated it traveling backward.

LEFT: Headdress frontlet. Worn as part of a bird-skin and ermine-pelt headdress commonly known today as a "peace dance headdress," a carved and inlaid wooden frontlet such as this would be made to display family and lineage crests. They were often richly adorned with blue-green abalone shell, which was obtained in trade from First Nations of California and Mexico. Local Northwest Coast abalone shells were small and pale on the inside, making them less desirable for inlays.

ago. Certain types that were drawn by the early Euro-American artists fell out of use and have not been seen since the mid-nineteenth century, though even these still survive today in model form. Other canoe types did not appear in the earliest drawings or accounts from the eighteenth century. These vessels were apparently developed in the early nineteenth century, when they begin to appear in various forms of historic documentation, such as paintings by both Native and Euro-American artists (for example, the Canadian painter Paul Kane). The canoe cultures were capable of dynamic and inventive change, creating new vessels or redesigning older ones that then took their place in the traditional flotillas.

The Value of Canoes to Coastal Societies

Along most of the Northwest Coast, especially in the northern regions (between the central coast of British Columbia and Yakutat Bay in southeast Alaska), food resources were and are highly seasonal, and, more importantly to the Aboriginal peoples, food-gathering sites were often far apart. The rugged outer coasts, where sea mammals, many species of fish, shellfish and seaweeds were once plentiful, required seaworthy vessels to navigate the channels, passages and open seas. Many miles away, at the heads of inlets that cut deeply into the rugged island and mainland shorelines, are the outlets of rivers and creeks where up to five species of salmon return to spawn through the summer season. Even in such a relatively harsh environment as the northern Northwest Coast (where winters are long and summers short), periods of intense labor could yield tremendous food riches at peak season for people capable of traveling optimally between resource sites. For the very survival of the Aboriginal people, canoes were the vital kingpins that made such an existence possible. The varied sizes of canoes carried not only the people to these seasonal camps, but also their house planks for shelters, their daily supplies and their specialized types of food-gathering equipment. The canoes would return to a more permanent winter village site after weeks or months of harvesting, smoke curing and drying of foods. The bounty of their efforts was loaded up and carried home in baskets and bent-corner boxes, to be stored and eaten throughout the long winter season or traded as surplus to distant peoples for resources not found locally.

Aboriginal Northwest Coast peoples lived out the shortest days of the year where the beds of clams, cockles, mussels and seaweed provided foods that were fresh and varied nutritionally. These seafoods would be supplemented by the harbor seals, deer, roots and berries that

LEFT: Steaming a large canoe. The regular pattern of thickness-measuring holes can be seen over the hull. The sailcloth used to contain the steam is pulled aside as the workers use split-wood tongs to remove cold stones and add new red-hot ones to maintain the water at a simmer.

were hunted or gathered from forest locations both near and far from the villages. Even resources closer to home were accessed with the aid of canoes, and it is said that people visiting from one end of the village to another would just as soon paddle over as walk along the beach.

Canoes carried the woodworkers to the areas where the best western red cedars grew—straight, tall and of a girth that staggers the imagination. Ingenious techniques using wedges made of antler and wood allowed Native artisans to split planks of regular width from trees that were still standing, as well as from those that had been felled by laborious burning and chiseling. These were the methods used in the days prior to the advent of Euro-American axes, with which even large trees could be felled much more easily. Prior to the period of direct trade with Euro-Americans, iron and steel tools were in use on the Northwest Coast, though mainly in the form of chisels, small adze blades and knives, rather than the larger and heavier Euro-American axes. Archaeological evidence shows that these ferrous metal tools were in use even three hundred to five hundred years ago at Ozette village, and presumably throughout the rest of the coast at that time as well. The material for these tools most likely arrived on the Northwest Coast by one or more possible means, of which three routes are the most readily apparent. One such route is the possibility of group-to-group Aboriginal trade from Asia across the Bering Strait and along the Gulf of Alaska coast southward. The second is the documented existence of Japanese (or other Asian) merchant shipwrecks, in which a few members of the crew sometimes survived, crossing the Pacific adrift. These shipwrecks or fragments thereof would have yielded structural metals as well as finished tools carried by the crew. The third route is the possibility of northward Aboriginal trade from the Spanish missions of Mexico and California, the earliest of which were established in the sixteenth century. After the arrival on the Northwest Coast of Euro-American traders and explorers in the late eighteenth century, many more steel tools of more sophisticated form became directly available to the carvers and canoe builders of the Northwest Coast. Captain James Cook, who anchored at Friendly Cove, west Vancouver Island, in 1778, noted the many steel knives carried by the Nuu-chah-nulth people and the existing words in their native language for iron and steel, proof that these substances were not altogether new to them. Fourteen years later, in 1792, Captain George Vancouver (who had sailed with Cook earlier) would bemoan the large number of firearms that had been transported into the region by British and American fur traders.

Though the forests were dense and the trees were unbelievably large (trunks up to fifteen feet in diameter were once fairly common), trees with the special characteristics necessary for canoes were very rare. Their scarcity sometimes required the canoe makers to journey far from their villages, and even far from the water's edge in order to locate the optimal section of log. Canoe trees had to be solid and had to have grown under the most appropriate natural conditions. They had to be protected from the storm winds that could cause cracks in the heart or break off treetops or branches. Such damage would let water and fungus spores into the moist interior of the tree, promoting decay. Many red cedar trees are standing hollow shells due to this type of interior decay, and consequently are not appropriate to use for canoes.

TOP: The ergonomically formed handle of this D-adze features the alert head of a wolf. The steel blade is bound to the wooden handle with rawhide strips, creating an extremely versatile tool for shaping and hollowing wood.

MIDDLE: Wooden wedges like this are topped with a rope-like cedar-withe (branch) ring to prevent splitting under the blow of a stone hammer. Made of either spruce or yew, wedges were always cut from the compression wood. This minimized the deformation of the wedge top caused by innumerable hammer blows.

BOTTOM: Stone mauls were formed by pecking a large cobble with a smaller, harder stone. After many days of relentless tapping, the maul took shape.

Once the right tree was felled, the canoe hull would be shaped out, rough hollowed, hauled with ropes and the aid of gravity out of the forest, pulled over the trunks of many small trees felled crosswise for the purpose. Then the rough hull was towed by canoe back to the village beach for finishing and fitting out. Thus canoes, already heavily involved in a myriad of tasks, were also used in the making of new canoes.

One of the most distinctive features of Northwest Coast dugout canoes is found in the technique of their construction, which is described in the following chapter by Eugene Arima. With the exception of some smaller vessels (and of course models), canoes from this region in their final form are actually made larger than the trees from which they were carved! This is possible because of the technique of steaming the canoe, to make the wood limber enough to bend, and widening out the sides to a

dimension that can be as much as fifty percent wider than the original log. Steaming-out not only makes the sides of the canoe wider, but makes the ends of the canoe taller as well, because the ends rise and move closer together (by the flexing of the bottom) as the gunwales are bent out and downward.

In addition to the dimensional changes the technique brings about, the sides of the hull are also made stronger than if they were only carved to shape. If the canoe is only carved to its final form, the wood fibers are largely cross-grained to the outward-curving line of the gunwale (from the bow or stern to the widest part of the hull). If the canoe is steamed and bent into its final shape, however, the long fibers of the wood follow the curve of the gunwale down the midsection of its length. In this way, the sides of the canoe have more in common with those of a vessel made of steam-bent planks than one that is merely carved to shape. This technique is not unique to the Northwest Coast area, but these may be the largest and most sophisticated vessels in the world to which the process has been applied. Canoes are also steam-widened in parts of South America and even in eastern European countries. In Estonia, and probably other parts of northern Europe, aspen-like trees were once carved and then steamed over a fire. When pliable, the sides of the canoe were rolled out to a much wider shape, after which crosspieces were set in place to hold the new dimension, just as is done on the Northwest Coast.

The Canoe's Pervasive Influence

The gracefully shaped and thinly carved canoe, perhaps more than any other Northwest Coast sculpture type, exemplifies the principle of "less is more." Spiritual inspiration and experiential development combined to produce vessels that contained only enough mass and sculptural form for optimum effectiveness in action. Each curve, each flare to turn off the waves and lift the vessel over the crests, had been established and pared down in design over the generations until just enough remained to do the job. The result was the creation of canoes that were both beautiful in form and perfect in function, superbly adapted to the requirements and characteristics of their world. Some of the largest canoes that survive, such as the forty-five-foot Brown Bear canoe of Chief Shakes at the Smithsonian in Washington, D.C., or the sixty-five-foot Heiltsuk canoe at the American Museum of Natural History in New York, are carved and refined until they are remarkably thin. The Brown Bear canoe is only one inch thick on the bottom, and somewhat less than that at the gunwales.

In all parts of the Northwest Coast, the forms of canoes influenced the design and decoration of numerous related articles—from carved or bent-corner bowls of wood, to carved, boiled and widened-out bowls and spoons of mountain sheep horn. These objects share in their conception, manufacture techniques and appearance several canoe-like traits: raised ends and low-curving sides; flat-topped, gunwale-like rims that are wider than the thickness of the sides below them; and outward-angled, sometimes flaring sides and ends that give the containers a stable, boat-like shape. In her book, *Out of the Mist: Treasures of the Nuu-chah-nulth Chiefs*, scholar Martha Black relates that leaders of Nuu-cha-nulth families say that the arched ends and downward-curving sides of carved and bent-corner bowls signify the mountains and valleys that rim the lands where their people made their homes. There are also carved bowls from the Northwest Coast that are precisely reduced canoe shapes. Short and nearly round, some almost as wide as they are long, these remarkable bowls mimic all the gracefully interrelated sculptural forms of the full-size canoes, foreshortened and compact like an embryonic vessel. Some bowls and ladles of wood or horn also have shallow, rounded grooves cut on their insides, just below and parallel to the rim. These grooves are visually analogous to similar forms carved below the gunwales on the inside of certain canoe types (in particular the Northern and indigenous Coast Salish canoe styles). These ladles and bowls were all made for serving and consuming foodstuffs that were harvested from canoes. It is appropriate that their forms are an homage and perhaps a prayer of thanks to the capable canoe—the bridge between the wealth of the sea and the reality of life.

Canoe Styles Among Northwest Coast First Nations

When looking at some of the early photographs taken on the Northwest Coast between 1860 and 1900, one is struck by the sheer numbers of canoes that appear in views of some villages. Along the gently slanting beachfronts, bordered by the large facades of the traditionally sea-oriented houses, there appear dozens of canoes in many different sizes. One sees in the many vessels found in such photographs an incredible consistency, a very close adherence to a traditional form and standard of workmanship. Though the minor differences that stem from the touch of an individual maker's hands are present, the consistency of line from one vessel to another is quite remarkable. The canoes are most often pulled up above the high-tide line, bows pointing out to sea, and often covered with bark mats or sailcloth to protect the delicate hulls from the drying and cracking effects of the sun (though clear days are relatively rare in this part of the world). They are pointed bow-to-the-sea (being traditionally landed in the same orientation) for two reasons: to protect the thinly carved bow entry from damage and wear when landing, and to place the canoes in their optimal position for immediate launching if necessary. Warfare and raiding among Northwest Coast groups was common prior to the late nineteenth century.

In addition to the recognized major types, there is also occasionally a rare or unique canoe form visible in such pictures, a canoe style that may have been limited in production to a particular region, village or individual maker. These appear as silent tributes to the design genius of the old masters: new forms created perhaps experimentally, by divine inspiration or trial and error, just as the traditionalized major types were first created. Each is either the answer to a particular requirement or the response to a desire to create something new.

The numerous canoe styles that have been employed by Northwest Coast Native nations have been fairly

Bella Coola Spoon canoe, thirty-six feet, six inches long, thirty-three inches wide. Though heavier and bulkier about the end than most finished nineteenth-century canoes, this example illustrates the straight sides and upcurved ends of a central coast river canoe, also called a Spoon canoe. The shallow draft and rounded form of the bottom on the ends kept the river's cross-currents from catching the ends and turning them abruptly about. Such a vessel would be poled through the channels more often than being paddled.

thoroughly documented by historical sources over the last two centuries in photographs and ethnographic texts. Beginning in the southern Northwest Coast, the major canoe styles that are distinguished in this region are:

River canoes: Shovelnose and Spoon
Nuu-chah-nulth/Makah canoe (for simplicity
   referred to as the Nootkan canoe)
Munka: a war canoe
Coast Salish canoe
Northern canoe
Northern ceremonial canoe
Spruce canoe
Head canoe

River Canoes

Rivers were the arteries that allowed the coastal people to travel to their traditional interior territories where they had access to hunting and gathering grounds, upriver village locations and inland trade routes. Though the big sea-going canoes were frequently used to sail or pole up the currents to conduct large-scale trade on the more important rivers, specialized river canoes were also valuable transportation for the individual or family. In Puget Sound and other Coast Salish regions, these vessels were called Shovelnose canoes (in English). They were shallow, narrow and squared-off on the ends. The undersides were gently rounded from side to side, so that cross-currents and spiral eddies in the streams wouldn't catch the ends of the canoe and turn them about. Euro-American settlers likened the appearance of the symmetrical ends to the shape of a shovel blade, and over time the name stuck. Farther north, among the Nuxalk and other mainland peoples, River canoes had a more rounded and raised-up shape to the ends, and so were called Spoon canoes by English speakers. Most often poled rather than paddled, River canoes demanded great balance and skill from their handlers. Aboriginal peoples literally grew up in canoes, however, and so even young children acquired these skills and techniques in a very natural manner.

The Nootkan Canoe
of the Nuu-chah-nulth and Makah

Of the canoe styles present on the southern coast today, the one with the widest distribution among First Nations is the Nootkan canoe. The Nuu-chah-nulth First Nations live on the rugged west coast of Vancouver Island in British Columbia. They are the cultural and linguistic relatives of the Makah tribe of Washington State; only the international boundary divides them into separate entities. They are the First Nations of the Northwest Coast who practiced the whaling tradition, and they created a most remarkable and beautifully designed canoe in which to undertake this and other traditional tasks of Nuu-chah-nulth/Makah life, including offshore fishing and fur seal hunting.

Also known as the Chinook canoe, this style of vessel was used from the lower Columbia River drainage, through the lowlands and coast of southwest Washington, north to Cape Flattery and along the west coast of Vancouver Island. By at least the late nineteenth century, this style of canoe was also in use through the territories of the Straits and Puget Sound Coast Salish. A very seaworthy vessel, it was adopted by First Nations neighboring on the Nuu-chah-nulth/Makah traditional territories and its use eventually spread over a wide geographic area.

The Nootkan canoe has several features that distinguish it from other Northwest Coast vessels. Most apparent are the shapes of the bow and stern. The line of the stern is vertical in profile, and topped with a flare that rises from the rear gunwale and turns sharply aft, creating a rectangular, sloping cap finial. The bow rises in a gentle curve from the gunwale line to a peak just above where the two gunwales converge. Ahead of that peak, a long, thin, narrow "snout" extends forward like the muzzle of a wolf, though it is a purely graphic shape and only suggestive of

an animal form. This profile serves to give these canoes a look of alertness, animation and vitality that makes them seem alive. There are several non-functional but traditional carved features that are always present in a complete canoe, and they were given various names in the different dialects of the Nuu-chah-nulth and Makah languages. For example, a little lump in the forward edge of the bow curve is called variously the "heart," the "Adam's apple" and the "uvula," depending on the dialect of language used.

Technical aspects of building the Nootkan canoe differ from those of any other vessel on the coast, except for the closely related Munka, or war canoe. On these vessels, regardless of size, a large measure of both the bow and stern are carved from separate pieces of wood and added on. This allows, among other things, for a canoe's hull to be made from just half of a log. If the interior of the western red cedar has active fungal decay present or is already rotten at the center (as many standing trees are), the separate end pieces allow for the affected wood to be cut out and replaced by the added sections. The canoe maker also takes advantage of the technique to alter the direction of the grain (the long wood fibers) in the added pieces. By having the grain angle up through the bow and stern, instead of running parallel to that of the hull itself, the delicate shapes of the end-flares and other features on these added pieces are strengthened and made more resistant to breakage.

Nootkan-style canoe, twenty feet, seven inches long, forty-six inches wide, circa 1870. This canoe appears very beamy for its length, but was likely made to carry a large load, perhaps for seal hunting. A crew of two would return home with as many seals as they could carry, and the meat and hides could be distributed among many families. The forward crosspiece in the canoe has a hole in it to support a mast for downwind sailing and reaching (with the wind off to one side or the other). The small step, or scarf, in the joint line between the hull and bow section can be seen in this picture, along with the alert, lifelike form that the graphic shape of the bow conveys.

First Peoples from all over Puget Sound and southern British Columbia journeyed to the Seattle area on a seasonal basis for trading and employment opportunities. Many people took harvesting jobs in the strawberry fields in the region or in the hop fields of the Puyallup and White River valleys. A number of temporary camps sprung up along the pioneer waterfront of Elliott Bay, below the growing town of Seattle. This location was one of the largest. Known as Ballast Island, it was formed in part by the dropping of stone ballast from hundreds of commercial sailing freighters that came to load lumber from the Yesler sawmill and others in the area.

An ingenious scarf included in the joining of the bow and stern pieces gives the joint itself remarkable strength. This small step (only about half an inch tall) in the curving line of the joint works in a geometric relationship with the remainder of the joint surface as it curves up to the level of the gunwales. Even before any pegs or other fastening techniques are used on the seam, the scarf alone allows the full weight of a small canoe to be lifted up using only the applied end-piece as a hand-hold. The lifting movement, countered by the rear of the end-piece against the hull at the gunwales, causes the joint surface to want to move up and forward. This upward/forward motion is stopped by the small step in the line of the scarf joint, completely preventing the raising of the end-piece. This pressure is the same as that applied by the lifting of a wave on the ends of the canoe, and such a joint would not be nearly as strong without this simple but very effective feature. Adding on the ends is far more difficult and time consuming than carving the

hull and ends of one piece, but the advantages gained successfully outweigh the amount of effort expended.

Nootkan canoes were made in a large range of sizes. One was for fishing halibut on the Swiftsure Bank near the mouth of Juan de Fuca Strait. Makah fishermen have said that a canoe of sixteen to eighteen feet is the best length suited to the frequency of the ocean swells in that area, where the long ocean rollers are driven closer together by the shoaling bottom. A shorter canoe would not have enough capacity to handle the catch loads, and a longer one would dive into the waves instead of gliding smoothly through the troughs and over the crests.

The Nootkan canoe in its most respected form was used for whale hunting on the open ocean, pursuing humpback and gray whales with a harpoon that was tipped with a mussel shell point and elk antler barbs. The details of this canoe's sculptured form are closely related to the structure of the frame and skin-covered umiaks of the Inuit whaling cultures of northern Alaska and

Canada. The late anthropologist Wilson Duff wrote a valuable essay on this intriguing comparative phenomenon, "Thoughts on the Nootkan Canoe," which details many of the characteristics these vessel types have in common.

Whale hunting required crews of eight specially trained crewmen to paddle their thirty-five-foot canoes offshore as far as fifty to sixty miles in search of migrating humpback whales. When they sighted the whale that their spiritual beliefs told them they were meant to have, they would harpoon and capture the leviathan, slowing its escape with inflated sealskin floats attached to the harpoon lines. Once it was killed, the crew would sew the mouth of the animal shut (to prevent sinking) and then the whale was towed back to the village for cutting out and dividing up the blubber, meat, baleen plates and bones among the people according to their social rank. All parts of the animal were considered spiritually valuable, and nothing was left to waste. Spiritual observances and rituals accompanied each step of the way, and the successful harpooner conducted four days of ritual and prayer songs addressed to the spirit of the whale in order to assure its safe and respectful return to the unseen realms of the ocean world.

Pelagic fur seal hunters in twenty-five-foot canoes would travel similar distances to encounter and harpoon their quarry, which were often spotted sleeping on the surface of the sea. Sealing canoes included a shallow, keel-like extension below the bow (running aft about four or five feet), to insure that the bottom of the canoe would not slap against the waves and awaken the sleeping seals.

One very dramatic statement on the seaworthiness of the Nootkan-style canoe comes to us from the historical account of Captain John Claus Voss, who in 1901 sailed a forty-foot dugout canoe he named the *Tilikum* from Victoria, British Columbia, through the Pacific Ocean (visiting many of its island communities), around the Cape of Good Hope in Africa and up to London, England. He decked over the hull and added a small cabin space, three short masts and a rudder to the traditional vessel, but relied on the original form of the hull and its sea-going capabilities to carry him and his part-time companions around the world. The voyage is recounted in Voss's book, *The Venturesome Voyages of Captain Voss*. The restored original canoe used in his journey is on display in the Maritime Museum in Victoria, British Columbia.

It has been said that the bow-form of the Nootkan canoe was the inspiration for the design revolution that brought about the fast and sleek clipper ships of the middle and late nineteenth century. The speedy clippers set numerous time and distance records for travel between Asian and Australian ports and those of the United States and Great Britain. Although there are knowledgeable people who dispute these claims, a fair examination of one of the surviving clippers, like the *Cutty Sark* moored on the hard in Greenwich, England, shows some direct similarities and relationships to the basic form of the Nootkan canoe's bowline and refined, narrow entry. Certainly when one compares the form of the clippers, first built in the 1850s, with the ships that preceded them, such as those that brought the first Euro-Americans to the Northwest Coast, there seems to have been a quantum leap in the efficient design and speed manifested in the clipper's form. The old "water-pushers" of the eighteenth and early nineteenth centuries were outclassed in design by the canoes of the "primitive" peoples they visited. The clear similarities between the bow of a fast and sure clipper and the lines of the forward end of a Nootkan canoe suggests a possible link that may indeed have bridged the gap from one ship design to another.

The biggest canoes in the Nootkan tradition were fifty to fifty-five feet long, made for carrying large numbers of passengers or freight between village sites. One of the largest on record was photographed in 1912 near the outlet of Nitinat Lake on Vancouver Island. This beautifully shaped canoe was over fifty feet long and more than seven feet wide. A comment that sometimes accompanies the published photo says that the canoe was "too hard to handle in the currents and tide rips, so it was hauled ashore." Knowing the seaworthiness and serviceability of such canoes, however, it is far more likely that the huge canoe had simply outlived its time. There were many canoes on the Northwest Coast of that size (and some bigger) that had served their owners and makers quite well for traditional purposes. There were other factors at work, however, that may have caused the abandonment of this great vessel in the woods of west Vancouver Island. By about 1910, Euro-American style gasboats, along with small skiffs and sailing vessels built by the planked method, had begun to displace the traditional canoes. Framed and planked boats were tougher and less prone to cracking than the thin, carved hulls of the traditional canoes, and the early gas engines were a boon to the coming generation of fishermen.

At the same time, strong acculturation pressures from outside the villages were being brought to bear on the old social and potlatch systems, which had brought the people of distant villages in their large canoes together for days or weeks of feasting and traditional dancing in the past. Laws were passed against Native gatherings and traditional dance performances, and some individuals even did jail time for participating in these once-respected and culturally important pursuits. Without these kinds of cultural motivations, the old traveling canoes like the one photographed at Nitinat Lake began to be set aside, to slowly decay back into the forests from which they came. In very recent decades, the making of large traveling canoes has once again gained support and enthusiasm from a new generation that has grown up without the repressive government policies of the past.

The Munka: A War Canoe

Munka is the Kwakwaka'wakw term for a highly specialized war canoe that once saw use among First Nations from Vancouver Island to southeast Alaska. The canoe is closely related in form to the Nootkan canoe, but is much more vertical at the bow, and the "snout" points up at a steep angle. The bow is also especially wide, with the gunwale flares turning well out to each side and following the upward rise of the stem. The broad shape of the bow led to one of its Native names, *hlukaku.úkw*, translated as "wide nose." This is the most significant feature of this canoe, and was used as a shield or cover when approaching or retreating from an enemy. English explorer Lieutenant Whidbey, one of Captain George Vancouver's officers, described an encounter with Tlingit warriors in a Munka in 1793. When fired upon from the ship, the canoeload of warriors swiftly turned the canoe to point bow-to (stern-away from) the musket shots and, shielded by the high, wide prow of the canoe that then faced the English ship, they paddled astern with all their might. Only their hands and paddles were visible from the ship on either side of the wide, shielding bowpiece.

The stern of this canoe type, instead of being essentially vertical like the Nootkan style, is slightly slanted aft, perhaps to give more lift to a canoe loaded with warriors in a following sea. This stern nevertheless retains a similar basic form and construction style to the more common Nootkan type of stern shape.

By the mid-nineteenth century, when traditional hand-to-hand warfare had been effectively supplanted by the use of firearms (whose power and accuracy had increased steadily), the Munka ceased to be of strategic value. Paul Kane, a Toronto artist who journeyed through the Canadian west with the Hudson's Bay Company, made field sketches of several Munka canoes and thoroughly measured one near Fort Victoria on Vancouver Island in 1847. Kane also field-sketched a model Munka with northern-style formline painting on it, and incorporated its image into an oil painting that was completed after his return to Toronto. In *The Tlingit Indians* George T. Emmons saw and remarked upon what could have been a Munka canoe alongside a grave near the Tlingit village of Klukwan, Alaska. "In 1885, I saw a very large old canoe with bow and stern almost perpendicular, a type of dugout which corresponds rather closely to the old wide-nosed Haida type." It was evidently one of the last surviving examples of a once-widespread canoe style, of which only a relatively small number of models can be seen today.

The Coast Salish Canoe

The term Coast Salish is perhaps the most broad of all the Northwest Coast culture names, covering many language dialects and a large geographic range. For the purposes of canoe comparisons, though, it's reasonably practical to combine the many related linguistic groups under one term. Coast Salish Nations' territories include the Puget Sound and Hood Canal basins in Washington State, the eastern shores of Juan de Fuca Strait and Admiralty Inlet, and the islands and mainland shores of the entire Gulf of Georgia in southern British Columbia. Scholar of Salish culture Wayne Suttles notes that this was the most densely populated area of the Northwest Coast in Aboriginal times. Throughout this broad range, though minor regional differences exist, a single primary style of canoe once served the needs of saltwater transportation. The indigenous type of Coast Salish

Coast Salish canoe, twenty-three feet, seven inches long, thirty-seven inches wide. The slim, graceful lines of this canoe are typical of the Coast Salish style of vessel, designed for the relatively protected waters of Puget Sound and the Gulf of Georgia area. Such a canoe was used for family traveling to food and material resource sites among the islands and channels of the region, as well as within the mouths of the many mainland rivers. The very slim and delicate end forms functioned well for turning off the choppy swells typical of these inland waterways, but were not designed for the much larger waves and rollers of more exposed coastal waters.

canoe was designed for the interior waterways that make up most of the Coast Salish homeland. The name for one version of this type of canoe in Lushootseed (Puget Sound Salish) is *s'dagwihl*.

Many Coast Salish people adopted the Nootkan style of ocean-going canoe for use on their native waters, probably due to its enhanced ability to handle stormy conditions and because a large canoe could be made from half of a hollow log. The making of a large Coast Salish style canoe requires a very sound-centered log, which became more and more hard to find. By the second half of the nineteenth century, Coast Salish territory in the Puget Sound and southern Gulf of Georgia area was increasingly being taken over by the influx of Euro-American settlers to the region. A gold rush on the Fraser River in British Columbia in 1858 brought thousands of miners (mostly Americans) to the region, and spawned many new municipalities in the area. Aggressive logging in Coast Salish territories at the end of the nineteenth century brought down the most accessible forests of cedar (as well as fir and hemlock), for the building of San Francisco, Seattle and Vancouver. As a result, Coast Salish people may have had to turn to more remote nations like the Nuu-chah-nulth and Makah for their traditional watercraft. Many Nootkan vessels (made by Nuu-chah-nulth and Makah carvers) were apparently traded into the area, while Coast Salish canoe makers may also have carved their own versions of the design. Coast Salish canoe makers today still often favor the Nootkan style of canoe, and many of this type can be seen being paddled by Coast Salish nations in the revived canoe gatherings now taking place on the Northwest Coast.

The indigenous Coast Salish style of canoe, however, is the one that originated in their area. Its design in turn appears to have influenced the development of another major canoe type farther north, the Northern canoe. The Coast Salish canoe is well adapted for the comparatively protected waterways of Puget Sound and the Gulf of Georgia. Strong storm winds and currents can quickly overwhelm both of these inland seas, but they are spared the much larger swells and breaking waves of the open ocean coast. The Coast Salish canoe is beautifully conceived to adapt to these conditions, and was used in a variety of sizes for long distance travel as well as more local hunting and gathering.

The Coast Salish canoe incorporates design features that make for a successful and seaworthy craft, even though the bow and stern do not extend especially far upward. The waterline of the Coast Salish canoe has a

Tlingit dugout, seventeen feet, four inches long, thirty-two inches wide, nineteenth century. This unusual canoe is from the northernmost portion of the Northwest Coast culture area, the region around Yakutat Bay on the shore of the Gulf of Alaska, in the territory of the Tlingit-speaking First Nations. The bow of this canoe has been incorrectly rebuilt after a breakage, but the remaining original parts are in the typical form of a Yakutat-style sea otter hunting canoe. The forward-angled cutwater is said to aid in breaking the thin surface ice sometimes encountered by hunters in the Yakutat area.

narrow entry (at the bow, or stem) and exit (at the aft-slanting stern). The bow features a nearly vertical cutwater that extends up to about half the total height of the bow's peak. At the top of the cutwater, the narrow entry angles abruptly forward, extending out over the water about twice as far as the cutwater is tall. The stern's narrow exit angles back at a steady rate to its peak, where it meets the rising line of the gunwales. From the peak of the stern to the same point at the bow, the gunwales curve down and out in a graceful sheer line. This curve (in all Northwest Coast seagoing canoes) is partly produced by carving and partly by the process of steaming the canoe and widening out the sides for increased width and stability.

Perhaps the most important feature in the design of this hull is the pronounced flare that is carved at a point below the gunwales along their run from bow to stern. This flare is most apparent where the vertical lines of the bow or stern converge with the rising horizontal line of the gunwales. This creates an extremely effective turnout for either approaching waves or a following sea. The flare serves to lift the canoe over the seas and prevent water from broaching the gunwale and washing over the interior of the vessel. Northwest Coast scholar Bill Holm has postulated in "The Head

Canoe" in *Faces, Voices, and Dreams* that the very closely related form of the Northern canoe was derived or developed from the Coast Salish canoe. They share the angled stern line, the bow cutwater with its overhanging prow and most especially, the flare that runs the length of the gunwales and becomes more pronounced at each end.

The Northern Canoe

In the upper Gulf of Georgia, the Northern Coast Salish culture area borders with that of the Kwakwaka'wakw (also known as Kwakiutl). The Kwakwaka'wakw territories continue northward to Queen Charlotte Sound, which opens out to the Pacific Ocean north of Vancouver Island. It may be these more exposed waters that motivated the upward development of the flared ends of the Coast Salish canoe into a vessel shape more capable of withstanding open-sea conditions. The drawings of the earliest explorers on the northern coast do not appear to clearly record the Northern canoe type in the eighteenth-century period, though the aforementioned transition may have already begun at this time. The accuracy limitations of these early drawings may obscure the characteristics that would help to distinguish between these canoe types. The fully developed Northern canoe does appear in a drawing as early as 1827, in a view made by a Russian artist in Sitka harbor, southeast Alaska.

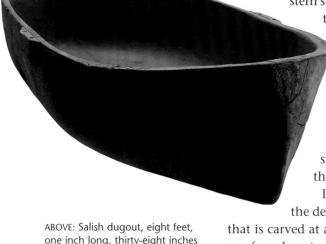

ABOVE: Salish dugout, eight feet, one inch long, thirty-eight inches wide. This dugout vessel is fitted with rowlocks, and was most likely made in the early twentieth century for use by a lone operator in trolling for salmon, digging clams or other kinds of inshore fishing. Its rounded, blunt shape would not move fast through the water, but would carry a fairly large payload.

RIGHT: Coast Salish dugout, twenty feet, seven inches long, thirty-three inches wide, circa 1900. This three-quarter-bow view shows the details of the bow area with its under-gunwale flares, which are designed to turn away the peaks of waves and swells. The harpoon-rest groove notch can be seen above the "mouth" slit in the peak of the bow, both of which are characteristics of these canoes. The mouth-like horizontal slit seems to have no clear function.

In a relatively short period, this important and innovative vessel design completely displaced older canoe types across the northern coast. If it was the canoe makers of the Kwakwaka'wakw who developed this revolutionary canoe form, they have unfortunately not been so credited. The vessel is known popularly as the Northern canoe, its name drawn from the fact of its distribution over all of the northern Northwest Coast, from Vancouver Island to southeast Alaska.

This canoe type was used by the Kwakwaka'wakw, the Oowekeno, the Heiltsuk, the Nuxalk, the Tsimshian, Nishga'a, Gitk'san, Haida and Tlingit First Nations. After this canoe style was developed, its increasing adoption and use completely displaced an earlier type of canoe that had once been used by all these nations. The Northern-style canoe proved to be more seaworthy (due to the extending outward flares on each end) and more maneuvrable than its predecessor, and in time the older canoe type ceased to be made. Known as the Head canoe in English, that older canoe style survives today in the form of models, most of which were made in the first half of the nineteenth century.

With its comparatively short waterline (in relation to its length) and gracefully upswept bow and stern, the Northern canoe became the primary vessel of the seas for the northern part of the coast. Northern coast First Peoples commonly journeyed as far south as Puget Sound (and some say even as far as northern California), conducting warfare and captive-taking in the early days, and trading or following seasonal labor jobs in the late nineteenth and very early twentieth centuries. These canoes could charge effectively through the waves and turn about much more swiftly than their predecessors, the Head canoes, even with an equal number of paddlers in each vessel.

In making a Northern-style canoe, the builder adds separate pieces to the bow and stern, but only a compar-atively small section at the peak of the ends. This feature gave rise to one of the Native terms for this canoe. The prolific scholar of Tlingit culture, George T. Emmons, records in *The Tlingit Indians* that the name *Ashaka siháayi yakw* from the Tlingit language means "bow-piece-put-on-canoe" (the older Head canoes were a one-piece vessel). As is done with the added-on bow and stern sections of the Nootkan canoe, the canoe maker also alters the direction of the grain from that of the hull in the smaller Northern-style end-pieces, in order to strengthen the delicate tips. This canoe, at least among the Tlingit, Haida and Tsimshian First Nations, was not commonly decorated with painted designs. Dozens of examples of this canoe type can be seen in nineteenth-century photographs of northern villages, and the hulls are all plain black in color. Like most Northwest Coast vessels, they were either scorched with torches on the outer hull and

The twenty-one or more people in this forty-six-foot canoe attest to the carrying capacity of the large Northwest Coast canoes. This one is known as the _Xoots Yakw,_ or Brown Bear canoe, and was the property of the Chief Shakes lineage of the Stikine Tlingit of Wrangell, Alaska. In about 1885, it was purchased by G. T. Emmons on behalf of the Smithsonian Institution in Washington, D.C., in whose storage facility it is housed today. The carved bear figures are attached to the bow and stern, and were sometimes removed for display at potlatches in the Shakes tribal house. This canoe was probably made in the Haida territory of the Queen Charlotte Islands (known as _Haida Gwaii_) and traded up into this more northern region.

rubbed with oil, or painted with black pigments. In the southern extent of its range, among the Heiltsuk, Nuxalk and Kwakwaka'wakw, such large traveling canoes were painted with designs, and some featured the addition of carved pieces to add dimension to the painted images. The everyday hunting and gathering canoes, however, which made up by far the largest number of vessels, were always just plain black on the outside of the hull.

The Northern Ceremonial Canoe

The Brown Bear canoe (_Xoots Yakw_) of the Wrangell Tlingit discussed earlier is an example of a subtype of Northern canoe that has not received a universally accepted modern name. Haida carvers may have developed this canoe type variation, though examples were also made by other First Nations of the northern area, as illustrated by the Heiltsuk canoe in the American Museum of Natural History, New York. This style of canoe, which was rare compared to its ubiquitous parent type, was nearly always painted on the ends with crest designs of the owner's clan. The Brown Bear canoe is one of the few that does not have painted ends. It does, however, feature a small sculptural bear mounted at both the bow and stern ends of the gunwales.

Matrilineal clans were the main divisions or social structures among the Tlingit, Haida and Tsimshian peoples, and these large ceremonial canoes were clan-owned objects, looked after by a succession of clan caretakers. Smaller, everyday Northern-style canoes were more likely to have been individually owned, like the family car today (as opposed to a corporately controlled vehicle, which would not have an individual "owner"). A very fine (though unusually small) canoe of this type, twenty-seven feet long, is in the collection of the Royal British Columbia Museum in Victoria. This canoe currently does not have design-embellished ends, but once did, as revealed in a historical photograph. Another canoe of this type, which was well known in the Wrangell village, was called the Killer Whale canoe (_Kéet Yakw_). This forty-five-foot canoe, the property of the Nanya.aayí clan, had an elaborate painting at the bow and the stern.

The style exemplified by these canoes is essentially a large version of the Northern type that has somewhat extended height to the gunwales, above the flare that runs the length of the canoe. Appearing almost like a plank that is added above the flare (though it's an integral feature of the hull), the "raised" gunwale extends clear

out to each end, terminating in added end-blocks that are of much larger size than those of the standard Northern canoe. Northwest Coast scholar Bill Holm, who has extensively examined and measured many vessels including the Brown Bear canoe, points out that these large, added end-pieces were hollowed out in order to reduce their weight. These very grand canoes fell out of common use by the early twentieth century, due to the kinds of external pressures mentioned in the discussion of the large Nitinat Lake Nootkan canoe.

In 1940, the Wrangell Killer Whale canoe was used in what that community called "the last great Potlatch." This was a celebration marking the completion of the tribal house reconstruction and totem pole replication project, which was undertaken by the Civilian Conservation Corps in some southeast Alaskan Native communities, employing Native artists and craftspeople. Unfortunately, this canoe later perished in a 1952 fire that consumed half of the Wrangell business district. In 1968, Bill Holm carved a thirty-five-foot canoe of this type that continues to be used in the outdoor programs of a summer camp that he is associated with in the San Juan Islands of Washington State. This was the first canoe of this type carved in over fifty years. In 1908, Alfred Davidson and Robert Davidson Sr. carved a fifty-five-foot canoe of this type that is now in the Canadian Museum of Civilization, Hull, Quebec. In 1986, Haida artist Bill Reid (along with a crew of younger Haida helpers) carved a forty-nine-foot canoe of this type for Expo '86, the World Exposition held in Vancouver that year. Since then, that canoe has taken part in numerous important journeys, including one unique trip down the Seine River in Paris, France. It was this same canoe, named *Loo Taas*, or *Wave Eater,* that carried its maker's ashes from Vancouver to his grandparents' village of Tanu on his final journey home.

The Spruce Canoe

One of the simplest seagoing canoe shapes on the Northwest Coast is probably also one of the oldest. Early nineteenth-century Russian artists in the Sitka area recorded their appearance, and they continued to be made into the twentieth century. Judging from the simplicity of their one-piece sculptural form, it is probable that these canoes were made on the northern coast for millennia. Unlike other Northwest Coast sea-going canoes, this canoe style has essentially the same form at the bow and stern—a straight, angling line truncated at the point where it meets the gunwale peak. Each end is a thin fin that is formed as the two sides come together

and turn to parallel the centerline, and there is no carved flare beneath the gunwale. The outward-angled line of the two sides' convergence creates the lift at the bow and stern that carries it over the swells.

These vessels are called Spruce canoes (in Tlingit, *seét yakw*), for the tree from which they were often carved, particularly in the northern Tlingit territory where red cedar trees are not to be found. In northern southeast Alaska, the climactic conditions are too extreme for the red cedar to flourish. As far north as Wrangell, the red cedar is close to the limit of its range (which is about 56º 40′ N), and few trees grow there that are large enough (or sound enough inside) to make a canoe more than about thirty to thirty-five feet long. North of that general latitude, canoe makers and other woodworkers turned to the Sitka spruce (*seét* in Tlingit) for their materials. Spruce is more dense and difficult to carve than red cedar, but when steamed it becomes extremely pliable. Spruce was also used for house planks and posts, bowls, combs and ceremonial articles, though it is seldom recognized as such in the ethnographic literature.

Spruce canoes were made large enough in some cases to handle a big crew and substantial freight, while smaller ones were used for seal and sea otter hunting by a two-person crew. Spruce canoes were used by Tlingit hunters well into the twentieth century in remote villages such as Hoonah. Only a very few models of this canoe type exist, and perhaps the only surviving full-size vessel of the Spruce canoe type is housed in the Wrangell Museum. That canoe is about eighteen feet long, and is made of red cedar rather than spruce, since there were cedars in that area that were appropriate for such a craft. Given a choice of the two woods, nearly all canoe makers would select the red cedar for its more carver-friendly qualities. Other variants of this style were made in the Chilkat River valley from cottonwood, a plentiful tree that grows fairly large and is readily workable. One such canoe, made by Tlingit carver Archie Klanie, is housed in the Sheldon Museum in Haines, Alaska. A twenty-five-foot Spruce canoe of the traditional type was carved in the village of Hoonah, Alaska, in 1988 by Steve Brown and Tlingit artist Mick Beasley, who worked under the guidance of a Hoonah elder, the late George Dalton, Sr. Mr. Dalton had worked on canoes with his father in the early twentieth century.

Though most Northern-style canoe bailers share the general hand-scoop appearance of this example, few are carved with such refinement and remarkable finish as this very beautiful one that is now in the Phoebe Hearst Museum of Anthropology in Berkeley, California.

The Head Canoe

The large, often decorated vessel known in English as the Head canoe is a variant of the Spruce canoe form, made with exaggerated extensions at the bow and stern. The fin-like ends of the Spruce canoe shape are in effect drawn out (to a length of several feet on a large vessel), and raised higher above the gunwales than the ends of a Spruce canoe. The forward line of the bow-fin drops at an angle just back from vertical, creating a very different appearance from that of the stern fin's rearward extension. If the Head canoe models that survive are an accurate indication of the standard treatment of the full-sized canoes, the bow- and stern-fins were usually painted with elaborate crest designs. Some models include sculptured features that were sometimes added to or carved into the fins. One of the Native terms for this canoe was recorded among the Tlingit by George Emmons as "long tail" (*lidikw layáat'*), an appropriate descriptive moniker referring to the elongated stern-fin.

The reason for the eventual replacement of the Head canoe by the Northern vessel type may in fact have been these large and often elaborately decorated integral fins. The load-carrying capacity of the Head canoe was obviously limited to the central, non-fin section of the vessel. This meant that a very long canoe could carry limited crew and no extra weight, especially when compared to a Northern-style canoe of the same total length. The only practical advantage of the end-fins would have been in

tracking the path of the canoe: keeping the vessel headed straight on its course. Conversely, these same fins would have made the canoe very difficult to turn quickly, which would have been a serious disadvantage in a close-quarters fight with a Northern-style canoe loaded with warriors. In a crossing wind, these end-fins would have proved most unwieldy. Also, the lack of a pronounced outward flare at the gunwale of a Head canoe would make it much less dry than a Northern-style canoe in a choppy seaway, a common condition on the major straits of southeast Alaska. Another advantage to a Northern-style canoe is its added lift and ability to turn out the tops of the swells. One early Tlingit speaker is quoted by anthropologist Frederica deLaguna in *The Story of a Tlingit Community* as remarking "The 'Anxaakhitan [a rival Tlingit clan] had Haida [Northern-style] war canoes. These could carry a lot and could outrun the others. There was more power in them, and there were more men to paddle" [in the same size canoe]. In a relatively short time, all the Tlingit clans had either traded with the Haida for the new Northern-style canoes, or carved their own versions of the type. The old and elegantly shaped Head canoes, once used over a large area of the Northwest Coast, were left to the elements one by one.

Head canoes appear in early Euro-American explorers' drawings from Yakutat Bay in the north to as far south as northwestern Vancouver Island. By the early nineteenth century, with the advent of universal preference for the

In 1881, Henry Brodeck made this photograph of a Tlingit man in the northern village of Hoonah, Alaska, in the process of carving a small Spruce canoe. Spruce canoes continued to be made in the Hoonah area well into the last century for use in sea otter and seal hunting, because they could approach the quarry in relative silence. In the backdrop are several traditional Tlingit houses, built of hand-split and adzed spruce boards. Red cedar, the wood more commonly used for houses and canoes, does not grow this far north.

Northern canoe style, the long-tailed vessel known today as the Head canoe was evidently no longer being made. Like the Munka canoe, no examples of the Head canoe style seem to have survived into the late 1800s, when the earliest photographs were being taken on the northern Northwest Coast. Native artists immortalized both the Munka and Head canoes in model form, and many elaborately painted model canoes of the Head canoe type can be seen in the museums of the world. Most Head canoe models are painted in the styles of the northern coast, but at least one exists (in the Peabody Museum, Harvard University) that was painted in an early nineteenth-century Nuu-chah-nulth style, a further indication of the broad distribution of the vessel type.

Northwest Coast Canoes in the Twentieth Century

With the many harsh and repressive policies propagated by both the Canadian and United States governments toward Aboriginal peoples in the late nineteenth and early twentieth centuries, the decline of the traditional Northwest Coast canoes was secured. The establishment of reserves (in Canada) and reservation lands (in the United States) robbed the First Nations of most of their traditional territories and sources of wealth: the food and material resources upon which many aspects of their cultures were based. The forests from which the great cedars and spruces were obtained were now off limits: they belonged to someone else. Rivers and other traditional fishing sites too, now belonged to someone else. The old means of building a home and feeding one's family were no longer viable in all but the more remote areas. People were forced to turn to other occupations to survive, as commercial fishermen, loggers, cannery workers, housekeepers and craft artists making small objects like model totem poles, model canoes and baskets for sale to outsiders.

As late as 1895, the canoes of the Northwest Coast were still comparatively numerous, their differing shapes and styles still conforming to a common traditional standard, which was passed from master to apprentice and adhered to by canoe makers from all the First Nations of the region. By 1914, however, only twenty years later, the numbers of traditional canoes were showing serious decline. Edward S. Curtis, the photographer and filmmaker who worked extensively among the Kwakwaka'wakw, was only able to round up five or six canoes of varying sizes, from about eighteen to fifty feet long, for use in the melodrama that he filmed that year. And this was in an area that had once had canoes in great abundance in many established village sites. His film, *In the Land of the Head-Hunters* (the

TOP: Thirty-seven-foot canoe of the Sitka Canoe Club, Alaska. This beautifully shaped Northern-style canoe was carved by Will Burkhart and Wayne Price at the Sitka National Park in 1998. Wayne Price went on to produce a twenty-foot Northern-style canoe at the Alaska Native Heritage Center in 2000, as part of a major, well-documented Native watercraft project, which also saw the creation of kayaks, bark canoes and umiaks in the traditional forms using Native materials. The revival of canoe making in Alaska has seen a steady increase in the last twenty years, and some of the most traditionally refined of the contemporary vessels are coming out of this area.

BOTTOM: Twenty-seven-foot Northern-style canoe made by Nathan Jackson, Tlingit, at its launching in 1995, at the village of Saxman, near Ketchikan, Alaska. Nathan carved this canoe, his first, with the depth and massive end-blocks typical of a much larger vessel. He wanted the canoe to convey the sense of scale and presence of the big canoes of the past, and yet be more manageable for purposes of transportation and storage. The canoe is used by the Cape Fox Village Corporation in its tourism and ceremonial programs.

name has since been changed to a less aggressive but equally graphic title: *In the Land of the War Canoes*), features some exciting and inspiring scenes of these canoes in action, paddled by a load of warriors or approaching a village with masked dancers in the prows. As Native Northwest Coast populations dwindled at the turn of the twentieth century, however, so did the sculptured canoes.

The new economies that were increasingly entrenched in the twentieth century brought new pressures on the canoe traditions as well as new possibilities. Planked boats, made in the construction style introduced by Euro-American shipwrights and powered by the first simple gas engines, were tougher, less prone to cracking and able to carry the much heavier loads needed for commercial fishing and a different kind of freight transportation. Men who were once canoe makers became boat builders in villages up and down the coast, making large seine boats (commercial fishing boats that carry huge purse-seine nets), gillnet fishing boats and small rowing craft for everyday use. The old traditional sculptured craft had diminished in importance, and one by one the grand vessels that helped to

make the Northwest Coast cultures what they were fell before the ravages of time. Although a few of the traditional types continued to be made for purposes such as seal hunting, exhibition or sale, or just to keep the skills and knowledge alive, attrition steadily took its toll on the overall numbers of surviving canoes. Drawn into the woods or left on the beaches, most of these old timers just rotted and faded away—leaving precious few survivors. The ones immortalized by Curtis's film eventually rotted and were broken up on the beach in Alert Bay and like so many others in all areas of the coast, the scraps were eventually used as kindling for starting fires.

Some types of canoes managed to survive in the twentieth century in an altered form, adapted for a new application. In the early twentieth century, Coast Salish carvers developed a unique style of canoe, many of which were made and photographed in the 1920s. There are still a large number of these long, slim racing canoes being made and used today. With proportions based on Euro-American racing shells, these canoes are employed in well-regulated events by eleven-person racing teams from villages around the Puget Sound and Gulf of Georgia areas. The older versions were carefully drawn

In this photo (circa 1900) the long sleek lines of a fifty-five-foot racing canoe stretch out alongside the line of canoe-pullers (paddlers) that make up the racing team. The racing of large, traditional style canoes had been popular along the Northwest Coast for decades. Around the turn of the century, Salish canoe makers took the inspiration of racing-style rowing shells and drew out the lines of traditional sea-going canoes into these knife-like hulls that pierce the water at great speeds. Today, these slim canoes continue to be made and pulled in races, though canoe makers of recent decades have dropped many of the traditional canoe's features, such as the flare beneath the gunwale that turns water aside as the canoe cuts through the swells.

out to long and narrow proportions from the traditional sea-going Nootkan type, and featured all the graceful flares and fine lines of their more traditional predecessors. Most racing canoes today have foregone these delicate and valuable lines and forms, though they retain the proportions of length and width that make for very swift passages (and not uncommon capsizings!).

The Canoe Nations Today

The current renaissance in canoe culture has grown remarkably since the first modern international canoe journey, which was undertaken by a Makah sealing canoe round trip from Neah Bay to Port Renfrew in 1976. This was followed in the 1980s by the making of the *Glwa* canoe at Waglisla village (Bella Bella) by Frank Brown and crew, and a large and well-organized assembly of canoes known as the Paddle to Seattle event of 1989. This gathering included nineteen canoes, some of which came from as far north as Bella Bella, British Columbia, and as far south as the Quilleute Nation on the Pacific coast of Washington State. Every four years, a different village takes on the hosting of the Canoe Nation gathering. Successive events have been held at Bella Bella (1993) and La Push, Washington

(1997), as well as in Victoria, British Columbia during the Commonwealth Games of 1996. This has been well documented in David Neel's book, *The Great Canoes*. Today, First Nations from all along the Northwest Coast have produced traditional-style canoes in both wood and fiberglass, and have paddled them over long distances to participate in these and other Canoe Nation gatherings, such as the Full Circle journeys undertaken to navigate the length of Puget Sound. These Canoe Nation gatherings are returning not only the physical sight of traditional Northwest Coast canoes to contemporary eyes, but they also return the spiritual strength and power that accompanies these undertakings to the individual members of the First Nations that participate.

The canoe was the backbone of the old Northwest Coast cultures, and today's canoe carvers and "pullers" (the commonly used Native name for paddlers) have fulfilled the revitalization of traditional Northwest Coast sea-going arts: the backbone is once again in place. In the twenty-first century, the Northwest Coast canoe is once again alive and well, and is helping in its own special and valuable way to heal and to repower the surviving cultures that first gave it life.

BUILDING DUGOUTS

EUGENE ARIMA

Making a canoe? That should be simple— like sharpening a pencil.

Tony Hunt, Kwakiutl artist

A dugout is in principle a simple thing to make, like a trough, but much thought, skill and sheer labor are needed to make a good one. Like many other crafts, Northwest Coast canoe making can be learned to different levels of competence. Traditional master canoe makers had such a high degree of skill that their creations are truly works of art, as demonstrated by the fine museum specimens saved from the past and by historic photographs. Builders in the recent revival of Northwest Coast canoe making still fall short of the best of the past, despite wonderful modern equipment and supplies, such as power tools and plastic resins. There was a near break in the building tradition around the mid-twentieth century, when much of the ancient knowledge was lost. Many of the old designs were discontinued, except for the odd small rowboat for old people who still wanted what they were used to from childhood. Some modified designs with motors (like the west coast Vancouver Island put-put for trolling) did continue into the 1960s, but even such modernization failed to ensure economic viability, and Northwest Coast dugouts as work boats disappeared. Only the odd non-utilitarian dugout continued to be built, not for Native use but for the white world for public display in museums or for private fancy by some non-Native builder. But now that the symbolic value of Northwest Coast canoes has come to the fore as part of a general cultural renewal, Native building for Native use has revived, at least for the moment.

Canoe making was approached in stages. Learning traditionally began almost at birth, since from infancy people were in contact with canoes in Northwest Coast

ABOVE: *The Spirit of Haida Gwaii* by Bill Reid. This epic masterpiece was the late Haida master artist's brainchild. Its general form is based on sculptural figure groups by Haida artists of the late nineteenth century, who used a soft black shale called argillite. The eighteen-foot cast bronze sculpture includes a great number of animal and mythical figures intertwined among human and semi-human personages. Reid's vision was expanded and transmuted from clay to plaster-on-steel to bronze with technical help from numerous assistants.

FACING PAGE: Giant Sitka spruce. Although red cedar is the preferred wood for dugouts, spruce is used in Alaska where cedar is not available.

Hayim or West Coast bailer, typically carved from alder, shown here upside down. The steersman holds it between his thumb over a long edge and his fingers on the back ridge, with the string loop placed taut around his wrist. The other long edge is repeatedly swept up the inside of the hull from the bottom to the gunwale, scooping out water in a stream like a pump.

BELOW: Older model West Coast canoe with broken nose, probably pre-1850. This fine model, thirty-one and one-eighth inches long, was the inspiration for Wilson Duff's idea that the Southern or Nootkan canoe originated when a flat-bottomed umiak arrived from the Arctic on Vancouver Island's West Coast and was copied as a dugout. Note how the bottom is higher amidships than at the ends. The bow is lower than in more recent craft, corroborating early historical drawings.

life, being constantly transported in them. Children played in them, sometimes in their own scaled-down craft made by doting fathers or uncles. Boys were canoe crazy from an early age. No doubt their canoe-making experience began with watching building, typically with the father or an uncle, who purposely took them along to the woods where the work began. They would be taught how to find and fell the right tree, and would observe the heavy or dangerous tasks. In less demanding, uncritical parts of the work, some physical participation might be allowed, such as gathering and preparing adjunct materials, like special cedar branches for lashing line, and pitch. There would be much to learn aside from carving the canoe itself. They would learn how to use the woodworking tools—adze, axe, carving knives, drill—almost as a matter of course from growing up in a culture with a wood-centered technology. From about nine or ten years of age, boys on the west coast of Vancouver Island made "flat models," cut-out board boats several inches long made of easily split red cedar. These model canoes, used for racing, were propelled by a sail of one or two salal berry leaves with a thin stick thrust through them for a mast. The winner picked up his boat and quickly hid it under his clothing so that the others could not pick up the secret to its success, the bottom shape. Already the secretive side of canoe making was in evidence. As strength and motor control grew with the teens, a youth could become a full-fledged assistant in canoe making. Then one day he would try building his first canoe by himself. It wouldn't be perfect, but no matter. To make mistakes was the recognized way to learn. In keeping with general practice, four

canoes had to be built before the craft was mastered. And, of course, there were different degrees of mastery. For the highest level of skill you had to be born with it, they said, and so the finest canoe makers tended to come in family lines.

At present in the Northwest Coast canoe making revival, most people who begin building craft are adults who have never had a canoe-making father or uncle with knowledge and experience to hand down to them. But the adult beginners who build on their own initiative are usually skilled Northwest Coast art carvers, not just of masks but of larger figures and poles, too. They can handle power saws and move canoe logs around. After some initial guidance by someone with a bit of canoe-making knowledge, they quickly forge ahead on their own. Usually mature family men, they work with sons who are young adults, bringing back the old tradition of family transmission of the skill. A modern twist is that younger boys tend to be excluded from learning canoe making because they are at school all day. Young adults

ABOVE: The Makah Nation of Cape Flattery employed this thirty-seven-foot whaling canoe, the *Hummingbird*, for their successful whale hunt in 1999, the first in over seventy years. The canoe was made by two Makah carvers working with Clayoquot canoe maker Joe Martin of Opitsaht, British Columbia.

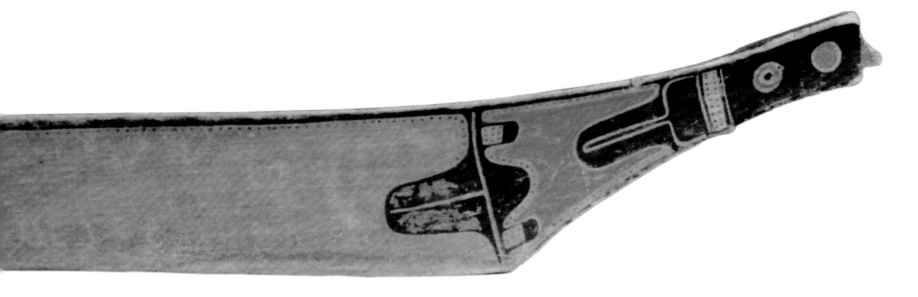

out of school have difficulty getting into canoe making on their own since they lack not only knowledge, but also the financial resources needed to buy the canoe log and the major tools (power saw and plane). On rare occasions a canoe-making project to involve them materializes, often with social rehabilitation as a rationale as much as culture transmission.

But a quite different construction development is most significant in the current Northwest Coast revival: molded fiberglass and Kevlar sea canoes. Their precursors were the glassed cedar-strip canoes, big and small, which were made as one-offs now and then by whites. Then in the 1980s Vancouver's Phil Nuytten (who designed the self-contained diving gear, the "Newtsuit") produced a molded eighteen-foot Northern-style canoe starting from a Kwakiutl design by Doug Cranmer. Only about a dozen were made, however, perhaps partly due to limited freeboard and crankiness from a V-bottom with a sudden transition to the sides.

In 1997 Western Canoeing Inc. of Abbotsford, the maker of Clipper Canoes, developed a thirty-one-foot Northern model in conjunction with Tsimshian artist Roy Vickers. Named the Clipper Northern Dancer, the canoe was manufactured in fiberglass and reinforced with Kevlar. Laminated with a foam core, the hull is strong enough without chine edges, but the hull design is a consciously non-Native one by the company designer, James Van Norstrand. He also shortened the stern from Vickers' overall design, cutting the tip flat on top for a peculiar look. The mahogany strip mold plug was tried out in the water, but was found wanting in stability. The gunwales were forced apart several inches, increasing the top width to fifty-four inches, which interestingly enough is the common width of the modern Native Band canoes. But the bottom widened less, of course, giving the Clipper product its idiosyncratic paddling qualities. At under five hundred pounds, this first Clipper sea model is lighter than a wooden dugout, slicker, faster and much cheaper at about $8,000. No wonder they have sold well: about a dozen annually, mainly to Coast Salish. With such success, the company wants to produce more models, larger and smaller, and in different styles (for example, Nuu-chah-nulth, although the hull shapes will be by Van Norstrand).

The mass Tribal Journey of July 2001 marked the success of the factory-built Northwest Coast canoe, when the Clippers ran circles around the more ponderous dugouts at Capilano, North Vancouver, at the end of two weeks of voyaging to the Coast Salish country. It is the dawn of a new era in Northwest Coast canoes.

Tlingit fishermen in Sitka, Alaska, circa 1908. A catch of salmon is unloaded and cleaned on the beach in front of the Sitka village, with Japonski Island in the background. This Northern-style canoe, more than thirty feet long, was probably made far to the south of this harbor and traded into the area, as red cedar does not grow on Baranof Island where Sitka is located. The high-curving, flared ends of the canoe, which give it the ability to travel in rough waters, show nicely in this view.

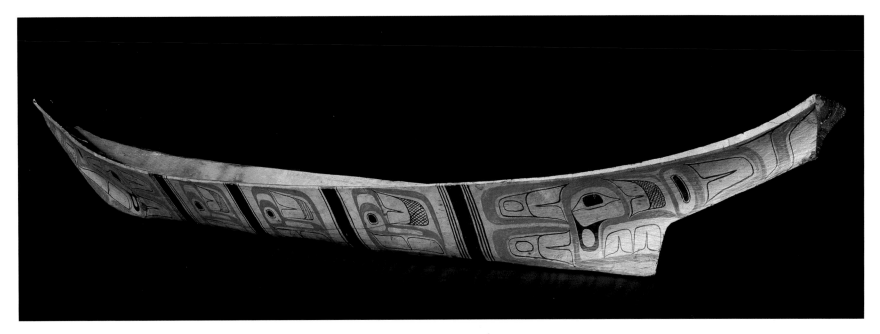

Getting the Log

Size is the first requirement in the canoe log, in particular a big diameter to make a beamy hull. The exceptions to this would be a log for a small canoe (sixteen feet or less) or for the odd canoe built for speed, like a sealer or a racer. Then good wood is sought, with few knots or defects like deep bark seams and cracks. But there is more than just finding the right wood, whether red cedar (yellow is rarely used for canoes) or Sitka spruce, or redwood in northern California. When the canoe maker searches the forest for his tree, he also has to consider how to get it out, especially in more traditional times when he had to transport it without the help of trucks or cranes. The hull was usually roughed out on the spot after felling the tree, and thus lightened, it was moved down to the water with skids, rollers, levers and ropes, pulleying as necessary. Felling had to be done with care not to crack the wood and, to soften the landing, small trees might be felled first to provide a cushioning bed.

That good wood, sound with few knots, is chosen for canoe making seems obvious and is generally true. Yet it should be noted that knotty cedar makes a stronger hull than clear, the crooked grain being more resistant to splitting. Hence the odd builder favored what might seem to be the worse wood. But because knots are hard to cut, it may be that this practice does not pre-date the iron tools that came with the Europeans in the late eighteenth century. When Northwest Coast axes, chisels and adzes had blades of stone, bone, antler or shell (large mussel shell), knots would surely have been avoided as much as possible.

ABOVE: This Haida model canoe, one of the finest known, is admired as much for its painted designs as for the shape. Made for sale to whites, it is completely covered with decorative painting, whereas real canoes were usually just black along the main hull body. The ends are exaggerated in size, as is usual with models.

LEFT: Cedar tree in the Queen Charlotte Islands with a test hole about eighteen inches wide. This was done to determine whether the condition of the inner wood was suitable for making a dugout canoe. The bark was stripped off in this section but over many years the tree grew out around the bare spot.

Carved for the Canadian pavilion at Expo '86 in Vancouver, Bill Reid's forty-nine-foot Haida ceremonial canoe was named *Lootaas,* or *Wave Eater.* It has since traveled on many of the Canoe Nation journeys undertaken in British Columbia and Washington State, and carried the remains of its maker on their final journey back to his grandparents' village of Tanu on Haida Gwaii (the Queen Charlotte Islands). Because the huge cedar log was used butt end to the stern, and the American racing yacht design of big behind and narrow forward was emulated, the bow is lacking in volume and *Lootaas* lives up to her name.

Traditionally, fire was used as a felling technique as well as a building technique. Usually during the dry spell in August ("the Burning Month" in Nootka), a fire would be lit around the base of a selected tree to burn away the base, with wet clay applied on the trunk to stop the fire reaching higher up the trunk. Fire was also lit under a pitchy tree so that the exudations melted and dripped down to be caught in large shells or other receptacles and used as a gum for caulking. The gathered gum was further heated to remove debris and then mixed with other substances, perhaps grease. The use of fire for hollowing the hull is not clearly known since it was dropped soon after iron cutting tools were obtained in quantity. It may have been optional.

The special Nootkan canoe log-cutting method of taking just half of the tree needs mention. Deep cuts were made above and below the desired length, then a split was begun from the top cut with a pole forced in crosswise. Left to work by the wind swaying the tree, the pole continued the split to the bottom cut in due time. With such a huge piece taken out of its trunk, the tree subsequently toppled over to that side. Some still remain in the woods of the West Coast, easy to spot when propped up off the ground by the branches. Presumably the method dates from back when the main Nootkan canoe-making tool was the elk antler chisel. Another sign of past canoe making sometimes seen on large trees is a rectangular slot taken out of the trunk to ascertain solidness. While such testing occurred, it should be noted

that a core loose with center rot is welcome, since it allows for easier hollowing of the hull. Solid blocks can be added to fill in at the ends as necessary.

The master canoe makers could build with what would seem to be bad wood. Even a log with the grain twisting along the length, as happens not infrequently, might be used. Once a man made a canoe with the grain spiraling all the way around for the fun of it. Another trick was to make a small second canoe out of the same log from the part removed to hollow the main hull. In a further refinement, the canoe might be made "inside out," so that the bottom was formed from the center of the log, the resultant grain pattern revealing the virtuoso achievement.

In view of the past riches in log choice and utilization, it is perhaps a letdown to hear that today one simply asks a logging company for a good big cedar for a canoe and waits for delivery, often not even going to the sorting yard to select one out of the pile. Indeed, the company may not welcome such intrusion into its busy commercial operation, particularly by choosy strangers who may not know too well what to look for or how to conduct themselves. The Native builder, however, is often known to the local superintendent and can select what he wants, even getting it gratis on occasion in recognition of the Native heritage of the land. Buying the log from a company and paying for delivery by truck remains the most efficient (and most expensive) way to get a suitable canoe log today. Logs are now cut to the more or less standard length of thirty to forty feet, weigh several tons if of good diameter (four feet thick midway) and cost starts at ten thousand dollars and goes up, depending on size and quality. Consequently, almost all the canoes being built in the present revival are of this medium-large size and serve as Band canoes. They could even be larger if it were easier to transport fifty- to sixty-foot cedars through the switchbacks of the logging roads. The exception is the Haida fifty-footer *Lootaas*, masterminded by their famous artist, Bill Reid (1920–98), who managed to get a huge tree specially cut. It is an unsurpassed example of reviving the truly big class of the past, the Northwest Coast War canoe.

Carving the Shape

With the canoe log on hand the builder has to decide how to use it and which side to make the all-important bottom. Generally the decision is a compromise, taking into account which plane will give the maximum diameter; where the wood is clear of the worst defects such as knots, cracks and rot; the extent of the curve overall (since a log is seldom really straight) and whatever other considerations the builder has in mind. If any factor is to be given preference over the rest, it is the good wood or, at the risk of sounding contrary, the worst and its avoidance.

Quatsino, 1998. Flattening the bottom on a Northern canoe by taking it down level a few inches reduces tippiness with the round cross-section. The transition to the bulged sides will be rounded later. At the stern Stan Wamiss is taking down the bottom corner, which is too prominent. Center rot will be replaced later with a filler block of solid wood. Alongside on the work-stand are the few layout tools used: straight-edge, level, square and plane.

Once the decision is made, the log is rolled to the right position, whether the hull is to be started right side up, as is usual, or upside down, as in the case of the Southern or Nootkan canoes. The latter method makes the bottom primary but may be more difficult for non-Nootka builders without the Nootka's familiarity with

A canoe maker used to do the rough shaping of the hull in the forest where the tree was felled, often alone. Sometimes he would have an assistant or two, usually a son or nephew. When the canoe was light enough to move, it would be hauled out of the woods and towed back to the village beach for final shaping, thinning out, steaming and spreading the sides, and finishing out the hull additions and thwart installation.

NORTHERN-STYLE CANOE

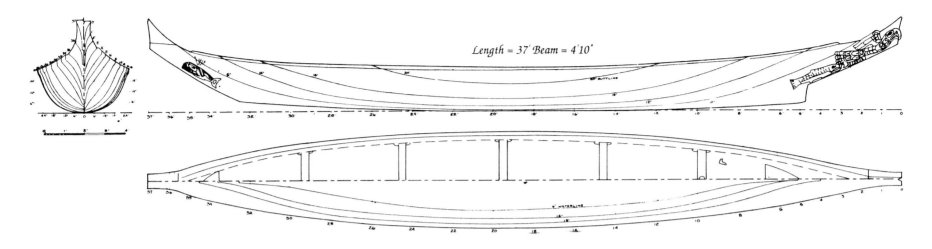

Length = 37' Beam = 4'10"

COAST SALISH–STYLE CANOE

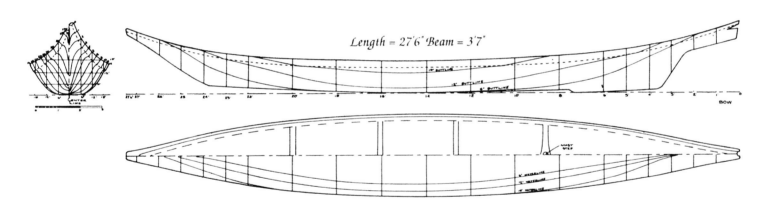

Length = 27'6" Beam = 3'7"

SALISH RACING CANOE

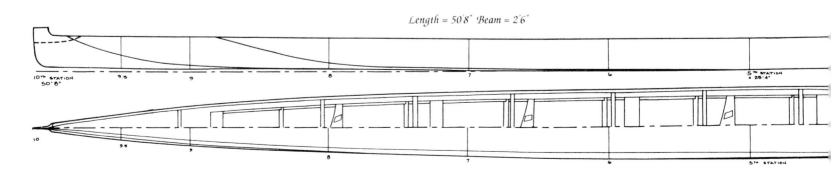

Length = 50'8" Beam = 2'6"

NOOTKAN-STYLE CANOE

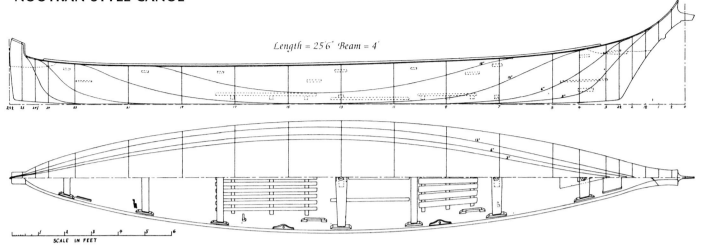

Length = 25'6" Beam = 4'

SCALE IN FEET

COAST SALISH SHOVELNOSE CANOE

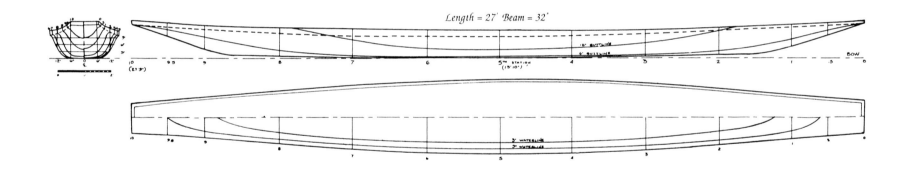

Length = 27' Beam = 32"

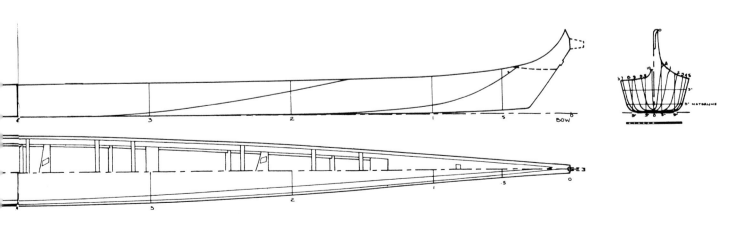

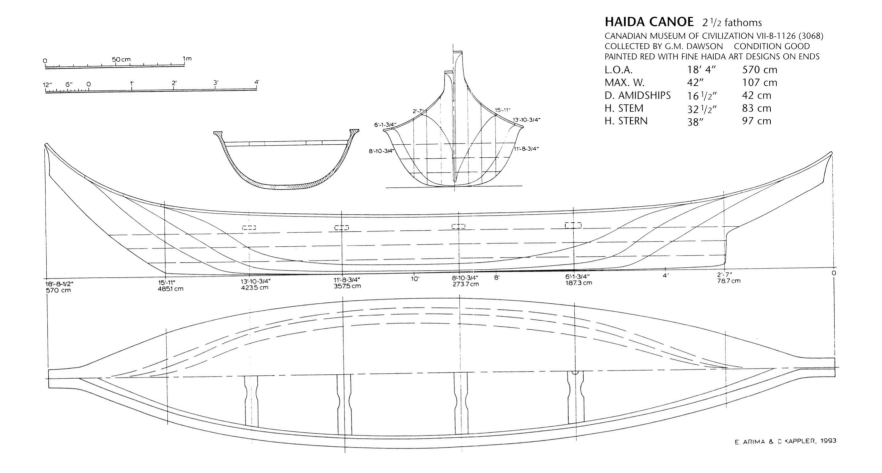

HAIDA CANOE 2 1/2 fathoms
CANADIAN MUSEUM OF CIVILIZATION VII-B-1126 (3068)
COLLECTED BY G.M. DAWSON   CONDITION GOOD
PAINTED RED WITH FINE HAIDA ART DESIGNS ON ENDS

L.O.A.	18' 4"	570 cm
MAX. W.	42"	107 cm
D. AMIDSHIPS	16 1/2"	42 cm
H. STEM	32 1/2"	83 cm
H. STERN	38"	97 cm

E. ARIMA & D. KAPPLER, 1993

ABOVE: Small Haida, length overall eighteen feet, eight-and-a-half inches. This canoe is a foot longer than the Yakutat canoe shown at the bottom of the facing page, but the waterline is actually shorter due to the great overhanging ends. Wider and deeper with a fuller, round hull section, it should be more stable than the Yakutat with larger capacity. The deeply scooped out sides toward either end will throw the waves off well. This canoe is an excellent sea design, affectionately called "Little Painted Haida," by Bill Reid, a master canoe builder and artist.

TOP RIGHT: Long Nootkan sealer, length overall twenty-four feet, four inches. This has the flat bottom and flared sides cross-section characteristic of the "Southern canoe" of the west coast of Vancouver Island and west Washington State. The beam of thirty-nine-and-a-half inches may seem ample, but with the strong side flare the bottom is only about two feet wide. Sealing canoes are supposed to be fast; occasionally they were used as messenger canoes. The narrow hull is not a problem for stability because the three-man crew sit low on the bottom. The one in the stern might have a low seat as steersman. Since the bottom is worn and indeed, in pieces, the way it is drawn here, dead flat with a sudden transition to the sides, may give too angular a cross-section. On the other hand, the comparatively flat sides do not indicate very well-rounded bilges. Traditional sealing canoes range from twenty-one to twenty-five feet length overall. Because they are fast they are used as messenger canoes in whaling, taking home news of a strike. A sixteen-foot harpoon shaft is held up as a signal while still distant from shore.

BOTTOM RIGHT: Small Yakutat, length overall seventeen feet, three-and-a-half inches. This canoe was one of the types used by the Yakutat people in South Alaska in the late nineteenth century. This looks to be a fast design, just thirty-three and one-quarter inches wide. With the sides flaring out, its bottom is narrower than on typical Algonquian-derived recreational sixteen-footers. The bow profile is correct for the style in the lower half, with the jut-jawed negative rake cutwater, but the zigzag leading edge of the reconstructed top half is a bit strange looking. Would-be builders might substitute a clean, straight edge, as is more common, angled up from the top of the big notch below with perhaps that point extended forward several inches. Museum specimens can't be launched for evaluation; however, this Yakutat gives all the appearance of being a good two-man dugout for recreational paddling today.

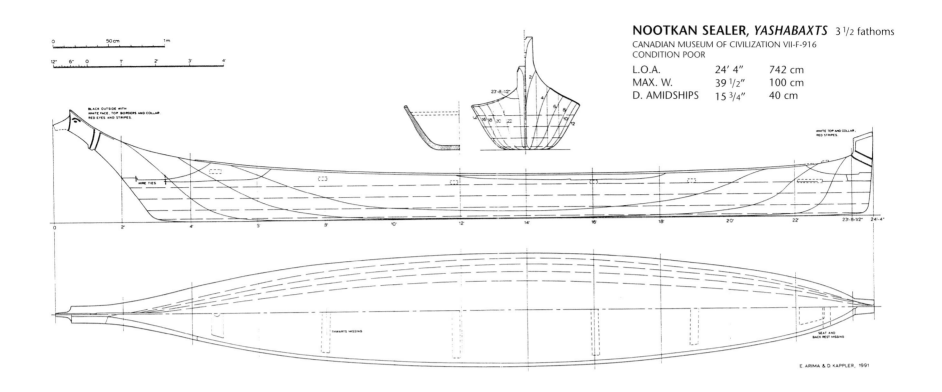

NOOTKAN SEALER, *YASHABAXTS* 3 ½ fathoms
CANADIAN MUSEUM OF CIVILIZATION VII-F-916
CONDITION POOR

L.O.A.	24' 4"	742 cm
MAX. W.	39 ½"	100 cm
D. AMIDSHIPS	15 ¾"	40 cm

BLACK OUTSIDE WITH
WHITE FACE, TOP BORDERS AND COLLAR.
RED EYES AND STRIPES.

WHITE TOP AND COLLAR.
RED STRIPES.

WIRE TIES

THWARTS MISSING

SEAT AND
BACK REST MISSING

E. ARIMA & D. KAPPLER, 1991

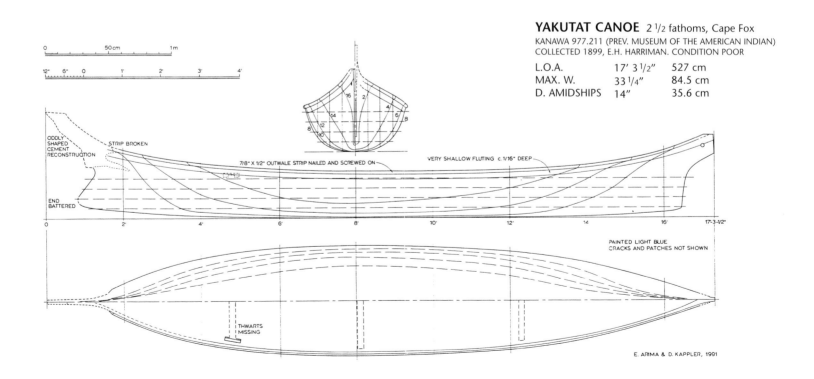

YAKUTAT CANOE 2 ½ fathoms, Cape Fox
KANAWA 977.211 (PREV. MUSEUM OF THE AMERICAN INDIAN)
COLLECTED 1899, E.H. HARRIMAN. CONDITION POOR

L.O.A.	17' 3 ½"	527 cm
MAX. W.	33 ¼"	84.5 cm
D. AMIDSHIPS	14"	35.6 cm

ODDLY
SHAPED
CEMENT
RECONSTRUCTION

STRIP BROKEN

7/8" X 1/2" OUTWALE STRIP NAILED AND SCREWED ON

VERY SHALLOW FLUTING c.1/16" DEEP

END
BATTERED

PAINTED LIGHT BLUE
CRACKS AND PATCHES NOT SHOWN

THWARTS
MISSING

E. ARIMA & D. KAPPLER, 1991

RIGHT: The ceremonial first cut for a dugout canoe is made on a huge red cedar. The chainsaw, not the axe or adze, is now the main tool in Northwest Coast canoe making.

BELOW: A lone Kwakwaka'wakw carver, surrounded by onlookers, carefully wields an elbow adze to fair and refine the outside form of a large Northern-style canoe. The ends of three other canoes are visible nearby, one covered with blankets and canvas to keep off the sun's rays. Two ermine-skin head-dresses are displayed on short poles on the far side of the canoe, perhaps indicating that a potlatch was underway at the same time.

the desired shape. Even Nootka neophytes might do better to start building right side up to establish the top plan outline first.

Before beginning work, the log should be raised off the ground on skids. For protection from sun and weather, a canoe-making shed is ideal, but putting up a plastic tarp is cheaper. With the log positioned as desired, a centerline can be marked on top down the length with the aid of a taut line, chalkline or plain line plus magic marker, placing it amidships at the center of the thickness to take full advantage for beam. Formerly marking was done by scoring or nicking the wood. At the ends the line can be off-center because they will narrow in, of course. If for some reason it is better to have it a little off-center amidships as well, that can be done, because in spreading the sides can be pushed out different amounts. In dugout making, alternative procedures are constantly available, and the builder should do whatever is common sense. This description simply outlines the general procedure.

Next, the centerline can be marked vertically on the ends with plumb or level, perhaps first cutting fresh faces with a power saw unless every possible inch of length is wanted. If the center rot at the butt, or small end for that matter, seems better reduced or eliminated, the log can be cut back accordingly, maybe several feet or more. However, a block of solid wood can replace the bad center so that less cutting back or none at all is possible. If just shortening for a smaller canoe, then the small end might be cut back to keep more log diameter for beam.

Blocking in for the initial rough shape can begin with taking off the top excess, leaving some spare above the gunwales, which can be marked on the sides using a level (a wooden bowl of water in the old days), and dropping down equally on both sides. Also to be marked is the spare or safety line, about two inches away from where the final cut line will be.

The amount of sheer depends on the planned model and the builder's preference, but for this discussion it can be drawn sweeping up to high ends from a level line drawn along the main length in between. With spreading about twenty percent, the middle should drop a couple of inches while the ends rise, and then the sheer can be altered further. High ends are suitable for the

Kwakwaka'wakw canoe from Kingcome Inlet, the still remote village on the mainland where electricity and television arrived only about a decade ago. Interestingly, this dugout seems to retain vestiges of the ancient Munka or war canoe in its end shapes. It is crewed by teenagers and was featured in a Japanese television special program on the 1997 Tribunal Journey to the North American Indigenous Games in Victoria. The red designs painted on the quarters are the four supernatural Wolves who founded this still proudly independent First Nation.

"Like sharpening a pencil." Big chainsaw with a five-and-a-half-foot bar proves handy for blocking in the bow of a fifty-foot double canoe started in 1997 for Port Hardy High School. Logger Alfie Matilpe is the saw man. Although this hull is too narrow, with just a three-and-a-half-foot beam, the canoe successfully completed the ten-day paddle to Victoria for the North American Indigenous Games, then went on to La Push.

Three canoes under construction at Fort Rupert, Vancouver Island, for the 1997 Tribal Journey to Victoria. Left to right: Quatsino Band canoe, Munka war canoe, Tlingit Head canoe.

Northern canoe, which is the style most commonly thought of when Northwest Coast dugouts come to mind. And a high bow at least can also be marked for the Southern or Nootkan canoe if it is made of a piece with the hull for simplicity. For Salish canoes, too, the ends can rise, though more moderately. For River canoes the ends can be raised still less, particularly if wide shovel-nose ends are planned to provide broad support there for poling. If more pointed tips are in mind for the Spoon-canoe style, they can be turned up more for a graceful profile. Another consideration in marking the sheer is the planned hull depth, and since this can be set later when cutting the bottom line, the only concern is to have the sheer high enough in the case of deep sea hulls, which will be spread to the maximum. Then it might be crowned (a convex bulge) above the widest point of the log for maximum spreading while keeping depth.

A pair of support blocks can be carved out of the wood and left attached to the canoe to make it easier to roll over while working. Make them about two-and-a-half feet long and cut in a little at each side to allow room to draw the outline of the sides on the newly created surface. Chainsaws are the speedy modern tools for this blocking-in work, but must be used with care not to overcut. Vertical cuts can be made to the safety line about three feet apart, and the intervening wood wedged off. Or large sections can be cut off directly with a big power saw used sideways. The top surface should be kept even to keep the work clean and controlled. The plan outline can be marked along both sides equidistant from the centerline with the maximum width coming a little before the halfway point. The bow is better placed at the bigger end of the log, except in some small canoes when the maker wants to make the butt the stern for some reason, like holding a heavy man while a lighter partner sits in front.

The top outline can be cut starting with the removal of large corner sections at the ends using a five-and-a-half-foot chainsaw bar, which is a good size for its reach and for its retention of the chain, which tends to come off too readily from a six-foot bar. This plan outline cutting can be done vertically, leaving flaring of the sides for later. If the amidships section is to be crowned up above the widest point of the log in order to gain more beam spreading, then the cutting leaves the width intact, of course. While the crowned sides shaping is most developed and best known for the Northern canoes of Sitka spruce in Alaska, it can be used farther south in red cedar country as well for achieving greater beam. A good example of this is the Kwakiutl Band canoe built in 1997 by Calvin Hunt, built with crowned sides for stability. The sides should be kept comparatively parallel for the main middle stretch to allow for the later increase in their curve by spreading. They are least curved in River canoes, which can be narrower than the sea-going types. A trough-like shape

Northern-style canoe, about thirty-three feet long, started in the summer of 1998 at Quatsino by Stan Wamiss. The head block set on the bow as a trial looks over-size. The sides are being roughed in vertically but will flare out a little when the hull is spread. The dark wood is rotten but only the worst parts will be removed and replaced with better wood.

results when the ends are wide and blunt, at least on top. They are blunt below as well to lesser degree, for a sharp cutwater tends to cause veering in the current. Easy entry overcomes resistance at the bow. Even with the sharp-ended sea canoes, at the blocking-out stage the ends should be left wide enough (one foot) to permit shifting of the centerline if so desired.

Little is known of the ancient techniques using stone, bone, antler or shell tools, aside from the extensive use of wedges, but with post-contact iron tools the axe was primary at this stage and throughout the shaping. Unlike a power saw, the axe, preferably double-headed for blade thinness and balance, is best used with the grain, and so in sharpening the bow and stern the chopping is to be done toward the ends, standing on them. Since a bit of width was left at each end for a work platform, the chopping was a notching in of the sides. Today when the power saw has ruled for a generation, and many new builders of the canoe revival have never used the axe, the foregoing may sound arcane. And yet the recreational dugout maker may actually prefer it over the noise, dust and vibration of power. Canoe carving with axe, adze and other hand tools can be most pleasant in a nice setting like on a beach by the sea.

When the plan outline is roughed in, both top and side surfaces can be smoothed for a foot or so from the gunwale edge with finer sawing, or chopping and adzing, and planing. Keeping the work clean helps you see the shape better. Shaping of the sides can begin, keeping the bulge of the log along the middle section and cutting in the flare toward the ends. While this roughing-in is essentially by eye, the balance between port and starboard can be checked by noting the amount cut in laterally on each side from a vertical dropped from the top edge with level or plumb, a method useful for checking bilateral symmetry throughout the work.

At about this point the log magically turns into a canoe, coming alive even though it is still buried in a bulk of excess wood. It is always wise to leave some spare, taking the wood down in stages rather than going straight to the final form, unless one happens to be very experienced and skilful. Such cautious procedure is often regarded with impatience by new builders, older as well as younger, but it is safer and lets you see better how to refine the shape. It is as if the canoe gradually shapes itself. When this roughing-in of the sides reaches halfway down to where the transition to the bottom begins, the canoe can be turned upside down. To facilitate the rolling, the hull can be lightened by partially hollowing it, leaving a lot of wood intact on the sides. The saw can be run lengthwise at a good slant to cut out a V-shaped trough except at the roller sections. A Southern or Nootkan canoe being built in the traditional manner would have been started upside down and so the rolling brings it right side up to shape the top.

Rolling can be done with jacks, preferably a Gilchrist

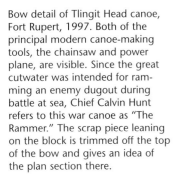

Bow detail of Tlingit Head canoe, Fort Rupert, 1997. Both of the principal modern canoe-making tools, the chainsaw and power plane, are visible. Since the great cutwater was intended for ramming an enemy dugout during battle at sea, Chief Calvin Hunt refers to this war canoe as "The Rammer." The scrap piece leaning on the block is trimmed off the top of the bow and gives an idea of the plan section there.

if this old logging tool is obtainable. With the pair of roller blocks left on top, the canoe will flip easily with skids coming under them and blocks placed to stop the roll. Then with level or plumb the work can be leveled again, using the vertical centerline on either end. In shaping the bottom three kinds of shapes can be distinguished: round, flat and V. If the flat cross-section is well rounded at the transitions from bottom to side, it can approach the round cross-section, which for its part tends towards a little flattening at the bottom. As for the V, it is shallow and rounded at the apex and bottom-side transitions. But the central part of the arms of the V are a touch concave, this cross-section being intended to dampen rolling and steady the canoe. It can be formed with minimal modification of the log section. Both round and flat sections entail taking down the bottom to different degrees. Whatever the section chosen, after roughing it in with a saw or an axe, the surface should be planed smooth. And the centerline can be drawn in, or redrawn since it may already have been put in before being obliterated by the bottom cutting. The rake of the ends can be roughed in.

Then for the finer shaping, repeated shallow passes with the power saw can take the wood down with control. Some like to use axe and adze in finalizing the shape. Templates can be used to duplicate line drawings, if such are being followed, and to match the sides. Power planing clarifies the shape. High spots needing reduction can be found by rubbing the surface with a thick, straight-edge coated with lumber crayon, a two-by-four several feet long serving nicely. Planing down the bumps to get smooth long curves fairs the hull. At either end, the sides should be scooped and lean out at the top to throw off waves, at least in sea canoes. River canoes tend to have less scooping, often none. Streamlining the shape makes for a fast canoe, but speed is to be balanced with stability and buoyancy, especially in the ends. Tracking and turning abilities also need to be shaped in, perhaps with skeg-effect end-blades or lack thereof, a slight V-bottom or a longitudinal rocker. The cutwaters on sea canoes can be thinned down to about three-quarter-inch thickness on medium and small canoes and left thicker on big models for strength. On top the ends can be built up higher with add-on pieces, as may be seen in the accompanying illustrations of the Northern and Southern types. Such additions are usually done after the hollowing is underway.

Hollowing and Patching

When the canoe has been shaped outside, it can be completely hollowed. While it is still upside down, dowels cut to appropriate lengths can be set about two to three feet apart in rows along the bottom and sides in order to hollow to the proper thickness, the hull getting progressively thinner from bottom to top. For canoes smaller

Making a canoe in Old Metlakatla, British Columbia, circa 1900. Three men work with big elbow adzes to hollow a large Northern-style canoe on the beach. One of the two spectators looks white. The round shape of the hull follows that of the log from which it was carved. When the canoe is spread with the aid of heat generated by adding hot rocks to water inside, the sides will lean out more, for upper volume and better resistance to tipping.

Nuxalk canoe, circa 1895. This bow three-quarters view of a good-sized Northern-style canoe shows the graceful curves and forms that are characteristic of the type. A combination of attached sculptural pieces and painted surface design depicts a big-beaked Eagle or possibly a Thunderbird in the bulbous Nuxalk (also known as Bella Coola) style.

than about thirty feet, the hull can be initially made about three inches thick on the bottom and two inches thick at the sides, anticipating further thinning in finishing. Bigger canoes might be made thicker by half an inch or so, but the hull shouldn't be too thick if it is to be spread very much. Traditional thickness reckoning was in finger widths. When the marker dowels are installed, the canoe is turned back right side up. As the hollowing reaches the planned thickness the dowel ends appear inside, their lighter color showing up against the darker cedar. The thickness gauge plugs might also be made of wood reduced to charcoal. Another marker was a blueberry dropped in the dowel hole for its stain. Today chalkline chalk can be squirted in. Another way of gauging hull thickness is to use big calipers. Holes can be bored and left open to measure thickness with splints, coat hanger wire, or thin tape.

The hollowing itself is best done with a power saw with a short blade, sixteen to twenty inches long. It can be run lengthwise at a slant in from the top of the sides. Crosscuts can be made and the intervening wood wedged out. Knots may require cuts to be made close together. Regardless of knots, if the transverse cuts are made just five to six inches apart, it is possible to quickly knock off the wood with a long-handled shipwright's adze. Scrap from both the outside shaping and the hollowing can be saved for firewood for the spreading. When the rough hollowing with the chainsaw is done, the finer work can be done with the adze and axes.

When the inside of the hull is basically hollow, cracks and knotholes can be patched in. Narrow cracks might just be cinched together with double dovetail inserts, dowels and ties. Heavy fishing line is sometimes used today. A traditional common lashing is the strong cedar branch rope, which is resistant to stretching. In spring when the sap is running, spindly, drooping branches with few twigs are sought among trees growing up the mountains. They might be about a finger thick at the butt end and an armspan and a half or so long. While the tip is anchored in one hand, the other end is rotated so the branch starts twisting from the small end, the grain separating into strands, which twist together into a strong rope (the bark coming loose in the process). As the rope making advances, the finished length is wrapped around the anchoring hand, and when complete, the coil is secured by winding the big end around it. This rope can be kept pliable in water for immediate use or stored dry. For tying it is threaded small end first through bored holes, then paired and looped through repeatedly until the hole is filled. To secure the end, a splinter is driven in. Other traditional tying materials were braided sinew and strong thong (elk hide). When the telegraph came into vogue the wire proved a good tie, particularly to secure add-on end pieces.

Another common European-derived fix is the tin patch, held by nails. Where holes and gaps exist, closely fitted wood patches can be inserted and held by glue (epoxy) and angled dowels. Such inserts can be quite large. Indeed, in Nootkan canoes a long section of the side might be an added piece at the top to gain more beam. Other long patches are common to fill in center rot toward the ends and bad bark seams. End rot can be patched with filler blocks. Close fitting of large pieces can be achieved by "bluing" with charcoal paste to find the high points on the joining surfaces. However, with the availability and good performance of modern silicone caulking, fitting need not be so exact as in the past when fragile gum was used.

Smoothing is done mainly with power planers today. Sanding is optional. Natural sandpapers of the past were sharkskin and sandstone.

Spreading

Hull spreading is done with heat and pressure. The canoe is partially filled with water and hot rocks are added. Then when the wood becomes pliable, the sides are forced out to the desired width with spreader sticks. Builders usually want to spread as much as possible, especially with a large canoe made from a log that is not quite big enough. "How much spread is possible?" you might ask, wanting some sort of quantification. Well, a suggestion might be about one-fifth of the width of a canoe with an unspread width-to-length proportion of about one to ten. For example, if

the unspread width is four feet and the length is forty feet, the spread might be about ten inches. With a well-thinned hull a one-quarter-width spread may be possible, but the danger of splitting grows. With a Northern-style canoe with very crowned-up sides, a greater than one-quarter spread can be done.

In preparation for spreading, the heating rocks are gathered, typically from the beach. Fine-grained dense stones, smoothly rounded and about the size of a large orange, are chosen, stones that are unlikely to shatter when put in the fire. Some choose bigger, grapefruit-sized stones, but they take longer to heat and reheat after immersion, which makes it harder to maintain high water temperature. Scrap iron can be used if suitable stones aren't available. Piping steam into the covered

Spreading a Tsimshian canoe. Heating and spreading the sides of a canoe usually lifts the ends. Although people commonly speak of "steaming" the canoe, the heating isn't really by steam, the visible water vapor notwithstanding. Since spreading curves the sides out to a nice wide shape, the hull can be carved beforehand with comparatively straight sides longitudinally, so that the grain stays more within the wood along the main middle part of the length for greater strength.

hull has been tried, but found to be less effective than heating water inside. Firewood will be abundant from the previous hull carving, some being saved for the purpose. Spreader sticks can be prepared as they are needed. The canoe can be raised a foot or so off the ground on two support blocks towards the ends. A lower, third block can be set amidships with a gap to the canoe bottom, which should bow downward as the top spreads wide and the ends rise. The height of the third block becomes a means of controlling the amount of longitudinal rocker. Like so many particulars in canoe making it is an option. If the as-carved-rocker is fine, the bottom is supported so it won't change. Spreading can also make the bottom more level, so all possibilities exist. Another control for width is to plant paired stakes in the ground at the sides amidships at the distance of the desired, or safe, spread.

Water is added to about a third of the inside depth, and the wood is allowed to soak it in for some hours, perhaps overnight. While it is the heat that makes the hull pliable, wet wood heats better through conduction. To increase water absorption, male urine might be added as a grease cutter, and today it is possible to substitute household ammonia. But adequate spreading is possible without either. Another additive sometimes used is oil, to raise the temperature; however, that's a waste since plain hot water short of the boiling point suffices. The amount of water to add is a matter of judgment, a large quantity being harder to bring up to spreading temperature, yet there should be enough to hold the heat and provide hot water vapor to steam the canoe, with the top opening covered. As there will be evaporation, add more water as needed during the steaming.

Today a tarpaulin (almost always plastic) is the common covering, wrapped down the sides. To keep the hot vapor from escaping at the high ends, quilts can be wrapped around them and tied in place. Keeping the heat trapped is important. Formerly, when stiffer mats were the covering, they stayed high above the sides, and it was possible to build fires along the sides to heat the hull from the exterior as well as the interior. Although these fires were controlled, scorching could develop, whereupon a clay-water mixture was swabbed on as required. With tarpaulin wrapped over the hull, such outside fires, efficacious as they may be, are no longer an option.

A bonfire is made to heat the stones "red hot," which in the past meant they had to be handled with large wooden tongs. Now steel shovels and wheelbarrows move them from fire to water. Since hot stones dropped into the water can still scorch when they hit the wood, seaweed used to be laid on the bottom. Today there are other substitutes, like wire fencing. If the stones are held in the water for a moment on the shovel before release until they lose some of their heat, such wood protection may not be necessary. At the other extreme the hot rocks can be dumped in directly from the wheelbarrow using a ramp, a method that loses less heat to the air. There should be enough stones to keep the water hot enough, perhaps three or four lots in rotation (since reheating takes time), although many make do with less. It is surprising how the hull will become pliable after several hours of heating with the water less than very hot.

Spreader sticks can be inserted when the wood softens and the sides bend with moderate hand pressure. They can be cut longer than the existing width, put in at a slant between the sides near the top and then pushed straighter to exert force outwards. If, as frequently

Heat-spreading a Tsimshian Northern-style canoe beside the University of British Columbia Museum of Anthropology in Vancouver, Canada. The Haida house in the background is reduced in size by the scale of the photo.

Spritsails and rudder-equipped Northern-style canoe near Haines, Alaska, 1898.

happens, one side is not bending out as much as the other and needs more pressure, spreader sticks can be inserted at a slant vertically from the opposite bottom "corner" of the inside, the ends sharpened if need be to hold them in place. While today these are more or less rigid spreaders, such as one-by-three-inch laths, formerly springy branches were often used. Many of them might be bent in place along the gunwales, pre-cut to the lengths that would give the desired top plan outline when they straightened out as the sides spread.

When the hull has spread to the final shape, the sides are held in place by a few laths across them nailed down to the gunwales and left in place until the spread sets, perhaps overnight. Removal of the stones and water will reveal a dirty interior that can be cleaned with sanding. Then it can be given some kind of finish, perhaps stained with alder or hemlock bark infusion and oiled with dogfish liver oil, if old practice is followed. The inside can also be painted, maybe red in the bark-stain tradition or blue-green after oxidized copper, another traditional color. Or boiled linseed oil can be applied for a darkened natural wood color.

Fittings

To solidify the canoe as a structure, permanent spreaders or thwarts have to be added to the hull. Since in more traditional times the crew seldom sat on them, they were usually comparatively slender laths set high near the gunwales. But in the big war canoes, at least in the Head canoes, plank thwarts about halfway down the high sides were used, sometimes with shaped seats for the pullers. By the twentieth century, low, wide thwarts for sitting on were common for all types. With milled lumber thwarts today a two-by-ten-inch plank is comfortable, preferably made from red cedar for lightness and warmth. They can rest on support laths nailed to the sides. With the old spreaders up near the gunwales, peeled springy young hemlock of about two inches in diameter is good. Use skinnier trees for small hulls. They can be let into the sides and tied with twisted cedar branch rope passed through holes drilled near their ends and holes in the sides. To have a little give in both the spreaders themselves and their attachment is advantageous when the hull moves in the waves. If stiff fir is used instead of hemlock, especially in the bow, it could happen that the hull will split in heavy seas. Currently canoes are not as stressed, since rough conditions are avoided, so give no longer seems so vital.

Gunwales should be protected with a cap strip. Although usually thin wood, say, half an inch thick, it can be deeper to add to the height of the sides. Since a thick strip may not bend readily enough to conform to the hull

sail of matting was known for a long time, European example and the introduction of canvas made sails a regular feature on Northwest Coast canoes. In the nineteenth century spritsails became the usual type. On bigger canoes with fore and mizzen masts, a pair of them could be set out to each side "wing and wing" to run before the wind. In the present canoe revival sailing is still timid with the canoes undercanvassed.

A rudder was also fitted sometimes on Nootkan canoes with their vertical stern. It was less common than sail and isn't used currently. Also no longer used, although very common before, are oars, adopted from Europeans.

Finish

A smooth surfaced hull is obviously best, yet today some canoe makers go for an adzed finish for its appearance. The canoe can be scorched and oiled for a darkened natural look, but today more often is painted. Decorative painting in a given Northwest Coast art style is quite common, although in Nootkan canoes it remains restrained. The basic Nootka scheme from the nineteenth century is black outside with a couple of stripes fore and aft. Salish canoes also look best painted quite plainly, say black or dull red. Northern canoes are more flamboyant, with family crests usually filling the end quarters or thirds of the length on a white or natural wood ground, while the middle length is plain black. Or a crest animal can be painted along the side without being restricted to an end section. Interior decoration with designs is possible, too, as was done in the past on rare occasions with special small canoes, for example, a wedding gift.

With use the surface becomes roughened, with slivers developing. These can be burned off, the traditional torch of a bundle of long cedar splinters still being easy to make and effective. Oiling and polishing with cloth will finish the job.

ABOVE: *Cumshewa*, 1912 by Emily Carr. She was fascinated by the aging remains of Haida villages, and painted many memorable scenes at a time when few North Americans saw the beauty and value in traditional Native cultures.

BELOW: Model of Haida canoe. Only the largest ceremonial canoes were decorated in this manner. The everyday hunting, fishing and work canoes were merely blackened on the outside.

FACING PAGE: Forty-foot Kwakiutl Band canoe, *Ugwamalis*, built in 1997 by Calvin Hunt, heading down the east coast of Vancouver Island to Victoria for the Indigenous Games.

curvature, the cap often has two layers. Or sections of wide board can be applied without bending in the wide plane and sawn to fit the curve. Metal finishing nails fasten the cap strip quickly, but some may prefer to dowel. Cutwaters more often than not are left unprotected, but again would benefit from a cap strip. A hardwood like yew or maple is good for cutwater strips since they serve as bumpers.

Sails are still used today, especially on the long Tribal Journey voyages; typically a small triangular one is set toward the bow for fair wind. Rigging is generally very simple, the sail being tied to a sapling mast without a halyard. Usually the sail is loose footed, the main sheet just a line tied to a thwart. While it seems that a square

The KAYAK and the WALRUS   KENNETH R. LISTER

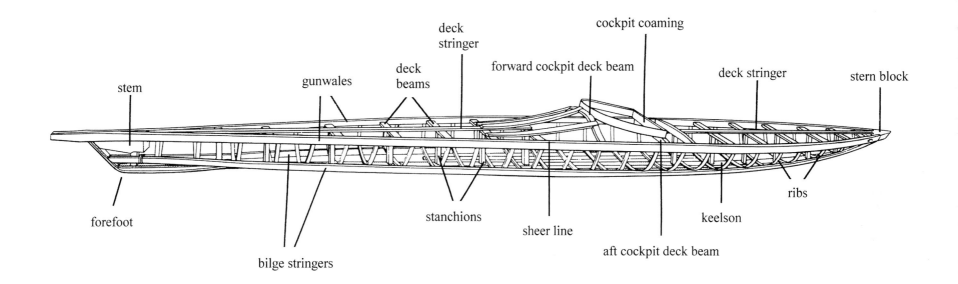

deck stringer

deck beams

forward cockpit deck beam

cockpit coaming

deck stringer

stern block

stem

gunwales

forefoot

bilge stringers

stanchions

sheer line

aft cockpit deck beam

keelson

ribs

They Used It For Hunting

It was nearing mid-August, 1991, and snow flurries were beginning to swirl around our tents when Andrew Oyukuluk and Simon Qamanirq completed the construction of a kayak frame. Oyukuluk had grown up on the land, and when he was young he used wood-framed kayaks covered with sealskin to hunt sea mammals in order to provide the food and raw materials necessary for his family's well-being. But many seasons had passed between those years and the summer of 1991, and the use of the kayak as a hunting tool had long faded from Inuit culture. In the community of Arctic Bay, northern Baffin Island, Oyukuluk was now the last living male elder who had constructed kayaks and used them for hunting. At the age of eighty-one, however, Oyukuluk—with a sense of urgency—was now anxious to pass his kayak knowledge along to a younger generation.

Simon Qamanirq, a young hunter and artist, shared Oyukuluk's keen interest in the traditions of their culture, and with each man possessing his own reason they partnered together and over an Arctic summer fashioned

pieces of wood laced with sealskin rope into a kayak frame, an object that had not been part of Arctic Bay's cultural makeup for well over thirty years. With Andrew Oyukuluk as his mentor, Simon learned the details pertaining to kayak dimensions, form and techniques of manufacture. The Royal Ontario Museum had supported this project and, with the assistance of the videographer Dennis Austin, I was fortunate to have the opportunity to record the construction process as it evolved from raw materials lying on the tundra to the finished kayak frame.

The frame is twenty-four feet in length by two-and-a-half feet in width. Consistent with the Eastern Arctic kayak style, the cockpit is positioned aft of the center point and the kayak's greatest width is located immediately behind the cockpit. The gunwales, stringers and stanchions are constructed of softwood, whereas the ribs and the cockpit coaming are made of oak. Oak is desired for its strength and for its good ability to bend after it has been softened through steaming. Each end of the oak ribs are fit into mortises (notches), which are chiseled into the underside surfaces of the gunwales.

FACING PAGE: Ice floes on the Arctic Ocean.

ABOVE: Drawing of a kayak frame constructed at Arctic Bay by Andrew Oyukuluk and Simon Qamanirq, 1991, twenty-three feet, nine inches long and twenty-eight inches wide. The frame has a very deep forefoot, longitudinal curve at the stern and rounded cross-section. The bow is quite different than the typical bow from northern Baffin Island, suggesting influences from the Netsilingmiut to the west.

In 1991, the hamlet of Arctic Bay and the Royal Ontario Museum undertook a project to construct a kayak frame. Tununirusirmiut elder, Andrew Oyukuluk, shares his kayak construction and hunting knowledge with Simon Qamanirq, a young artist and hunter.

Simon Qamanirq lashes the gunwales to the stem with sealskin rope. Channels are cut between pairs of holes to recess the rope so that the rope lies flush with the wood surface to prevent abrasion against the skin cover.

The ends of the ribs are then secured with wooden pegs. The remaining parts of the frame are lashed together with sealskin rope.

In profile, the bow has a deep forefoot formed by a length of softwood sheathed with oak and fastened to the keelson. From the forefoot to the cockpit, the bottom of the frame is flat but behind the cockpit the bottom bends upward in a gentle curve to where the keelson meets the gunwales and their connections to the stern-block. The unique longitudinal shape of the bottom is an efficient design for a kayak devised for hunting sea mammals in that the forefoot will dig deep into the water, while the back of the kayak, with its curve upward to the stern-block, has much less depth. The bow grips the water while the stern, which provides minimal resistance, swings around so that the kayak naturally heads into the waves. This is the safest orientation for a hunter to float in as he waits in anticipation of sighting sea mammals rising from the depths for air.

This kayak frame made on a beach near Arctic Bay was one of the longest and widest of the Inuit kayaks and after its completion I was surprised to hear Oyukuluk state, "I would prefer the kayak to be longer and a little bit wider." Oyukuluk saw the kayak as part of his hunting equipment: its size and design was individually tuned for the purpose of pursuing seals, narwhals and walrus, and he wanted maximum stability in an unforgiving environment.

To paddlers of smaller, modern-day kayaks, however, these grand dimensions are astounding, and non-Inuit kayakers who see such a craft may question the ability of a sole paddler to maneuver it effectively. But the kayak is being looked upon by two different sets of eyes and two different cultural backgrounds. "They used it for hunting!" exclaimed Oyukuluk, and indeed the kayak design characteristics, developed over hundreds of generations of Inuit use, were well tuned to that role. But for the modern-day paddler the kayak is not a hunting tool; it is for touring, the ideal craft for those who search for the wilderness through the softness of a paddle. Thus, when Oyukuluk views a modern kayak, with its sleek, smaller dimensions, we can understand his point of view when he states, "No! That's not a kayak!" To different paddlers, the kayak has different associations, and it elicits different responses and emotions.

To give another example, my family and I live on a boat that is referred to as a trawler. The boat is forty-two feet long and the lines of its semi-displacement hull are based upon those of fishing vessels that trawl large fishing nets. However, if we were to invite a Nova Scotia fisherman on board, he would look at its two bathrooms, sleeping cabins, teak-lined interior, and non-existent fish hold and state with disdain, "That's not a trawler!" To a Nova Scotia fisherman, a trawler is a working boat used for making a living at sea. To my family, it's our home. The Inuit hunter and the Nova Scotia fisherman used boats that played fundamental roles in their methods of making their livelihoods. Both of these boats, however, have now evolved into something else. Although they bear the original names, their functions differ.

Greenland Kayak, date unknown, seventeen feet long, twenty inches wide. This kayak is a West Greenland style and likely comes from the Upernivik district along Greenland's northwest coast. The sharp rise in the bow and stern were common features, but the deck profile was straightened out with the introduction of firearms to lessen the kayak's chance of being hit by a misplaced shot. The pattern of lines stretched across the fore and aft decks were used to secure hunting equipment.

Wood, Skin, Baleen and Bone

The traditional Inuit kayak consists of a frame that, with the exception of those areas occupied by single (or in some cases multiple) paddlers, is completely enclosed within a skin cover. The following early nineteenth century account by Lieutenant Edward Chappell, in his *Narrative of a Voyage to Hudson's Bay in His Majesty's Ship Rosamond,* provides an interesting description of the eastern Canadian Arctic kayak.

... these were built of a wooden frame-work of the lightest materials, covered with oiled seal-skin, with the hair scraped off; the skin being sewed over the frame with the most outstanding exactness, and as light as parchment upon the head of a drum. But the most surprising peculiarity of the canoes [kayaks] was, their being twenty-two feet long, and only two feet wide. There was but one opening in the centre, sufficiently large to admit the entrance of a man; and out of this hole projected the body of the Esquimaux, visible only from the ribs upwards. The paddle is held in the hand by the middle; and it has a blade at each end, curiously veneered, at the edges, with strips of sea-unicorn's horn. On the top of the canoe were fastened strips of sea-horse's hide, to confine the lance and harpoon; and behind the Esquimaux were large lumps of whale blubber, for the purposes of barter. These canoes are only capable of containing one person, for any useful purpose; the slightest inclination of the body, on either side, will inevitably overturn them; yet in these frail barks will the Esquimaux smile at the roughest sea; and in smooth water they can, with ease, travel seven miles an hour.

The frame is largely constructed of wood, shaped into gunwales, stringers and stanchions, and secured together with pegs of wood and bone and lashings of baleen and skin. In the treeless Arctic, wood is highly valued, and prior to contact with European culture the Inuit depended upon driftwood, or they sometimes made long journeys south to gather wood from below the treeline.

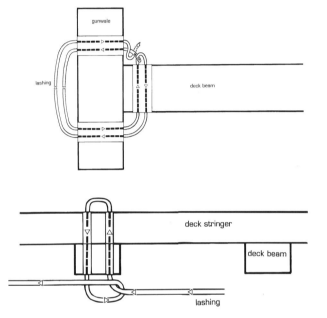

gunwale

lashing

deck beam

deck stringer

deck beam

lashing

TOP: Traditionally, kayak frames were held together with sealskin rope and wood pegs. A single female ringed sealskin can produce 183 feet of continuous rope. The Arctic Bay kayak frame is held together with more than 252 feet of rope.

MIDDLE: In the Arctic Bay kayak frame, continuous rope lashes the deck stringer to the deck beams. Through pairs of holes in the stringer and each beam, the rope passes up through one hole and down the adjacent hole. Underneath the deck beam, where the rope enters the initial hole, it hooks around itself and then continues on to the next pair of holes in the following beam.

BOTTOM: Inuit hunter with harpooned white whales and kayak, eastern Hudson Bay. The primary technological elements in sea mammal hunting by kayak are illustrated in this photograph: the hunter holding a harpoon beside a slain white whale, the sealskin float tethered to the whale and the Eastern Hudson Bay kayak.

This kayak was constructed by the Inuit of Povungnituk at the Ontario Science Centre in Toronto between June 15 and July 4, 1976. The kayak construction demonstration was a program run during an exhibition celebrating Native heritage. The following sequence of six photo-graphs illustrates the traditional division of labor, with the men largely responsible for the construction of the frame while the women do the preparation and sewing of the skin cover. The kayak is now part of the Canadian Canoe Museum collection.

1. The two gunwales are the main structural elements of the kayak frame. The gunwales and deck beams are temporarily held in position with lashings of commercial cord. The forward cockpit deck beam has been lashed into place and the remaining beams are being secured with sealskin rope.

2. With the deck beams in position, the shape of the deck is set. The kayak has been turned over for the installation of the ribs. Holes are drilled into the bottom edges of the two gunwales to accept the rib-ends. The ends of the ribs are whittled to shape and then forced into their two aligned holes.

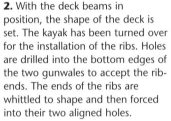

Kayak frame, East Hudson Bay type. Early to mid-twentieth century, sixteen feet, eight inches long and twenty-seven inches wide. This kayak frame represents the Eastern Canadian Arctic kayak type noted for its flat deck, deep bow and low stern. Regional kayak styles are marked by differences in size and shape. The rounded hulls in the north contrast with the flat bottoms further south. The long Hudson Strait and Atlantic Labrador kayaks contrast with the shorter kayaks from eastern Hudson Bay.

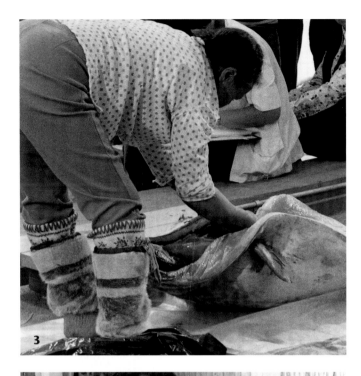

3. The cover of the kayak is made from depilated sealskins. After the skin has been removed, the hair, subcutaneous fat and connective tissue are scraped away. For this work the skin is spread over a scraping platform. Great skill is necessary for shaving the hair and scraping the fat without nicking the skin. They are using an ulu, a semi-lunar knife often referred to as a woman's knife.

4. Sinew thread, made from caribou tendon fibers, is used for sewing the sealskins of a kayak cover. An over-lapping, waterproof stitch is used to sew together enough prepared skins to span the length of the kayak frame. The cover is placed along the bottom of the frame and the two sides are pulled over the gunwales. The two opposing edges of the cover are tied with rope over the top of the deck and gradually tight-ened until the edges come together.

5. Where the edges of the kayak cover meet, they are sewn together. In the areas where the edges do not touch, the gap is patched with additional sealskin.

6. After the skin cover has been sewn onto the frame, the last task is to mount the wooden cockpit coaming. In this kayak type, the coaming is not attached directly to the frame. It is held in position by the skin cover itself, which runs beneath the bottom edge of the coaming and then is lashed to the coaming's inner face.

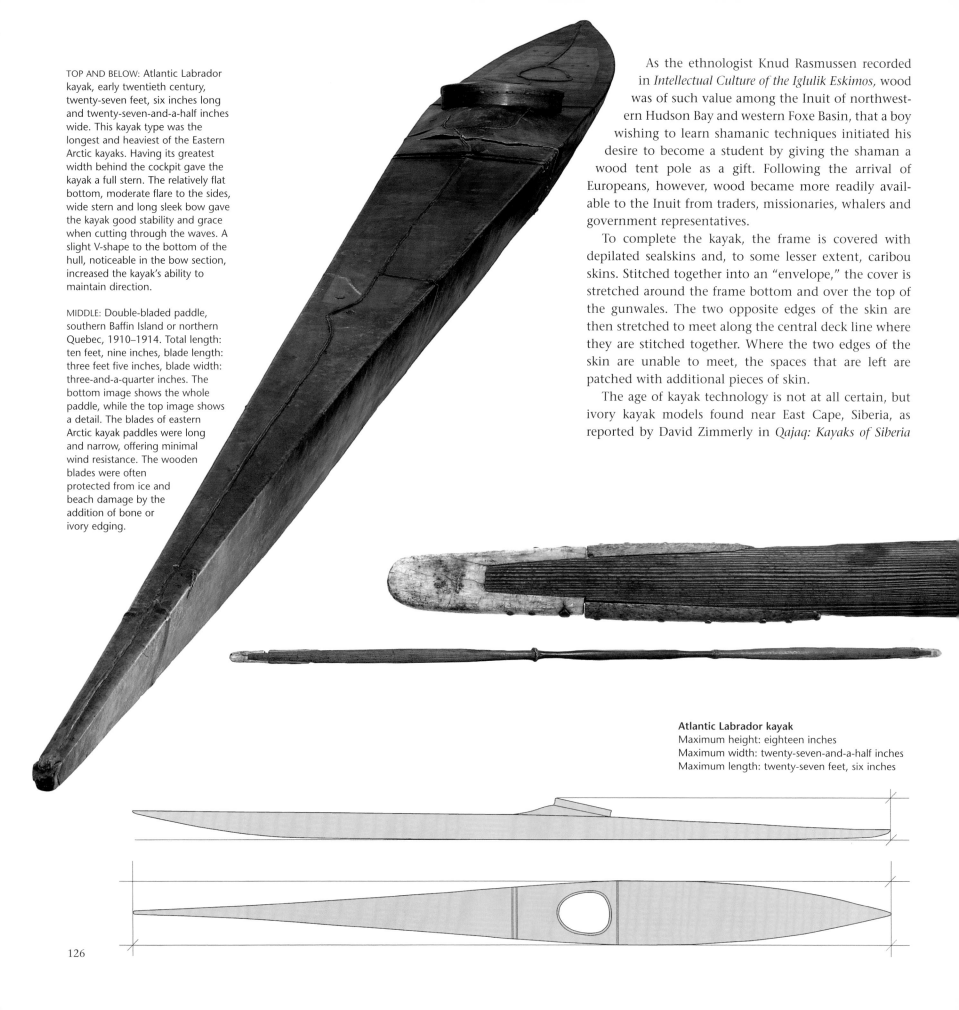

TOP AND BELOW: Atlantic Labrador kayak, early twentieth century, twenty-seven feet, six inches long and twenty-seven-and-a-half inches wide. This kayak type was the longest and heaviest of the Eastern Arctic kayaks. Having its greatest width behind the cockpit gave the kayak a full stern. The relatively flat bottom, moderate flare to the sides, wide stern and long sleek bow gave the kayak good stability and grace when cutting through the waves. A slight V-shape to the bottom of the hull, noticeable in the bow section, increased the kayak's ability to maintain direction.

MIDDLE: Double-bladed paddle, southern Baffin Island or northern Quebec, 1910–1914. Total length: ten feet, nine inches, blade length: three feet five inches, blade width: three-and-a-quarter inches. The bottom image shows the whole paddle, while the top image shows a detail. The blades of eastern Arctic kayak paddles were long and narrow, offering minimal wind resistance. The wooden blades were often protected from ice and beach damage by the addition of bone or ivory edging.

As the ethnologist Knud Rasmussen recorded in *Intellectual Culture of the Iglulik Eskimos,* wood was of such value among the Inuit of northwestern Hudson Bay and western Foxe Basin, that a boy wishing to learn shamanic techniques initiated his desire to become a student by giving the shaman a wood tent pole as a gift. Following the arrival of Europeans, however, wood became more readily available to the Inuit from traders, missionaries, whalers and government representatives.

To complete the kayak, the frame is covered with depilated sealskins and, to some lesser extent, caribou skins. Stitched together into an "envelope," the cover is stretched around the frame bottom and over the top of the gunwales. The two opposite edges of the skin are then stretched to meet along the central deck line where they are stitched together. Where the two edges of the skin are unable to meet, the spaces that are left are patched with additional pieces of skin.

The age of kayak technology is not at all certain, but ivory kayak models found near East Cape, Siberia, as reported by David Zimmerly in *Qajaq: Kayaks of Siberia*

Atlantic Labrador kayak
Maximum height: eighteen inches
Maximum width: twenty-seven-and-a-half inches
Maximum length: twenty-seven feet, six inches

and Alaska, indicate that kayaks have been part of Arctic cultures for at least two millennia. The arctic ethnologist Eugene Arima, in his article "Barkless Barques" in *The Canoe in Canadian Cultures*, identifies an artifact shaped like a kayak rib found at a Saqqaq Culture site in West Greenland, suggesting the possibility that kayak technology may indeed reach back as much as four thousand years.

Across Arctic North America and into the eastern extremity of Eurasia, the kayak's primary function was that of a hunting tool. However, kayak designs varied and design characteristics were influenced by the specific functions the kayaks served and the waters paddled. For instance, the form of the Greenland kayak is a balance between the needs of the hunter and the conditions he worked in, as the Greenlandic authority H.C. Petersen explains in his book, *Skinboats of Greenland*:

The kayak must be able to transport its owner in very rough seas; not just in the swell of the waves but in the churning, choppy seas where the waves break unpredictably from all sides. It must be able to shoot river rapids. It must carry the catch and animals killed, and

Sculpture of family sewing and building a kayak, artist unknown, 1969. Black stone, bone and sinew: four and three-quarter inches by sixteen by ten-and-a-half inches. The sculpture expresses a story translated by Joni Pov of Povungnituk. A family stranded on ice were fortunate to capture a bearded seal. From its skin they made a kayak cover and from its bones they made a kayak frame, and they were able to paddle to safety.

LEFT AND BELOW: Hudson Strait kayak, 1910–14, twenty-one feet, eleven inches long and twenty-six inches wide. Collected by Robert Flaherty, filmmaker of *Nanook of the North* (1922). In this film, which includes several kayaking sequences, Flaherty interwove the lives of real people with a dramatic story. Although he has been accused of staging his scenes, the film is nevertheless an invaluable record of Inuit reality in the early twentieth century. Characteristic of the Eastern Arctic kayak type, the maximum width of the Hudson Strait kayak occurs behind the cockpit, giving it a full stern. The wide stern, side-to-side flat bottom and flared sides provided good stability.

Hudson Strait kayak
Maximum height: eighteen inches
Maximum width: twenty-six inches
Maximum length: twenty-one feet, eleven inches

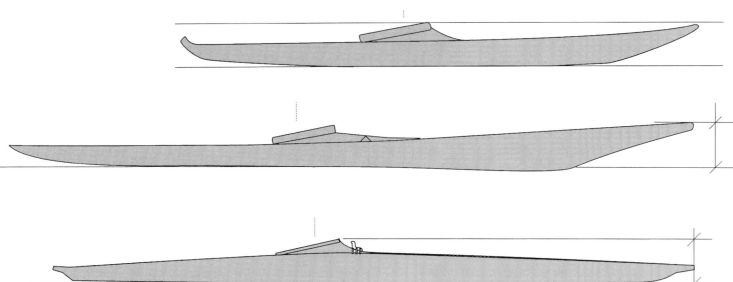

Eastern Hudson Bay kayak, 1976
Maximum width:
twenty-nine inches
Maximum length: sixteen feet

Northern Baffin Island kayak
Early twentieth century
Maximum width:
twenty-seven-and-a-half inches
Maximum length:
twenty-one feet, six inches

Netsilingmiut kayak
Mid-twentieth century
Maximum width:
twenty-and-a-half inches
Maximum length: twenty feet

ABOVE: The Eastern Hudson Bay kayak (top) and the Northern Baffin Island kayak (middle), were kayaks from the eastern Canadian Arctic, which were used for hunting sea mammals. The Netsilingmiut kayak (bottom), from the central Arctic, was used for hunting caribou as they swam across rivers and narrow lakes. The Northern Baffin Island kayak often had a deep forefoot, which gripped the water and helped keep a heading into the wind. The rounded cross-section differs from the flat-bottomed hulls to the south, indicating a possible influence from kayaks of the central Arctic.

RIGHT: This photograph of a Copper Inuit man carrying a kayak was taken by John J. O'Neill, the geologist with the Southern Party of the Canadian Arctic Expedition, 1913–16. Under the leadership of zoologist Rudolph M. Anderson, the purpose of the expedition was to undertake scientific investigations of the Coronation gulf region of Arctic Canada. The ethnologist with the expedition, Diamond Jenness, assumed the studies of the Copper Inuit.

other goods as well. It must be serviceable in ice-filled waters and able to manoeuvre between floating ice. It must be transportable over large distances resting on the kayaker's head so that both hands are free to carry things, over ice as well as uneven terrain. On thin ice the hunter must be able to carry it between his legs so that he can get into it quickly if the ice cracks under him.

Petersen identifies four main Greenland kayak types. The Flat kayak is built and used in southern and eastern Greenland. This kayak type is quite shallow with a flat bottom. It is narrow with straight gunwales, and its ribs, with only a slight shortening of the aft section, are generally the same height along its length. The Curved kayak type is found along Greenland's southeast coast. The middle section of the sheer line is straight; however, the bow and stern ends of the gunwales curve up slightly to form a concave profile. This is the deepest type of the

Greenland kayaks. Interestingly, it displays a sinuous keel line, in that the keel in the bow section is convex shaped, whereas in the stern section, the keel takes a concave configuration. The *Avasisaartoq* kayak type seemed to have had widespread use until the beginning of the twentieth century, but now only vestiges of this kayak type can be seen along Greenland's west coast. The main feature of this kayak type is its concave sheer line and its sharply curved ends. In comparison to the curved type, this kayak type has a much more concave profile and shallower sides. Finally, the North Greenland kayak type represents the shortest of the Greenland kayaks: it seems that this type only appeared during the twentieth century after the demise of the *Avasisaartoq* kayak. In profile, the shape is slightly concave with very short bow and stern tips.

Across Arctic Canada and Alaska, kayaks differed greatly in size and shape, with their individual characteristics influenced by local needs and conditions. In eastern Canada, four general kayak styles can be

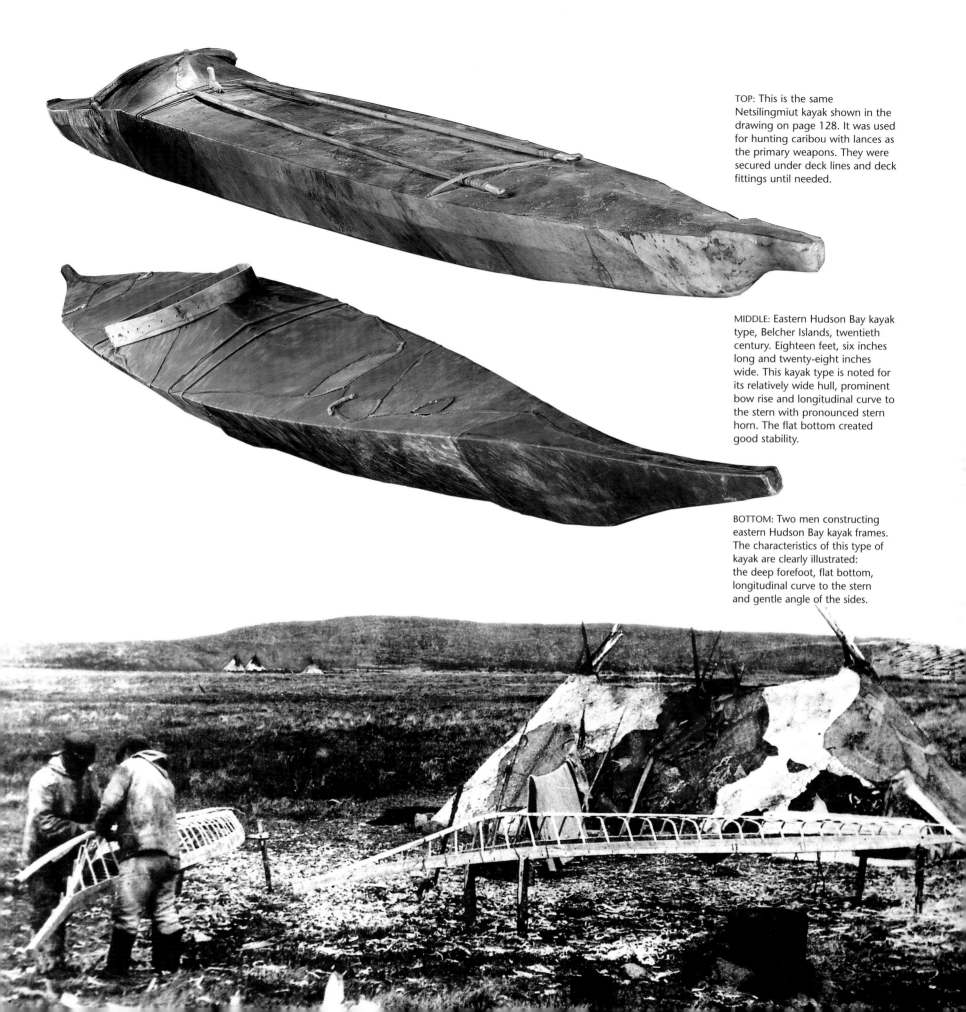

TOP: This is the same Netsilingmiut kayak shown in the drawing on page 128. It was used for hunting caribou with lances as the primary weapons. They were secured under deck lines and deck fittings until needed.

MIDDLE: Eastern Hudson Bay kayak type, Belcher Islands, twentieth century. Eighteen feet, six inches long and twenty-eight inches wide. This kayak type is noted for its relatively wide hull, prominent bow rise and longitudinal curve to the stern with pronounced stern horn. The flat bottom created good stability.

BOTTOM: Two men constructing eastern Hudson Bay kayak frames. The characteristics of this type of kayak are clearly illustrated: the deep forefoot, flat bottom, longitudinal curve to the stern and gentle angle of the sides.

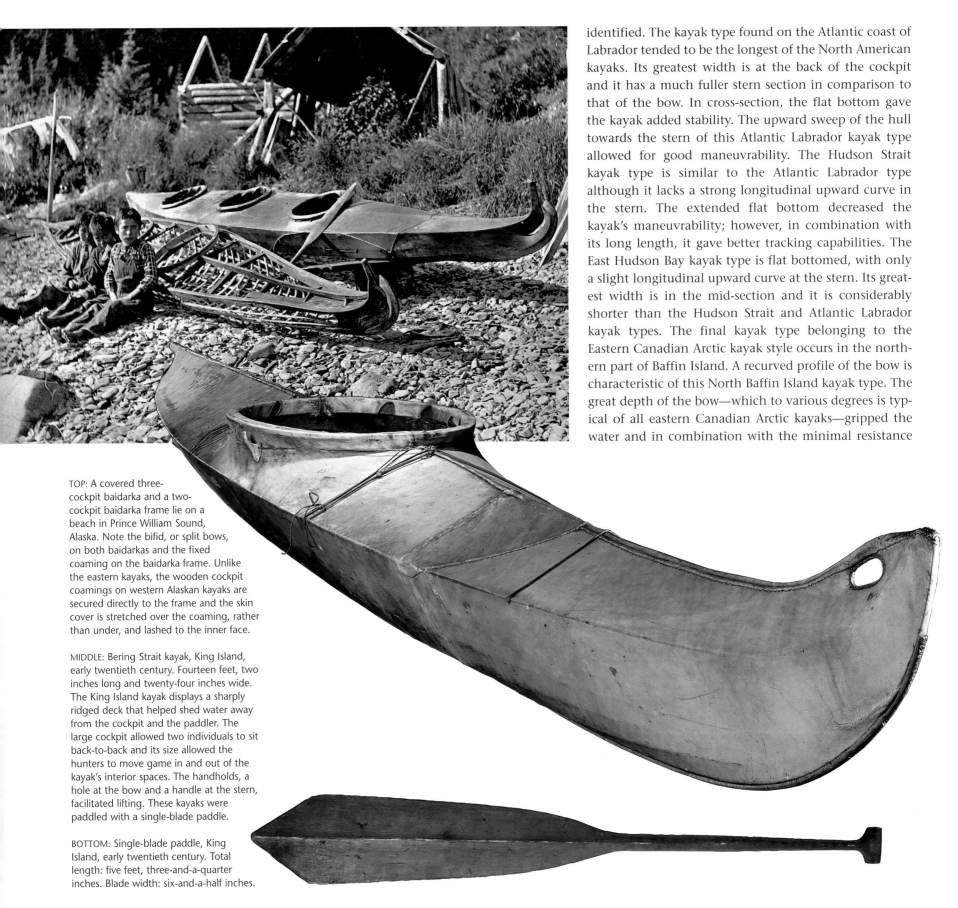

identified. The kayak type found on the Atlantic coast of Labrador tended to be the longest of the North American kayaks. Its greatest width is at the back of the cockpit and it has a much fuller stern section in comparison to that of the bow. In cross-section, the flat bottom gave the kayak added stability. The upward sweep of the hull towards the stern of this Atlantic Labrador kayak type allowed for good maneuvrability. The Hudson Strait kayak type is similar to the Atlantic Labrador type although it lacks a strong longitudinal upward curve in the stern. The extended flat bottom decreased the kayak's maneuvrability; however, in combination with its long length, it gave better tracking capabilities. The East Hudson Bay kayak type is flat bottomed, with only a slight longitudinal upward curve at the stern. Its greatest width is in the mid-section and it is considerably shorter than the Hudson Strait and Atlantic Labrador kayak types. The final kayak type belonging to the Eastern Canadian Arctic kayak style occurs in the northern part of Baffin Island. A recurved profile of the bow is characteristic of this North Baffin Island kayak type. The great depth of the bow—which to various degrees is typical of all eastern Canadian Arctic kayaks—gripped the water and in combination with the minimal resistance

TOP: A covered three-cockpit baidarka and a two-cockpit baidarka frame lie on a beach in Prince William Sound, Alaska. Note the bifid, or split bows, on both baidarkas and the fixed coaming on the baidarka frame. Unlike the eastern kayaks, the wooden cockpit coamings on western Alaskan kayaks are secured directly to the frame and the skin cover is stretched over the coaming, rather than under, and lashed to the inner face.

MIDDLE: Bering Strait kayak, King Island, early twentieth century. Fourteen feet, two inches long and twenty-four inches wide. The King Island kayak displays a sharply ridged deck that helped shed water away from the cockpit and the paddler. The large cockpit allowed two individuals to sit back-to-back and its size allowed the hunters to move game in and out of the kayak's interior spaces. The handholds, a hole at the bow and a handle at the stern, facilitated lifting. These kayaks were paddled with a single-blade paddle.

BOTTOM: Single-blade paddle, King Island, early twentieth century. Total length: five feet, three-and-a-quarter inches. Blade width: six-and-a-half inches.

provided by the stern's longitudinal bottom curve, the kayak tended to point bow-first into the wind when the kayaker was resting.

In the central part of the Canadian Arctic, kayaks were used to intercept caribou as they swam between areas of land. The Caribou Inuit and the Netsilingmiut kayak types have hulls that are long and narrow, reducing draft and overall water resistance and giving these craft the capability of high speed. The acute rise of the deck from the aft section of the bow to the front of the cockpit—a characteristic of these kayak types—deflected water away from the cockpit and the paddler.

Among the kayak types from Canada and Alaska, the Inuvialuit kayak type from the region of the Mackenzie River Delta was one of the shortest. Characterized by a strong convex bottom curvature and a rounded cross-section, this kayak type is noted for its easy maneuvrability.

Four general kayak styles are noted from Alaska: the North Alaska type stretching from Kotzebue Sound around the north Alaskan coast to the Canadian border; the Bering Sea type from Bristol Bay to Norton Sound in southwest Alaska; the Pacific Eskimo type from the Prince William Sound and Kodiak Island area of south Alaska;

and finally, the Aleut type from the Aleutian Islands.

The North Alaska kayak type has a long but narrow hull with a round cross-section. In combination with a rockered bottom this kayak type possessed ideal characteristics for speed. Similar to kayaks further east, the decks are flat with the exception of a sharp rise in the deck between the aft section of the bow and the front of the cockpit.

The Bering Sea kayak type has a deep hull, wide beam and a rounded cross-section. Its strongly-ridged deck increased interior space and, like the raked coamings of the eastern Canadian Arctic kayaks, the ridged deck served to shed the water away from the cockpit and the paddler. A stern projection and bow hole served as hand grips for lifting the kayak in and out of the water. A wide cockpit facilitated ease of entry and exit, as well as the interior storage of captured animals.

The Pacific Eskimo and Aleut kayak types are referred to by the Russian term baidarka. Perhaps the most intriguing feature of these kayaks is the bifid (split) bow, which may have served both figurative and functional roles. Symbolically, the two "arms" of the split bow may symbolize an otter swimming on its back where the forward arm represents its head and the aft arm represents

This photograph shows a group of paddlers in North-Alaskan-style kayaks. The photograph was taken by Edward S. Curtis, who wrote in *The North American Indian*: "These skin-covered craft, of marvellous lightness and efficiency, are of outstanding importance to the Eskimo. Remarkable too is the manner in which they are handled by their owners, who are exceedingly expert even in rough water."

its front paws. Functionally, the two-part bow is an ingenious design that furnishes a sharp bottom surface for cutting the water and a larger upper surface for buoyancy. In the words of David Zimmerly, the split bow "... allowed the bottom portion to be sharp and narrow like a cutwater, while the upper part was large and triangular in shape to give more buoyancy." Both kayak types were long, with narrow beams and rounded cross-sections. The Pacific Eskimo type, however, had distinguishing construction differences, such as a wider beam and a distinct stern configuration. Both kayak types were constructed with one, two or three cockpits. The three-hole variety, however, seems to have been developed after contact with the Russians. The middle cockpit held Russian missionaries or traders while the two end cockpits were occupied by the Native paddlers.

Dashing Kayaks and Splashing Paddles

The kayak was born in the hunting world of the Arctic peoples and to be understood it must be seen from their perspective and within a hunting context. An ivory sculpture (see page 134) of an Inuit hunter paddling a fully equipped kayak, which comes from the Cumberland Sound area of the eastern Canadian Arctic, is a fitting image of the kayak in a cultural context. By letting this image fill our minds, we can see and almost smell the Arctic waters and imagine the generations of kayak hunters who paddled from the banks of their camps fixed with their own visions of seals and whales.

The harpoon is positioned on the right and the toggling harpoon head, which is secured to the harpoon's foreshaft and attached by line to the sealskin float, waits for the throw. The lance, the implement that will impart the final death blow, is within easy reach on the aftdeck behind the paddler. And the bird spear, with its end point and its three barbs at mid-length, rests in position on the foredeck should its need arise. This kayak sculpture with its associated hunting equipment symbolizes the significance of the kayak in the Inuit harvesting-oriented technology. The kayak provides the means by which hunters are able to approach targeted animals such as seals, walrus, whales, narwhals, sea otters, waterfowl and caribou.

In the western Arctic, during the period of intensive hunting to support non-Native demands for furs, the sea otter was hunted almost to extinction and the baidarka played a decisive role in the hunt. An early nineteenth century Russian explorer, Urey Lisiansky, in his book *A Voyage round the World in the Years 1803,4,5&6*, describes a technique of hunting sea otter where a number of Aleutians in baidarkas cooperate in hunting a single otter:

A number of Aleutians, more or less, go out together in separate baidarkas. As soon as any one of them perceives an otter, he throws his arrow at it, if he can, and ... pulls to the place where it plunges. He here stations his boat, and lifts up his oar. The rest of the hunters, on observing the signal, form a circle round it. The moment the animal appears above water, the hunter that is nearest throws his arrow, and then hastens to the spot where the animal replunges, and makes it known, as in the preceding instance, by raising his oar. A second circle is then formed; and in this manner the chase continues, till the poor beast is perfectly exhausted by the blood flowing from its wounds. I was told by very expert hunters, that these animals were sometimes easily caught; whereas, at other times, twenty baidarkas would be employed half a day in taking a single otter: and this animal has been known to tear the arrow from its body in order to escape. The first plunge of an otter exceeds a quarter of an hour; the second is of shorter duration, the third still shorter; and thus the intervals gradually diminish, till at last it can plunge no more.

The sea otter hunt was a communal event, as was the whale hunt among the Inuvialuit, which sometimes involved upwards of two hundred kayaks. C.E.Whittaker, in his book *Arctic Eskimo, a record of fifty years' experience and observation among the Eskimo*, describes the hunt as follows:

When the look-out raises and lowers his arms several times rapidly, the time has arrived for action. This signal was given and the new master of the hunt launched his kayak and headed for the open sea, his men, at about forty-yard intervals, followed in his wake.

When the fleet had got below the school the leader turned across the stream until a barrier was formed between their quarry and the sea. Silently they approached

Nunivak Island kayak, Bering Sea. Collected during the late nineteenth century, this kayak is shown equipped with a single-blade paddle, harpoon line and line rack, and skin float. Inside the cockpit the port side coaming stanchion can be seen, with the upper portion of a carved face visible. In Nunivak Island kayaks, carved face images on the two coaming stanchions depict smiling and frowning faces that relate to good and bad luck. The outside surface of the kayak is painted with the image of a mythical water being and the lines on the stern projection represent the hunter's personal identification markings.

the feeding whales, as nearly as possible, when at a signal every man shouted with all his might. Alarmed by the din of voices, the darting kayaks, and the splashing paddles, the whales dashed madly up-stream, to left and right, and soon floundering in water too shallow for diving.

The hunters now rushed in, and with their harpoons attacked their prey. Each harpoon had an inflated bladder attached, to prevent sinking and to show its course in case it got into deep water.

The harpoon seldom kills, this being accomplished with a long-handled, light spear, by frequent thrusting. Then to ensure floating, the hunter also inflates his whale, blowing his breath into the viscera through a spear thrust, and stopping the wound with a wooden plug.

Caribou were also communally hunted from the kayak, for example among the Netsilingmiut in the regions of the Boothia, Simpson and Adelaide Peninsulas. The Norwegian explorer, Roald Amundsen, described such a hunt in the account of his epic journey through the Northwest Passage:

When the kayak is fitted out for the reindeer [caribou] chase, the hunter has his two reindeer lances ready beside him, fixed in straps in the kayak skin so that they may not fall overboard. The reindeer have a fixed track to the north for their spring migration. When passing Nechilli they take such a course as to make it easy for the

ABOVE: For kayak hunting expeditions, clothing generally consisted of sealskin parka, pants, boots and mittens. Sealskin is excellent for spring and summer clothing as it is durable, light-weight and water repellent. In some areas of the Arctic, a gutskin jacket made from seal-intestine casings was worn like a raincoat and protected the layer of sealskin underneath from rain and sea-spray. The Greenland jacket illustrated has drawstrings around the face and wrist openings, as well as around the bottom, where it was secured to the cockpit coaming to prevent water from entering the kayak.

BELOW: Kayak sculpture from Cumberland Sound, Pangnirtung area, Baffin Island. Artist unknown. Ivory and skin, nine-and-a-quarter inches long, 1933–42. This delicately carved sculpture of a kayak and a hunter with his hunting equipment close at hand symbolizes the importance of the kayak in the Inuit culture. See page 132–33 .

Eskimo to drive them into the water. The huntsmen divide into two parties, one with the kayaks and the other without. The kayak men station themselves on the bank opposite to the one from which the deer are coming. When a herd of reindeer approaches, the drivers make a wide circle round them and drive them into the water. As soon as the deer are well into it, the kayak men jump into their boats and spear one reindeer after another. The animals are towed to the bank and taken care of by the huntsmen on shore.

The larger whales, such as the right and the bowhead whales, as well as narwhals, walrus and seals, were hunted in the eastern Canadian Arctic with the kayak equipped as shown in the ivory sculpture on the opposite page. Ernest Hawkes, an anthropologist with the Geological Survey of Canada, recorded in his 1916 publication, *The Labrador Eskimo,* the following description of kayak hunting equipment and its placement on the decks of the kayak:

Two thongs are sewn into the kayak in front to hold the harpoon rack and harpoon on one side, and the bird spear on the other; and behind the hole, two small loops are sewn to hold the seal hook and killing lance. The position of these weapons on the kayak is regulated by their use, the chief weapon to be used being at the right hand front of the hunter. Ordinarily, the harpoon occupies this position, and the bird-spear and throwing-stick are placed on the left front, the seal-hook on the right back, and the lance on the left back. The line of the harpoon lies in the rack in front of the hunter; the harpoon is held in the right hand and the coil in the left when the harpoon is thrown from the kayak. If the harpoon line has a float attached, it rests on the boat just back of the hunter and is thrown into the water after the harpoon is launched. In northern Labrador, a circular hoop-like float ... is attached to the float, and being dragged at right angles through the water, soon lessens the pace of the fleeting game.

The primary weapon for capturing sea mammals from a kayak, as Hawkes suggests, was the harpoon with an attached sealskin float. The harpoon rested on the side-deck in a ready-to-throw position pointing to the stern. The sealskin line joining the harpoon head to the float was coiled on the harpoon-line rack immediately in front of the cockpit. The lance, positioned on the left-hand side of the aftdeck, was employed in concert with the harpoon: the harpoon caught the prey, but the animal's death was completed with the lance.

As indicated by Hawkes, a bird spear was also carried on the kayak and it was generally positioned on the left-hand side of the bow deck. The bird spear was the primary weapon for capturing waterfowl and sea birds. To throw the spear, the butt end was placed along the channel of a throwing board and held in place by the thumb. With the increased thrust created by the throwing board the spear could be accurately thrown over great distances. Albert P. Low, Officer in Charge of the 1903–04 Canadian Arctic Patrol to assert Canadian sovereignty over Hudson Bay and the Arctic islands, wrote the following in his 1906 report about the Inuit use of the bird spear:

This instrument consists of a light wooden shaft five or six feet long, with a trident of deer horn at its upper end. The pieces of horn are from six to eight inches long, about half an inch in diameter; their sides are notched by a number of barbs pointing downwards, and they are so set at the head of the shaft as to project outwards at an angle of 45 degrees, while each piece of horn makes an angle of 120 degrees with its neighbours. Similar barbed prongs are attached to the shaft.... The lower end of the shaft is flattened, and made tapering to fit a groove in a throwing board held in the hand of the hunter. This dart is very skilfully thrown many yards, and entangles itself about the necks or in the wings of the ducks.

Two Inuit male dolls from southern Baffin Island dressed in the summer clothing worn during kayak hunting expeditions: sealskin parka, pants, boots and mittens. Early twentieth century. The doll on the left is thirteen-and-a-half inches high, and the doll on the right is twelve inches high.

This is a unique view of a hunter positioned to throw his harpoon from an Eastern Canadian Arctic kayak. Holding his double-blade paddle in his left hand for balance, the harpoon is thrown with his right hand. The harpoon head is attached by sealskin rope to the sealskin float resting on the back deck behind the cockpit coaming. The socketed harpoon head is held secure to the harpoon foreshaft through tension between it and a pin on the harpoon handle. After the harpoon is cast, the sealskin float is thrown from the back of the kayak and acts as both a drag for the harpooned animal and a marker.

During the nineteenth and twentieth centuries, Inuit contact with foreigners gave them access to European and North American materials and practices. In turn, these influenced both the economic and the social realms of Inuit culture. The introduction of the wooden boat, the whaleboat and later the motorized canoe, modified the Inuit need for their traditional kayak. No longer did they have to find and prepare materials and undertake the time-consuming process of assembling wood, skin, bone and ivory into a kayak. The wooden boat was more forgiving in terms of care, and, unlike the kayak with its vulnerable skin, it did not require constant diligence in keeping voracious dogs a safe distance away. The introduction of firearms also modified traditional cultural practices. Replacing the bow, arrow and harpoon, firearms improved the efficiency of hunting and the quantity of animals captured. Firearms also made solo hunting feasible and therefore decreased the traditional need to maintain cooperative communal hunts. With the gun, for instance, caribou could be hunted as the opportunity arose, rather than by organized communal caribou hunts by kayak at water crossings. As the Inuit adopted new technologies and practices the kayak gradually lost its vital function, and by the 1960s it was no longer part of Inuit hunting.

The Kayak and the Walrus

Over the thousands of years that the kayak was part of the culture of the Arctic, it played an essential role in the Inuit material system. During the ice-free periods of the year, the kayak enabled the Inuit to procure a living from their physical surroundings. To Inuit hunters, though, the kayak was more than the sum of its parts. It was part of a complex relationship between the hunters and the animals hunted. The Inuit and the animals they hunted represented participating communities in a shared environment linked together through harvesting. The association between the hunters and their prey was a relationship of equality between two groups of sentient beings. The Aivilingmiut hunter, Ivaluardjuk, expressed this concept to anthropologist, Knud Rasmussen:

All the creatures that we have to kill and eat, all those that we have to strike down and destroy to make clothes for ourselves, have souls, like we have, souls that do not perish with the body, and which must therefore be propitiated lest they should revenge themselves on us for taking away their bodies.

Hunting success depends on the generous intentions of the hunter, for the animals can sense a hunter's attitude and will only allow themselves to be caught when the hunter embraces respect for the hunted and generosity with the catch. Another Native hunter, Herbert O. Anungazuk, of Wales, Alaska, quoted in *Inuit, Whaling and Sustainability* by Milton Freeman *et al*, expressed it this way:

Whaling is a sacred affair to the Iñupiat hunter.... The belief that spirits are embodied in sea mammals is very strong among the northern Inuit.... An appropriate ceremony must be conducted when a whale is landed by the whaling crew to avoid insult to the spirit of the whale and other sea mammals.

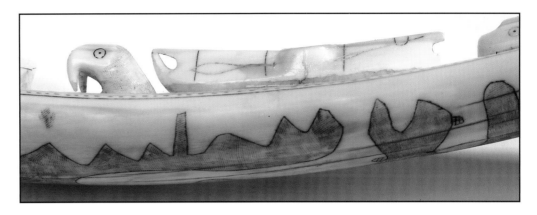

Like the ivory model of an equipped kayak from Cumberland Sound, the sculptured image of a kayak and walrus on a cribbage board from Norton Sound in Alaska, on the opposite side of the continent, symbolizes the Inuit-animal relationship. From a side view, the kayak is positioned behind the head of a swimming walrus and the relationship between the hunter and the hunted is clear. However, if the image is rotated and the view is oriented from above, a skilful interplay of two and three dimensions shows that the kayak forms the body of the walrus. The two in essence have become one, tied into a relationship based upon mutual respect and understanding. As represented so skilfully in the Norton Sound sculpture, the kayak functioned within a cultural system that viewed itself and the physical world as a single integrated whole.

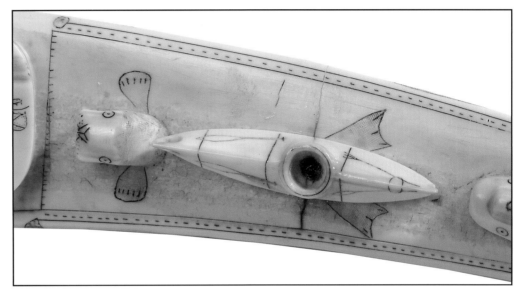

The final word, in the poetry of song expressing the interrelationship of hunter, kayak, walrus, and spirit is given to the Inuit shaman, Aua, as recorded in the early 1920s by Knud Rasmussen:

Detail of a walrus and kayak on a cribbage board, from Norton Sound area, western Alaska. Artist unknown. Ivory, twentieth century, eighteen and a half inches long. From the side view (top), the kayak is pursuing the swimming walrus, but from above (bottom) the kayak forms the body of the walrus. This represents the world view of the Inuit, where hunter and hunted are joined together as part of the integrated physical world.

I could not sleep,
For the sea lay so smooth
near at hand.
So I rowed out,
and a walrus came up
close beside my kayak.
It was too near to throw,
And I thrust the harpoon into its side,
and the hunting float bounded over the water.
But it kept coming up again
and set its flippers angrily
like elbows on the surface of the water,
trying to tear the hunting float to pieces.
In vain it spent its utmost strength,
for the skin of an unborn lemming
was sewn inside as a guardian amulet,
and when it drew back, blowing viciously,
to gather strength again,
I rowed up and stabbed it
With my lance.
And this I sing ...

BUILDING UMIAKS

EUGENE ARIMA

The umiak is used for hunting big game: big seals like the bearded and bladdernose, and whales like the beluga and narwhal, as well as some of the bigger whales, above all the bowhead. It is also used for general transportation, for moving from place to place during the annual round and voyaging afar. In this role it is often rowed by women, hence the European characterization "women's boat" in the East Arctic, where umiak hunting faded in the nineteenth century. In the West Arctic the umiak has never lost its identity as a hunting boat operated by men, paddling. It was also the war boat.

Umiaks and kayaks are complementary sister craft used over a huge region: from northeast Asia, around the Bering Sea (including the Aleutians), across the Bering Strait and along northern North America from South Alaska to Greenland. This vast area includes Hudson Bay and Atlantic Labrador and parts of the Gulf of St. Lawrence, with quite varied expressions of the two skin boats. The umiak, being open, is the less unique watercraft. It could be up to about sixty feet long, but more typically ranges between eight to forty feet. The smallest are for retrieving seals killed from the floe edge; the largest are for moving. Wider and deeper than the kayak, the umiak is more stable and comfortable. The light but strong frame and skin construction enhances speed, maneuvrability, carrying capacity and manhandling. Structural flexibility softens the shock of waves and hard things, the sea mammal skin cover being quite strong, especially when made of bearded seal or walrus.

The pinnacle of umiak purpose is whaling, still done in Northwest Alaska in the spring when leads (channels in the icefields) open and the bowheads migrate east. Surrounded by religious ritual, whaling climaxes with the harpooning, described for Point Barrow as follows by Robert F. Spencer in *The North Alaskan Eskimo*:

From the prow the harpooner, waiting until the boat was as close to a surfacing whale as could be managed, let his harpoon go ... throwing with all his strength. He twisted the harpoon lightly so that the head would turn in the body of the whale. As he threw, he sang his songs. Once one line was secured in the whale's body, an attempt was made to secure other lines. The seal floats on each line, usually two or three in number, served to make the wounded whale surface again. When the animal did so, the skill of the crew members and of the helmsman were taxed to the utmost. The umiak had to be maneuvered so that the whale could be approached from the side.... Once the craft was close to the whale, the lance, with its stone or slate head locked into a haft with a bone wedge, had to be used to advantage. The whale had to be stabbed in some vital organ, preferably the heart or kidneys.

FACING PAGE: Man guides umiak to shore, in the Tasiilaq/Ammassalik area in East Greenland, circa 1961.

BELOW: Modern print (1979) of an umiak from Cape Dorset, South Baffin, with oars, square sail and rudder. It is boxy and clumsy looking, unlike its archaeological Thule Culture ancestors on the bow drill in the illustration on page 144. The round shape on the bow looks like a sealskin float to buoy up the front end in waves.

The harpooner thrust his lance again and again in the effort to kill the whale. For an average-size whale, one running thirty to thirty-five tons, and a corresponding number of feet in length, two lines and one lance were regarded as sufficient. The crewmen held the lines and drew the umiak near the whale. When the whale was dead, it tended to turn over and was kept afloat by means of the floats which were fastened to the carcass.

An ideal situation occurred when two boats came together, one on each side of the whale. The seal floats would then be fastened equally and the animal could be lanced from each side.... The principal danger lay in a "spinning" whale. If the quarry fouled up the lines and surfaced under the umiak, tragedy could result for the crew.

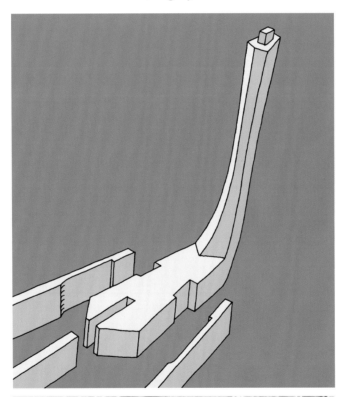

This method of joining stem and stern to the keel and chine stringers is often used with Greenland umiaks.

A stern post or stem would be cut from a piece of tree root driftwood like this one, found on St. Lawrence Island, in the Bering Sea.

Framework Construction

Wood (principally spruce) for the umiak framework is gathered both as driftwood and live, cut from sheltered river valleys where trees grow farthest into the open northern lands. The driftwood is often well inland at the highest lake on a major river, where trees uprooted at breakup get stranded. Bark indicates newness and flexibility, which is wanted in certain parts. Since the advent of Europeans, dressed lumber is also used. In the west, since the 1920s when bent-rib multi-chine umiaks (with several lengthwise edges in the hull surface along the stringers) developed in Alaska, including St. Lawrence Island, hickory and oak from Seattle are preferred for the steam-bent ribs. A chine is a longitudinal line of transition between hull surfaces, such as where the bottom meets the sides. If the transition is gradual over some distance transversely, it is a "soft" chine, as when the bottom rounds smoothly up to the sides. If the transition is quick, forming a more or less sharp edge, it is a "hard" chine.

Inuit are discriminating about wood. Greenlander skin boat scholar H.C. Petersen writes in *Skinboats of Greenland*:

The framework of an umiak makes certain demands on the properties of the wood, and the boat builder must try to meet these. First the strength and toughness of the wood must be considered. Flexibility is also a desirable characteristic. Some kinds of wood are more water absorbent than others. They may be light or heavy and the color is also significant. In addition to all these, the availability of the wood is an important factor.

Certain parts of the umiak are important for the strength of its structure, others can be viewed with a less critical eye. The weight of the wood is also significant, as the umiak has to be transported for long stretches overland [also over ice], and this factor is therefore taken more seriously than the others by many boat builders. The keel, side ribs, chine stringers, bottom ribs, and stem and stern posts should preferably be of a tough wood. The grain of the stem and stern posts is very important....

Niaqunak or tree root is ideal for end construction, its sharp turn into the trunk providing a strong knee for the post to keel juncture. The umiak is generally built right side up, but at the start it may be handier to have the work inverted for the posts and keel assembly. The keel, the principal structural member, is called *ku* in East Canadian Arctic Inuit, *kuyaaq* in Greenlandic and *kuyak* in Siberian Yupik on St. Lawrence Island. In Greenlandic the umiak is *umiaq* as in Canada, but in Yupik it is called *angyapik*. The keel is dressed rectangular or, less often,

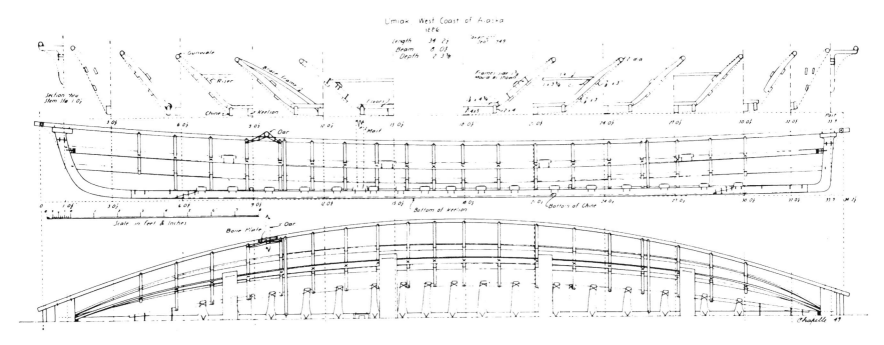

Lines drawing of an 1886 umiak from
King Island, on the west coast of Alaska.

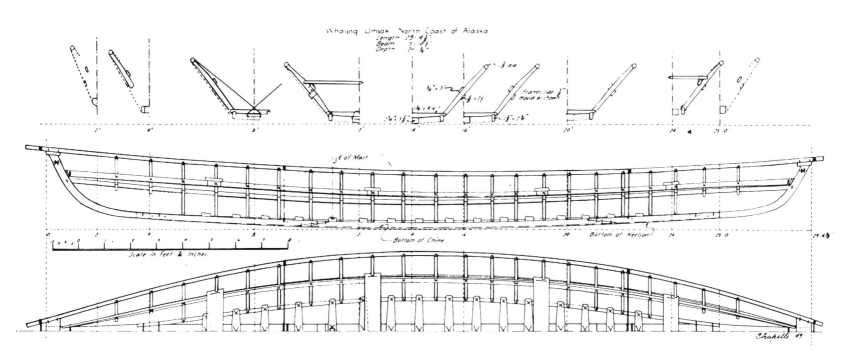

A North Alaskan whaling umiak built
in about 1890. The lines drawing
was done from a damaged frame,
which has since been destroyed.

These drawings, seen from both the side and from above, show the various shapes of the joins between the stem and stern to the keel of an umiak.

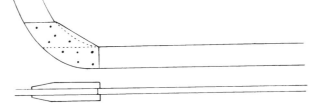

Here the pieces are made from planks.

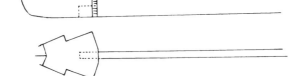

Here the keel is rabbeted into the foot of the stem and stern.

This is a simple join made with metal nails.

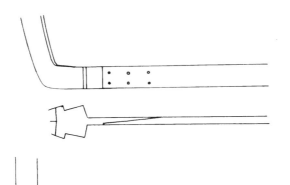

Here a hook scarf has been made and the pieces joined with wooden nails.

Side ribs were made in a variety of shapes.
A. Straight
B. Bent at an angle
C. Curved
D. With a hole for the inner stringer to go through

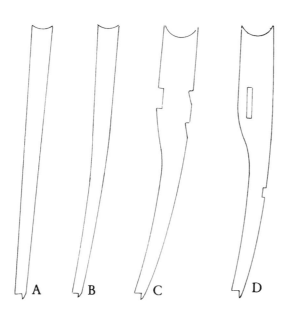

square, and is about three by five inches or four by six inches for a moderate sized umiak of twenty-five to thirty feet in length overall. Usually it is laid on the flat but, recently on-edge construction has come into vogue in both Greenland and Alaska. The end-post is narrower laterally as it is the cutwater, but still sturdy.

The bow is typically more upright and taller than the stern by a couple of inches, the latter being about two feet tall in a medium size umiak. The longitudinal bottom rocker will raise the ends another couple of inches, while amidships sheer height might be several inches less, but such dimensional relations are quite variable. In the west the bow is often strongly raked while the stern has a slight rake, or both ends may be well raked. Also the ends may be convexly curved in profile, particularly in the lower bow, a shape that is good for hauling up onto ice or gentle sandy beaches. Siglit or Mackenzie Inuit umiaks had raked and rounded ends as in their kayaks. At the bottom of the East Canadian Arctic umiak bow, the full width of the tree base is kept for volume and buoyancy, the wood scooped out for lightness but still thick enough for joining on the bottom side or bilge stringers. If the right trunk with side root is unavailable, an intermediate bottom end-block can be used. Such a bow base piece is about one-and-a-half feet wide and long like the front flap on a woman's parka or *kiiniq*, and called the same. Rounded in front, it might be three to four inches thick and have mortise slots to receive the bow post, keel and bilge stringers. A separate stern base block, narrower and deeper than the bow base piece, is called *niaquyaq* after the white whale head it resembles. In another kind of end assembly, a separate post can be joined directly to the keel and bilge stringer, as is commonly done in Greenland. The joining of pieces in this critical area has to be secure. Joints are fastened with strong line and/or tree, bone, ivory or iron nails. Lines of bearded seal and, in the west, baby walrus, are strong but best is baleen (*suqqaq*), which neither loosens nor tightens when wetted and remains flexible. All lashings are baleen in the North-Alaskan-style thirty-five-foot migration umiak found in northeasternmost Greenland, which has been radiocarbon dated to about 1440 CE.

The keel and posts assembly, righted if need be, is put on skids (at least on St. Lawrence Island) with the ones at the end higher so that the keel can be weighted down at the lower middle skid to create the longitudinal rocker, which facilitates sliding over snow and ice. The parts are lined up and cross-braced at the ends to hold the alignment. Each end-post top is cut to have a tenon to fit into the headboard, which can be given a slant on a line to the keel amidships if strongly upswept ends are desired. Or the headboard slants, along with the sheer, can be more restrained overall.

The bottom framework is filled in with crosspieces, which traditionally have their middles widened and flattened underneath to sit on the keel. Their narrowed ends are notched underneath to hold out the bilge stringers to the desired bottom outline. Bottom width amidships can vary greatly, from around two-and-a-half feet to four feet. Floor crosspieces are usually spaced about one foot to one-and-a-half feet. Recently these floor timbers tend to be straight-sided rather than spindle-shaped in plan, commonly about four by one-and-a-half inches laid on the flat. In the west they can be tenoned into the bilge stringers, and they are thinner. In Greenland the floor timbers have come to be set on edge, notched below to house the longitudinals while the sections in between are partly cut away to be up out of contact with the skin cover, which bulges in when soaked and soft.

Bilge or chine stringers are usually rounded, at least on the outer lower sector, while the inner and upper surfaces are often straight, as will happen when the stringers are prepared by quartering raw timber. Their thickness is variable but a two to two-and-a-half inch diameter suffices for up to about thirty-foot-long boats. Where conditions call for stronger construction (such as in the Bering Strait) they can be heavier. Often in the west and in Greenland they sit a little higher than the keel strip to give a shallow V-bottom. The truly flat bottom seems usual in the east Canadian Arctic. In West Greenland since the nineteenth century, bilge stringers are commonly of milled one- by three-inch strips, set on edge. Though left sharp-cornered all around, they are sometimes leaned inward to the bottom to ease the transition to the side.

In the east Canadian Arctic the stringers commonly expand inward in large flag-like shoulders. The end assembly is well rounded to the front outside, with an upward sweep, giving a big smooth bulb broadening into the wide bottom behind. Stringer flags aren't new, for they occur in the bow bottom assembly of the already mentioned 1440 CE western umiak found in northeast Greenland, in which they are set into the upper surface of the stem base with ivory nails. With the bottom framework thus assembled, the ribs are erected along the bilge stringers at intervals about the same as those of the cross-floors but not coming at the same spots. At the joins with the stringers the ribs are cut at the right angle to sit flat on the upper stringer surface at

ABOVE: The bow of an *angyapik* in Gambell, St. Lawrence Island, Alaska in 1973. The rib and stringer construction is very clear in this picture, as is the joint where the stem joins the keel, a join where the stem was lengthened and an additional piece was added to the gunwales to make them stronger.

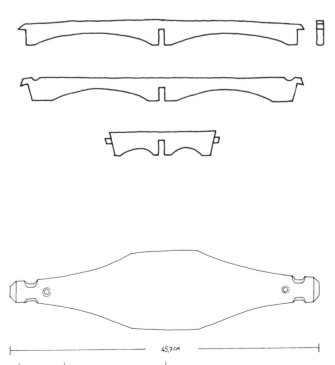

LEFT: For the past two hundred years, the bottom ribs of umiaks made in West and East Greenland have been made from pine planks one-and-a-half-inches thick. Upright chine stringers were used with this bottom rib and lashed (top). Slanted chine stringers were lashed to this bottom rib (middle). This bottom rib, used mostly in East Greenland, was mortised into slanted chine stringers (bottom).

Bottom rib of an umiak dating from 1721, which was found in the Nuuk area, Greenland.

143

RIGHT: Construction of flat-bottomed *angyapik* in 1932 in Gambell, St. Lawrence Island, Alaska. The framework parts appear to have been laid out for the photograph.

BELOW: Thousand-year-old engraved bow drill handle found at Mittimatalik, North Baffin. A bow drill is a drill turned by a bow, with the string of the bow twisted around the drill.

the desired lean-out, notched to grip the bilge stringer. The ribs are temporarily braced in position until the gunwale rails are attached, their top ends being notched to receive the long poles, which are commonly about two inches thick. Ribs are cut to fit to them, of course, all being calculated to produce a desired sheer to the top of the hull with the desired hull depth, usually about one-and-a-half to two feet, quite deep. In Greenland in places the ribs have become wide boards set on edge, and with the greater breadth laterally, they are notched on the inside edge or even pierced in the body to receive the inside stringer, which holds the cover lashing line and supports the thwarts. In the west the ribs are sometimes thinned down laterally and tenoned into the bilge stringer. The Siglit or Mackenzie umiak from Toker Point in the Canadian Museum of Civilization in Ottawa (IV-D-1913) has this kind of tenoned assembly between all the transverse and longitudinal members of the framework, except for the keel-floor and headboard-gunwale unions. This tidy construction may be recent, following the advent of good quality milled lumber in the later nineteenth century.

Atop the bow and stern posts sit the already mentioned transverse slots fitting over tenons in the post tops. In the east they have apparently widened in recent times as the transport role of the umiak grew, becoming three to four feet across, but in the west, where hunting remains predominant, they are still only half as wide. Traditionally carved saddle-like pieces rounded in plan to the ends, they have in recent times become plain boards about one-and-a-half to two feet thick by four to eight inches or so broad. Since the ends of the gunwale rails sit over the headboards, the latter are fastened to the end-posts first. If round poles, the gunwale rails are given a flat face where they sit on the headboards. The gunwales extend several inches or more past the headboards to serve as hand grips. While long end-horns may look nice and racy, they are more prone to breakage. Yet there is evidence that prehistorically they may have been much longer, which was handy for landing or launching at shallow, rocky shores. A couple of umiak profiles are engraved on a profusely decorated Thule Culture bow drill handle found in North Baffin. Even allowing for artistic license, the horns are extra long, especially at the bow, where they have a jog up at their base in the same fashion as in Caribou and Natsilik Inuit kayak horns. Moreover, the stern horns angle up in Caribou kayak fashion and in the lead umiak at least, the gunwale is

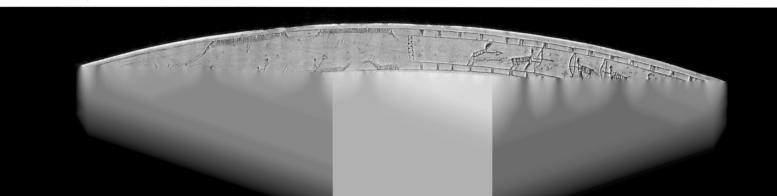

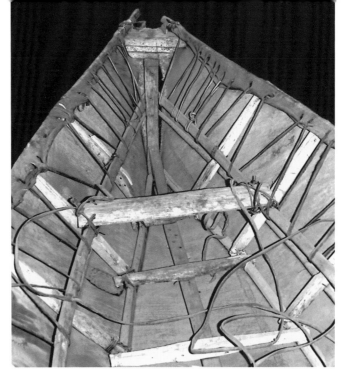

humped up amidships and falls off to the stern, all very much like Caribou kayaks. But the bow drill's engraved kayaks are of stylized East Canadian Arctic form. It's one of those tantalizing glimpses of strange things in the past with Arctic skin boat design.

On the inner side of the ribs is a strong stringer, which anchors the cover lashing line and helps support the thwarts. Around Hudson Strait, the inner stringer is high up near the gunwale rails because the thwarts are set just under the gunwales. In Greenland it is a lathe, which in some umiaks goes through wide ribs of board. On the outside of the ribs about halfway down, a light stringer is attached to keep the skin cover from contacting the ribs. Either side stringer can be housed in shallow notches cut in the rib edges, but usually is just tied on the surface. The inner stringer can serve to hold the ribs together during assembly. Thwarts are the last basic parts of the framework. There are also some secondary parts, like additional half-ribs to reinforce the upper end structure between the inner stringer and the gunwale rail. At the bow the horns sometimes join together, reinforcing each other. All surfaces that will contact the cover are well smoothed.

Covering

Sealskin is the usual covering for umiaks, with the outstanding exception of split walrus hide, which is used in the Bering Strait region. Bearded seal, which can be about nine feet long, is very strong and the first choice in the East Arctic. Hooded or bladdernose seal, which can reach nearly seven feet, is commonly used in Greenland south of Disko Bay. Both large seals, laid crosswise, can reach around the hull. Harp seal is also used in Greenland, but at less than five feet long it has to be sewn together in pairs whether used crosswise or lengthwise. Gaps between the narrow ends of the sealskins are filled in with patch pieces. Whether the preference is for spring skins for smoother grain and elasticity or fall skins for thickness, in actuality it is hard enough to amass the skins required regardless of season. Because of this practical economic factor, umiak size, like that of

Women covering a twenty-foot umiak reconstructed in 1960 at Ivuyivik, southwest Hudson Strait, for the National Museum of Canada. They are filling in the gaps between the ends of the bearded sealskins under the gunwales.

kayaks, is reckoned by the number of skins needed for the cover. In *Skinboats of Greenland* Petersen writes:

> South Greenlanders used the number of hooded seal skins in the cover as a measure of the size of their umiaks. Nine-skin umiaks are the smallest. Then came medium-sized boats with 12 skins. If 14–15 skins are used the boat is large and if 16 or more skins, very large indeed. Boats of that size, however, are rare.

With bearded seal, seven skins covered the twenty-foot-long Hudson Strait umiak made at Ivuyivik in a 1960 reconstruction for the National Museum of Canada.

In skinning the seal a ventral cut is usual, but there are other cuts adapted to hull shape or assembly arrangement. There are various procedures of skin preparation to remove fat and subcutaneous membranes: dry, bury in snow, roll up, soak, partially rot, dehair, scrape and so forth. Skins are sewn together with waterproof double seams that vary regionally. During assembly they are hung on sharp-ended sticks tied to a raised beam. Braided threads of caribou or whale sinew are used, which swell when soaked to stop and seal the imbedded

stitches. Needles are steel now, preferably triangular glover's, but were made of fox or hare sesamoid bones before. The assembled cover is draped over the upside-down framework and pulled taut by crosslines run through the edges. Then the umiak is righted to lace the cover down to the inner stringer. Any gaps or holes are patched. After several days, when dry, the cover is coated with aged oil and the seams with a thicker kind. Boat covering is a special occasion, as in the following festive picture from north Disko Bay, described by Petersen in *Skinboats of Greenland*:

> Angunnguaq's umiak was covered with bearded seal skins. The year before he had collected enough skins for this and they were now softened to give them the right elasticity. One August day the women gathered outside Angunnguaq's house. The old cover was taken off the umiak and the framework laid upside down on some wood beams. Its beautiful structure was silhouetted against the green grass. A happy mood prevailed. Angunnguaq himself led the measuring and cutting. The women sat talking, laughing and sewing. They talked constantly. Delicacies were served—fresh and dried meat,

coffee and tobacco.... The sun shone down on the happy group and their gaiety infected the rest of the settlement.

Covering the umiak with walrus hide is both fascinating and important, for without it the umiak would not still exist today. A thorough description of the process on St. Lawrence Island is provided by Stephen Braund in *The Skin Boats of Saint Lawrence Island, Alaska*. Too heavy as is, walrus hide has to be split for cover use. The skins (female for smoothness and strength) come from the spring hunt and are worked upon in early summer when umiaks are renewed. Any flesh or blubber still on the inner side is scraped off, then the hide is folded and wrapped in old skin or put in a big wooden dish and set to ripen in a warm place for a week or longer. When the hair loosens it is scraped off with the hide laced to a wooden frame by the top edge. Then with the hide laid out on the ground, the edge is slit an inch or two deep all the way around to make small lacing holes eight to twelve inches apart in the inner side. The skin is laced hind end up to half of a big strong rectangular wood frame propped up with its shorter dimension vertical. From top to bottom a woman carefully splits the hide evenly in two with her semi-lunar knife. This generally takes four to eight hours, preferably done when the sky is overcast so the skin doesn't dry in the sun and become hard to work.

How the result is used varies. On King Island and at Wales only the outer side is usually used. On St. Lawrence Island the halves are left attached by a strip at the neck end, turned sideways and stretched across the whole length of the frame, and then dried for two to four weeks, laid on the flat to catch less wind. The double-length female skin, prepared like this, is typically eight feet by seventeen feet, and can be stored away until needed. Two-and-a-half to three split skins cover a typical St. Lawrence Island *angyapik* or umiak, with two additional calf skins used for the cover lashings. Before use the skins are soaked in a lake for four to seven days to soften, with a final half hour in saltwater if sunny, to slow drying out. Draped over the upside-down boat framework, they are trimmed to fit along straight lines for sewing together. The bow is covered with inner-blubber-side-out skin, which is the toughest, to best resist young sharp ice. Since the skins used lengthwise commonly won't reach gunwale to gunwale, patches are added at the top, preferably along one side only for less sewing, though that limits hull width and beam.

The waterproof double seam is sewn with the edges overlapped about two inches, with the needle imbedded in the skin, which is still one-quarter- to one-half-inch thick after splitting. The needle does not go through the skin from one side to the other so there is no channel for the water to leak through. The braided whale or caribou sinew thread used for sewing will swell when wet to stop up the holes in the skins, which exist on one side only with the imbedded stitches. A thimble or flat stone is needed to push the needle through, each stitch pulled tight with the woman's whole body weight. The patch seam is sewn with one length of thread by two women who anchor it at the midpoint then sew out to the ends. Since the seam isn't in a stressed area, the needle is imbedded only in the bottom skin and goes right through the patch piece. Rolling up the sides exposes the inner side to sew the second seam in the same manner. If two split skins are joined with a transverse seam, the sewing is started at the keel and taken out to the gunwales. The skin is fitted, trimmed and sewn over the bow, the seam offset from the midline or cutwater edge where ice abrades the cover. As the cover usually dries during this assembly work, it is rewetted by soaking for half an hour in salt water. Then it is slid back on the inverted boat framework again and patches are added as necessary.

Cover fastening starts at the bow where its end is trimmed even with the headboard and then laced on tightly with bearded seal or baby walrus line run through holes in both skin and headboard. Men pull the cover toward the stern, holding it with temporary line while working and stretching it tight. Then the umiak is turned right side up to lace the cover down inside to the inner stringer. For even tightening the lacing is done on both sides simultaneously, beginning from amidships

Femmes cousant les peaux de l'umiaq. (Women sewing skins on an umiak.) Soapstone. Charlie Inukpuk, pre-1975. Nine inches by thirty-two inches by twelve inches.

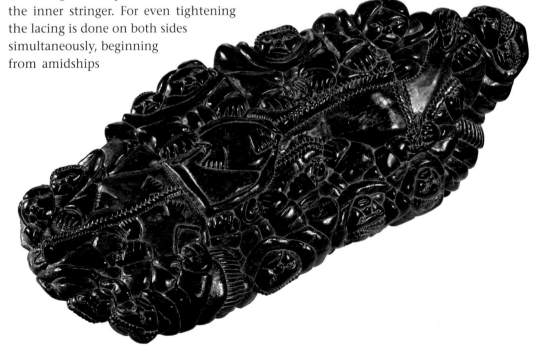

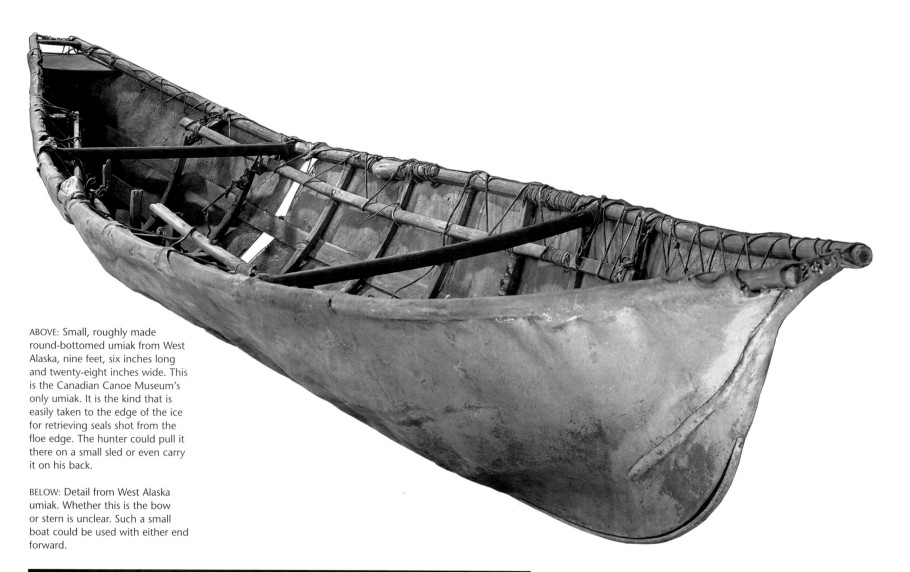

ABOVE: Small, roughly made round-bottomed umiak from West Alaska, nine feet, six inches long and twenty-eight inches wide. This is the Canadian Canoe Museum's only umiak. It is the kind that is easily taken to the edge of the ice for retrieving seals shot from the floe edge. The hunter could pull it there on a small sled or even carry it on his back.

BELOW: Detail from West Alaska umiak. Whether this is the bow or stern is unclear. Such a small boat could be used with either end forward.

and working towards the bow. The lacing line is preferably anchored in the cover over each rib and looped around the stringer in the intervening sections. Then the cover is laced down toward the stern. The lacing is further tightened down the whole length of the umiak with a pair of whale-rib belaying sticks, with the process repeated as necessary. At the stern the cover is laced to the headboard and excess skin is trimmed off. For the vertical stern seam the skin need not be overlapped but is simply sewn with two parallel seams, with the stitches of the two staggered to each other. Cover completed, the umiak is left to dry for a week or two. It is then painted. While the whole procedure is technically complex and laborious enough, compared to covering with sealskins, using walrus entails fewer seams for much less sewing and gives a far stronger result.

The efficacy of the walrus covering is a major reason for the continued viability of the umiak in the Bering Strait region. Also contributing to its survival are the qualities of the boat's design: light, strong, commodious and fast, and the very rewarding pursuits of whale and

walrus hunting in the Bering Strait region. Compared to the walrus-covered umiak, the wood-planked whaleboat used in the commercial whaling era broke too easily (lacking the skin boat's shock-absorbing flexibility in collisions with ice), was harder to repair and was too heavy for launching, beaching and portaging across moving ice fields. Not that walrus was invincible, for as Edward Nelson said in his 1899 report "The Eskimo About Bering Strait," "Sometimes umiaks are driven out to sea by storms and their occupants are unable to regain the shore, when the dashing spray and the waves soak the cover and the rawhide lashings of the frame until they relax and the boat collapses, drowning all on board." Finally, since the 1920s the umiak has had the addition of the outboard motor, although it is still paddled for silence during the whale hunt itself. Elsewhere, whether along the Asian North Pacific Coast southwest of the Bering Strait down to Kamchatka, in the Aleutians, in Alaska south of Bering Strait, in the Mackenzie Delta–Liverpool Bay region, or in the Eastern Arctic including Greenland, the umiak is gone.

Performance and Use

When it comes to performance, recreational paddlers usually want to know how fast the boat goes. While no top speed figures seem available for umiaks of given sizes, they are fast unladen because of the comparatively light weight, smooth skin, and the shape of the bottom (flat or slightly V with hard chines), which makes for shallow draught and maybe low turbulence. The fastest kind was probably the V-bottomed Aleut *nigilax*, which was narrower than others. Whether it was as fast as the fastest kayaks is hard to say, although with many paddlers and a long waterline in bigger models it may be expected to hold its own up to the practical limits of non-planing speed. Umiaks generally are faster than plank boats of comparable size (e.g., whaleboats), so we might guess that one around thirty feet long could do six to seven knots if necessary. Umiak races were known to take place, during the summer gatherings in West Greenland for harp seals and capelin at Sydost Bay, for example.

Under sail they go quickly downwind with no keel. Though they cannot tack into the wind, umiaks are

Sirlik camp in the Mackenzie River region, showing an overturned umiak behind a kayak, circa 1901. Both the umiaks and the kayaks from the Mackenzie Delta have upcurving ends.

capable of a broad reach. But they are not as responsive under sail as a whaleboat with centerboard. Adoption of the sail from Europeans extended voyaging capabilities. If Asian sail introduction occurred, it would be fairly recent as well, since the engraved representations of umiaks made during the Thule Culture (1000–1500 CE) don't show sails. In "The Eskimo About Bering Strait" Nelson says, "In ancient times sails sometimes were improvised by sewing together grass mats and putting them up between two long sticks, which were fastened to the framework of the umiak and stayed by means of cords so as to extend upward and outward in V-shape form, one from each side of the boat." This sounds Polynesian. Oars and rudders, adopted in the East Arctic, facilitated voyaging with laden boats.

Like the beamy East Canadian Arctic kayak of similar hull shape, the umiak has high initial and final stability. It also has high load capacity. Yet draught remains comparatively low for a given load because of the wide flat bottom and light initial weight, so that the umiak can go in shallower waters, as when it is being tracked along the shore. When summer caribou hunting trips inland used to be common in eastern Canada and Greenland, the umiak could be tracked up rivers with dogs, such as along the Payne River off west Ungava Bay. For north Disko Bay, West Greenland, Petersen, from his unique vantage point as an Inuk, gives absorbing details on the tracking with dogs in *Skinboats of Greenland*. They were going from Saqqaq to Qallu, fifteen miles away, mainly to gather driftwood:

At the end of August the family prepared for another hunting trip to Qallu. The umiak was loaded with the necessary items, including a long skin strap. Angunnguaq put the reins on his dogs, rolled up the traces and tied them securely on the backs of the dogs so they would not be bothered by them. As soon as the umiak pulled away from the shore the dogs took off to the northwest and soon disappeared in the mountains.

The umiak sailed along the coast towing the kayak behind it. When they approached the north coast of the headland Angunnguaq took his binoculars out. "Yes, there they are, on the mountain looking down at us. One, two, three…. They are all there." They sailed on. At the next place, where the dogs were expected to sit and wait, Angunnguaq would tie the dogs to the umiak if the weather was good and the sea calm. He left the steering oar to another and sat at the next to front thwart with the line for the dog traces tied loosely around the thwart. He gave the signal and the dogs pulled away along the flat sand beach. He made sure the steersman maintained the proper distance from shore. He watched for rocks and checked that the dogs did not run too far inland. When they met an obstacle he would immediately loosen the line and steer the boat around it. The dogs were happy, the boat shot along at a good pace and the water foamed at the bow. Everyone enjoyed the trip.

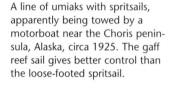

A line of umiaks with spritsails, apparently being towed by a motorboat near the Choris peninsula, Alaska, circa 1925. The gaff reef sail gives better control than the loose-footed spritsail.

Good descriptions of caribou-hunting umiak expeditions in Greenland are provided by Petersen, like those into the great fjord of Kangerlussuaq or Sondre Stromfjord, which goes 109 miles into the interior of central West Greenland. While the umiak's relatively light weight has been cited as conducive to portaging, carrying it several miles over poor footing and climbs up to lakes was arduous, with mosquitoes adding to the hardship. Still, it enabled people to reach the caribou and obtain a supply of the fine meat and the warm fur so good for winter clothing, plus antler for assorted artifact-making purposes. But umiaks were generally essential for movement during the open water season whether or not caribou were involved. Besides hunting, trade and wider social contact were important objectives attained through the travel means of umiaks. For example, in West Greenland the most important trading place was Taseralik, on Nassuttooq Fjord, where many umiaks gathered from up and down the coast. Petersen reports in *Skinboats of Greenland*:

> Baleen, valuable kinds of driftwood, stones for the blades of weapons, knives, walrus tusks and much more were traded here. People also came to meet old friends, settle arguments and to take part in the festivities. Just outside the camp at the mouth of the fjord the best halibut fishing in the whole country was found.... There were many cultural activities, songs, dances and sports games in the 1 1/2 months they stayed in this summer camp.

Greenland Inuit society realized its potential at Taseralik, thanks to the capacious umiak, which could carry both family and goods over long distances. Because of their traveling capabilities, umiaks were instrumental in social and cultural maximization throughout their range.

> Kayaks were usually along as well, with the men in them ever ready to hunt. If an umiak ran into bad conditions or sprang a leak and was in danger of swamping and capsizing, a kayaker could help steady it. He could also race ahead for help for whatever problem occurred. More frivolously, a young kayaker might court a girl, throwing his harpoon into the little whirlpool left by her oar.

When stopping for a while, the umiak is turned upside down for shelter and to dry the cover. It is propped up on one side with three or four sticks about two feet long stuck in the ground, which prevent warping and joint weakening of a perhaps 400-pound structure. While the length of possible prolonged immersion time varies with

This umiak is being used as a wind-break and a shelter in Alaska. It may also be drying out. A great many goods are visible. They did not all necessarily belong with this umiak, which suggests that the picture was taken at a store.

the kind of skin and preparation (including oiling), around forty-eight hours seems a wise limit before the cover is thoroughly dried out. This is to keep the seams from failing when the sinew thread cuts through the waterlogged skin edges. In Greenland, while the skins are well coated with aged and oxidized seal oil (*puyaq*), the seams are stopped with *miniq*, a paste of oil and ground ashes or, recently, chalk. If the umiak is not used a lot, one spring waterproofing suffices for the season, but with long voyaging another oiling is usually done over the summer. A second old cover might be put on outside for prolonged immersion, at least in South Baffin.

Weather cloths can be propped up on the sides against big waves; also inflated sealskin floats are tied along the gunwales. Floats also serve as rollers on shore. With snow or ice the umiak can be moved by dogteam. Since its ends usually overhang the sled, they are held up by lines tied high on a pole raised amidships.

War was an important use, especially in the Bering Strait region, where umiak raids continued into the early twentieth century. In this region whaling from umiaks flowered in the first millennium CE, becoming the central focus in the Punuk Culture period of 500–1000 CE. The disciplined whaling crew, with the authoritative leadership of the boat owner-captain (*umialiq*) contributed to the waging of organized warfare. Thus for centuries the umiak was an integral part of the greater Native political scene in the conflict-ridden region. In the 1890s

large their designs in a given place bear resemblances to each other; not surprising, since their builders are usually the same individuals with certain ideas on basic watercraft design. Although their thinking is usually unrecorded and unknown to us, reasonable guesses can be made from the hull forms, physical conditions and whatever is known of use. The greatest variation in umiaks occurs with the distinctive shapes in the Kamchatka region, Aleutians and South Alaska. The Koryak umiak, with its long V-shaped bow section and top rail curved continuously around the ends, has best preserved the coracle ancestry, with the pronounced cutwater underlining the umiak's main developmental history of sharpening the rounded coracle ends for sea-use conditions. Whaling was the primary purpose of the Koryak boat. The short, broadly proportioned Koryak kayak preserves the rounded end only at the stern in some cases, while in others both ends are sharp. Its bottom is V-shaped (no doubt to counter the swiveling of a short, wide hull), in a further departure from the coracle hull form.

End sharpening is most developed with the Aleut and South Alaska bulged cutwater bow. This umiak "bifid bow" seems more basic than that of the corresponding kayaks. For all its virtues of both cutting through and riding on the waves, the bifid bow is likely a more recent imitative refinement. A circa-fourteenth-century carved wood Aleut kayak model from the Islands of the Four Mountains still lacks the split bow, having instead a unitary upcurved one, as on Bering Strait kayaks. It does have the wide-shouldered stern with just a short cutwater blade behind. A prototype is suggested by the Koryak kayak variant, which has a rounded wide stern with a short handgrip projection. The Aleut umiak stern has a non-projecting raked cutwater board under a wide rounded end at the gunwales. With the coracle as the assumed starting point, a nice progression appears for

ABOVE: West Greenland umiak drawn up to shore in the Tasiilaq/Ammassalik area in East Greenland, circa 1961. The oars with the bola bat-shaped blades are characteristic of Greenland. Only women rowed, and so the chamber pot was a necessary accessory. When men crewed a boat, they faced forward and used paddles.

RIGHT: This is a well made Greenland model umiak with very long end horns. The bottom is very slightly V-shaped.

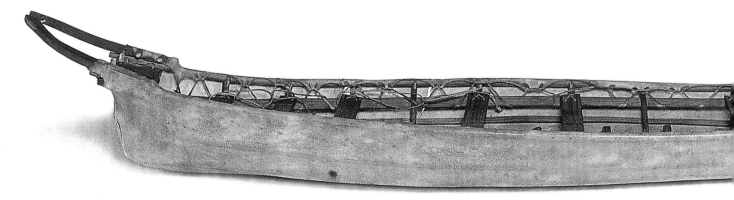

umiak top plan development, from the still coracle-like round ends of the Koryak *gatwaat*, through the Aleut *nigila̱x* with its sharp bow and round stern, to the Eskimo and Chukchi umiaks with gunwale rail projections joined sharply at the bow but ending separated at the stern, and finally to the East Arctic umiaks with the gunwale ends separate at both bow and stern. While a number of possible determining factors are to be considered such as use, physical conditions, and construction materials and techniques, this top outline series from a distance seems to be largely stylistic, passing and changing from group to group, though physically functional reasons also appear at closer view. Dated archaeological remains (whether actual, models or engravings) are needed as space and time cultural markers to confirm the apparent development.

Mackenzie Delta region umiaks have upcurving ends like the Mackenzie kayaks. North and West Alaska umiaks generally seem to have curved ends. In Greenland straight ends, only slightly raked, are common although there are the odd ends with curved or "round" profiles as Petersen calls it. The outstanding round profiled umiak found in Greenland is the circa 1440 CE "Peary Land umiak." It looks like the voyaging umiak of Birnirk-culture-descended late Thule migrants from North Alaska, who found Greenland already occupied by earlier Punuk Thule arrivals except in the extreme northeast. The abandonment of the magnificent boat suggests a sad end to an epic Arctic journey.

At the other northwestern end of Arctic umiaks in northeast Asia, on St. Lawrence Island and the Bering Strait Islands, the characteristic profile combines a well raked curved bow with an upright straight stern, again paralleled by the kayak profiles of the region. For umiaks the combination is efficient, providing a sharp bow whose overhang facilitates landing by letting a man

jump off in front and ease the boat ashore on a skid to avoid damage to the skin cover. Launching is similarly helped. Gunwale end-projections add to the bow over-hang, of course, improving reach and grip if long and joined at the tips. Long stern gunwale horns are also possible, as in some Greenland umiaks. The near upright rather than well raked stern gives more waterline length for speed and load carrying, including the umiak owner-captain-steersman, who would sit there. This profile together with the general umiak cross-section with flat bottom, hard chine and flared slab sides resembles East Asia plank boat design, and while no definite link is attested, some influence around 500 CE seems possible in view of other exchanges (trade goods like iron and

Photo of the Inuit family Kituk, taken in Nome, Alaska, in the Lomen Brothers photo studio, 1903. A miniature umiak is on the floor. It could be a handicraft. The man holds a small drum.

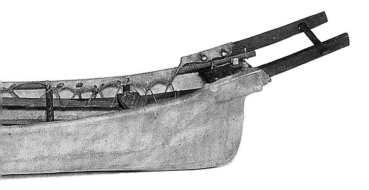

The RECREATIONAL CANOE

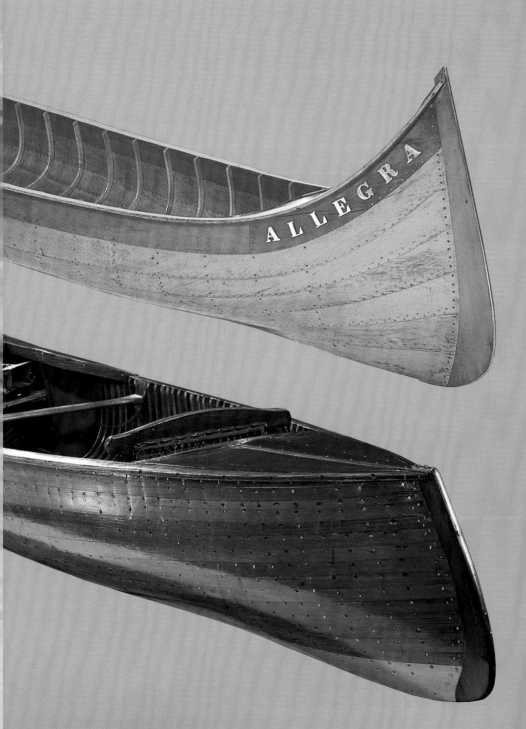

In the mid-nineteenth century, the role of the canoe changed drastically from a work boat to a pleasure craft. Although it was still used for transportation and exploration in the wilderness, it enjoyed growing popularity as a recreational vehicle, for racing, canoe tripping or just a Sunday afternoon paddle on a pond or a river.

The transformation occurred more or less simultaneously in Canada and the northeastern United States over several decades, with an interesting contribution from an Englishman, whose written accounts of his adventures in a little decked canoe through the rivers of Europe inspired a generation of canoeists in England and North America. John MacGregor wrote eloquently in a series of books about the joys of paddling his solo *Rob Roy* canoe and camping out with an adventure waiting around every corner.

Soon the canoe became the most wanted vehicle for recreation, and the race was on to build a good canoe that could be made in quantity and sold for a reasonable price. Many of the early developments in creating a manufactured canoe took place in the town of Peterborough, Ontario, and the surrounding area, where canoe building became a major industry.

Canoe clubs sprang up in cities and towns everywhere. The formation of the American Canoe Association in 1880 reflected the canoe's new status as a gentleman's plaything. The members met once a year to hold races and debate the finer points of the rules of competition and canoe classification. In 1900 some of the Canadian delegates formed the Canadian Canoe Association.

The wooden canoe reigned supreme until the end of the Second World War. With the development of materials such as fiberglass and Kevlar in the mid-twentieth century, canoeing changed again. The canoe has now become more popular than ever, while still retaining the basic shape and function of the original Native canoe.

From Forest to Factory: Innovations and Mass Production   162
TED MOORES

Paddling for Pleasure in the Northeastern States   194
HALLIE E. BOND

Fast Paddles and Fast Boats: The Origins of Canoe Racing   212
C. FRED JOHNSTON

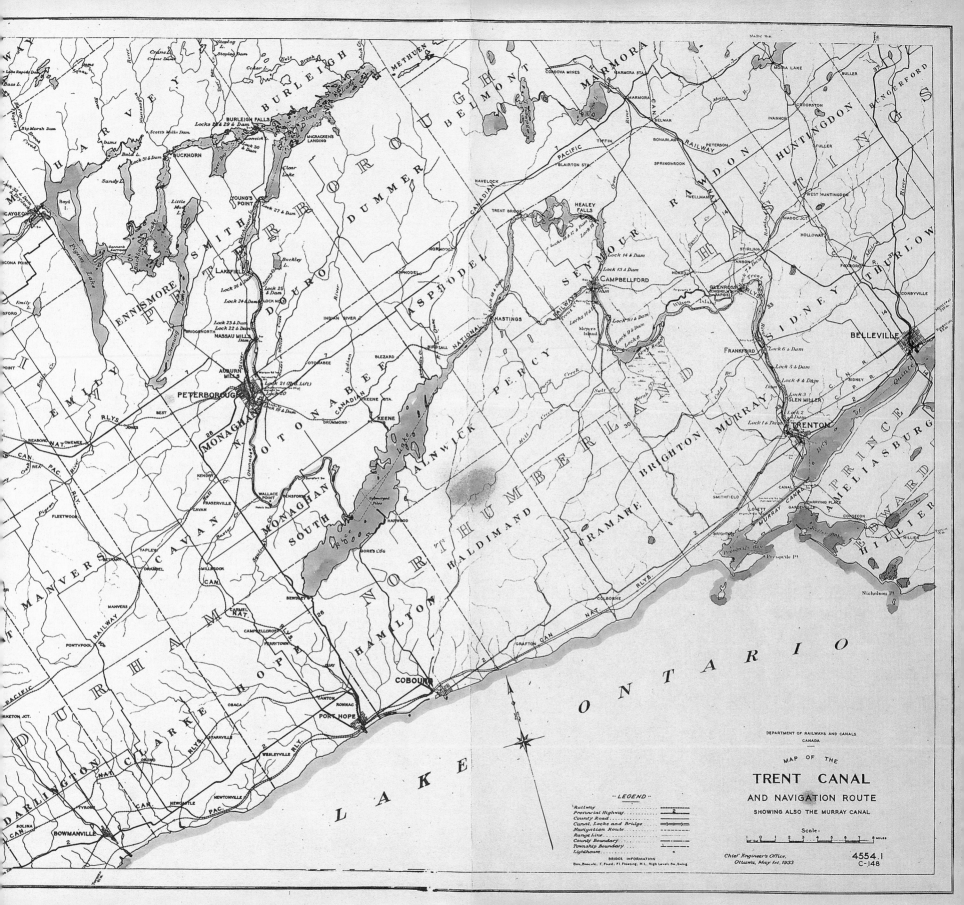

PETERBOROUGH, ONTARIO, and SURROUNDING AREA

In the latter part of the 19th century, Peterborough was the center of a thriving canoe-building industry.

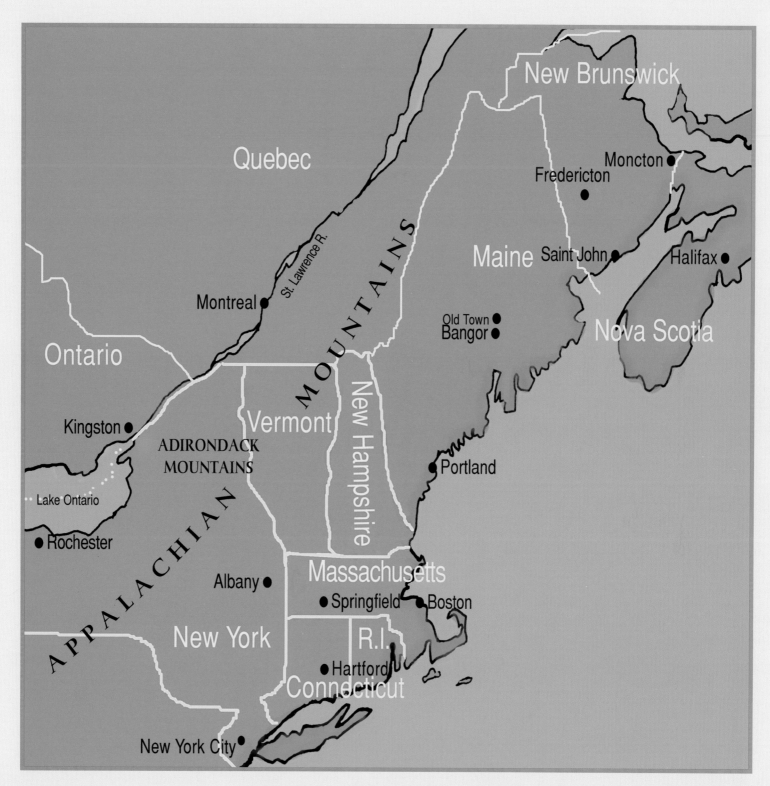

NORTHEASTERN STATES and CANADA

In the late nineteenth century, canoeing became a popular recreational sport for people who lived in the cities and towns of northeastern United States and eastern Canada. Canoe-building companies in the area struggled to supply the increasing demand for canoes. Competition was fierce, particularly between the Old Town Canoe Company in Maine and the Chestnut Canoe Company in Fredericton, New Brunswick.

From FOREST to FACTORY

TED MOORES

INNOVATIONS AND MASS PRODUCTION

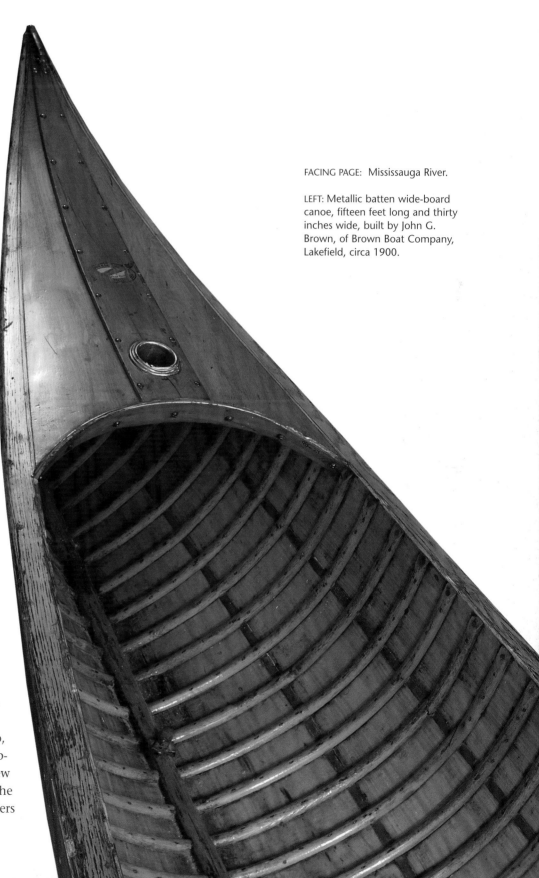

The evolution of mass production began with the dugout. Peterborough, Ontario was the site of a revolution in canoe building techniques. Most of the most significant steps in the transition from traditional Native dugouts and birchbark canoes to modern manufactured canoes took place in and around this town in the latter half of the nineteenth century.

Around 1800, European settlers, first loyalists fleeing the American Revolution, and then English, Irish and Scots immigrants, had begun to move into the region stretching north from the shores of Lake Ontario between present-day Toronto and Kingston. The whole area was by this time administered as a British colony, Upper Canada, and land grants were made available to new settlers. The land was covered with dense forest which, once cleared, made good farmland, with gentle hills caused by glacial deposits from the Ice Age, and a winding river now known as the Otonabee in its upper reaches and the Trent lower down. About thirty-five miles north of Lake Ontario lay the Canadian Shield, the vast plate of hard rock that covers much of the northern part of Canada, land that is rocky and mostly unfarmable and dotted with lakes and small streams.

The local Native population was not large and was comparatively recent. The earlier inhabitants had been reduced by European diseases and then driven out during the disastrous Iroquois wars in the seventeenth and eighteenth centuries and the region was more or less vacant until it was occupied in the 1790s by Aboriginal people moving up from what had become the United States. They had established semi-permanent communities, and combined agriculture with hunting and fishing, and made and used both crude dugouts and finely crafted birchbark canoes.

The first choice of land for settlers was close to Lake Ontario, but by the 1820s they were taking up land further north, establishing what became the town of Peterborough and later, a few miles up the Otonabee River, the village of Lakefield, close to the northern boundary of farmable land. For the most part the settlers

FACING PAGE: Mississauga River.

LEFT: Metallic batten wide-board canoe, fifteen feet long and thirty inches wide, built by John G. Brown, of Brown Boat Company, Lakefield, circa 1900.

had amicable relations with the Native people and quickly became fascinated by their canoes. The Native people used the craft in their everyday lives for fishing and for such tasks as harvesting the wild rice that grew in Rice Lake, and for hunting and trapping expeditions to the rocky wilderness and lakes further north, such as Stony Lake at the head of the Otonabee River.

For the settlers, who were mostly concerned with lumbering and with the commercial businesses and services related to farming, canoes could be useful for occasional fishing or hunting excursions, but were used mainly for transportation. Birchbark canoes were purchased from the Native people, as this building technique was unfamiliar to the European settlers. But the dugout canoe, which could be shaped with the tools and skills familiar to every settler, quickly became a refined craft for work and play.

During the early 1800s, the settlers' dugout canoes developed at a slow yet determined pace. The dugout canoe made with European woodworking tools was a beautifully shaped and exquisitely finished craft. The form and design features were copied (in a stylized fashion) from the birchbark canoes of the local Mississauga Indians. The polished basswood or butternut hulls were smooth and fair, the symmetry controlled through the use of patterns. Decks of butternut or walnut were fitted below the edge of the hull and the outside trimmed with an outwale of white oak. Maple or oak thwarts were fastened into rabbeted thwart blocks. By 1850 the settlers' dugout was a beautiful, highly civilized craft that had evolved to the practical limit of the material.

Boatbuilders throughout the centuries have been driven by the search for perfection in their craft. The assumption of this responsibility is part of the magic of the boats they build and ensures that the evolution progresses in a positive, safe direction. The satisfaction and reward for most wooden boatbuilders comes from being part of this elusive pursuit. Long before the development of the Peterborough canoe, the search for perfection was fueling the evolution of the skin boats, bark canoes and dugouts of North America. A perfect canoe would be swift and strong, light enough to portage, easy to maintain and repair under field conditions, durable in and out of water, affordable and attainable, safe and beautiful. When the factories began to produce canoes in quantity, building and selling at a profit was added to the requirements.

The first recorded backyard canoe builder in the Peterborough area, Sam Strickland, is said to have built a crude dugout around 1830. He was later to admit that it "looked more like a hog trough than a boat." This was a crude beginning to a fascination with canoe building that would follow the Strickland family through the next seventy-five years. It was not all work around Strickland's sawmill, but there were a lot of shavings being made. George Strickland, no doubt with the benefit of his father's experience, continued to perfect the dugout canoe. He is said to have devised a method of duplicating the fine lines of the bark canoe into the dugout hull. Guided by a series of templates, the basswood or butternut log was worked down with axe, adze, drawknife and plane until the outside shape of the canoe

Basswood dugout, fifteen feet, nine inches long and thirty-and-one-half inches wide, built by William Alfred Payne, of Warsaw, Ontario, in the late nineteenth century (see page 245). During the early 1800s, the settlers' dugout canoe shaped with European woodworking tools developed into a beautifully shaped and exquisitely finished craft. Though the hull thickness had been reduced to a thickness of one-half-inch, demonstrating a remarkable sophistication in construction, it still could not match the lightweight bark canoe for portability.

was reached. Pegs representing the thickness of the hull were most likely driven into the hull at critical places as a thickness gauge for shaping the inside. Shaping on the inside would stop when the end of the peg was reached. This was not an easy task, even with sharp tools, as there was a lot of material to be removed. By 1855 George had completed a beautiful finished dugout with a shape reminiscent of the Native bark canoe. When the Prince of Wales visited the area in 1860, he was presented with a racing dugout by the Stricklands.

Regattas were an important event for the Strickland family, as they were for the other families along the river system. The community turned out to watch their neighbors compete in skiffs and sailboats and the Native people paddling bark canoes and dugouts. Soon the settlers were competing in dugouts that they had constructed specifically for the race.

The 1857 Lakefield Regatta was organized by Sam Strickland with his son Henry as secretary treasurer. George paddled his dugout *Shooting Star,* a shallow, long and slim hull he had designed and built for racing with paddle or oars. Carved down to the minimum hull thickness, the shape had long fluid lines with hints of a rowing shell. He easily defeated all challengers in three races at the Lakefield Regatta. With great confidence in his canoe, he entered the Peterborough Regatta, but was defeated by *Bell of Peterborough,* a dugout paddled by Mr. Armstrong, and by *Flying Cloud,* entered by the Rice Lake Indian Band. That September he again suffered defeat in the Rice Lake Regatta, the race going to *Flying Cloud.* Paddled by a local Native, this racing dugout from Rice Lake was better suited to the rough chop that was kicking up on the shallow lake. Had it been a calm day, there might have been another victory for *Shooting Star* and John Stephenson would have had an opportunity to show off his radical new "board" dugout. It was still called a dugout even though it was not "dug out" of wood, but built on a solid form, in an attempt to recreate the dugout without the labor involved in a true dugout. Stephenson's new canoe was shaped along the lean lines of *Shooting Star* and required flat water to perform without sinking. John Stephenson and his friend Mr. Armstrong entered the race in a borrowed dugout to be beaten by Sam and George Strickland; presumably not in *Shooting Star.*

Not a great day for racing but it was a day that would change the course of boat building history. Adapting the dugout as a solid mold, or "form" as it would be called, was the stroke of genius that made the mass production of wooden canoes feasible.

ABOVE: The design features that distinguish the "Peterborough" canoe were a product of the dugout, worked out long before manufacturing began. This basswood dugout, shaped by William Alfred Payne in Warsaw, Ontario, in the late nineteenth century, is representative of the work of George Strickland in 1850s.

LEFT: In spite of the seriousness of carving out a new home in the bush while adjusting to a harsh unforgiving environment, the early settlers enjoyed the camaraderie of sporting events. Regattas were a time for the community to catch up on the latest news and enjoy the company of their neighbors. In the beginning the settlers competed in clinker built skiffs and sailing craft as well as log (dugout) canoes constructed specifically for racing. Perhaps because of their superior paddling skills, the Natives competed against each other in birchbark and log canoes. Soon after the 1849 Rice Lake Regatta, settlers and Natives began competing as equals.

Village Economy: Lumber, Road and Railroad

RICE LAKE REGATTA.

TO take place on Rice Lake on Wednesday, 12th September, 1849, at 12 o'clock M.

	PRIZE.	ENTRANCE.
1st Class, Sailing Boats, open to all,	£10 0	Purse added £1 5
2nd Class, Sailing Boats, 16 feet keel and under,	7 10	Purse added 1 0

(The second boat in the above two races to save her entrance.)

1st Class, Rowing Boats, 4 oars, Ran-dan,	£4 0	Purse added £0 15
2nd do. do. 2 do.,	2 10	Do. 0 10
Skiff Race,	2 0	Do. 0 5
1st Bark Canoe, 4 Indians,	2 0	}Four canoes to
3rd single Log Canoe, for Indians,	0 15	start or no race. No entrance.
2nd Log Canoe, 2 White men,	2 0	Purse added £0 10

Three Boats to start in all cases or no race. All Boats to be entered on or before Monday, 10th September, 1849, on which day the committee will keep the book open for entrance at Harris's Hotel, Gore's Landing, Rice Lake, from 11 o'clock, A. M. until 3 P. M., when it will be closed.

CHARLES BAKER, Esq., *President.*

Committee of Management.

Thos. Gore, and Thos. Mercer, Esq's, *Rice Lake ;* Sheriff Conger, Capt. R. Buck, *Peterboro';* G. S. Daintry and G. Perry, Esq's, *Cobourg ;* Jas. Scott, J. A. Ward, and Jas. Smith, Esq's, *Port Hope.*

GEORGE LEY, *Treas. & Sec.*

Rice Lake, 23rd August, 1849.   30

Thos. Gore, Thos. Mercer and George Ley were on the committee of management representing Rice Lake.

The Invention of the Solid Building Form

The board dugout that John Stephenson had brought from Peterborough had been built over the hull of last year's racing dugout. Ribs had been bent over the inverted dugout and fastened at the sheer. Two thin, wide basswood planks per side had been bent over the dugout and nailed to the ribs. The joints between the planks were backed up with short pieces of rib stock, a technique that was no doubt familiar from repairing dugouts. A solid carved stem had been fitted from the inside and the hull was trimmed with outwales, thwarts and decks in dugout fashion.

Boatbuilder Tom Gordon from Lakefield was probably in the crowd and would have taken some interest in the reaction to Stephenson's new canoe. Gordon and Stephenson were friends and were known to be hunting and fishing partners, so there is the possibility that he had been involved in this experiment from the beginning. Tom Gordon was twenty-four years old in 1857, lived in Lakefield and had just completed his boat building apprenticeship.

John Stephenson was born in Peterborough, Ontario, in 1831. Growing up on the edge of the wilderness, he loved the outdoors and became an ardent sportsman. At age seventeen he had apprenticed to a blacksmith in Cobourg, Ontario. After returning to Peterborough, he worked for Duncan MacDonald, a blacksmith and woodworker. In 1857 he was twenty-six years old and a partner in a planing mill with his brother Jonathan and his brother-in-law John Craigie. His combination of blacksmith and woodworking skills would have been useful in creating the machine jigs and fixtures for making the laths, moldings, barrels and shingles produced by their planing mill.

Who actually invented the solid building form? I believe that Stephenson and Gordon were both involved from the beginning and together they possessed the combination of skills and experience that could make this unconventional idea work. Without further documentation, any conclusion remains speculation. Since there is no evidence of Tom Gordon coming up with many novel ideas in the future, it might be safe to say that it was the fertile mind of John Stephenson that was

ABOVE: Tom Gordon, foreground (1833–1916). Lakefield, Ontario boat builder who sold his first canoe in 1858 and became the first manufacturer of wooden canoes, officially in the canoe business by 1861. At the age of seventeen he began building punts and skiffs and would remain active in his boat shop well into his seventies. In addition to his contribution to the evolution of the wide-board canoe, he also built steamboats, motorboats and skiffs.

RIGHT: Thomas Gordon building form, fifteen feet long and twenty-nine inches wide. Lakefield, late nineteenth century. The solid building form controlled the canoe's shape and made the building process repeatable. A keelson for the next canoe rests in the groove down the center of the form. Stems that have been steamed and bent to shape on a form will go on next to complete the backbone and define the shape of the bow and stern. The canoe's skeleton will be complete with the addition of steam-bent half-round ribs.

Deep furrows from the nails of countless canoes define the rib position on this ancient form. The row of holes along the bottom of the form are to capture the end of the hot rib before being bent over the form and secured with a "button" on the opposite side. Above the holes can be seen the aftermath of cutting the ribs off at the sheer line to release the planked hull from the form.

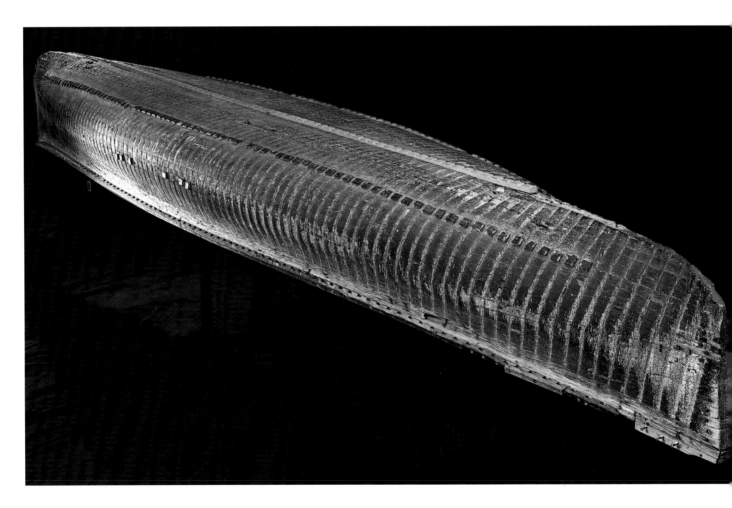

responsible for this new system of canoe building. He had a track record of lateral thinking, and as a non-boatbuilder, he had a lack of prejudice for traditional techniques. Stephenson probably came up with the idea of bending wide planks over a dugout and talked it over with Mr. Gordon, the boatbuilder. Together they could have worked out the technical details and then gone home to work out the finer points of construction.

The building method was deceptively simple and used basic, well known technology: a combination of techniques that would be familiar to builders of boats, carriages, wagons, sleighs, furniture and containers. The board dugout canoe began on an overturned dugout canoe with the outwales removed. Ribs of three-eighths by five-eighths of an inch elm or white oak were steamed and bent over the dugout on about six-inch centers and clamped temporarily at the sheer. Two wide basswood planks per side were planed to one-quarter-inch thickness, cut to shape, then hot water was applied judiciously to the outside of the dry plank, causing the outside surface to swell and the plank to curl. When the plank could be pressed around the curving sides of the hull, it was nailed to the ribs; the nail going through rib and plank into the dugout. After all the planks had been nailed to the ribs, the hull was pried off the dugout and the copper nails clinched on the inside. The open ends of the planking were nailed to a stem carved from a solid block of softwood. Plank seams were then backed up with short lengths of rib stock fit tightly between the ribs and nailed over the seam. The hull was completed with outwales and decks and then painted.

Before production could begin, the dugout building form needed a few modifications. Over the next two or three years, Stephenson and Gordon made changes that made it more convenient to use and developed the patterns for duplicating the plank shapes.

The immediate problem facing Stephenson and Gordon was to find a way of clamping the ribs around the edge of the dugout. In addition, there was the awkwardness of fitting stems from the inside. A major construction problem came from shaping the dry plank and being able to anticipate the shape of the plank after being bent to the shape of the hull. As they struggled with the wide basswood plank that changed shape as it bent in two directions at once, the idea of patterns for all the parts could not have been long coming.

The new form was strip-planked with narrow basswood or pine planks about three-quarter-inch square over station molds set on twenty-four-inch centers. As each plank was nailed to the station mold, it was also edge-nailed to the plank below it, effectively recreating the dugout. To accommodate clamping the ends of the ribs that would be bent longer than needed, the form was built three or four inches deeper than the desired hull. Fastened in this space were small wooden C-shaped buttons that clamped the ends of the ribs in position when a screw was tightened.

Now past the experimental stage, the builders incorporated the components of traditional wooden boat construction. To accommodate the keelson (inner keel), a slot was made down the middle of the form to allow the five-quarter-inch white oak keelson to sit below the surface of the form. When built on the dugout, the bottom planks were simply joined down the centerline of the hull and backed up on the inside with seam battens. Lack of a longitudinal support down the centerline allowed the bottom to flex. When the nails through the seam battens and planks began to work, the holes were enlarged, creating a potential place for the canoe to leak, and making maintenance a challenge.

Before the keelson was assembled on the form, grooves were cut along its length to match the size and position of each rib that crossed it. When the keelson was lowered down into the form, the rib fit snugly in the groove, making both outside faces flush to receive the plank. Aside from the added structural integrity of the longitudinal member, the premachined grooves in the keelson defined the position of the ribs and saved fitting individual seam battens between them.

Fitting the solid stems from the inside was appropriate for an experiment but added little to the structural integrity of the hull. They also required much trial and error for a good fit and a reliable watertight joint. It had been necessary when building on the dugout to leave the ends of the planking open in order to pry the hull off the form. To accommodate the recurve of the stem when the hull was removed from the form, the ends of the new form were missing. The end profile was defined by the shape of the pre-bent white oak stems. With the form controlling the shape, and patterns controlling the shape of the parts, the process became repeatable.

Deciding on the plank width and devising a method of sealing the joint were the main source of future innovations in the evolution of the Peterborough-style canoe.

The Innovators

The year 1861 was a good time for starting a small business and canoe building provided the perfect niche to use available materials, supply an interested market and benefit the local economy. Tom Gordon, the Lakefield

Sam Strickland (1805–67) had been raised as a gentleman on his family's English country estate, but he found the rough life and challenge of homesteading in Upper Canada to his liking. His fascination with canoe building began around 1830 when he constructed his first dugout. Three generations of Stricklands were involved in refining the settlers' dugout and manufacturing canoes for a world market.

John Stephenson (1831–1920). The major contributions the Peterborough canoe builders made to wooden boat building were the solid building form and the use of machine-edged planking, which made possible the transition from craft-built to manufacturing. The uninhibited John Stephenson was instrumental in both of these accomplishments but never profited from becoming a manufacturer. He was an inventor, the master of many trades in both wood and metal who preferred the creative space of working alone.

boatbuilder, sold his first canoe in 1858 (according to his son Gilbert) and became the first manufacturer of wooden canoes, officially in the canoe business by 1861. Gordon had the support and encouragement of the Strickland family. George Strickland's experience with the use of patterns and templates would have been useful in the construction of a dedicated building form. He had a ready supply of wood and many social and sales contacts. A few miles down the Otonabee River in Ashburnham (now part of Peterborough), John Stephenson, while still an active partner in the Stephenson and Craigie planing mill, continued to perfect his building form and patterns. Although fascinated with the development process, he was not ready to go into the canoe business full time.

In 1857 there were two other young men in the area who would become significant canoe builders: William English, son of a Peterborough blacksmith, and Dan Herald, who lived in Gores Landing, a small village on the south shore of Rice Lake. English had acquired a combination of skills, which could be put to good use building canoes, growing up in his father's blacksmith shop building wagons and sleighs. In 1861 he purchased a mold and patterns from John Stephenson and set up shop at 182 Charlotte Street by the dam on Jackson Creek. English appears to have been unassuming yet ambitious, happy to do a hard day's work without creating a lot of stress. While never an innovator, he was well respected as an honest businessman and fine craftsman. He had a small shop with the boss working at the bench, and the subtle details in his canoes show a love of the craft. He found a niche in custom building, later supplying the growing market for sprint racing canoes.

At peak production, the shop employed five or six workmen building a variety of small craft. Initially canoes were built "wide-board-and-batten," but as the innovative John Stephenson developed new techniques and their benefits were proven, English adopted these methods. After the death of William English in 1891, the company was taken over by his brothers, James and Samuel W. English.

They sold it to the Peterborough Canoe Company in 1914, who acquired it for their racing canoe business, which had continued to be a steady though not major source of sales.

Dan Herald was born in Ireland in about 1832. He apprenticed as a shipwright in England before immigrating to the United States in his late teens. He settled in Gores Landing in the late 1850s. Attracted to the possibilities of the board dugout, he was working on the details of the canoe building form at the same time as Gordon and Stephenson. The Herald Canoe Company was formed in 1862 to build wide-board-and-batten canoes in basswood and cedar. Dan Herald possessed a dynamic balance of craftsman skills with an aggressive understanding of business. The men who would later shape the industry would be businessmen with an appreciation of the craft, but they would lack Herald's questioning approach and innovative skill as a builder. Herald's competitive nature put an edge on his relationship with the Peterborough and Lakefield builders. The search for the perfect canoe had now taken on the element of competition between businesses. This competition, which appears to have been friendly, stimulated new ways of using the solid building form.

Early wide-board-and-batten basswood custom-made racing canoe, twenty feet long and twenty-three inches wide, built by the Lakefield Canoe Company circa 1900. The first wide-board-and-batten canoes were built with two wide basswood planks per side. Over time this would be increased to as many as four to reduce the amount of expansion and contraction each plank was expected to absorb.

Dan Herald and the Double-Cedar Canoe

One attractive advantage of the dugout over the bark canoe was the clean, uncluttered interior. As it developed, the Peterborough canoe retained its roots in the dugout, as seen in the attempt to use the widest plank possible and the inventions that were patented to preserve this attribute.

Wood changes shape when it takes on or releases moisture, a feature that was used to advantage in getting the wide boards to curl. The problem of the dugout checking (cracking) when allowed to dry out was also a problem in the wide basswood planks of the board-and-batten canoe. Adding more battens over the cracks might have become routine for some but it was not acceptable to Herald or Stephenson.

Dan Herald was the first to do something about it. On November 28, 1871, Herald made an application to the Canadian Patent office for protection of his new idea. Patent #1252 for "Herald's Boat and Canoe Mould" was granted on December 15, 1871. While Herald's new canoe became known as the "Herald Patent Canoe" or "double-cedar," the patent was for a mold that was adjustable for size and for the use of metal bands around the form to clench the cut tacks as they came through the inner layer of planking. Ten years later the cedar-canvas canoe emerged from the Maine bush. It was built on a solid form with metal bands to turn the tacks.

Two continuous layers of thin cedar planking were used to achieve a smooth interior and exterior. The inner layer ran perpendicular to the centerline, the ends temporarily fastened below the sheer. The outer layer ran fore and aft in a traditional manner but with a Herald twist. A sheet of canvas duck, set in a thick mixture of white lead-based paint, is sandwiched between the two

Patent Drawing #1252. Herald's Boat and Canoe Mould, 1871. Daniel Herald designed this adjustable building form with metal bands to turn the seven thousand tacks holding his Herald Patent Canoe together. The patent stated that the form was "built so as to turn the points of nails in driving and clenching them." By spreading the four sections shown and presumably inserting additional sections into the space, canoes of different sizes could be built on the same form. A building form with steel bands was adopted in the early 1880s for the mass production of the cedar-canvas canoe.

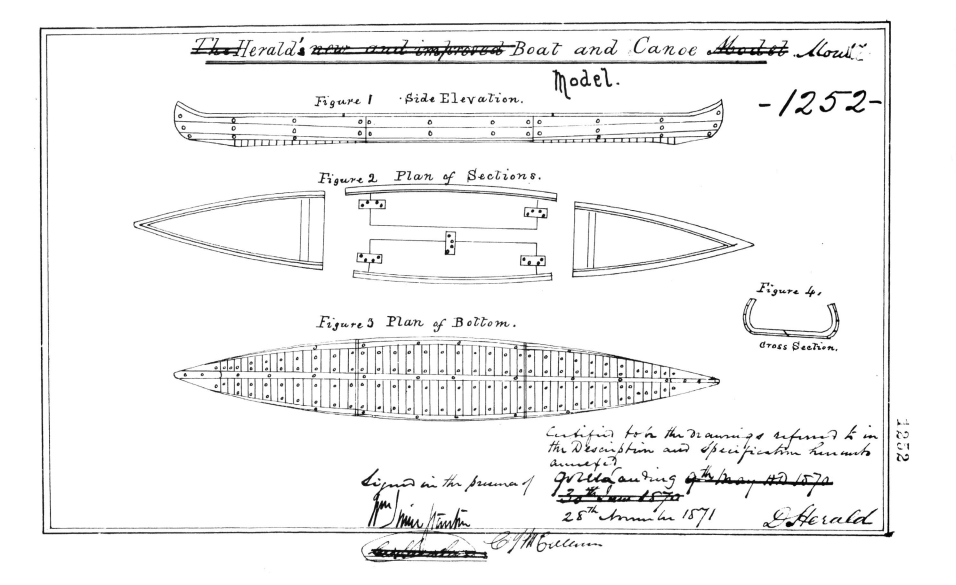

Dan Herald was a young apprentice shipwright when he left Ireland in about 1845. He eventually settled in Gores Landing, Rice Lake, where he found work with William McBride, a builder of coffins and boats. Herald was in the canoe business by 1861, building wide-board-and-batten canoes. In 1871 he patented a building form that was adjustable for size as well as having steel bands for clinching the thousands of tacks used in the production of his unique double-cedar canoes. This patented form was adopted in the early 1880s for cedar-canvas canoe manufacturing.

layers of planking. Before the paint hardened, the two layers were drawn together with about seven thousand closely spaced copper or brass cut tacks.

Herald probably tried this idea out on his wide-board-and-batten building form. The main problem was holding the layers together with the unclenched tacks until the paint could dry. The objective was to glue the layers together so that water would not be able to penetrate between them. But the form would be full of nail holes from building board-and-batten canoes and the tapered shape of the cut tack provided little holding power to draw and keep the layers together. With a forest of seven thousand tacks holding it on, it would have taken much wedging and prying to release the hull from the form.

Perhaps taking his cue from the shoemaker's metal last, a tool that had been familiar for centuries, Herald added metal bands to the form. When the cut tack was driven through the two pieces of wood, the tip hit the metal band and began curling over and turning back into the wood. As it curled back, it drew the two layers up tight together.

Herald's Patent Canoe successfully addressed many of the objectives of the perfect canoe. It was strong, beautiful,

light enough to portage, waterproof and could be produced in quantity. Production time was reduced with the use of cut tacks, since they were faster to use than the brass canoe nails used by the Peterborough builders. Canoe nails required drilling through the plank and hardwood rib before the nails could be inserted and driven home, and the ends of the nails had to be clinched after the hull was pried off the form. The cut tack required only two motions: pressing the sharp tip into the wood and then driving it in.

The two layers of planking with a layer of waterproofed canvas in the middle completely eliminated the problem of leakage and cracking. And with the employment of patterns, the building system had became quite repeatable. But the high level of finish and use of the best materials kept it from becoming the canoe for everyone.

Dan Herald's double-cedar canoe met the objective of recreating the dugout with a smooth outside surface and an interior uncluttered with ribs. The weight was reasonable and as an object of beauty, it was unsurpassed. Aside from beginning with Stephenson's solid building form, the new system offered a fresh approach to building a thin

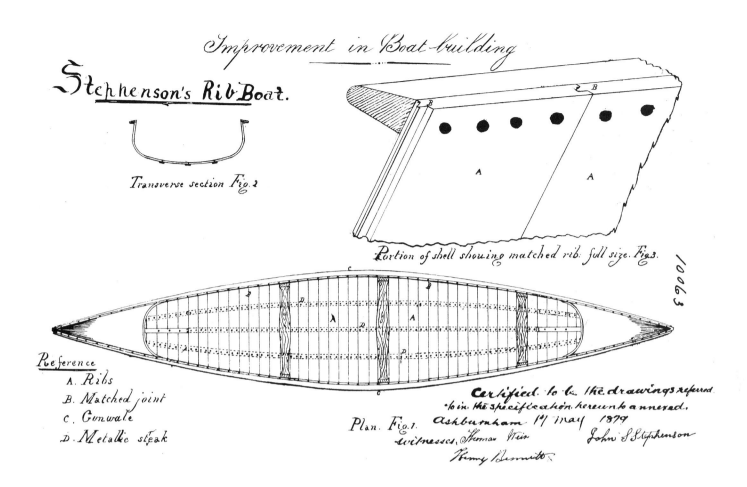

Improvement in Boat-building

Stephenson's Rib Boat.

Transverse section Fig. 2

Portion of shell showing matched rib full size. Fig. 3

10063

Reference
A. Ribs
B. Matched joint
c. Gunwale
D. Metallic streak

Certified to be the drawings referred to in the specification hereunto annexed.

Plan. Fig. 1. Ashburnham 1st May 1879

Witnesses, Thomas Weir   John S Stephenson

Henry Bennett

wooden hull that could remain watertight through cycles of wet and dry.

Esthetics as well as function played a major role in the development of the Peterborough canoe. The glistening varnish and clean interior of the double-cedar canoe built by Herald had a degree of finesse that could not be approached by the fanciest wide-board canoe, and his innovations had overcome the drying-out problem. This must have troubled John Stephenson and the Peterborough builders, as they were all striving for the same objective of building a canoe that combined function with beauty.

John Stephenson and the Cedar-Rib Canoe
During the latter half of 1870, John Stephenson was building canoes in a shop beside the big dock on Little Lake at the foot of Burnham Street while working on his own perfect canoe. On the same quest as Herald, he continued to search for the perfect craft with a clean interior and a hull that didn't open up when it dried out. His response to Herald's double-cedar was a technique that was equally as beautiful and, like Herald's canoe, featured

the dugout's uncluttered interior. On May 17, 1879, Stephenson was granted a patent for "Stephenson's Rib Boat," a technique that would become known as the cedar-rib canoe. Patent #10063 was for a building technique that featured narrow tongue-and-groove planks running from gunwale to gunwale. The patent refers to "metallic strakes" or longitudinal battens running from bow to stern on the inside of the hull to hold the cedar ribs together. There is also a reference to a canvas covering that suggests that perhaps Stephenson was unsure of being able to make this elaborate structure watertight; or knowing that Herald was on to something with the use of canvas, he included it just in case. However, there is no evidence of canvas being used on the surviving examples of this craft, and instead of metallic strakes, the battens appear to be white oak.

Comparing these two solutions to the same problem, we have a glimpse into the personalities of these two men. The uninhibited and innovative craftsman, John Stephenson, designed a system to build a canoe that was beautiful and met the functional objective but missed on the commercial end; the canoe was very labor-intensive

Stephenson's Cedar Rib Patent, #10063. John Stephenson was granted this patent for "Stephenson's Rib Boat" on May 17, 1879. Known as the cedar-rib canoe, this patent was for a building technique that featured narrow tongue-and-groove planks running from gunwale to gunwale, held together with longitudinal battens fastened on the inside of the hull. Though very labor-intensive to manufacture, it did introduce a radical new concept for joining thin planks with a machined edge. Tongue-and-groove, shiplap, metallic batten, flush batten and bead-and-cove are variations of this technique.

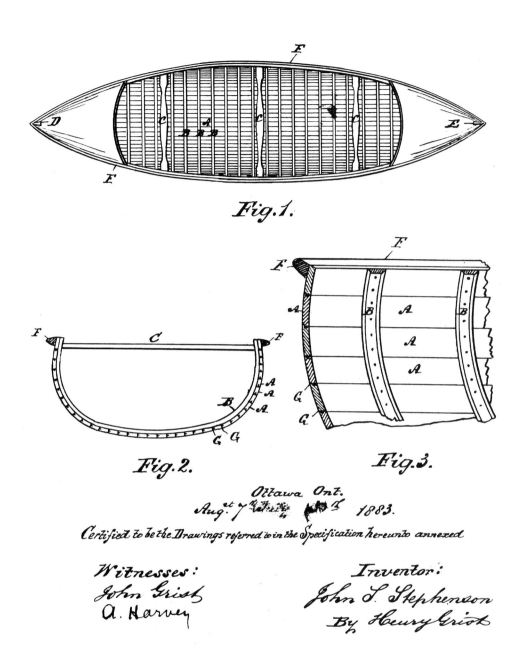

Fig.1.

Fig.2.   Fig.3.

Ottawa Ont.
Aug.st 7 .... 1883.

Certified to be the Drawings referred to in the Specification hereunto annexed

Witnesses: Inventor:
John Grist   John S. Stephenson
A. Harvey   By Henry Grist

Patent for Stephenson's longitudinal rib canoe. John Stephenson's most significant patent was a combination of the traditional carvel planking technique with the tongue-and-groove joint first used in the cedar-rib canoe. Soon to be known as the cedar strip, Stephenson's invention fulfilled all the current criteria of the perfect canoe. This building method would eventually be used by all the Peterborough area builders in the production of canoes, skiffs, sailboats and runabouts.

to manufacture. But it was his use of the machined edge that would revolutionize small craft construction. Herald, the businessman and innovator/craftsman, developed a system that met the main objectives and in addition, his canoe was striking in appearance, straightforward and reasonably economical to build. In the future his patent building form would be combined with the birchbark canoe shape to take manufacturing to the limit.

Stephenson's new technique showed some similarities to Herald's double-cedar method in that the first layer of wood to go over the form ran from gunwale to gunwale. On the Herald canoe, this layer is one-half the thickness of the total planking, but Stephenson's is the full one-quarter-inch planking thickness. The double-cedar technique relies on the outside layer of fore and aft planking to provide longitudinal strength and tie the pieces together, while the cedar-rib canoe is held together on the inside with a few longitudinal battens.

The cedar-rib method is significant in that it introduced a whole new concept of joining thin planks with a machined edge. This radical new approach was the beginning of an entirely new direction in boat building methods and a positive step towards building the perfect canoe. The use of a machined edge to seal the joint was more reliable, and proved faster and simpler than nailing numerous battens over the seams. The tongue-and-groove joint addressed the problem of the planks shrinking and cracking by acting as an expansion joint that would allow some movement in the joint. By reducing the width of the planks, the amount of movement each joint was expected to absorb was reduced. In the future, tongue-and-groove, shiplap, metallic batten, flush batten and, eventually, bead-and-cove would become variations of this concept.

Showing a realistic and serious commitment to the canoe business, Stephenson's next effort was to combine the structure of traditional carvel planking with the machined edge planking. Patent #32701 for "Stephenson's Longitudinal Rib Canoe" was granted four years later. The Canadian patent was granted on August 7, 1883, and the U.S. patent on August 13, 1883, for the building method that made Peterborough famous. Soon to be known as the cedar-strip canoe, the method would eventually be adopted by all of the Peterborough area builders.

The hull was built on the same form that had been used for the board-and-batten and cedar-rib canoes and incorporated the same stem and rib set-up. It is curious that there is no keelson in the drawing as it was in common use by this time. Perhaps he was still after the clean

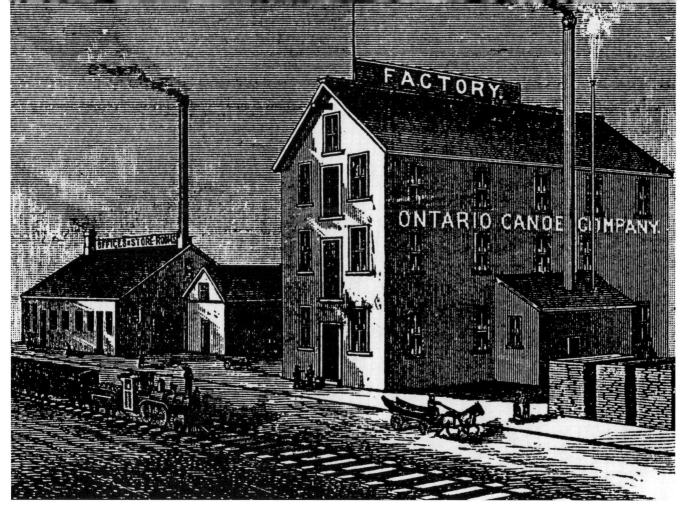

At the height of its production in 1892, the Ontario Canoe Company factory, under the ownership of J. Z. Rogers, supported twenty builders working six days a week. It was located in the former lumber warehouse of Ludgate and McDougall in the Ashburnham railway yards, expanded to accommodate the thriving boat-building company. The main factory building was thirty by sixty-five feet on four floors, plus a warehouse and office in a thirty-five by ninety-foot one-storey building. Machinery for the shaping of the parts was run off a long line shaft powered by a twenty-horsepower steam engine. A devastating fire in May of 1892 destroyed it, and Rogers sold his shares to the newly formed Peterborough Canoe Company, where he became manager.

James Zacheus Rogers traveled to England in 1879 with a Stephenson's cedar-rib canoe to explore market potential and contact dealers and sales agents. Convinced of an international market for the Canadian canoe, he purchased John Stephenson's canoe business and patents in 1883 and created the Ontario Canoe Company. He devoted the remainder of his life to canoe manufacturing in Peterborough; when he died in 1909 at the age of sixty-seven, he was still the manager of the Peterborough Canoe Company. A Peterborough newspaper reported that he had worked in the morning and was resting at home in the evening when he suffered a heart attack.

interior and had a lot of faith in the strength of the tongue-and-groove joint. A keelson soon became a standard component of the cedar-strip canoe. The patent drawing shows narrow tongue-and-groove parallel-sided planks running fore and aft parallel to the centerline. What the drawing does not show is what would happen on the side of the boat when parallel-sided planks were laid in this fashion. Because the hull is wider in the middle than it is at the ends, the plank line would end up an uncomfortable U-shape when it reached the sheer line. The common boat building technique of spilling or shaping the planks wider in the middle than at the ends would have to be incorporated to make the invention look right. The wide rib spacing that is shown appears to be the same as was being used on the board-and-batten canoe. It would soon become obvious that the narrow planks and fragile edges would need more support. Rib spacing would soon be reduced to two inches by adding two extra ribs between each of the original ribs. The look of the canoe continued to echo the dugout by using the same style of deck, thwarts and outwales.

The tongue-and-groove joint would soon be replaced with the shiplap or half-lap joint that was much easier to work with and served the same purpose. The tongue-

and-groove was necessary on the cedar-rib to hold the ribs (planks) in line, but it was also the source of the builders' frustration and aggravation. Putting up with the fragile edge was not necessary on the cedar-strip, since the ribs were close together and the nail, positioned close to the lap, pulled the joint up tight. Curiously missing in the patent is any reference to the use of canvas. Stephenson must have been satisfied that the machined joint was reliable and would not require an additional canvas covering.

J.Z. Rogers and the Transition to Industry

In 1883 John Stephenson sold his canoe-building company along with his patents and forms to James Zacheus Rogers of Ashburnham. All the pieces were now in place for canoe building to become a major industry and John Stephenson must have known that to take responsibility for it would take more capital and energy than he had to give. Forty-one-year-old J.Z. Rogers was an old friend and neighbor of John Stephenson and had followed the progress of the canoe's evolution and sensed the growing market potential. In 1879 Rogers took a Stephenson cedar-rib canoe to England to investigate the market potential and make contact with dealers and sales

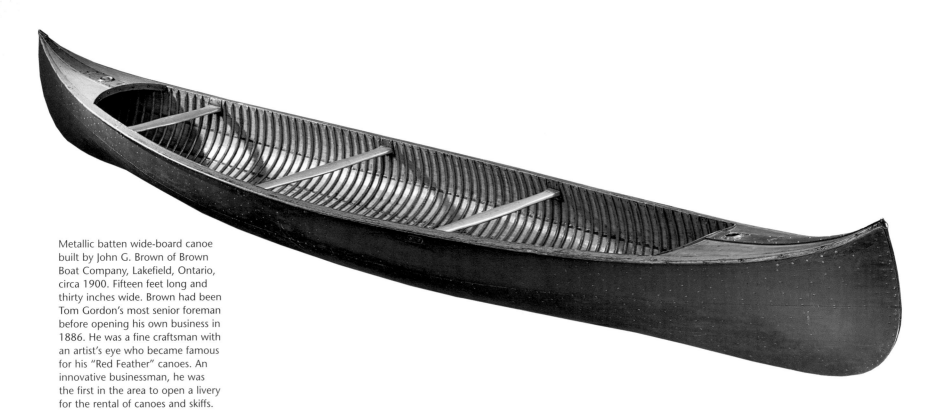

Metallic batten wide-board canoe built by John G. Brown of Brown Boat Company, Lakefield, Ontario, circa 1900. Fifteen feet long and thirty inches wide. Brown had been Tom Gordon's most senior foreman before opening his own business in 1886. He was a fine craftsman with an artist's eye who became famous for his "Red Feather" canoes. An innovative businessman, he was the first in the area to open a livery for the rental of canoes and skiffs.

Detail of Brown's canoe. The metallic batten is a channel of light metal resembling a long row of short-legged staples. The channel straddles the joint between the two planks on the inside of the hull with one leg embedded in each plank and is held in place by friction and the ribs.

agents. The response must have been favorable because he was back in the early 1880s exhibiting at the Fisheries Exhibition in London, England. Expositions were the first means of mass marketing and would be used by all the builders to cultivate interest in their canoes to a broad international market

By now the definition of the perfect canoe had started to undergo a significant change in emphasis, moving from technical development to focus on manufacturing at a profit. An efficient building method had been invented and an effective system to sell canoes in quantity had been established. What was missing was a strong leader who could put it all together and show a profit.

J.Z. Rogers fit the bill. He grew up in Ashburnham, where his father was a successful businessman with a sawmill, flour mill and store. Rogers clerked in the store and managed the lumber business, as well as serving in the military, where he commanded the 57th Battalion. With his considerable management skills and his family's business connections, Rogers was well positioned to develop canoe building into a successful manufacturing business.

Under his enthusiastic direction, the Ontario Canoe Company flourished. The former lumber warehouse of Ludgate and McDougall in the Ashburnham railway yards was expanded to accommodate the large crew of builders that would grow to twenty-five by 1892. The new company began by offering six sizes of canoes in three types of construction: the board-and-batten, cedar-rib and the cedar-strip, for a total of eighteen models in all. The number of models would increase to 120 to supply the evolving sport of canoeing. By 1892, they were offering folding canoes, decked and sailing canoes, oars, sails and canoe fittings, plus duck boats, lapstrake skiffs and twenty- to fifty-foot steam launches. Sales were made through agents and dealers as well as international exhibitions. Catalogs became an important sales tool and the mail was used extensively to communicate with customers in far flung places.

The Metallic Batten Canoe

During this period, the Gordon Canoe Co. in Lakefield had been growing in a similar fashion. Anchored in the dugout tradition, Gordon continued to explore the possibilities of the board-and-batten canoe. The problem of the wide planks shrinking was addressed (but not eliminated) by using narrower planks. While this helped to cure one problem, it created others. More planks also meant more joints to be backed up with seam battens, each joint between batten and rib taking time to fit and providing more potential places to leak. Gordon knew that Stephenson was on to something with the machined edge that created an unbroken seal between the planks from bow to stern. But he was still thinking along the lines of covering up the joint rather than fitting one part

of a plank into a space in another when he started using metallic battens, the next step in the evolution of the wide-board canoe. The Lakefield Canoe Company claimed to have used this method prior to 1880.

The metallic batten was a channel of light metal, either galvanized steel or brass, that resembled a long row of short-legged staples. The channel straddled the joint between the two planks on the inside of the hull, with one leg embedded in each plank, held in place by friction and the ribs.

Building a wide-board canoe using the metallic batten began with the usual keelson, stems and ribs. While the metallic batten would back up the joint, allow for expansion and keep the water out, it would not support the plank edges between the traditional six-inch rib spacing. Without the support provided by the raised batten, the span would eventually need to be reduced. As Stephenson had done with the cedar-rib, Gordon simply added two extra ribs between the old rib positions on his wide-board form. This increased the number of ribs without having to change the form.

To install the plank, a slit about one-sixteenth of an inch deep was cut parallel to the edge of the plank with a cutting gauge (similar to a marking gauge) and one leg of the batten was carefully pressed into it. The plank was then nailed to the ribs and stems. The next plank, with the slit cut in the edge, was pressed over the other leg of the

batten and the plank nailed into position. This is much easier said than done, considering that the plank, which was under a great deal of tension from being bent in two directions at once, had to be fit up to the last plank then pressed straight down over the leg of the batten without bending it over or breaking off the edge of the plank.

Incredibly beautiful canoes were built using this technique, none finer than the Sunnyside Cruiser built by

ABOVE: Large freighter canoe with Cree and Naskapi (Innu) paddlers on the Kaniapiskau River, Quebec, in the 1920s. Most of these canoes were made in the south and brought north by the HBC, as manufactured cedar canoes replaced Aboriginal bark canoes. Northern Aboriginal peoples quickly adopted these southern canoes, as they had previously adopted other European technology through the fur trade, to continue their traditional way of life.

LEFT: Canadian Canoe Company finishing department at 439 Water Street. The company was started here in 1892 by Arthur Tebb, a former Ontario Canoe Company foreman, and Felix Brownscombe, a young entrepreneur. Arthur Tebb sold out soon after and Morley Lyle became the manager. Brownscombe and Lyle ran an excellent company until 1929 when the company was purchased by the Peterborough Canoe Company.

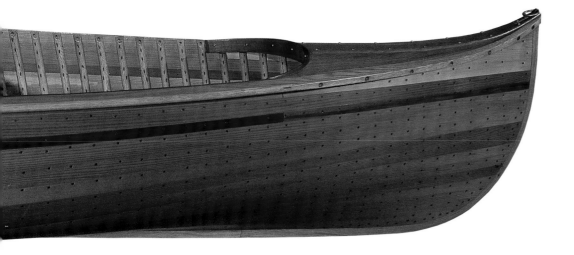

ABOVE AND RIGHT: Cedar strip built by Walter Walker, 1998, fourteen feet long, twenty-nine inches wide. See building sequence, page 190–93. The cedar-strip canoe invented by John Stephenson and patented in 1883 became the favored building method used by all the Peterborough area wooden canoe manufacturers. This canoe was built for the Canadian Canoe Museum in 1998 by Walter Walker, the last of the factory trained builders. Now in his nineties, Mr. Walker is reluctant to give up the pleasure that comes from combining red cedar, white oak, cherry and butternut to produce exquisitely functional canoes.

RIGHT: Tools were adapted or redesigned to make building more efficient. Walter Walker's hammer is a rare pattern that was cast for the Peterborough Canoe Company. The head has a large flat face with softly rounded edges that won't bruise the wood; claws are designed for removing the short copper canoe nails. Dubbing irons (also known as holding irons, backing irons or bucking irons) are shaped for clinching nails in a variety of inside curves and confined spaces.

Walter Dean in Toronto. Dean combined Spanish cedar planking with brass battens and lots of varnish to take this method to the extreme. He opened his boat shop at Sunnyside Beach in Toronto in 1888 when he was nineteen. A very inventive builder and mechanic, he had a great imagination and an eye for beauty. He became known for his exquisite paddling and sailing canoes that populated the Toronto Islands and Sunnyside Beach.

Competition and Expansion

There was no doubt that wooden canoes could be manufactured with great finesse but the demand for a cheaper, serviceable canoe was growing and could not be ignored. Up to the late 1880s, the builders were able to devote themselves to this private search for excellence. It was a self-indulgent time for canoe builders; they were the only source of supply and the public had to buy what they had to offer. Each model was offered in a variety of construction methods that gave the consumer a choice of quality and price. The finishes were varied, ranging from painted basswood with steel nails to highly varnished Spanish cedar with brass seam battens and walnut trim. The people who bought the lower-priced canoes wanted a boat for work or hunting and fishing. Getting on the water was the objective rather than looking elegant tied up at the church dock on Sunday. Low maintenance and durability were high on the list of desirable characteristics. There was a growing impatience with the devout attention demanded to maintain all-wood canoes. The paddlers' definition of the perfect canoe was no longer the same as the builders'.

When the change did come, it was from outside the area from builders who didn't possess the same obsession with craftsmanship. In order for builders to consider compromises in construction methods, the business had to be driven by the tough atmosphere of love for commerce rather than love of the board dugout. The Peterborough builders would ultimately be forced to adopt the cedar-canvas technique, the building method that made serious mass production of the wooden canoe possible.

This burdensome change began in the form of a disastrous fire at the Ontario Canoe Company in 1892. As the summer of 1892 approached, the Ontario Canoe Company was working at capacity as it entered the busy season. Stephenson's lumber shed had been replaced in 1884 when a new factory was built. The facilities continued to grow. The main factory building was thirty by sixty-five feet on four floors, plus a warehouse and office in a thirty-five- by ninety-foot one-storey building. Machinery for the shaping of the parts was run off a long line shaft powered by a twenty-horsepower steam engine. The factory was becoming plugged with orders waiting to be shipped, while more than twenty craftsmen worked six days a week to build more. The company was working at a frenzied pace with an optimistic future.

On May 9, 1892, disaster struck. Rogers later wrote of his loss in *The Peterborough Examiner:*

On Monday morning, the 9th of May, the factory of the OCC was set on fire and burnt, factory, machinery, plant, sheds, store houses and everything but office and one store house. We lost over $25,000 and had no insurance, the rate being prohibitory. I owned all the stock in the company and lost everything.

Never had we such a large and expensive stock of canoes on hand.

We had over $3,000 worth of ordered work burnt: and although we had over twenty men working, we could not keep up to our orders, and had just sent away for more men. We went on building in our store house and built a good many canoes during the summer, but we were working to a great disadvantage.

The summer found Rogers scrambling to salvage his business while trying to decide on the best of his options. Others were poised ready to fill the void left by the Ontario Canoe Company's curtailed production. Building in the store house could fill the orders on hand, but it would take capital to rebuild the lost momentum.

While the local builders benefited from the fire, it was the activity in Peterborough that caused Rogers the most consternation. A number of wealthy businessmen formed the Peterborough Canoe Company. The company was registered on June 3, 1892, with a capital stock of about $10,000. Rogers was fifty years old and had to accept that he was undercapitalized and would now have to compete for workmen as well as sales. That fall he sold the assets (including patents) of the Ontario Canoe Company to the Peterborough Canoe Company and became the manager. By February 1893 they had built a new factory and manufacturing had begun. The factory was designed for efficient production with ample floor space, office space, a power plant and improved machinery.

Meanwhile the local competition became more active. The Lakefield Canoe Works, Strickland and Company was started by Robert Strickland and his son George Arthur in 1892 to build wide-board canoes exclusively for export. George Arthur Strickland had learned the trade working with Tom Gordon and had previously operated a small shop of his own. Robert Strickland, who was now living

in England, handled sales. By 1898 they had exported a total of six hundred canoes to England and were promoting their canoes in Europe, Africa and Australia.

Another significant competitor was Arthur Tebb, a smart, resourceful and ambitious former Ontario Canoe Company foreman. Tebb rented the former Peterborough office and sales outlet of the Ontario Canoe Company at 439 Water Street in 1892. Assuming the goodwill of the location was the first of many astute decisions that would make the Canadian Canoe Company one of the most successfully run canoe enterprises. The choice of name was another; the open canoe was internationally known as the "Canadian" canoe, and in effect he assumed an established brand name. With twelve years of experience as a canoe/boatbuilder and foreman, he knew how to run a shop and manage workers. Felix Brownscombe, an ambitious young Peterborough businessman, provided financial backing for the venture and worked there full time as secretary-treasurer.

Throughout the 1890s, the canoe companies' growth and success was due to hard work, perseverance and resourcefulness. The number and variety of models increased to keep up with new applications of the canoe

The Lakefield Canoe Works, Strickland and Company, opened in 1892 to build wide-board canoes exclusively for export. George Arthur Strickland learned the trade working with Tom Gordon and previously operated a small shop of his own. His father, Robert Strickland, who was living in England at the time, handled promotion abroad. When fire destroyed their factory the following year, they moved to this building, the former People's Christian Association Hall. The Gordon and Strickland companies amalgamated in 1904 to form the Lakefield Canoe Building and Manufacturing Company.

An advertisment showing the first Peterborough Canoe Company factory at the corner of Water Street and King Street. The Peterborough Canoe Company was incorporated on June 3, 1892. Work began in October on this factory that was estimated to cost $5,000. Designed on the vertical manufacturing plan, the construction process flowed smoothly from department to department, ending at the varnishing room on the top floor. Elevated walkways connected the factory to a large storage shed, conveniently located on the water.

in work and play. A common problem for all the builders was keeping the factory busy twelve months of the year; the canoe is a seasonal craft in this country and sales drop off in the fall. As early as 1895, the Peterborough Canoe Co. was offering to build custom furniture, doors, moldings and verandah chairs. Marketing became more aggressive as competition grew. In 1893 all of the Peterborough builders were represented at the World's Columbian Exposition in Chicago.

The Flush-Batten Technique
In spite of rapidly expanding markets in the 1890s, the search for a luxury canoe with the dugout's clean interior was not forgotten. Used to build exquisitely beautiful canoes, the flush-batten was the last technique developed by the Peterborough builders.

A 1910 catalog from the Lakefield Canoe Building and Manufacturing Company states: "The Flush Batten system of building canoes is an invention of the Lakefield Canoe Company." The Gordon and Strickland canoe companies had amalgamated in 1904 to form the Lakefield Canoe Building and Manufacturing Company, so the flush batten was most likely a Gordon contribution to the partnership.

The flush batten was used with wide planks to make a continuous joint between the planks on the inside surface. It was similar to the metallic batten in that it covered the joint, but did not require close rib spacing. The flush batten was an easier method to work with and repair than the metallic batten, but it was more labor-intensive to install. The edges of the quarter-inch thick planks were rabbeted on the inside one-eighth of an inch deep by three-eighths of an inch wide. When the two planks were put together, they created a channel three-quarters of an inch wide by one-eighth of an inch deep. A continuous piece of one-eighth of an inch by three-quarters of an inch hardwood was fitted into this groove to span the joint, secured with closely spaced brass tacks. The flush-batten canoe was built on the standard solid form in the same order as the previous methods and required a similar degree of craftsmanship.

In the early 1900s, John Stephenson made a bold move away from the solid form and developed an inverted mold that was a series of steel hoops with spaces between them. This prototype production fixture allowed both sides of the hull to be worked on at once for the production of the flush-batten canoe. The machine could have been adapted to increase production of the cedar-strip, but by this time the market for mass-produced canoes was in the low price range, making his invention redundant.

By the early 1900s, the Peterborough builders' experimentation with new techniques had come to an end. Future development focused on diversification into related products and new models of outboard-powered boats that could be built in cedar strip or cedar canvas.

The Development of the Cedar-Canvas Canoe in Maine
When Peterborough, Gordon, Strickland and Canadian went into business they were ready to supply the world with their style of all-wood canoes. Although they were aware of the developments in Maine, they failed to take the canvas-covered canoe seriously. Before they knew it, a new industry had been established and paddlers were embracing the utility-grade canoe that met so many of the objectives of the perfect canoe. The American sporting press and American Canoe Association (ACA) were also slow to accept the cedar-canvas canoe; they did not acknowledge it until 1910, when the cedar-canvas canoes were flooding the market.

The ACA did not officially recognize the wood-canvas canoe as a class until 1934. American recreational paddlers were members of the elite, gentlemen who liked to

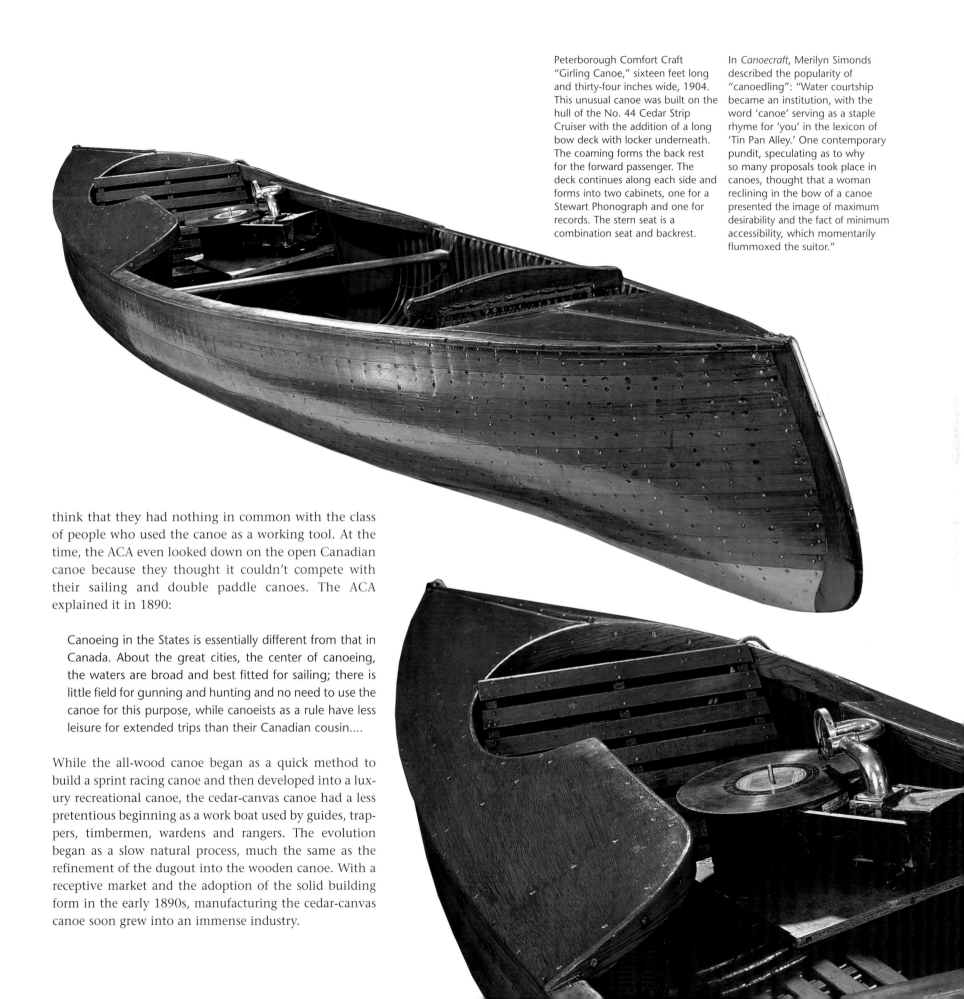

Peterborough Comfort Craft "Girling Canoe," sixteen feet long and thirty-four inches wide, 1904. This unusual canoe was built on the hull of the No. 44 Cedar Strip Cruiser with the addition of a long bow deck with locker underneath. The coaming forms the back rest for the forward passenger. The deck continues along each side and forms into two cabinets, one for a Stewart Phonograph and one for records. The stern seat is a combination seat and backrest.

In *Canoecraft*, Merilyn Simonds described the popularity of "canoedling": "Water courtship became an institution, with the word 'canoe' serving as a staple rhyme for 'you' in the lexicon of 'Tin Pan Alley.' One contemporary pundit, speculating as to why so many proposals took place in canoes, thought that a woman reclining in the bow of a canoe presented the image of maximum desirability and the fact of minimum accessibility, which momentarily flummoxed the suitor."

think that they had nothing in common with the class of people who used the canoe as a working tool. At the time, the ACA even looked down on the open Canadian canoe because they thought it couldn't compete with their sailing and double paddle canoes. The ACA explained it in 1890:

> Canoeing in the States is essentially different from that in Canada. About the great cities, the center of canoeing, the waters are broad and best fitted for sailing; there is little field for gunning and hunting and no need to use the canoe for this purpose, while canoeists as a rule have less leisure for extended trips than their Canadian cousin....

While the all-wood canoe began as a quick method to build a sprint racing canoe and then developed into a luxury recreational canoe, the cedar-canvas canoe had a less pretentious beginning as a work boat used by guides, trappers, timbermen, wardens and rangers. The evolution began as a slow natural process, much the same as the refinement of the dugout into the wooden canoe. With a receptive market and the adoption of the solid building form in the early 1890s, manufacturing the cedar-canvas canoe soon grew into an immense industry.

Although the cedar-canvas canoe owes its roots to the birchbark canoe, the manufacturing technique comes from the wooden canoe. The use of the solid dugout form made mass production possible. Canvas had been used as a substitute for birchbark long before the canoe became a manufactured item. Canvas and birchbark are both tough, waterproof materials that are available in sheets; given the availability of canvas, the substitution was not surprising. The Cree canoe builders of northern Quebec, who built canoes for trade with the Hudson's Bay Company, had for many years used canvas as a substitute for birchbark. In the Romaine region of Quebec, on the far northern shore of the St. Lawrence, where birchbark has never been available, the Native people built exquisite canvas-covered canoes using traditional bark-canoe building techniques. Canvas was also a common material used to repair bark canoes.

Settlers in the Maine bush had always depended on the Native birchbark canoe to get around in a land that was as much water as forest. The Penobscot River was the link between the lakes and the ocean and had been an access and trade route for centuries. When the Native builders could not supply bark canoes in sufficient quantity to the meet the demand, non-Native builders began taking up the craft. Guy Carleton from Old Town, Maine, began by building bark canoes and bateaux for the Penobscot lumbermen. Lowell, a small town several miles up the river, was home to two non-Native builders.

In the 1870s, J. Darling and Bill McLain set up bark-canoe building factories. Bill McLain and his son built over seventy-five canoes a year and many of them went to the Bar Harbor Canoe Club. While it was a business with very low overhead, production was limited to the availability of the bark. It takes a very large birch tree to produce a usable piece of bark, and not all trees of sufficient size produced bark that could be shaped and sewn without separating. By the mid- to late-1870s, the Penobscot builders had run out of local bark and were forced to buy it further afield. Necessity was truly the mother of invention when they started using canvas as a bark substitute.

The new canvas-covered canoe did not impress the local paddlers. It took some time for the builders to get used to working with the new material. Canvas was less rigid than birchbark, so any inconsistency in the ribs or planking would show through. *The Industrial Journal*, a Bangor, Maine, paper, commented in 1885: "Bark will never be driven out by canvas, for it bends prettier and is a more romantic material than duck." In the early part of the 1880s, the problem of keeping the hull fair (smooth lines) was solved with the adoption of the solid building form to control the shape.

The invention or adoption of the solid building form by the Maine builders is shrouded in as much fog as Penobscot Bay on an early fall morning. The lack of documentation suggests that there was nothing to document

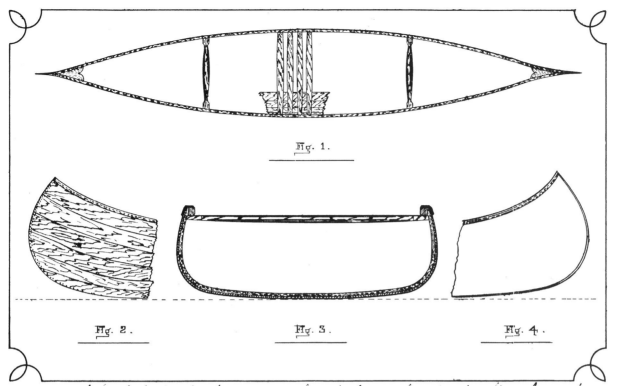

Fig. 1.

Fig. 2.   Fig. 3.   Fig. 4.

Certified to be the drawings referred to in the specification hereunto annexed

William F. Chestnut

Fredericton, N.B.   *Witnesses*
Dec 20th   *H. G. Chestnut*
1904   *N. B. Atherton*

LEFT: This patent for the cedar-canvas canoe building technique was granted to William Chestnut on February 28, 1905. Although the intended bluff was meant to thwart the builders in Ontario, it was never enforced. Curious that a process in use by builders in both Canada and the United States could be granted letters of patent by a builder new to the trade. Builders of all-wood canoes were reluctant to build in cedar-canvas but could not ignore a canoe that was in demand and could be produced at a profit.

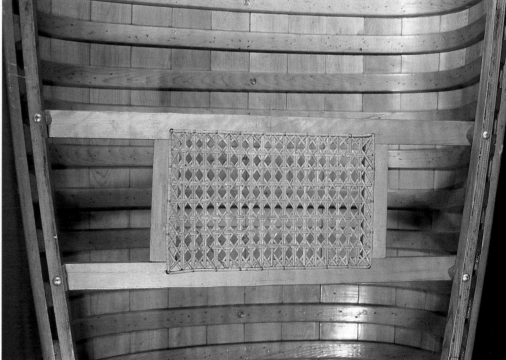

Boatbuilder Jack J. Moore built lapstrake canoes for hunting and fishing across the street in his Phoenix Square workshop. Business had been falling off as the guides who had been his customers became acquainted with the Maine cedar-canvas canoe. This lull in business ended when the Chestnut brothers hired him to build a replica of the Morris canoe on display. The canoe must have been a success because within two years, Moore and his assistant, Allan Meads, were working at capacity in their crowded little shop.

The Chestnut canoe began in 1905 when R. Chestnut and Sons began building cedar-canvas canoes in the second floor of the J.C. Risteen Co. To drastically increase their production capacity in a short time, they needed to hire more experienced builders. In a shamelessly aggressive move that would unfortunately become typical of the Chestnut management, William Chestnut journeyed to Old Town, Maine, and proceeded to interview potential employees. He was able to convince five builders (in the end only two stayed) to move to Fredericton and join the canoe company. Naturally, Old Town was not impressed and filed a lawsuit as well as threatening to set up manufacturing in Canada.

Chestnut was granted a patent for the cedar-canvas canoe building technique on February 28, 1905. In an attempt to control the canoe builders in Ontario and thwart Old Town's expansion into Canada, they obtained a patent for a building process that was in common use by many builders in Canada and the United States. A message in the 1908 Chestnut catalog warns: "We hereby warn anyone in Canada against using our construction!" Chestnut's 1909 suit against the Peterborough Canoe Company for patent infringement was settled when Chestnut failed to respond to a motion for dismissal and the case was dismissed for want of prosecution. By 1910 all the canoe builders, including those in the

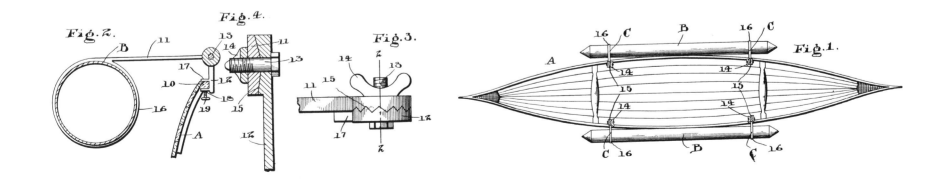

Peterborough area, had accepted the inevitable and began building for this new, unsophisticated market.

The canvas-covered canoe proved to be more appropriate for work in the bush. The Peterborough Canoe Company lost a major customer when the Hudson's Bay Company began buying canoes from Chestnut. This account would eventually grow to the point that Hudson's Bay was purchasing almost the entire production of the Chestnut factory. By 1910 Chestnut had sales agents in New Brunswick, Quebec, Nova Scotia, Alberta, British Columbia and Manitoba, with foreign agencies in Newfoundland, New Zealand, Australia, England and Germany.

Recreational canoeing had reached a peak before the First World War, when new forms of outdoor recreation such as the bicycle, the outboard and the motor car began to grow in popularity. Stony Lake saw its first Evinrude Detachable Engine in July 1913. Following the war, sales of all-wood canoes improved but they did not experience the same growth as they had in the optimistic first decade of the century. Recreational canoeing had redefined itself again; canoe sailing was not significantly revived after the war and the recreational paddler, without the company of a guide, had returned to the original habitat of the canoe. Competitive paddling in Canada survived primarily as sprint racing and was

The Canoe, Tom Thomson, 1914. A distinguished member of the Canadian artists known as the Group of Seven, Tom Thomson added to the mystique of the canoe with his haunting paintings of canoe country in Northern Ontario. He died mysteriously while canoeing on Canoe Lake in Algonquin Provincial Park in July 1917.

American tourists in Ottawa, 1925. Following the First World War, the motor car, now accessible to the vacationer of modest means, changed the way people traveled. No longer limited by the schedules of railroad and steamer, they were free to assume a gypsy lifestyle. The cedar-canvas canoe complimented the car as it was also affordable, light enough to carry on the roof or running board, and could withstand the drying-out effect of the sun and wind.

doing well, with many clubs active in Central and Eastern Canada. The cedar-canvas canoe flourished because it was better suited to the needs and budget of the new recreational paddler. The serious market for the canvas-covered canoe lay in its initial role as a work boat; the original demand for canoes in the fur trade, exploration, hunting and fishing had continued a steady growth.

Chestnut made the best of this opportunity and continued expanding to meet the demand. Their good fortune came to an abrupt halt in 1921 when fire destroyed their York Street factory. The Chestnut brothers wasted no time in rebuilding the factory along with replacing all the forms, jigs, patterns and machinery lost in the fire. Precious time and orders were lost and their debt load increased by $60,000.

In 1923, William Chestnut was fifty-six years old and his younger brother Harry was fifty. It could be that the fire had taken some of the fun out of the canoe business and it was time to think about retirement and bringing fresh management in to sustain the company. The time had also come to end the fierce competition with the Ontario builders and introduce some order and stability to a fragmented industry up against a fickle consumer.

Canadian Watercraft: Chestnut and Peterborough Join Forces

Canadian Watercraft was created in 1923 as a joint operating company that owned both the Chestnut Canoe Company and the Peterborough Canoe Company. A joint operating company allowed the manufacturers to use competition to stimulate and regulate sales without losing control. The combined working capital could be used as leverage to raise more capital and was a legal way of moving money around for a tax advantage. The companies continued to manufacture canoes under their own brand names and compete against each other. Chestnut concentrated on the canvas-covered canoe market and supplied Peterborough with canoes to sell under their own label. Peterborough provided all-wood canoes for Chestnut and continued to build all-wood canoes, boats and accessories.

Throughout the first quarter of the twentieth century, the Canadian Canoe Company continued to grow at a conservative yet determined rate. They survived the lean years of the war, achieved a stable financial condition and took advantage of the boating trend created by the outboard motor.

In 1926 a fire damaged the factory they had occupied since 1911 and brought production to a halt. The loss was completely covered by insurance and Morley Lyle and Felix Brownscombe set about rebuilding the business. The Canadian Canoe Company was back in production in 1927 and finished the year with a profit and $21,000 worth of boats in inventory.

Canadian Canoe Company president Homer Fisk and secretary-treasurer Felix Brownscombe were both sixty-four years old. They were founding members and majority shareholders who had faithfully guided the company since its inception in 1892. The manager, fifty-seven-year-old Morley Lyle, was the other major investor with thirty-four years of service to the company. Fisk and Brownscombe were soon to retire and plans for the future of the company were due to be made. Canadian received a favorable offer to purchase from Canadian Watercraft Limited. The sale was made final on January 12, 1928, with assets valued at $25,000 for real estate plus an inventory worth $21,142.32. Fisk and Brownscombe and Lyle had the distinction of making a profit in the canoe business and living to enjoy a healthy retirement. For the next thirty years, the Canadian Canoe Company was owned and run by Canadian Watercraft Limited. The company built both cedar-canvas and all-wood canoes; their specialty in the group was manufacturing cedar-strip outboard runabouts.

Now that there was solidarity within the industry, the system was in place to control the supply of wooden canoes and small boats. This proved useful in surviving the turbulent business environment over the decade. The depression years of the 1930s were extremely tight for the canoe builders. Most people were able to live

without a new canoe in hard times. The canoe companies continued to operate but the employees were forced to accept significant wage cuts. According to one former employee, just prior to the Second World War the company cut single men's wages in half and married men's wages by a third. The factory workers were now getting paid $ .12 an hour with no time-and-a-half for overtime.

This astute ad from the Old Town Canoe Company in 1919 suggests that paddling an Old Town canoe helped prepare the soldier for survival on the battlefield. While perhaps stretching the point, survival in the wilderness requires a similar degree of resourcefulness and adaptability.

Boom and Decline Follow the Second World War

Following the war, the recreational canoe market made a rapid recovery as returning veterans indulged themselves in some of the freedom they had been fighting for. The 1950s were good to the wooden canoe industry, with both major companies showing substantial profits. Chestnut had their best year in 1958 and the market continued to show signs of solid growth. This good

CONSTRUCTION OF A
WIDE-BOARD-and-BATTEN
BASSWOOD CANOE

In 1998, Walter Walker, then in his early nineties, was commissioned by the Canadian Canoe Museum to build the canoe pictured in the following sequence. He was assisted by three canoe builders closely associated with the Canoe Museum: Ted Moores, Ron Squires and Fred Forster. The craft is a wide-board canoe, built on a nineteenth-century Thomas Gordon (Lakefield) form and made with three basswood boards per side. This early form of building has not been done commercially for at least seventy-five years. Walter Walker, who for many years was a foreman at the Peterborough Canoe Company, is one of the few living canoe builders who knows the original way of building a modern canoe. Walter was the first canoe builder inducted into the Canadian Canoe Museum's Hall of Honour. At age ninety-four he is still building canoes and volunteering at the Canoe Museum.

1. Preparing stems
Building the all-wood Peterborough-style canoe begins by steam-bending a pair of white oak stems and setting them aside to dry on their form. The stem-bending form is an integral part of the tooling, as it defines the shape of the bow and stern for a particular model or series of models. To keep the stem from splitting as the bend is being made, a metal band is used to keep the outside surface from stretching and force all of the distortion into compression on the inside. The white oak keelson and basswood planking are also prepared beforehand as well as ribs of straight-grained white oak.

4. Shaping stems
Using the ribs as a reference, the stem is shaped first with the drawknife to take off the bulk of the material then smoothed up with a bench plane to receive the planking.

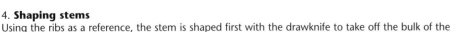

5. Caulking
A strip of cotton is fastened to the stem to insure that the craft will not leak in this area. While all wood canoes rely on the wood swelling to be watertight, the cotton absorbs moisture faster than the wood, providing a first line of defense. Another precaution that will contribute to the long life of this canoe is the application of a mixture of boiled linseed oil and a preservative between mating surfaces.

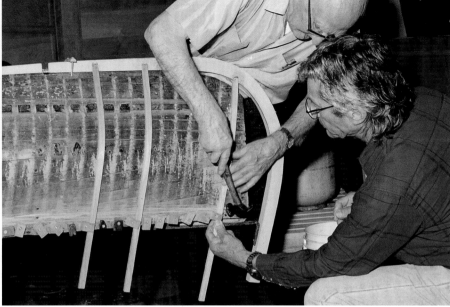

2. Bending ribs

Bending the ribs is a two-man job. After the ribs have been in the steam box for about thirty minutes, the first man takes a hot rib from the box and inserts it into a hole in the retainer on one side of the form. He begins the bend, handing over the rib to the second man who completes the bend, fastening his end with a twist of the wooden button. While he is doing this, the first man has nailed the rib to the keelson and is heading back to the steam box for the next rib.

3. Half-ribs

When the hull shape becomes a sharp V-shape at the bow and stern, the ribs can no longer be bent from gunwale to gunwale in one piece. Here the ends of the half-ribs are fit into mortises cut into the stem.

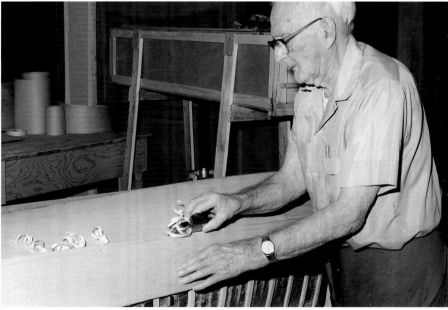

6. First plank

Planking begins by cutting the one-quarter-inch thick basswood plank to shape and nailing it to the keelson along the centerline of the canoe. Hot water is then applied judiciously to the outside of the dry plank, causing the outside surface of the plank to swell, which in turn forces the plank to curl. When the plank can be pressed down to the rib, it is fastened to the rib with copper canoe nails.

7. Second plank

The next plank is carefully shaped for a perfect fit along the edge of the first plank. Much skill and judgment is required to anticipate the change in shape as the wide flat plank is bent in two directions at once. In the factory, much of this judgment would be incorporated into accurate patterns, but there is no substitute for the skilful use of hand tools.

8. Outside stem

The outside stem seals the end grain of the planking from moisture absorption and protects it from physical damage. The metal backing band being used here is similar to the one used on the inside stem but with an ingenious twist. Holes have been punched in the band on about six-inch centers, allowing the screws and nails that will hold it in position to be placed while the stem is hot and the band is in place.

9. Keel

The keel is the last component to be installed before the hull is released from the form. Guided by a stringline that has been stretched down the centerline, the keel is fit between the outside stems and screwed through the planking into the keelson. The keel will act as a skid, protecting the bottom from abrasion as well as adding some directional stability.

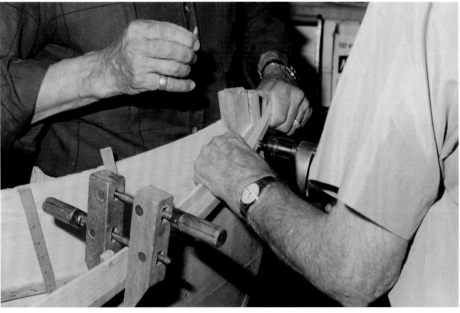

12. Outwales

The Peterborough-style outwale is a distinct feature that is firmly rooted in the dugout tradition. To remove weight, both visual and real, the outwales are tapered in cross-section as well as becoming narrower as they converge at the stem. Inwales, as seen in the cedar-canvas canoe and skiff construction, are not used on the Peterborough canoe.

13. Decks

Decks are another design feature that developed in the settlers' dugout. Butternut and chestnut, both lightweight, beautifully figured hardwoods, became the signature deck material in the Peterborough-style canoe.

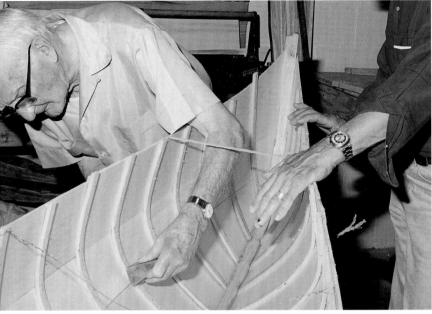

10. Clinching nails
After the hull has been pried off the form, the next step is to clinch the nails protruding from the ribs. The outside surface of the planking is wet down with hot water, to allow the head of the nail to be set slightly below the surface and to swell out bruises from the hammer. First the ends of the nails are bent over (dubbed off) with all the tips pointing towards the keelson. While holding a shaped iron weight (dubbing iron) against the bent-over nail, the nail is gently driven from the outside, causing the end of the nail to curl into the rib and sink below the surface.

11. Battens
Battens are short pieces of rib stock that fit between the ribs to back up the joint between planks. No two battens are the same length or angle, so precise measuring and cutting is necessary for a watertight seal. Notice the wires that are keeping the sides of the canoe from spreading as the ribs try to straighten out. Decks, outwales and thwarts will eventually stabilize the shape.

14. Deck caps
A coaming of walnut, oak, cherry or mahogany is steamed and bent to follow the graceful curve of the deck. More than a refined detail, the coaming covers the vulnerable end grain that is prone to check. The deck is completed with deck caps of the same hardwood to cover the joint down the center of the two-piece deck.

15. Paint and varnish
Basswood canoes were traditionally painted outside and varnished or painted on the inside. Our green canoe with varnished interior and trim has a timeless beauty that is as fresh today as it would have been coming out of Gordon's Lakefield shop over a century ago.

PADDLING for PLEASURE in the

NORTHEASTERN STATES

HALLIE E. BOND

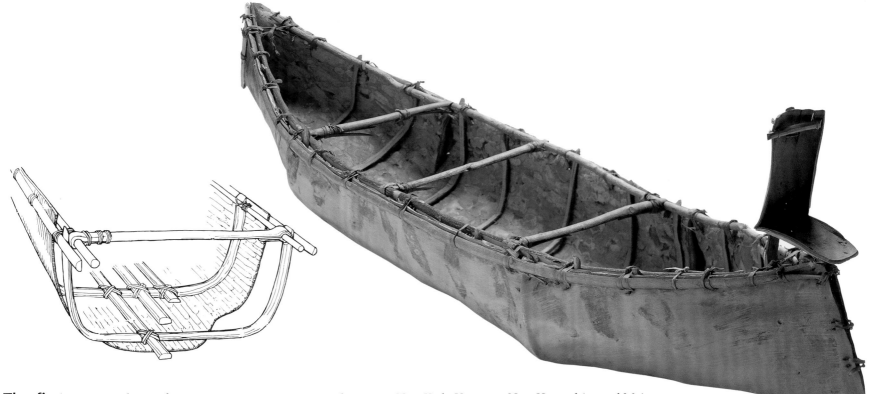

The first canoes to enter the Adirondack region of northern New York State were paddled by a couple of whitewater enthusiasts in 1880. Or so proclaimed one of them, Charles Farnham, in an article he published in *Scribner's Monthly* in April of the next year. Farnham and a companion took their decked cruising canoes from the Glen below the Hudson River Gorge in the present Adirondack Park, to the city of Albany at the junction of the Hudson and the Mohawk rivers.

In his ethnocentric view of his trip, Farnham was of course ignoring the canoeists of the preceding several millennia, Algonquin and Iroquois peoples who had traversed the region in dugout and bark canoes. Farnham's boat was not even what the Aboriginal peoples of the northeast would have recognized as a canoe, even though it was directly descended from a Native North American boat. Farnham's Shadow model canoe was European in construction, built with wooden planks attached to wooden frames with metal fastenings, but it was very similar to an Inuit kayak in shape and configuration.

Charles Farnham may have been the first white man in a plank-on-frame canoe to shoot the rapids of the upper Hudson River, but he was certainly only one of the many people of European descent to adopt and adapt an Aboriginal boat to his own ends in the regions now

known as New York, Vermont, New Hampshire and Maine. This chapter is the story of that adoption and adaptation.

The northeasternmost four states present a varied landscape to the canoeist. The region's waterways are now interrupted by dams, and have always been interrupted by mountain ranges, but they have probably been used as transportation corridors for at least seven thousand years. In the east, they wander through the uplands and around the mountain clusters of Maine, trending generally south and southeast towards the Atlantic Ocean. From east to west, the St. John and St. Croix (which form parts of the border with Canada), the Penobscot, the Kennebec and the Androscoggin have been major highways and major centers of canoe construction.

New Hampshire and Vermont are defined by mountain ranges running lengthwise through them: the White Mountains in New Hampshire and the Green Mountains in Vermont. The small rivers that drain these hills and the lakes along their lengths have provided good canoeing for Native peoples and whites alike, particularly if they have had portable boats. Between the two states runs the Connecticut River, historically the major avenue of settlement and travel.

On the western border of Vermont lies a waterway that practically determined the course of colonial history, and was a significant transportation corridor for thousands of

ABOVE LEFT: Construction of an elm bark canoe was similar to that of a birchbark. The builder removed the bark from the tree in one piece, laid it on the ground with its inside down, flattened it, and then rolled it up for transportation to the building bed. Here it has been bent into the canoe shape with the bark on the inside of the boat. The thwarts and inner and outer rails are lashed into place with split spruce root.

ABOVE: Elm-bark canoe model. Few historic bark canoes survive, so it is difficult to know just exactly what they looked like. This model from Huron territory gives us a glimpse of the simple construction and rough lines of an elm-bark boat.

FACING PAGE: Long Lake, New York, in the Adirondack Mountains.

years previous. Lake George drains northwards into Lake Champlain, which tumbles out through the Richelieu into the St. Lawrence and thence into the Atlantic. A short trek overland southwards from the Wood Creek, the inlet of Lake Champlain, takes one to the Hudson River, which leads south to the Atlantic as well, many coastal miles from the mouth of the St. Lawrence.

Between the Lake George–Lake Champlain corridor and the lowest Great Lake, Lake Ontario, lies the massive uplift of the Adirondack Mountains, with over forty peaks higher than four thousand feet, as well as thousands of lakes and five significant rivers that run off the dome in all directions. The Adirondack region has a forbidding climate and was probably not inhabited year round by Aboriginal peoples.

Native peoples did live in most of the rest of the northeastern states, beginning with the retreat of the last glaciers about ten thousand years ago. These groups typically moved their homes seasonally to take advantage of the natural bounty of the forests. In the Northern Forest,

ABOVE: "Dug-out on Beaver Lake," circa 1890. Frank "Pico" Johnson and William H. Ballard are carrying on a long tradition. Dugout canoes were cheap to build and could survive being left on shore, or even submerged for months, to be ready for checking traps or an afternoon of fishing.

TOP RIGHT: Charles Fenton is the probable builder of this remarkable dugout. Rather than being a result of necessity or whimsy, as are most historic Adirondack dugouts, this one seems to have been built as a test of skill with hewing tools by a man well familiar with contemporary boat types. It has a little wineglass transom and a hewn-in stern seat as well as outrigger oarlocks, and the elegantly shaped hull has a well-defined chine.

BOTTOM RIGHT: Ancient dugout canoes like this one turn up periodically on the bottoms of lakes across the Northern Forest. Many of them were probably put there for protection from porcupines or unauthorized borrowers, by a native hunter who never returned. This dugout was built between 1344 and 1504 with stone tools and fire, and then used on Lake Ozonia in the northern part of the New York State.

196

for example, in spring they moved to the seacoast or to waterfalls in the great rivers for fishing. In the early winters they broke up into small family bands for moose hunting deep in the forest. Small boats that could be carried from waterway to waterway or around beaver dams or rapids were essential to this lifestyle. For long-distance travel, Native peoples preferred fine birchbark canoes, but bark of the paper birch was not always available. When it wasn't, they built boats of spruce or elm bark, or even of moosehide.

The northeastern states are at the southern limit of the paper birch tree, so important in the canoe culture of Canada. South of Cape Ann, just north of Boston, it doesn't grow, and even north of that, at the higher altitudes such as in the Adirondacks, it is scarce. It is for this reason that the Iroquois, who inhabited central New York, did not build birchbark canoes, and why early travelers in the Adirondacks and southern reaches of the northeast found the Native peoples building canoes of other bark. In 1747 Peter Kalm, a Swedish naturalist and favored student of the great Linnaeus, headed up the Champlain valley in search of useful plants for northern climates. Near Fort Anne his guide built them an elm-bark boat big enough to carry four people with all their baggage. Kalm worried about the fragility of the craft, feeling that if they ran against a sharp branch, half the boat would be torn away, and wrote in *Travels in North America* "if one is rowing energetically, exposing the people in it to great danger, where the water is very deep, and especially if such a branch also holds the boat fast." In the event, the vessel carried Kalm and his companions safely. Native peoples, and later Europeans, also built boats of spruce bark. Neither elm nor spruce can be formed to the fine shapes of the more pliable birchbark. The results were, in the words of one paddler writing in *American Neptune* in July 1949, "clumsy craft, unsuited to long voyages, dangerous for crossing lakes, and suicide in white water."

While a portable boat was essential for long-distance travel, for shorter voyages on a single waterway dugout

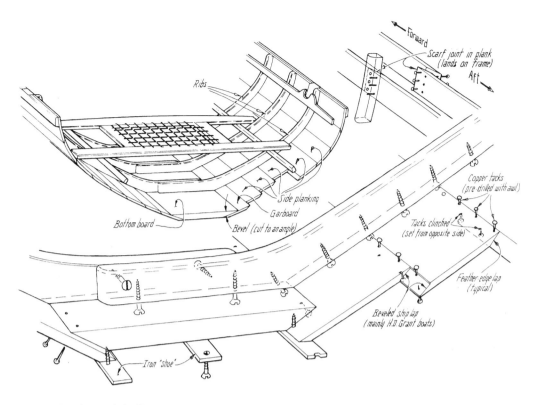

Forward

Scarf joint in plank
(lands on frame)

Aft

Ribs

Side planking

Garboard

Copper tacks
(pre-drilled with awl)

Bottom board

Bevel (cut to an angle)

Tacks clinched
(set from opposite side)

Feather edge lap
(typical)

Beveled ship lap
(mainly H.D. Grant boats)

Iron "shoe"

ABOVE: Framing and planking an Adirondack guideboat. The early guideboat builders of the Adirondack region of New York State refined bateau construction to the ultimate. These two drawings describe the two distinguishing construction features of the guide-boat. The upper one shows their peculiar flush-lap planking. Technically, guideboats are planked lapstrake, rather like a clapboard house, but the overlapping edges are beveled to a feather edge to form a smooth skin. The lower drawing shows a detail of the framing along the bottom of the boat. Guideboat frames, or ribs, are sawn (not steam-bent) from naturally curving spruce roots.

RIGHT: Adirondack guideboat. Fully equipped, standard, sixteen-foot Adirondack guideboats weigh between fifty and seventy pounds. The equipment includes one pair of "pinned" oars (with fixed thole-pins that fit into oarlocks on the boat), three caned seats, one or two with backs, a carrying yoke and a paddle. The paddle is used in tight places (the pinned oars can't be pulled shorter) or for sneaking up on deer. This boat was built around 1900 in the area of Blue Mountain Lake, probably by George W. Smith or John Blanchard.

canoes were used. Archaeologists have uncovered stone tools and bone and copper gouges probably used for carving dugout canoes that date from as early as 3,000 to 1,000 BCE. Actual examples exist from the fifteenth century; radiocarbon dating has established a construction date of around 1424 of a dugout found submerged in a lake in the northern part of the Adirondacks.

Although many canoeists of the nineteenth century, like Charles Farnham, declined even to consider "prim-itive" canoes such as birchbarks and dugouts worthy of notice, these craft continued to be used, by whites and Native peoples, well into the nineteenth century. The great American artist, Winslow Homer, sketched and painted several dugouts in use in the Adirondacks by trappers and guides in the 1870s. The country's pre-mier nineteenth-century canoe builder, J.H. Rushton, recalled in the 1880s the use of dugouts in his childhood, in a 1906 catalog for his canoes. These boats "were not make-shifts, but highly cherished by their owners."

Bark canoes continued to exist alongside plank-on-frame boats in even greater numbers. In Maine, they faded from common use only when the supply of good canoe birch ran out. Until the 1870s the standard boat to take into the north woods was a bark canoe, or perhaps a plank-on-frame bateau. Large bateaux, long, narrow, flat-bottomed plank-on-frame boats, could carry more cargo than the average woods canoe, but were corre-spondingly harder to carry over the portages.

And even well into the twentieth century birchbark canoes survived as an important feature of the idealized North Woods. Nineteenth century "sports" purchased them for their romantic associations and artists painted them in pictures. The artist A.F. Tait, whose paintings lithographed by Currier and Ives did so much to bring the Adirondack region to the attention of the nation, invariably put his subjects in birchbark canoes. This, in spite of the fact that he himself was rowed around in Adirondack guideboats—as was practically every other visitor to the region at the time.

Adirondack guideboats and Maine bateaux were both descended from a colonial ancestor, the bateau. Both the French and the British built colonial bateaux in tremen-dous numbers across the northeast. They were long, narrow flat-bottomed craft sharp at both ends, with frames (or ribs) sawn out of naturally curving roots or branches, and had lapstrake planking, with the planks overlapped like the clapboards on a house. The larger bateaux, around thirty feet in length, were commonly used as troop transport on the inland waterways of the northeast and were rowed. Smaller bateaux could be paddled.

By the middle of the nineteenth century these bateau descendents had become essential to what were fast becoming the main industries of the region, logging and tourism. Across the northeast, the logging business depended on crews in large, heavy bateaux to herd sawlogs downstream in the annual spring drives from the woods to the mills. In the Adirondack region, an extremely refined version of the bateau was known as the Adirondack guideboat by the 1880s. They were generally between fifteen and eighteen feet long with frames and planking made so thin that the boats weighed only fifty to seventy pounds, light enough to carry. Their skins were smooth. Although technically lapstrake, guideboat-style planking is nowhere thicker than any given plank because the overlap is beveled to a feather edge. Each guideboat was equipped with a yoke, the form of which was obviously borrowed from yokes then common around farms for carrying buckets of water or maple sap. Carrying a wooden boat this size on one's shoulders seemed "as impossible as carrying a man-o-war" to Thomas Bangs Thorpe, a visitor to the Adirondacks in 1859 who was used to coastal boats. In 1857, Samuel H. Hammond, a New York judge, watched in wonder as his "boatman

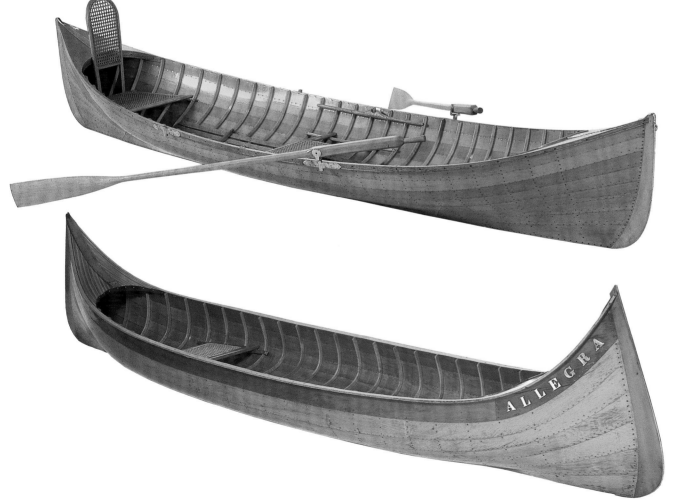

ABOVE: *Going Out: Deer Hunting in the Adirondacks* (1862). The English-born artist Arthur Fitzwilliam Tait always put his Adirondack "sports" into birchbark canoes, even though he himself traveled in a guideboat. Tait was one of the most prolific and well-known artists to publicize the Adirondacks. Many of his paintings were reproduced by Currier and Ives.

TOP LEFT: This Adirondack guide-boat, known as a Brown's Tract Boat, is one of the most distinct guideboats. In the 1890s H.D. Grant flared the upper ends of his ribs outwards near the bow and stern, for greater buoyancy and deflection of rough water. Because this looked "podgy" to Grant, he tipped the stems outwards towards the vertical. The resulting "Brown's Tract" stem profiles are easily distinguished from the tumblehome stems of most other guideboats.

BOTTOM LEFT: This canoe is built like an Adirondack guideboat with a sawn frame and smooth-skinned, flush-lap planking. *Allegra* was reportedly one of four identical boats, one of which ran the rapids of the Hudson gorge and survived.

199

marches off, with his boat, like a turtle with his shell upon his back."

Samuel Hammond was part of a new group of people coming to the north woods, a group that was rapidly increasing in size and that would have a tremendous impact on the economy of the region, and on the boats used there. The settlers who rowed him around and pointed out the good brook trout holes or the deer runs called him a "city man" or simply "sport." We would call him a tourist. All across the northeast people were looking to the wilderness as an antidote to industrial civilization. The north woods were seen as a place to go for moral and spiritual regeneration. For even while Americans were enchanted with the technology that produced such advantages as inexpensive, high-quality cloth, telegraphs and steam transportation, they were aware of the negative aspects of the new age. Crime and poverty were already apparent among crowded workers in the rapidly growing cities, and the air and water around the mills and factories were becoming polluted. The routines and specialization of factory and office work alienated workers from their work.

The ability to escape from these conditions was not available to everyone, nor did everyone who could take advantage. Until the economic boom and technological advances of the post–Civil War period in America, travel to the region was an adventure in itself. The average visitor until the 1870s was an upper-middle-class man, a professional or a high-level manager. Average working people had neither the money nor the leisure to spend a

month or two on vacation. "Roughing it" didn't appeal to many women, nor was it socially acceptable.

The desire to get out of the cities and away from the comforts and conventions of civilized life was not peculiar to North America. Nor was the interest in doing so in a small boat. On a sort of Grand Tour in reverse in 1859, a Scot named John MacGregor sampled several Native boat types in Upper Canada and the north, paddling a birchbark canoe, a dugout and a kayak. When he returned to Britain, he had a boatbuilder there build him a small boat of the general form and size of a small kayak, but with European plank-on-frame construction. MacGregor had a double-bladed paddle made to go with it, as he had seen in the Arctic, but he added a tiny lugsail and jib, which had not been used there. The sails were only intended as auxiliary power. There was no centerboard or leeboard, and MacGregor used his paddle as a rudder. The size of *Rob Roy*, named after the original of the character in Sir Walter Scott's novels and an ancestor of MacGregor's, was determined by the maximum size allowed on German railway carriages, for MacGregor proposed a European cruise using trains to travel between watersheds. *Rob Roy* was fifteen feet long, had a beam of twenty-eight inches, was nine inches deep and weighed eighty pounds.

MacGregor set off down the Thames for the Channel on a hot day in July 1865, with all his duffel for the three-month trip in a little black bag one foot square and six inches deep: a change of clothes, a black Sunday coat, a few extra collars, handkerchiefs and socks, a testament and a pair of blue spectacles. As he stated in his subsequent book, his object was to try "a new mode of traveling on the Continent, by which new people and things are met with, while healthy exercise is enjoyed, and an interest ever varied with excitement keeps fully alert the energies of the mind."

MacGregor thoroughly enjoyed himself, and when he returned he wrote *A Thousand Miles in the Rob Roy Canoe on Rivers and Lakes of Europe* (1866) to introduce the new pastime to others. His first and subsequent books about his journeys (he eventually made five trips, each with a different *Rob Roy*) were well received. The idea of traveling the countryside in a tiny yacht, with no timetables to adhere to, no appearances to keep up and with a chance to get off the beaten tourist path, was extremely attractive to men of leisure and means who wanted to escape the cities—the same sorts of men who, like Hammond and the other "sports" in the northeastern states, were attracted to travel in the backwoods. The sports and the yachtsmen differed primarily in their interest in hunting

General E.A. McAlpin and his guide Jack Richards circa 1890. The Adirondack guideboat has the reputation of being the fastest fixed-seat traditional rowboat in the world. Its speed, a result of refinements meant to make the boat easy to row for many miles through the Adirondack wilderness, was a great help in getting the "sport" his deer. One of the most popular hunting techniques of the late nineteenth century was "hounding," which is what Messrs. McAlpin and Richards have been up to. Along with several other hunting parties, they stationed themselves around the shore of the lake while the hounds were set on the deer. The deer were driven to the water, and the boats leapt forth in pursuit. If they caught up with a deer before it reached the safety of shore, the hunter had his shot at close range. If he missed, the guide could always club the animal to death. Hounding was outlawed in the 1890s.

and fishing. The canoe cruisers often carried rods and guns, but their primary interest was scenery and recreation. These different interests naturally had an impact on where they chose to cruise.

Instead of venturing into the wilderness, the majority of cruising canoeists kept to the more civilized waterways of the northeast, rivers like the Connecticut and the Hudson, and routes along the coast. These waterways, like the rivers of Europe, were perhaps even more civilized then than they are today. Canoeists could paddle along canals across country, occasionally hitching rides on canal boats. They could count on towns, villages or farms along the way for hot meals or camp supplies, or for an occasional night between sheets. Mill dams forced canoeists to portage, but smoothed out upstream rapids, and a farmer with a cart or a gang of small boys could usually be counted upon to help with the trip overland.

Like MacGregor, American cruising canoeists wrote about their adventures. Canoeists today read, and are inspired by, published accounts, letters and articles in periodicals that tell of their exploits, including: *The Voyage of the Paper Canoe, From Quebec to the Gulf* (1874) by Nathaniel Holmes Bishop; the Glens Falls, New York, photographer Seneca Ray Stoddard's 1882–83 trip from the Bay of Fundy to New York; piano manufacturer Siegfried Wulsin's attempt to find the source of the Mississippi; and a pseudonymous canoeist's retracing of Benedict Arnold's ill-fated trip up the Dead River in Maine towards Quebec. "Without question the foremost of all manly sports is yachting, encouraging as it does, in the highest degree, self-reliance, decision, quickness of thought and action, endurance and daring, while open to none of those objections on the score of cruelty," wrote W.P. Stephens in an article entitled "The Poor

Rushton advertised this Vesper model decked canoe as the "ultimate cruising canoe." Watertight cargo hatches kept duffel dry and made the boat an "unsinkable life-boat," and the boat was easily paddled if the wind died. The patented Radix centerboard was constructed of seven sheets of brass. The boat's fine lines and great spread of sail also made her fast and fun to race. It had no permanent ballast. Instead, the sliding hiking board allowed the sailor to get his weight out to windward to keep the boat upright in a fresh breeze.

LEFT: *A Cruising Canoeist* (circa 1880). Frederic Remington is best known for his defining images of Western cowboys and Indians, but he was born in New York's North Country and was a friend and contemporary of the canoe builder J.H. Rushton. He made this sketch for Rushton, perhaps as an advertisement. It depicts a gentleman of leisure (with a tam to suggest Scotland) paddling Rushton's first cruising canoe model, the American Travelling Canoe, his version of John MacGregor's famous *Rob Roy*.

RIGHT: "A Carry Between 2 Lakes." George Whitfield Butts took this picture. He and his wife took a long cruise through the Adirondacks in 1907, shortly after their marriage. The region was popular with canoeists for its combination of natural, unspoiled beauty and amenities. At the major "carries" (portages are never called by their French name in the Adirondacks) locals stood ready with a wagon and team of horses to do the hauling, for a fee.

BELOW: "*Diana* at the campsite," photo by Richard Walker. Every yacht must have its cabin, and the "poor man's yacht" was no exception. John MacGregor of *Rob Roy* fame designed the first canoe tent, which looked much like this one. Here it is shown on exhibit at the Adirondack Museum on the Rushton-built Princess model canoe *Diana,* built in 1882.

Man's Yacht" in *Forest and Stream* in 1881. Stephens was an early canoe cruiser and builder, and later canoeing and yachting editor for *Forest and Stream* and one of the country's foremost yacht designers. "But yachting even on a small scale is costly…. The canoe offers a means of exercise at once safe, pleasant and easily learned at a reasonable cost."

Part of the fun of cruising in little yachts was sleeping at night in their "cabins." MacGregor invented the first canoe tent, which was slung from the mast so that the canoeist could pull the boat ashore and sleep on board, his legs under one deck and his head under the other. "Perhaps one of the most important things tending to a comfortable cruise is the matter of shelter," wrote an anonymous canoeist in 1881 in *Forest and Stream.* "Under [a tent] the writer has, on a rainy evening, seated in the canoe with a small alcohol stove between the knees, prepared his 'Leibig' soup, coffee, and toasted crackers, written up his log, read awhile by lantern light and turned in snugly to 'sleep the sleep of the just,' oblivious to the elements."

Many canoeists felt quite strongly about "proper" cruising. In 1878, W.L. Alden, an early cruising canoeist and canoe builder, wrote in a charming little book, now rare, called *The Canoe or the Flying Proa, or, Cheap Cruising and Safe Sailing,* that "the canoeist who does not sleep in his canoe is guilty of treason, and deserves the lasting scorn of all loyal paddlers." A practical editor at *Forest and Stream* countered in July 1874 that "sleeping in the canoe is to be avoided, if possible; it is very uncomfortable for one thing, and strains the craft and causes her to leak, for another. A much better plan is to carry a small cotton tent and make camp in the usual way." It was Alden himself who named "MacGregor's Line," an abrasion on the nose suffered by canoeists who woke up suddenly and forgot where they were.

As the popularity of canoe cruising grew in North America, several men set themselves up as builders of the craft and began reaching out to customers beyond their local area, via advertisements in popular sporting periodicals such as *Forest and Stream* and through catalogs and circulars. A group of canoeists sitting around a parlor fire on a damp November evening in the 1870s could discuss the boats of W.P. Stephens of Rahway, New Jersey, or any of the New York State builders: James Everson of Williamsburgh, on Manhattan Island, George Ruggles in Rochester, A. Bain and Company in Clayton, Herbert M. Sprague of Parishville, or J.H. Rushton of Canton.

Early in 1880, Nathaniel Holmes Bishop, whose long-distance cruise in a paper canoe had captivated small-boat enthusiasts across the country, issued an invitation to his fellow canoeists to attend a "canoe congress" to be held in August on Lake George, on the eastern edge of the Adirondack Mountains. His primary aim, as he reported in the widely read sporting periodical *Forest and Stream* after the meet, was to bring canoeists together "for the feature of sociability about the camp fire in the evenings, the swapping of yarns and experiences, the learning of kinks from each other, and a spread of that fraternal spirit essentially characteristic of a body of men engaged in furthering ends at once honest, moral, and strengthening alike to body and mind." As we shall see, the meet ended up becoming a trade show and a racing venue, as well. For the first meet Bishop arranged for a group of Native people (probably Abenaki living in the area) to attend to "paddle on the Horicon of Cooper," an allusion to the popular and well-known book by New York author James Fenimore Cooper, *The Last of the Mohicans*. It was only a token appearance, however, intended to evoke the romance of the past. The meet was intended to attract the "modern" canoeist primarily, the man who paddled or sailed a brass- and copper-fastened, plank-on-frame boat.

By the end of the congress, the organizers had established the American Canoe Association, an institution that, at this writing, continues to promote canoeing and hold annual encampments. One of the first orders of business at that initial meeting was to establish five classes for racing. At one end of the scale were birchbarks and Canadian-style canoes, canoes propelled only by paddle. At the other end were sailing canoes not adapted to cruising, where auxiliary power would be needed. In between were sailable paddling canoes with qualities equally divided, and paddleable sailing canoes with sailing qualities predominant.

The ACA was originally conceived as an international organization, and Canadians participated from the beginning. At the first meet, Thomas Henry Wallace of Rice Lake, who reportedly crossed the finish line calmly smoking a pipe, won the one-mile paddling race. In the nineteenth century, the organization met several times

ABOVE: Early members of the American Canoe Association at an Annual Meet, circa 1885.

LEFT: A seventeen-man, custom-built war canoe leaving the shop of J.H. Rushton, Canton, New York, circa 1900.

ABOVE: Cover to the 1881 catalog of J.H. Rushton, Canton, New York. Rushton was a pioneer in catalog advertising.

BELOW: "The Canoe *Dimple*: A Close Call." Photo taken by Seneca Ray Stoddard at an American Canoe Association meet on Lake George, 1888.

in Canada, and when it chose a permanent home in 1901, it was in the Thousand Islands of the St. Lawrence River, on the international border. But several factors contributed to a declining interest in the ACA on the part of Canadians, and the foundation of the Canadian Canoe Association in 1900. The strong emphasis on decked canoes may have discouraged Canadians, with their strong and vibrant tradition of open canoes. The majority of annual ACA meets were held in the States, and not convenient to most Canadian members. Also, the leadership of the organization in its first two decades, which included W.L. Alden and W.P. Stephens, tended to come from the ranks of the upper-middle-class men who perceived the standard canoeist as a man who could afford his own decked canoe. Young men who wanted to get started in the sport often couldn't afford such a vessel. In Canada many such canoeists joined clubs that owned so-called "war canoes," canoes twenty-five to thirty-five feet long paddled by eight to twelve paddlers, but the ACA as an organization had only minimal interest in these craft.

The designs of open paddling canoes and decked canoes with sails were affected by the drive to win races. From Wallace's victory on, aficionados of the open canoe recognized the long, sleek Canadian canoes as the forms to copy. Several American builders advertised what they called "Canadian-style" or simply "Canadian" canoes. J.H. Rushton offered five different Canadian models over

his forty-year career. His were long boats characterized by narrow beam, V-bottoms, light weight, and flat, wide outwales. They did not have the characteristic sharp upturn at the ends of the Peterborough area builders, however (probably an aesthetic decision on Rushton's part), and Rushton used the construction methods with which he was familiar. His smooth-skinned Canadian canoes were planked flush-lap like a guideboat.

The effect of racing on the design of the decked cruising canoes was more extreme than it was on the open paddling canoes. While it is conceivable that one might go cruising in an open racing paddler like Rushton's Arkansas Traveler, the decked sailing canoes rapidly evolved into much more specialized machines. In 1896, in an article called "Back to the Grindstone: The Canoe Camp," R.B. Burchard, an editor at *Outing* magazine, wrote: "the perfection of the racing-machine and the extreme acrobatic skill required in attaining perfection in its handling, has driven busy men for the most part from the sailing courses." The early cruising canoes, like MacGregor's *Rob Roy*, had had no centerboard, or indeed anything for lateral resistance except for the keel. Sails were only used for auxiliary power. Steering was done with the paddle. By the mid-1880s, however, sailing canoes not only had two or three sails, but rudders and centerboards. As sails increased in size in attempts to go faster, canoeists had increasing difficulty in keeping their boats upright. Here the English and North American traditions diverged. While the English built their boats heavier and ballasted them (usually sandbags fitted to the bottom of the boat), the Americans built lighter and lighter boats and used themselves for ballast. Initially they just got up and sat on the side decks, then they found themselves leaning out backwards over the water, and then they devised hiking boards. These were narrow thwartships planks that slid back and forth in a wooden bracket that clamped across the cockpit of the canoe. The canoeist sat on the windward end, slid out as far as he dared. When he came about, he had to slide the board across the boat while handling the sheets and the tiller. Although one had to be a bit of a monkey to sail them, sailing canoes were tremendously exciting. Even today, they are the fastest single-hulled boats afloat.

The amount of notice given the decked racing canoes of the ACA and its member clubs tends to obscure the fact that during the same time the tradition of backwoods travel in open canoes was growing ever more popular. After the American Civil War, travel to the north woods became easier and cheaper with the expansion of railroad and steamboat routes throughout the northeast.

A vacation in the woods became available to greater numbers of people as the vacation became established as an American institution, and more popular as enterprising entrepreneurs built hotels and settlers opened their homes to visitors.

In the Adirondacks visitors still tended to hire a resident guide and these men almost invariably preferred their regional type of boat, the Adirondack guideboat. But in Maine backwoods travelers hired Native guides, who came equipped with birchbark canoes or bateaux. As the demand for the guides and their boats increased, canoe builders along the Penobscot River prospered. Natives, such as those on the reserve on the island at Old Town, couldn't keep up with the demand. Soon, white men began building birchbark canoes. In Old Town itself, Guy Carleton built both bateaux and bark canoes, and upriver in Lowell both J. Darling and Bill McLain had bark canoe factories. McLain and his son produced over seventy-five canoes a year during the 1870s.

But good birchbark was becoming increasingly scarce in the area. Builders had to import it from a considerable distance and began using canvas for a substitute. At first canvas was used for patching, and probably also to cover leaky bark boats. By the mid-1870s there were, according to the Bangor, Maine, newspaper, "a great many" canoes built like birchbark canoes but with painted canvas used in place of the bark. But it wasn't until the building method was completely changed to a European-style

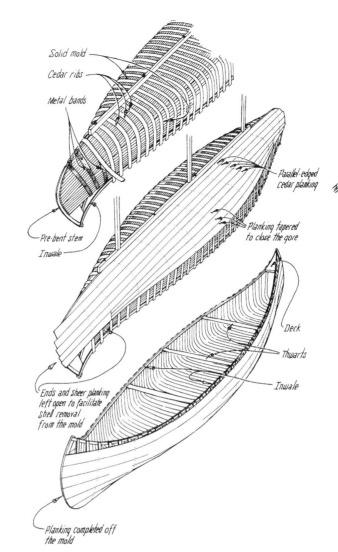

LEFT: Wood-canvas canoes are built over a solid mold. The upper drawing shows the mold with cedar ribs steamed and bent over it. The metal bands below the ribs will turn the points of the tacks when they are driven through the planking, which is what is about to happen in the middle drawing. The bottom drawing shows the shell of the canoe after it has been removed from the mold and had its thwarts and deck put in. In the right-hand drawing is a detail of how the canvas covering is secured before being tacked to the shell.

BELOW: Standard designs for decoration of Old Town canoes, 1926.

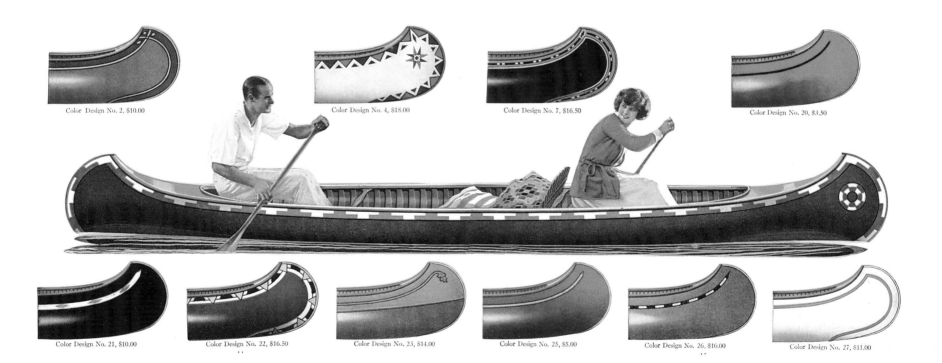

Color Design No. 2, $10.00
Color Design No. 4, $18.00
Color Design No. 7, $16.50
Color Design No. 20, $3.50
Color Design No. 21, $10.00
Color Design No. 22, $16.50
Color Design No. 23, $14.00
Color Design No. 25, $5.00
Color Design No. 26, $16.00
Color Design No. 27, $11.00

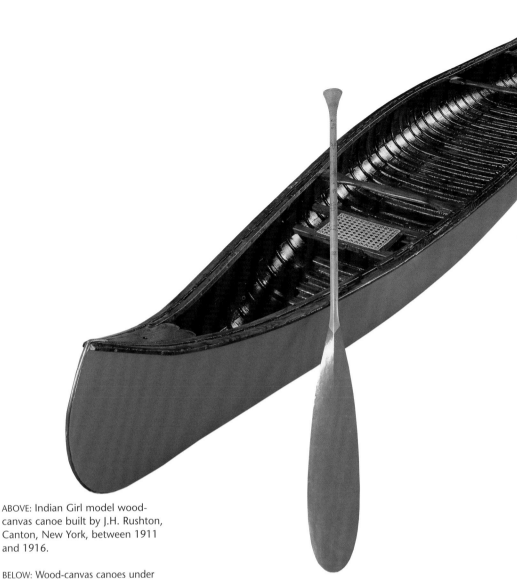

technology that canvas-covered canoes caught on among the white visitors to the north woods.

Instead of continuing to build their canoes by eye, or with a simple building bed that provided basic plan dimensions, as had been used for production of quantities of bark canoes as early as the late eighteenth century, the new builders built their canoes over a solid form, which guaranteed a uniform shape for each new canoe. Builders of European heritage build many types of small craft over forms. In most cases, these forms are sets of cross-sections through the boat, representing different points on the hull. The frames and planking are bent to conform to this general outline. The Peterborough area builders used a solid form, but there is no evidence of direct transfer of this idea from them to the Maine builders. The Maine builders constructed a solid form using the dimensions of the inside of the canoe. Metal bands the width of the ribs are attached to the form at the places where the ribs will fall. The ribs are steamed and bent over the form at these bands and attached to an inwale. The planking is then fastened to the ribs, the copper canoe tacks clinching themselves as they are driven through the planking and ribs and hit the bands. This wooden shell is then removed from the form and canvas stretched tight over it. Finally, the canvas is waterproofed with a thick mixture that traditionally included white lead. When dried and cured, the canoe is painted.

Although it was built in an entirely different fashion than a bark canoe, the new wood-canvas canoe retained the main distinctive features of the birchbark canoe: thin planking over thicker, flat ribs, covered with a flexible material. These elements were assembled in the opposite order to a bark canoe. Instead of the skin being filled by the planking and then the ribs, the ribs of a wood canvas canoe go on first, then the planking and lastly the covering.

Not only did the wood-canvas canoe solve the problem of availability of materials, but it actually improved the craft from the point of view of profit and marketing. Because of the form, an infinite number of canoes of the same shape and size could be built. Because the planking did not have to be fitted watertight, the canoes could be built by workmen of less skill than all-wood canoes like the *Rob Roy*-style cruisers. With simplified construction came lowered prices—just the thing to appeal to the increasing numbers of people wishing to enjoy the outdoors from the seat of a canoe.

ABOVE: Indian Girl model wood-canvas canoe built by J.H. Rushton, Canton, New York, between 1911 and 1916.

BELOW: Wood-canvas canoes under construction in the Canton, New York, shop of J.H. Rushton, circa 1900.

By the 1890s, aspiring "outers" had choices not only in the types of canoes they might use, but in the way they might enjoy the wilderness. While the sports of their father's generation generally hired a local guide, whether it was an Adirondack Yankee rowing a guideboat or a Penobscot Indian paddling a canoe, people looking for a canoe trip in the north woods in the final years of the nineteenth century were increasingly able to "go it alone." That they were able to do so was due in part to the hotels, steamboats and railroads of the post-war era, but also thanks to the writings of "Nessmuk."

Nessmuk was the pen name of George Washington Sears, nominally a shoemaker from Wellsboro, Pennsylvania, but at heart a wanderer. He liked nothing better than to abandon his shoemaker's last and travel the world. By 1880 his travels had taken him to the Amazon and the lumber woods of Michigan, but he was slowing down and planned a trip closer to home. Sears was a small man, standing about five feet, three inches tall and weighing around one hundred and ten pounds. In 1880, when he planned his first Adirondack trip, he was fifty-seven years old, and probably suffering from consumption. He studied the catalogs of a number of different builders, after having tried several other types of boats (some of which he built himself), but finally settled on J.H. Rushton, who was making a specialty of light-weight construction and advertised the smallest, lightest canoes on the market. Even so, Rushton's boats were not light enough for Nessmuk; in 1879 Nessmuk ordered a light canoe to weigh less than twenty pounds—ten pounds lighter than the lightest stock boat Rushton offered at the time. The builder rose to the challenge, however, and the result was the ten-foot-long, seventeen-pound, nine-and-one-half-ounce *Nessmuk*.

Rushton subsequently built four more tiny canoes for Sears. He was a canny businessman, and soon offered "Nessmuk" model canoes in his catalog. The boats were quite popular with the public—and indeed have remained so to the present day. Their popularity puzzled the builder, however. "The trouble is," he wrote to Sears in 1886, "every d—— fool who weighs less than 300 thinks he can use such a canoe too. I get letters asking if the Bucktail will carry two good-sized men and camp duffel and be steady enough to stand up in and shoot out of. I told one fellow that I thought he'd shoot out of it mighty quick if he tried it."

Although they were canoes, and as such direct descendants of the Native craft of North America, in construction and propulsion the Nessmuk canoes were products of European traditions. They were built like

George Washington Sears (1821–90), whose pen-name was "Nessmuk," was a widely read proponent of "going it alone" in a solo canoe. For many years he contributed articles, called "letters," to *Forest and Stream*, describing his adventures exploring the Adirondacks by canoe. His vivid accounts inspired readers to follow his lead and take to the water.

"I hope at no distant day to meet independent canoeists, with canoes weighing twenty pounds or less, at every turn in the wilderness, and with no more duffle than is absolutely necessary."
—George Washington Sears (Nessmuk), in *Forest and Stream*, 1883.

(and probably simply smaller models of) the double-ended lapstrake skiffs of the St. Lawrence Valley, boats used by the Loyalists who moved to the region after the American Revolution. These boats seem to have migrated south; according to Rushton, small canoes eleven to thirteen feet long and typically paddled by two paddlers were common in his childhood. In the 1850s in the northern Adirondacks, however, canoeists paddled their boats with single-bladed paddles, as the Indians had. Nessmuk "modernized" the use of these small canoes; he paddled his with the double-bladed paddle of the Inuit, which he had inherited via the *Rob Roy*-style canoeists. Nessmuk's canoeing style was truly North American, a blend of two different native traditions, each showing the unmistakable mark of European craft and fashion.

As the nineteenth century drew to a close and cities became increasingly crowded and city life more stressful, the outdoors became increasingly more attractive and accessible. And the "outdoors" didn't have to be the deep woods. For many people it was a city park or the nearest shore or riverbank. By the 1890s canoe liveries on the outskirts of Boston and Cambridge on Massachusetts's Charles River and Springfield and Hartford on the Connecticut River were in business renting wood-canvas canoes to hundreds of people each warm-weather weekend, people who took the streetcar out from the city centers to the rivers not to go anywhere in particular, but simply to get out in the fresh air and socialize. Maine canoe

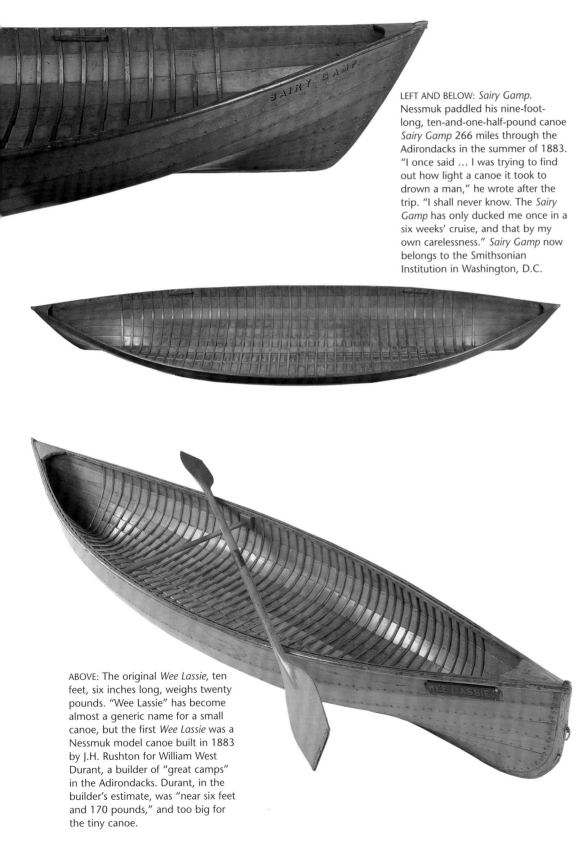

LEFT AND BELOW: *Sairy Gamp*. Nessmuk paddled his nine-foot-long, ten-and-one-half-pound canoe *Sairy Gamp* 266 miles through the Adirondacks in the summer of 1883. "I once said … I was trying to find out how light a canoe it took to drown a man," he wrote after the trip. "I shall never know. The *Sairy Gamp* has only ducked me once in a six weeks' cruise, and that by my own carelessness." *Sairy Gamp* now belongs to the Smithsonian Institution in Washington, D.C.

ABOVE: The original *Wee Lassie*, ten feet, six inches long, weighs twenty pounds. "Wee Lassie" has become almost a generic name for a small canoe, but the first *Wee Lassie* was a Nessmuk model canoe built in 1883 by J.H. Rushton for William West Durant, a builder of "great camps" in the Adirondacks. Durant, in the builder's estimate, was "near six feet and 170 pounds," and too big for the tiny canoe.

builders responded and modified the sleek, fast canoes designed for eating up the miles on the upper reaches of the Penobscot or the Allagash or the lakes along the West Branch, by making them wider and with flatter floors for stability, and by adding sponsons, which were separate air chambers running most of the length of the canoe just beneath the outwales, intended to increase stability. They tacked on exterior keels for help in tracking, seats for both paddlers (or for a paddler and a passenger) and made aesthetic changes such as higher bows, long fancy decks and decorative paint jobs.

J.R. Robertson of Auburndale, Massachusetts, was one of the first builders to build particularly for this recreational market. He was well-versed in the business of building canoes for recreational paddling; he began his career as a workman in the Rushton shop, and even advertised after he had gone out on his own that he had designed "Adirondack Boats and Canoes (Known as Rushton's Portables)." In 1902 he entered a brief but high-profile relationship with a fledgling canoe company in Maine, but by 1903 he had returned to Massachusetts and that company was incorporated under the name it would keep and make almost synonymous with wood-canvas canoe, the Old Town Canoe Company.

The Old Town Canoe Company reflected a new trend in small boat building, and indeed in American business generally. The founders, George and Herbert Gray, were not boatbuilders themselves, but entrepreneurs. They and other members of their family dealt in patent medicine, carbon ink, luggage and hardware, and had interests in several aspects of the lumber business. In 1900 George and Herbert became interested in canoe building as a promising business, and brought Alfred Wickett, an experienced builder, into the picture.

When the Indian Old Town Canoe Company was established in 1900 (the term "Indian" apparently added simply to establish the new company's part in a tradition), there were a number of other builders already well established in Maine building wood-canvas canoes. E.H. Gerrish was probably the earliest, setting up shop in Bangor in 1875. B.N. Morris, upriver from Bangor in Veazie, had begun building boats in 1882. E.M. White, further up in Gilman Falls, had commenced operations in 1888. Gerrish, Morris and White were all builders themselves, and although they became respected names in the business, they didn't have the capital, marketing and management skills that the Gray family swiftly used to make the Old Town Canoe Company the country's leading canoe builder.

The other wood-canvas canoe builders of the northeast did not disappear from the scene, however. No

single American company was able to acquire the patent for the wood-canvas process as Chestnut was able to do in Canada. In New York State the J.H. Rushton company, and then the Penn Yan and Thompson Boat Companies built wood-canvas canoes through the first fifty years of the twentieth century when there was plenty of business to go around.

As there were many choices of canoe, so also backwoods travel got ever more popular and easier. Residents of what the tourist industry now calls "gateway towns" like Old Forge, New York, on the eastern edge of the Adirondack Park, established canoe liveries, from which campers could rent a complete canoe camping outfit with tent, cookware, canoe and paddles, and head off into the woods for a week or two. The most popular routes were so well known, guidebooked and marked that one need not fear getting lost. And if it rained for too many days in a row, or the camper ran out of grub, there was seldom a village too far distant.

Many of the canoe campers of the twentieth century had been introduced to the craft at a children's camp. Many city dwellers who saw an Adirondack canoe trip as a "grand good tonic" for themselves sought a similar draught for their children by sending them to camp for the summer. The theory was that spending a summer in the balsamic air, without the distractions of family or, until the 1920s, the opposite sex, children could grow in health and character away from the "dust, dirt, and dangers" of the city streets. Eighteen camps were established nationwide in the 1890s, one hundred and six between 1900 and 1910, and by 1929 over a million campers attended seven thousand summer camps in the United States, ninety percent of which were in the northeast. In the first three decades of the twentieth century, children's camps aimed to teach woodsmanship and cooperation and build character, as well as give campers plenty of healthy outdoor exercise. Boating accomplished all these aims. The inexpensive, durable and widely available wood-canvas canoe was frequently the choice of the camp director for the character-building watercraft program.

In a report on the boating scene on Lake Placid in the Adirondacks, *MotorBoat* magazine wrote in 1910, "everyone recognizes the necessity of the motorboat and its superiority, but it is interesting to watch the genuine enthusiasm of the old guides and backwoodsmen whenever they see a neatly modeled speed boat cutting through the water. So popular is the gasolene [*sic*] engine becoming that a number of St. Lawrence skiffs and guide boats have been equipped with motors...." The correspondent might also have mentioned that boaters eagerly figured out ways to motorize canoes, as well. As early as 1910 J.H. Rushton offered a wood-canvas canoe with a three-horsepower inboard motor in it. In the 1930s, as outboard motors grew more reliable and cheaper, they became Everyman's choice for motorizing

War canoes, usually built in twenty-five- and thirty-five-foot lengths, were popular at children's camps, where they helped teach teamwork and paddling skills.

canoes. The up-to-date canoeist simple made or purchased a simple thwartships bracket that clamped onto the gunwales at the stern of the boat and hung the outboard off to the side.

The "gasolene" motor in a very different vehicle, the automobile, began to transform patterns of tourism after the First World War. Automobiles gave tourists freedom to travel when they liked, where they liked. The low cost of automobile ownership made recreational travel cheaper and more accessible—just as the railroads and steamboats had for previous generations. And while many of these people came to the north woods to hike or just to see the sights, canoeists used their cars to get them closer to the paddling waters, quicker. It was several decades before vacationers routinely brought their canoes with them on their vacations, however. Until the 1930s car tops wouldn't support the weight of a canoe, so the local liveries continued to thrive.

Over the Memorial Day weekend in 1944, as the Allied Forces in Europe massed for the invasion of Normandy, William J. Hoffman took a short fishing vacation in the Adirondacks. Hoffman was chief tool engineer for the Grumman Aircraft Engineering Corporation, which was busy building aluminum airplanes for the navy. On his Adirondack trip he took his aged thirteen-foot Old Town. After carrying the boat into Squaw Lake from Limekiln and becoming convinced that it weighed considerably more than its advertised fifty pounds, Hoffman decided that what the country would want after winning the war was a lighter canoe. He felt certain that one could be made out of aluminum. When he returned to the factory, he worked up a prototype the same length as his Old Town, but weighing just thirty-eight pounds. The end of the war was in sight, and Hoffman apparently had little trouble convincing Leroy Grumman to plan the switch from producing equipment for war to equipment for recreation. By the end of 1945 Grumman had ninety-five orders for its new aluminum canoe, and within two years Grumman was the nation's largest canoe manufacturer.

At about the same time as Grumman was developing aluminum into the country's most popular material for canoes, other entrepreneurs were adapting fiberglass, another new technology developed in the war effort, to small craft production. Fiberglass had become commercially available in 1948, right after the Second World War, but boatbuilders took a few years to realize the great advantages of the material for watercraft in both production and maintenance: fiberglass was virtually care-free and could be mass-produced by unskilled labor in about one-quarter of the man-hours needed for a wooden boat. In 1960 the Old Town Canoe Company introduced its Rushton model canoe, a ten-and-one-half-foot long fiberglass canoe, with lines inspired by Nessmuk's Bucktail model of 1884.

Post-war prosperity fueled the recreation industry all over the country. Canoe manufacturers began courting not only the traditional audience of those with experience in the out-of-doors, but also a more general public not familiar with small craft. Stability and sturdiness were, to many, more important in a canoe than the fine lines, traditional appearance and handling—characteristics that took experience to appreciate. Price was also a consideration; factory-built aluminum and fiberglass boats were even cheaper than the products of the big wood-canvas building shops. In 1947 a seventeen-foot Old Town Otca model wood-canvas canoe weighed eighty-five pounds and cost $199 in the highest grade. A contemporary Grumman of the same length weighed sixty-seven pounds (fifty-three in the lightweight version) and cost $157.

The trend towards ever cheaper and more "user-friendly" canoes continued with synthetics used for canoe manufacture. In the 1970s the Coleman Company, an outdoor

It wasn't until the mid-1920s that car tops were sturdy enough to carry a canoe. "Automobilists" who wanted to go canoeing had to resort to creative solutions to the problem of transporting their gear to the put-in.

equipment manufacturer known for its camping stoves and picnic coolers, introduced its polyethylene canoe. The Old Town Canoe Company was only one builder that came out with a canoe made of Acrylonitrile Butadiene Styrene (ABS), a hard rubber product that sheathes a layer of foam. Canoeists soon had their choice of these materials, composites and canoes of Kevlar, a DuPont product also used in bulletproof vests. Kevlar and some of the lighter synthetics were also used in construction of racing canoes, the designs of which followed the pattern of the sailing and open paddling canoes of the 1890s in becoming so extreme they were completely unsuitable for ordinary paddling.

Several times every year a small party of canoeists paddles down the West Branch of the Penobscot River in Maine. The canoes are eighteen- and twenty-foot wood-canvas models designed by the E.M. White Company of Old Town. They are loaded with cast-iron and enameled steel cookware, bags of potatoes and onions, and several white canvas wall tents. If the season is late there is also a small sheet-iron stove aboard. The expedition is just like a professionally guided expedition of a century before, but for the bright fleece and nylon clothes of the "sports." The guides are Garrett and Alexandra Conover of Willimantic, who studied woods ways with the Chesuncook guide Mick Fahey and are committed to his style of nineteenth-century guiding—and to doing it in wood-canvas canoes. They feel that the canoes are flexible, maneuvrable, fast, and just nice to paddle. The Conovers are obviously continuing the nineteenth century tradition of canoe travel in the northeastern United States. And across the northeast there are builders and users of bark canoes as well, continuing a tradition going back much farther. But even if modern canoeists paddle an ABS canoe on an overnight trip to the other side of a lake, cooking freeze-dried chili for dinner and sleeping snug in down bags in a nylon dome tent, they are part of the living tradition, as well, a tradition that has perhaps less to do with materials or construction than it does with form and feeling.

Fiberglass, developed as part of the war effort in the 1940s, revolutionized the small-craft manufacturing business. In this photo U.S. Senator Robert Kennedy paddles an early fiberglass whitewater kayak in the Whitewater Derby on the Hudson River, 1967. The kayak was designed and built by Bart Hauthaway of Weston, Massachusetts.

Fast Paddles and Fast Boats

THE ORIGINS OF CANOE RACING

On the afternoon of Saturday, September 1, 1860, Albert Edward, Prince of Wales, and his entourage journeyed out to Victoria Island in the Ottawa River to ride a log raft down the huge timber slide that carried timber around Chaudière Falls. For the nineteen-year-old prince, the ride was a thrilling and dramatic entrance to the waters below the falls, where he was met by a flotilla of one hundred and fifty birchbark canoes manned by lumbermen, brilliantly costumed in scarlet shirts and white trousers. Crowds by the thousands were present to see the young prince and to view the rare event: a lumbermen's regatta organized by the local lumber barons. Prize money was offered for races of approximately a mile

distance, from the moored scow where the royal party was positioned downstream to where the canoes circled a turning buoy then back to the start and finish line.

Reporters wrote of the magnificence of this "sporting event." But if this was sport, it was a dying sport. It was not a manifestation of a burgeoning interest in a sport that attracted both participants as well as spectators. Competitors in the lumbermen's regatta were seasoned veterans of the large bark canoes, whether it be in lumbering or the fur trading industry. Voyageurs, primarily French Canadians and Natives, had crossed the country in huge, thirty-six-foot Montreal canoes from Montreal to the Lakehead, where freight was transferred to smaller,

C. FRED JOHNSTON

twenty-four-foot North canoes for transport to the distant fur-trading posts in the northwest. These traders had to get back to their posts before snow and ice barred their way, while the Montreal canoes, heavily laden with the inland furs, returned to their point of origin at Lachine. The transcontinental canoe trip across Canada was a race against time.

But there was more to the speed of the canoes than meeting a schedule. Voyageurs were proud of their calling and took every opportunity to demonstrate their strength, endurance, skill with the paddle and domination over their peers. Portage sites were likely spots to witness speed play. The first crew to reach the portage controlled the pace; they had the luxury of getting through the portage first, with the best choice of location if the next campsite should be close at hand. Paddling eighteen hours a day at a routine forty strokes a minute was a wearisome, boring activity, particularly on large bodies of water. As crews came together it did not take much encouragement for one crew to break out with a blistering stroke rate and for other crews to make chase.

There were elements of sport incorporated in the regatta on the Ottawa River in 1860; but this event was more pageantry than sport, recalling images of the frontier. While there were still remnants of these passing days in the remote, unsettled regions of North America, few

Lumbermen's Regatta, Ottawa River, 1860. This drawing of the spectacle appeared in the *Illustrated London News*. It was a remarkable feat to assemble so many birchbark canoes, since manufacturing had declined since 1821 when the North West Company merged with the Hudson's Bay Company, marking the beginning of the end of the great fur trade brigades. Before the emergence of organized canoe sport and the adoption of amateur codes governing competition between gentlemen and professionals, there was nothing to preclude friendly tests between sportsmen and the legendary reputations of Native canoemen. Huge lumber mills along the Hull side of the Ottawa River sustained the birchbark canoe's presence near Ottawa. Occasional challenge races between "gentlemen" sportsmen and Native crews sustained the bark canoe's visibility until it was replaced in the 1870s by the white man's carpentered canoe.

TOP: British forces racing with double blades in Mi'kmaq birchbark canoes in Halifax Harbour, 1881. With spare time and the need to maintain top physical condition, British Forces promoted the cause of sport for its forces throughout the British Empire. Here the British troops race in Mi'kmaq birchbark canoes, forfeiting the Native single-blade paddle for the British sportsman's double-blade paddle.

BOTTOM: *Perdita II*, a decked canoe that belonged to Campbell Mellis Douglas (see page 221). The modern Canadian canoe owes much to the development of the racing dugout in the Peterborough region during the period 1840–70, but regretfully very little material evidence of the racing dugout remains. For this reason the *Perdita II* takes on greater significance. *Perdita I* was a dugout canoe fished from the waters of Katchawanooka Lake, north of Lakefield, Ontario, between 1883 and 1893 by Douglas' young sons George and Lionel. The refined lines of the dugout distinguished it from an ancient, primitive craft and the boat was used by Douglas to make a mold from which the hull of *Perdita II* was produced by the Lakefield Canoe Company. The decking was a "contemporary" addition to the lines of the dugout hull. Now at the Canadian Canoe Museum, *Perdita II* remains a reflection of the sophisticated dugouts that plied the waterways of the greater Peterborough region in the mid-nineteenth century.

Emergence of Canoe Sport in Canada 1820–80

The first recorded regatta in Halifax Harbour took place in 1826 on the occasion of the visit of His Excellency, the Earl of Dalhousie, Governor General of Upper and Lower Canada. But the lackluster appeal of the slow-moving cutter races, with crews drawn from the British ships in harbor, was in stark contrast to the enthusiastic response that attended the canoe races staged by the local Mi'kmaqs. In all the regattas during the 1830s, Native races dominated the festivities. Their popularity might account for the trend to small boat races—gigs, wherries, flats and jolly boats. This prompted the change in the regatta site in 1846 from the unpredictable waters of Halifax Harbour to the smooth waters of Lake Banook on the west side of the harbor.

British officers stationed at Halifax in the late 1860s founded the first canoe club in North America, the Chebucto Canoe Club. It was operational in 1869 when the Canoe Club in England extended an invitation to a Canadian paddler to compete for the World Canoe Championships. Like the mother club in England, the Chebucto Club was a cruising club. They used birchbark canoes acquired from local Native people and the occasional decked *Rob Roy* canoe that accompanied military personnel on their tour of duty.

Lacking a Native settlement in the immediate vicinity, aquatic sports in the community of Toronto were dominated by yachting and rowing. Despite continuous regatta activity from 1839, a paddling race did not appear on the program of the Toronto Rowing Club until the 1870s. The appearance of canoe races at that time can be accounted for by the emergence of a new type of craft, the "modern" Canadian canoe.

Canoeing was a common sight about Montreal, going back to the days when Lachine, located above the rapids of the same name, was the embarkation point for the canoe brigades of the North West Company. Canoeing skills and traditions nurtured in the fur trade were sustained by the Iroquois voyageurs who lived on the

reserves of Kahnawake, across the St. Lawrence from Montreal, and Kanesatake, on the Lake of the Two Mountains. The military garrison at St.-Jean on the Richelieu River, south of Montreal, organized regattas in the late 1830s. The St.-Jean Boat Club organized its first regatta in 1840 and competed at a Montreal regatta in 1844. With the canoeing tradition in the Lachine area and its growing popularity as a summer retreat for affluent Montrealers, it was understandable that this community should be attracted to aquatic sports. The first Lachine Regatta took place on Saturday, September 3, 1864, and was reported in *The Montreal Gazette* two days later. Six races were on this first program: single scull, sailing, four-oared, double scull and two canoe races, one for Native men and one for "squaws." Little is written about canoes used by the Native competitors, except that they were made of wood; there is nothing about their size, form or method of construction. Native canoe races became the highlight of the annual regattas at Lachine.

By 1880 modern canoe racing was a minor sport, tenuously established on the regatta programs of the majority of aquatic clubs; but it was a minor activity compared with rowing, which dominated the five general purpose boating clubs that were formed in the Montreal area in the 1860s and 1870s: Lachine (1864), Longueuil (1867), Grand Trunk (1875), Ste.-Anne (1878) and Pointe Claire (1879). It was the Native peoples from the Kahnawake and Kanesatake reserves who popularized

canoe racing, preparing the way for a different kind of canoe, a wooden canoe built along the lines of the traditional birchbark. This was another "civilized" canoe but quite different from the *Rob Roy* that MacGregor popularized from his base in England.

Origins of the "Modern" Canadian Canoe, 1850–75

In the backwoods region of the Otonabee Valley in Ontario, the Native concept of the canoe was subjected to the industrial technology of European culture, and the product was the modern, open Canadian canoe. British settlers moved into the region in the early 1820s. Isolated and dependent upon the river as highway, settlers had a choice of three different watercraft: a birchbark canoe made by the local Mississaugas; a log dugout, also used by the Native peoples; and a wooden plank canoe.

North of Peterborough, in the vicinity of the village of Lakefield, George and Robert A. Strickland, sons of Samuel Strickland, a prominent settler in the Lakefield community, transformed the log canoe into a racing machine. A modest challenge, a tandem match race in 1854 on Katchewanookah Lake between the Strickland brothers and the team of Matt Young and A. Edmonson, initiated a battle on the water. The Stricklands had produced a log canoe eighteen feet long and twenty-five inches wide, described by Robert in an article for *Forest and Stream* in 1888 as "a great improvement over the former canoes ... it was both fast and steady," due to the

ACA Meet of 1881, Canoe Islands, Lake George. Base camp for the founding meeting of 1880 had been at Crosbyside Park, at the south end of Lake George. To insure a more appropriate environment in the future, Nathaniel Bishop, supported by Judge Nicholas Longworth and Lucien Wulsin of the Cincinnati Canoe Club, purchased and took possession of three small islands in Lake George on August 21, 1880, to be used as a "home" for the ACA meet. Lorna Island, the largest of the three Canoe Islands, was selected as meet headquarters for 1881. At this second meet the three Canadian clubs—ten paddlers representing Peterborough, Ottawa and Toronto—were led by E.B. Edwards, Captain of the Peterborough Boating Club. Here the leadership of the ACA is assembled at the "Council Wigwam," fronted by a decked sailing canoe on the left and two "Canadians" on the right.

TOP: Paddling Race, ACA Camp, Jessup's Neck, Long Island, New York, 1890. The superiority of the double blade over the single-blade paddle had now been established. A "shell" was replacing the traditional open Canadian canoe. There was experimentation with technique, such as paddling from a standing position.

form of the hull. The Native log canoe retained the basic round shape of a tree and was said to be cranky to paddle and downright dangerous to shoot from when used for hunting; the Stricklands flattened the bottom of the canoe hull to take the "crank" out of it. That race, won by the Strickland brothers, prompted a canoe designing and building competition over the next ten years that produced successively longer and narrower dugouts, culminating in *Lightning*, a tandem canoe, thirty-three feet long and seventeen inches wide.

The formative regatta was held on Little Lake at Peterborough, September 23–24, 1857, where John Stephenson engaged in the competition in the log canoe, *Comet*. Henry Thomas Strickland, the brother of George and Robert, acting as regatta secretary, wrote in 1884 in *The American Canoeist* (the publication of the American Canoe Association) that John, at this regatta "first conceived the idea of building the Canadian bass wood canoe, of which he built several in the spring and summer of 1858." By 1861, modern, "improved" wooden canoes, rib-and-batten in structure, with carvel-constructed, basswood planks, were being turned out on uniform molds from the shops of John Stephenson, Thomas Gordon and Dan Herald. But it would take ten years for the modern Canadian canoe to drive the elegant racing dugout from the annual regattas in the Peterborough/Lakefield/Rice Lake region. This new boat on the water began to work its way into the competitive programs of the aquatic clubs that developed in the 1870s in the waterfront communities of Dartmouth-Halifax, Montreal Island, Toronto and other urban centers throughout central and eastern Canada. As in so many human endeavors, the quest for speed proved to be a significant stimulus to technological development. Certainly the emergence of the modern Canadian canoe owes much to those innovative racers in their log canoes and the canoe builders who dabbled in racing.

The American Canoe Association, 1880–1900

A meeting of canoeists at Lake George in the Adirondack Mountains of upper New York State in the summer of 1880 led to the formation of the American Canoe Association, an organization that was to have a dynamic impact on the organization and development of canoeing in the United States, Canada and even Great Britain.

"The Call" for the Canoe Congress, endorsed by twenty-four canoeing enthusiasts, largely from northeastern United States, was sent out under the hand of Nathaniel Holmes Bishop, a man of independent means, who summered on Lake George in upper New York State. As recorded in the American Canoe Association Constitution, the Congress at Lake George in 1880 called for an organization of "persons of respectable character, of any age, who possess a true love of nature, and are in earnest sympathy with the brotherhood of cruising canoeists." The intention was to connect these individuals with newly formed local clubs to stimulate contests of canoeing skills. But somewhere between "The Call" and the distribution of the constitution in 1881, the plan for a national association gave way to an "American" canoe association, which was meant to include the vast territory of Canada. And it was taken for granted that membership was to be associated with the ownership of a canoe: one man, one canoe. That was the vision in the beginning.

It was not a simple task for the founders of the ACA to take existing boats and organize and classify them on the basis of functional design for racing purposes. Within the founder's group there appears to have been some unorganized vision of what the association was to be all about: small, manageable boats propelled by sail and paddle combined in a variety of ways; an adventurous, physically active lifestyle (but not too strenuous, particularly when the boat was under sail); eating and sleeping in the out of doors (but not necessarily all the time). Their concept of canoeing was very much molded by the literary images created by John MacGregor.

Coming up with a workable boat classification system for the first meet was not too difficult. The organizers for the meet in 1880, who weren't entirely sure what kind of boats would appear at the founding meeting, categorized boats for racing purposes into five general classes, based on canoe models then in use:

Class I. Paddling canoes propelled only by paddle such as the birchbark or *Rice Laker.*

Class II. Sailable paddling canoes in which paddling qualities dominate, such as the *Rob Roy.*

Class III. Sailing and paddling canoes with qualities equally divided, such as the *Shadow, No. 3 Nautilus, Jersey Blue,* etc.

Class IV. Paddleable sailing canoes with the sailing qualities predominate, such as the *Pearl.*

Class V. Sailing canoes, not for cruising, such as the *Nautilus 5* and *6.*

BOTTOM FACING PAGE: ACA Camp, Grindstone Island, St. Lawrence River, 1884. On the starting line for the One-Mile Canoe Race for canoes not over sixteen feet in length, not less than twenty-six inch beam. Left to right: M. Fisk Johnston, Toronto, J.L. Weller and Frank Adams, both of Peterborough. Racing rules prescribed specifications of the boat but the paddle was the choice of the paddler. Johnston, paddling from a high sitting position, used a double blade, the other two, single blades. Johnston won the race in 10:34; Weller was second in a very respectable 10:44.

BELOW: Toronto Canoe Club, The Harbour, 1906. In 1893 this magnificent Victorian aquatic building was built, the toast of the Toronto Harbour waterfront. There was no canoe clubhouse like this one anywhere else in North America. No wonder the TCC attracted young gentlemen from the very best families of Toronto society and dominated Canadian canoe racing in the period before the First World War.

Robert Tyson seated in his canoe *Isabel*, 1886. An avid cruising canoeist and a correspondent with Nathaniel Bishop, Robert Tyson was a primal force in the establishment of the Toronto Canoe Club and the first Toronto paddler to attend an ACA meet, in 1881 at Lake George. Here Tyson sits in his canoe with his sails set, getting ready to move his boat out into the St. Lawrence River from the meet center on Grindstone Island.

While races could be organized around a boat classification, it was more important to make provision for competition between classes.

Two Canadians heeded "The Call" and journeyed to Lake George in 1880. Robert W. Baldwin, an employee of the federal government, made the trip from Ottawa to Lake George in a *Rob Roy* canoe recently purchased from the Governor General of Canada, Lord Dufferin. Representing the Canadian school of canoeing was a hunting and fishing guide from Rice Lake, Ontario: Thomas Henry Wallace. Because canoes were classified for competition according to primary design features, Wallace had some difficulty fitting into the program with his open canoe, which was constructed by Dan Herald of Rice Lake and propelled with a single-blade paddle. It became obvious that organizers had not anticipated that there would be many Class I boats in camp at Lake George. Notwithstanding the fact that the other boats in camp were decked canoes and, no doubt, heavier than Wallace's Herald canoe, he was allowed to race against them in two races: the race for paddling canoes and in the open race for all types of canoes, including sailable paddleable canoes, one of the feature races. Winning a paddling race against decked canoes with double blades was unexpected but there was widespread acknowledgement and appreciation of Wallace's skill with the single blade. In the open race, lack of wind

disadvantaged the sailing and paddleable canoes, enabling Wallace to win a victory over his more sophisticated sporting adversaries. To have him smoking his pipe as he raced down the course did not endear him to his competitors.

Aside from the problem posed by the Canadian canoe, problems developed with the perceived fairness of time allowances on some sailable canoes in paddling races and paddleable canoes in sailing races, which was essential for competition between canoes from different canoe classes. A review of the technical rules governing competitions became an annual exercise for whoever was responsible for the annual meet.

Canadians responded enthusiastically to the ACA. The first membership from Canada in 1881 was that of Elihu Burril Edwards, a Peterborough barrister, a member of the Peterborough Boating Club and an acquaintance of Nathaniel Bishop, who became member number five. Edwards was followed by number sixty-seven, Robert Tyson, an avid canoe sailor from Toronto and a prime mover in the formation of the Toronto Canoe Club in December 1880.

At the 1881 meet, the Canadian delegations from Ottawa, Toronto and Peterborough represented a substantial bloc of the fifty paddlers in camp. On August 13 the reporter for *The New York Times*, observing the arrival of the Peterborough representatives, commented on the Canadian canoes that were: "... wholly different than ours and carry no sail. They are propelled entirely by the paddles and the paddle has only a single blade, instead of a double one, as the Americans have.... Their boats are the perfection of strength in canoe building; but our American canoeists want a boat to sail and one they can live in when on a long cruise."

Canadians fared well at Lake George this second year. Predictably, they won the Open Hunting Canoe race, and E.B. Edwards was elected vice-commodore.

A man who was to severely test the ACA rules and patience of the organizers throughout the decade of the 1880s, was M. Fisk Johnston. A young, inexperienced paddler from the Toronto Canoe Club when he attended his first ACA meet in 1882, he could do no better than win the one-mile paddling race in the Junior class. At that, he had to forfeit his victory because he was unaware that a previous victory in a Toronto Club race had undermined his Junior status. H.B. Weller of Peterborough opened a few eyes when he won the open Junior sailing race in an open Stephenson canoe "using a lateen-rigged sail and steered with a single-blade paddle instead of a rudder," as reported in *The Toronto Mail*

on August 10, 1882. That result complicated the common perception of the open Canadian; it was more than just a paddling canoe.

After having the first three meets at Lake George in the Adirondack Mountains of New York State, pressure mounted to move the annual meeting to other sites to allow ACA members from regions remote from Lake George to attend. With that decision, it was only proper that the camp for 1883 should go to Stony Lake, north of Peterborough in the "true wilderness" of Ontario, the home of the first Canadian commodore of the ACA, E.B. Edwards. The task of reconciling technical problems from 1882 for the 1883 meet was left to the new commodore and Robert Tyson, the canoe sailor from Toronto.

By this time, the annual technical review began to focus in on a very basic problem. After the Stony Lake meet, E.B. Edwards and Robert Tyson attempted to explain in *The American Canoeist* the complexity of the task that confronted them. "We were at our wits' ends how to reconcile in one definition or class the totally conflicting requirements of a paddling race and of a sailing race." Tyson, in exasperation, succinctly targeted what he considered to be the root of the problem: the conflicting pressures from the canoe paddlers, who promoted reducing the beam of the canoes to create a faster paddling canoe, and the canoe sailors, who advocated increasing the beam of their canoes to get a faster sailing canoe. The rules governing competition at Stony Lake failed to resolve the problem. At the time, Edwards and Tyson were not aware that the Royal Canoe Club of England had resolved the conundrum with a rather practical and simple solution, an acknowledgement that there is no such thing as an "all-round canoe" in the Royal Canoe Club Races. "Canoes in the paddling classes will not come into the sailing classes and vice versa," wrote Tyson in *The American Canoeist* in November 1884.

The Stony Lake Camp of 1883 was unlike the camps on Lake George. The only amenities at Stony Lake were the goods available at the store that had been installed on Juniper Island. It was impossible at Stony to combine the luxury of hotel life with the rousing fun of the campsite, as was the case at Lake George.

Fisk Johnston from the Toronto Canoe Club was able to enter and win the Junior paddling race in 1883 as a result of a change in the definition of Junior. For this race all paddlers used a single blade, except Johnston, who used a double blade. Questions arose from the 1883 camp that did not relate to the boat as much as to the paddle.

Initiating the annual technical debate was a Canadian from Toronto, Campbell Mellis Douglas, who joined the ACA in 1883 so that he might participate in the Great Canoe Meet at Stony Lake. Born in 1840 on Grosse Isle, in the St. Lawrence River below Quebec City, he was the son of Dr. George Douglas, medical superintendent of the island's Quarantine Station located downriver from Quebec City. Douglas studied medicine in Scotland,

At headquarters for the Stony Lake Meet of the ACA's Northern Division, 1887. Because it was not always convenient for some ACA members to get to the annual meet, the organization of regional associations was recognized in 1886, so that regional meets might be held when the annual ACA meet was remote. In 1887 Canadian clubs formed the second regional association, the Northern Division of the ACA. It held its first meet in 1887, returning to Stony Lake, the site of the Third ACA meet. Formation of the Northern Division and the introduction of annual Division meets in Canada did much to attract new Canadian members to the Association.

meet on Grindstone Island in the St. Lawrence River to challenge the best America had to offer.

Robert W. Gibson in *Vesper* and E.H. Barney in *Pecowsic*, selected to defend ACA honor, soundly defeated their British visitors, coming in first and second. The verdict of sailing connoisseurs was that the *Pecowsic* was a superior canoe to *Vesper*, but Gibson was a superior sailor to Barney. For his victory Gibson won the new ACA Sailing Challenge Trophy, paid for by public subscription to initiate the challenge race with the Brits. The race resolved the question as to the superiority of the American or the British schools of canoe sailing. It was a victory for the smaller and lighter American boats. But in victory, there was also an element of defeat; the win signaled a triumph for a specialized racing canoe over the general purpose cruising canoe that was popular in Britain as well as the sentimental favorite of the majority of American canoe sailors.

Pecowsic had a smooth skinned hull with a suite of five interchangeable standing sails, each designed for different sailing conditions. As well as differences in the sailing canoe, Americans had modified sailing technique. They sailed from a high seating position, which made it possible to control the boat by shifting their bodies. More revolutionary was the innovation of the sliding seat, which allowed the sailor to hike outside the hull—and still control rudder and sail—to achieve the effect of a wider beam and greater stability under sail. To the emerging paddling racing machine was added the sailing machine. After having created the Record Trophy in 1884 to reward and stimulate the canoeing generalist, the introduction of a dedicated Sailing Trophy Race in 1886 profiled the racing sailor.

Atwood Manley, the biographer for the canoe builder Henry Rushton, marked the significance of the event for the ACA. "Eighteen-eighty-six marked a crest in the popularity of the decked wooden cruiser adapted both to sailing and paddling and requiring materials and craftsmanship of high quality. Over the next decade, the decked wooden canoe was to evolve as a specialized racer. And racing was for the few."

In 1889, the clubs in Canada that formed the Northern Division were responsible for selecting the site and planning the annual meet. The formation of sub-regions within the ACA was a consequence of criticisms from ACA members who were not conveniently located to take advantage of the annual meet. In 1886, an Eastern Division of the United States was formed, followed in 1887 by a Northern Division, which included all of Canada. The Canadian Division, as host for 1889, went all out to plan and execute an improved annual meet.

A frivolous novelty at the 1889 ACA camp at Stave Island in the St. Lawrence River was a large open Canadian canoe, thirty feet long and inappropriately referred to as a "war canoe" because of its size. Built for the Toronto Canoe Club by the Ontario Canoe Company of Peterborough, the *Unk-ta-hee* ("Lord of the water") was an imposing sight: crimson-red on the blue water, framed by the forest-green landscape. Sixteen paddlers wielding single-blade paddles and wearing whimsical triangular hats, manned the huge "club" canoe, which caught the attention and imagination of meet participants from the United States and Canada. Over the winter months a building spree took place and by spring it was rumored that five war canoes would be at the meet in summer of 1890, at Jessup's Neck, Long Island, New York: Toronto's *Unk-ta-hee* and four others from the northeast United States. Unfortunately, only one canoe was able to overcome the transportation complications and actually make the meet: the huge thirty-five-foot *Ko-ko-ko-ho* from the Yonkers Canoe Club, New York City. It proved to be as much a hit on the salt waters as the Toronto canoe was on the St. Lawrence the year before.

But there was something insidious and subversive about the effect of the big canoe; like a Trojan Horse, the club canoe attacked the "one man, one boat" principle of membership that was fundamental to the structure of the ACA. Throughout central Canada, clubs in Montreal, Ottawa, along the St. Lawrence River and in Toronto invested in a boat that was owned by the club or a group within the club, and not by an individual member. It now became possible to join a club and to paddle without the burden of ownership of a private, personal canoe. Without doubt, the innovation had a democratizing effect on club memberships and it had another, more subtle effect: new members to the club were directed to the war canoe where they learned single-blade and not double-blade paddling. Because Canadians were more attracted to the war canoe and that community was more concentrated than in the United States, its introduction increased the differences between the two schools of canoeing. At virtually any regatta in Canada, war canoe events proved to be the most exciting races on the regatta programs; club rivalries enhanced training for conditioning and renewed interest in technique and style, focusing on any factor that might bring victory. The impact was felt in the individual clubs first, but eventually it reached the ACA proper.

And in 1889 Fisk Johnston, as usual, came to camp with a new canoe, the *Adair*, facetiously described in

Forest and Stream the following September as "a nominal sailing craft ... of matchbox construction, brought out for the paddling races, a shell of the flimsiest sort, built of stuff little thicker than vaneer [sic] with decks and side decks so light that they were badly broken in ordinary racing use." As questionable as the quality of the canoe was, the *Adair*, made for Johnston by the English Canoe Company of Peterborough, managed to win two races for decked Class II and III canoes, and more importantly, the Paddling Trophy Race.

Paddlers had pressured the officers of the Association to institute a Trophy Race for paddlers to match the Trophy Race for canoe sailors that was introduced in 1886. The first Paddling Trophy Race was run on Lake George in 1888. The new race brought forth a cornucopia of nautical creativity that impacted on boat design, style and technique. Two blade wielders from Springfield rose to the occasion to challenge Johnston for what he thought was to be his victory. Johnston's new boat for 1888 was *Bonnie*, an open Canadian with decks at the bow and stern. (Americans over time would call these Canadian racing shells "peanuts.") Johnston stood upright in the canoe, "using two paddles spliced together to make a twelve-foot blade, and stooped forward at the beginning of the stroke, to all appearances working very much harder than his antagonist." (*Forest and Stream*, August 30, 1888.) *Agawa*, paddled by E.C. Knappe of Springfield Canoe Club, Massachusetts, took Johnston at the start but he also was passed by *Narka*, paddled by H.E. Rice, also from Springfield. Rice was a new man at the summer meet, "the latest star among paddling racers ... who uses a fourteen-foot blade, standing in his canoe." (*Forest and Stream*, August 23, 1888) Paddling from a standing position had been around since time immemorial; Native peoples had paddled from a standing position in bark canoes. While more challenging to stand and paddle in a light racing canoe, it was conceded that as long as balance could be maintained, the speed was far greater than in the traditional sitting position. Johnston was able to overtake Knappe but not Rice, and he collapsed in exhaustion and defeat in the bottom of the boat as he crossed the finish line. Rice was the first winner of the Paddling Trophy Race.

The significance Johnston attached to the second running of this race in 1889 was understandable and he was not disappointed. Victory was sweet on the water, but he was less successful when the Regatta Committee assembled to consider an appeal lodged by a competitor against Johnston's canoe, *Adair*. The Committee ruled the *Adair* was not a properly fitted decked sailing canoe and therefore ineligible to compete and win. The second Paddling Trophy victory went to another Canadian,

Unk-ta-hee, Lord of the Waters, thirty-foot open canoe, Stave Island, St. Lawrence River, 1889. This was a unique canoe for the ACA but not for its manufacturer, the Ontario Canoe Company. For some time it had produced large, heavy-duty canoes for special situations such as government surveys and exploration expeditions. This canoe, built to order for the Toronto Canoe Club, was a lighter version of these special purpose freighter canoes, on the scale of an oversized sixteen-foot canoe. The large club canoes were facetiously referred to as "war canoes" because of their size and the numbers of paddlers they would hold. Eventually war canoe became a respectable name for this boat, which was very popular in racing clubs as well as boys and girls summer camps.

War canoe race at Lachine, Quebec, 1892. At the meet of 1886, the St. Louis Club, taking advantage of the long tradition of Native "war canoe" racing at Lachine regattas, borrowed two canoes from the local bands so that gentleman paddlers might race in the big canoes. The excitement and popularity of the thirteen-man Native canoe races soon spread to other canoe clubs. The number of clubs in the Montreal area guaranteed the success of war canoe racing in that region. Here on the Lachine waterfront in 1892, local clubs vie for local honors. Little did the Native paddlers from that first regatta in 1864 realize the contribution they would make to the adoption of a big club boat into Canadian paddling.

use the open canoe with single blade would not only increase the use of the open canoe at the annual meet, it would also result in a fairer canoe race for decked cruising canoes in a paddling race, pitting a lighter open canoe with single blade against a heavier decked canoe with double blade.

Between December 1886 and March 1887, Will MacKendrick argued against the proposal in a series of letters with Robert W. Gibson, published in *Forest and Stream*. The demise of the single blade happened because the ACA failed to provide races for single-blade paddlers. To MacKendrick, it was that simple. Paddlers who wished to keep to the front of the pack in paddling races had little choice but to adopt the double-blade paddle. Requiring a paddler in an open canoe to use the single blade was just another way of handicapping the versatile open canoe. Moreover, he did not believe the intent of the change would be achieved, because anyone who wanted to win a paddling race could deck over the open canoe with cotton, canvas or cedar and then qualify the boat as a decked canoe eligible for use with a double-blade paddle. While the intent of the recommendation was to promote the use of the single-blade paddle, it did so as a handicap in order to equalize racing between decked and open canoes. The consequence of the rule change would be to drive the open canoe out of the racing program.

Perceptively, MacKendrick realized that the future of the open Canadian canoe in the ACA was in jeopardy.

His advice to the Committee at the time, if it wished to resolve boat problems in general and the open canoe problem in particular, was to identify or confirm the canoe type or class the ACA was advocating to the membership and then take a serious look at the canoe specifications for each class that was to be supported in the program. Developments between 1887 and 1897 confirmed his analysis of the problem, with detrimental consequences for single-blade paddling and the open Canadian canoe as a result of the 1887 rule change. Not until 1897, as the country slowly emerged from the throes of the depression, did the ACA tackle the problem of the continuing decline in the use of the open canoe and the single blade.

John N. MacKendrick, the third of the MacKendrick brothers, was elected commodore of the ACA for 1897. Given his canoeing heritage and his family background it was not surprising that he tackled issues associated with the Canadian canoe and single-blade paddling on the ACA program. The problem was dealt with in two stages. For 1897 the Technical Committee avoided structural rule changes, favoring instead the adoption of a program of races that effectively isolated open canoes from decked canoes in competition; single-blade paddlers were not required to race against paddlers in decked canoes with double blades. Manipulation of the program bought time. Throughout 1897, meetings were held within the divisions to explore more substantive rule changes. The Northern Division of Canada played a significant role in generating the recommendations for rule changes that were eventually considered and adopted by the Technical Committee for implementation in 1898.

The Technical Committee, with responsibility for the rules and program for 1898, adopted the advice given by Will MacKendrick in 1887. Real change had to start with the specifications of the canoes the Association wished to promote in the sport.

To take advantage of the emerging popularity of the open Canadian canoe, the Committee for the 1898 meet proposed a change that would reverse the line of development of the open paddling racing canoe, which had a mandated beam of no less than twenty-six inches, replacing it with a canoe sixteen feet in length with a minimum beam of thirty inches and half an inch of variance allowed in measurement. This change clearly represented a return to the traditional, general purpose open Canadian that canoeists were purchasing "off the shelf" throughout Canada and the United States. The change was intended to undermine the ongoing development of the paddling "racing machines" and make the general purpose open Canadian canoe a class boat for competition. It remained to be seen how competitor and builder would react to the new specifications for the open canoe.

Acknowledging the problems of four-in-a-boat crews trying to race in a sixteen-foot tandem canoe, the Northern Division recommended (and it was accepted by Committee) that specifications be conservatively set for a fours canoe at a length of twenty feet, a beam of thirty inches and a depth of twelve inches.

And finally the Committee tacked the war canoe problem, which had become more frustrating and troublesome with each passing year. Following the introduction of the *Unk-ta-hee* in 1889, club boats were purchased throughout the ACA, more so perhaps in Canada than in the United States. Mr. Barney, writing to *Forest and Stream* in December 1891, waxed eloquently on the dramatic impact war canoe racing could have on the ACA. "Anyone who has seen a war canoe like the *Unk-ta-hee*, the *Ko-ko-ko-ho* or the *Mohican* underway can form an idea of what a race would be with four of these canoes, manned by seventeen men each, the crews uniformed in bright colors and the big single blades flashing." Barney called for the adoption of boats of the same size and model. The only occasion when two war canoes were in camp at the same time

between 1889 and 1897 was in 1891 when two canoes took to the water, one the thirty-foot *Mohican* with a crew of thirteen and the other the twenty-foot *Googoozenia* from the Puritan club, with a crew of six. The failure to establish the war canoe as a class boat with uniform specifications throughout the ACA was having a disastrous impact on the development of crew boat racing at a critical time in the Association's history.

The Northern Division lobbied for a thirty-five-foot war canoe with a crew of fifteen; others, notably those in the eastern United States, lobbied for a smaller boat, preferably thirty feet long, because anything larger could not be easily transported in a railway boxcar. The Committee's compromise set the length of all new war canoes at thirty feet with a maximum crew of fifteen. However, existing thirty-five-footers could continue to be used.

Between the announcement of the new specs for the open Canadian canoe and springtime, the William English Canoe Company was offering for sale a new open canoe, sixteen feet in length, with a beam of twenty-nine-and-a-half inches. Reporting on the meet of 1898 in August of that year in *Forest and Stream*, W.P. Stephens commented on the new class of boat, which did not turn out exactly as the planners had anticipated. The boat came out in two models: a service model and a racing model. The service model, which had been available for

Brockville, Ontario, on Regatta Day, circa 1900. Three clubs, none of them canoe clubs, were involved with canoe racing in Brockville: the Brockville Rowing Club, the Bohemian Amateur Athletic Association and the Brockville Young Men's Christian Association. What engaged young men from the three clubs was a common interest in war canoe racing, a team and canoeing event. Around the turn of the century, war canoe racing in Brockville was a popular spectator sport that brought out the whole community, hence its selection as the site for the first Canadian National Canoe Championships in 1900.

War canoe race, Kelowna, British Columbia, 1910, on the turn. Ostensibly a national association in 1900, the Canadian Canoe Association was restricted to the provinces of Ontario and Quebec. In 1909 a war canoe racing community developed in splendid isolation in the Okanagan Valley in the interior of British Columbia. War canoe events on the Okanagan lakes raced with a turn at the halfway point, allowing spectators to see both the start and the finish of the race. What few spectators saw away from the crowds was the classical "Canadian turn" executed by a fifteen-man war canoe. Many a war canoe race was won and lost at the turn. Here the Kelowna Fire Brigade crew turns the flag: stroke left reaches to the right for a bow plug while the second right reaches out assisting in the turn with a hanging draw; while rights combine sweeps with draws, lefts combine back strokes and draws.

some time, had a "rockered keel, rounded ends below water (to facilitate turning), graceful sweep of bow and stern, flat floor amidship." The new canoe had a keel "practically straight from end to end, the least possible rocker, full right angles where keel joins stem and stern." While Stephens admitted "such a canoe is fit for straight-away race course" he also said, "For the present, at least, the new class will tend to revive racing...." And it did. Within a year several canoe manufacturing businesses in Canada—William English and the Canadian Canoe Company in Peterborough, and the Capital Boat Works in Ottawa—were turning out their versions of the ACA-approved, sixteen-foot open racing canoe for both single-blade and double-blade paddling as well as the approved twenty-foot racing fours. The same sixteen-foot canoe was to be used for singles and tandem paddling.

The program now began to take on some semblance of practicality as well as rationality. A subtle, but significant change in the single-blade events (single-blade singles and single-blade tandem), was the absence of any reference to canoe designation (such as "open" or "decked") in labeling the event. The kind of paddles used with the fours was left open, but the only ones ever used in the fours were single blades. It was assumed racers would use the new William English open racing canoe for these races. The Committee also added two races for decked canoes: One Man Paddling and Two Men Paddling. But there were no entries for these races.

Additional positive effects of the changes were to be confirmed the following year at Hay Island on the St. Lawrence River when the new open racing shell was favorably accepted for both double-blade and single-blade singles races. As a consequence there was no need to designate paddling races by boat; designation by paddle was all that was necessary. Moreover, the resolution of the longstanding boat problems that had confounded the paddling program of the ACA in the singles paddling events, would serve as a template for similar decisions dealing with tandem and fours racing. The way was open for separation of tandem and fours events into separate single-blade and double-blade races when interest and numbers warranted.

The specifications for the racing shell adopted by the ACA in 1898 was to serve both the ACA and the soon-to-be established Canadian Canoe Association well into the twentieth century. Not until the 1950s was the Canadian racing shell, the "peanut," replaced by boats that adhered to specifications developed by the International Canoe Federation.

The war canoe races in 1899 aroused an enthusiastic response never before seen at an ACA meet. Seven war canoes, all from the Northern Division, turned up to race at the meet. The request to hold the war canoe races on the first day, August 14, was agreed to, although the old timers lamented the way the "racers" changed things to suit their purposes. Seven crews, all from Canada, journeyed to Hay Island to race: two crews from Brockville, the Rowing Club and the Bohemian Club; two from Ottawa, Britannia and the Ottawa Canoe Club; the Dorval Juniors from Montreal; the Toronto Canoe Club and the Kingston Yacht Club. No ACA camp had ever seen 105 paddlers on the water at one time. The regatta at Hay Island attracted hundreds of spectators in canoes, skiffs and yachts, which lined the course to watch the great war canoe race.

Before the race could begin, the Committee was required to meet to contend with visible anomalies. The Brockville Rowing Club had metal steering fins attached to the hull of its canoe. Deemed to be an unfair advantage, the illegal fins were ordered removed before the race. And while there was concern by paddlers from a number of canoes about the boat to be used by the Rowing Club, nothing could be done to prevent them from racing. The oarsmen from Brockville brought to camp a new war canoe that was not of the "cruising type." This canoe, built by Mr. Gilbert of Brockville was "light, well cut away at the ends, and with a turtleback deck forward, a straight sheer and full lines of the bow … giving the appearance of a torpedo boat," reported *Forest and Stream* in August 1899. This was a racing war canoe, a very big racing machine! But the oarsmen did not walk away with the race by any means. The steersman of the Brockville Rowing Club boat, minus its fins, had a very difficult time steering his boat, crossing the course and fouling several of the crews that were well back, out of contention. The Bohemians with the short blades executed very fast, short strokes, which brought them to the finish line ahead of the Britannias of Ottawa, followed by the Dorval Juniors from Montreal. A second race for Northern Division crews only, this time a half-mile race that included a turn, was again won by the Bohemians and proved their first win no accident.

There is little doubt that the presence of seven war

canoe crews in camp resulted in additional entries in single-blade singles, tandem and fours races; and there was even a good field in the double-blade singles race. "Altogether these were the greatest canoe events ever held," complimented the Special Reporter to *The Commercial Advertiser*. With 329 registered paddlers in camp, many of the officials were ecstatic. But some of the old timers were not impressed with the large registration of paddlers, particularly when the majority left after the war canoe races. They had no commitment to the sport or to the association.

At the business meeting in 1899, the ACA selected William MacKendrick as its next commodore for 1900, to take the Association into the twentieth century. He had been a prominent competitor and a leader within the ACA since 1885, when he initiated his membership. MacKendrick would have to contend with rumors that some Canadian clubs were of the opinion that they should set up their own association, a Canadian canoe association that would be independent of the American Canoe Association.

Britannia War Canoe Crew Champions of Canada, 1906. The Britannia Boat House Club was situated on the Ottawa River on Britannia-on-the-Bay, just west of Ottawa. The club was not involved with the American Canoe Association, in part because it was founded in 1891 as a general boating club where sailing, rather than canoe sailing, was a popular activity. But during the 1890s Britannia became a very competitive canoe racing club, with exclusively single-blade paddling in singles, tandems, fours and especially war canoes. Britannia was an active force in the formation of a separate Canadian canoe association.

Decked sailing canoe, fifteen feet, one inch long, thirty-four inches wide, 1890. Canoe sailing in both Canada and the United States became very popular at the end of the nineteenth century. This craft, *L'Hirondelle*, is a decked sailing canoe built in about 1890 by the Ontario Canoe Company of Peterborough. It is built of red cedar in the cedar-rib style with walnut decking, chrome-plated brass hardware and a Radix folding fan centerboard that is worked by a lever. The canoe combines the traditional shape of the Canadian open canoe with decking that is usually associated with American sailing canoes. This kind of all-purpose open cruising canoe, for use with sail or paddle, has virtually disappeared.

clubs to renew membership for the year, and the failure of the Eastern Division to come forward with a regatta site for 1915, the Executive Committee refused to consider suspending the event. Under the leadership of commodore Robert F. Wilson from the Toronto Canoe Club, a Championship was held on Toronto Harbour, hosted by the Toronto Canoe Club.

But the suspension of the Championship was inevitable. At the annual meeting on May 13, 1916, a motion was passed to suspend the National Championship for 1916; the new commodore, S.J. Milligan from the St. Lambert Boating Club in Quebec, could do little more than pledge that he would "endeavour to hold things together during his term of office." Outgoing commodore Robert Wilson informed the membership that he had taken it upon himself "to write a letter of condolences to the family of Alister MacKenzie on account of the death to one of our greatest paddlers, at the front." With the singing of "God Save the King," the seventeenth annual meeting of the Canadian Canoe Association was brought to a close.

The Golden Age Between the Wars 1919–39

Between the two Great Wars, canoe sport enjoyed an expansion in membership, spectator popularity, competition and international recognition, so much so that the period might appropriately be described as the "golden years" of Canadian canoeing. The period began with the restoration of the National Championships in 1919 after a three-year hiatus. A major shift in the development of canoe racing was marked by the initiation of a demonstration of canoeing at the 1924 Paris Olympics, in which four Canadians and four paddlers from the Washington Canoe Club participated. The golden age reached its climax at the 1936 Berlin Olympics when Frank Amyot won the Gold Medal in Canadian Singles and the twosome of Warren Saker and Harvey Charters from the Toronto Balmy Beach Club won the Bronze and Silver medals. It ended with the outbreak of yet another war in 1939. The 1940 Tokyo Olympics were cancelled and the promise of the 1940 Olympic Canadian canoeing team was not to be realized.

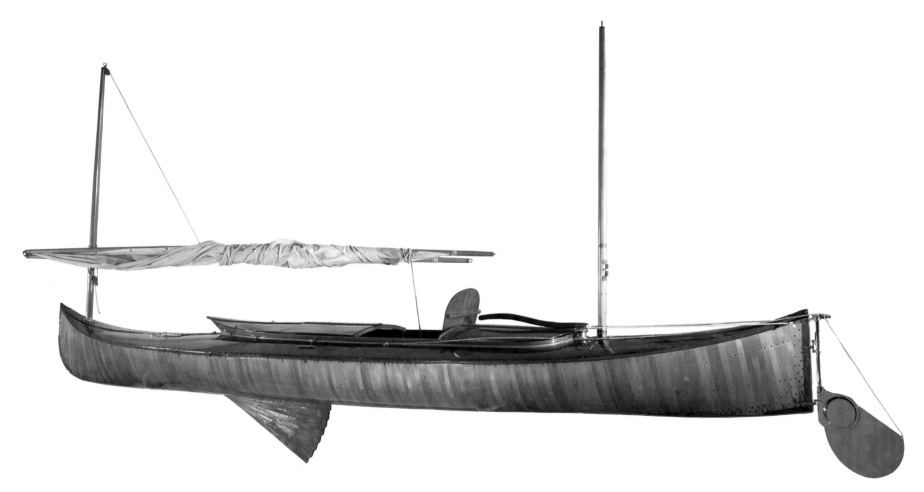

The Second World War 1939–45

Not unlike the First World War, the Second World War had a devastating impact on canoe sport. As the young men responded to the need and volunteered their services, club memberships were decimated. In the Gananoque Club, 114 members volunteered for active service, greatly depleting the Senior, Intermediate and Junior ranks. But the Association responded to wartime need and the call of the government for sport organizations to persist with their programs in order to maintain physical fitness amongst Canadian youth. For the 1940 Championships a Juvenile Class (sixteen and under) was recognized, and the first Juvenile event added to the program was a war canoe race. Ralph Adams, from *The Montreal Daily Star*, complimented the efforts of canoe sport from his vantage point: "instead of hiding their heads in crying towels, they turned their energetic efforts towards molding a powerful juvenile section to take care of the boys coming up." By 1942, "with practically all our paddlers above our juvenile class, either in uniform or in war work" (Minutes of CCA Annual Meeting 1942), it was futile trying to maintain a National Championships. It was discontinued in 1942. But the minutes of the Eastern Division meeting of April 15, 1942, echoed in similar meetings of the Northern Division in Ottawa and the Western Division in Toronto, accepted the suspension of the annual competition and recorded the decision that was to sustain the sport over the war years and give it a foundation for renewal at war's end. "It was generally agreed that this Division continue to function and that juvenile races be encouraged." Each year from 1942 to 1945, an annual meeting was held to keep the three divisions and clubs working together. By 1945 ten clubs responded to the call for the annual meeting. The report of commodore Cecil Powers, a brief eight lines, terminated with the hope "that the CCA regatta may be resumed in 1946."

Amateur Sport Goes International 1945–2000

The Second World War marked a turning point in the development of canoe sport in Canada in many ways. The image of canoe sport in 2000, when the CCA celebrated its hundredth anniversary, was in stark contrast to the pre-war years. Paddlers qualified for the National Championships in six regionally organized Divisional Trials and journeyed from across Canada to compete in several racing classes: Midget, Juvenile, Junior and Senior for both males and females in open canoe and kayak events. (Canada is virtually alone internationally in the provision of open Canadian canoe races for females in all age classes.)

Nearly all the boats used in what is now referred to as sprint or flatwater racing are international in design and manufacture: kayak singles (K-1), kayak tandem (K-2) kayak fours (K-4) and Canadian singles (C-1), Canadian tandem (C-2) and Canadian fours (C-4). Few are made in Canada except for the war canoe and the Canadian fours. But those sleek, molded open canoes used in international competition, constructed from fiberglass and carbon fiber, are still referred to as "Canadians" after the country from which the craft originated.

Top billing at National Championships goes to national team athletes, particularly those who are international stars. Canadian athletes who make the national team train year-round in order to be competitive at the international level, receiving athletes' training allowances from the federal agency, Sport Canada, for doing so. Federal funding to the CCA is essential to

In 1991 Renn Crichlow, from the Rideau Canoe Club, Ottawa, won the first World Kayak Championship for Canada, in the 500-meter K-1. He is paddling a Van Dusen Eagle II model. Starting in the 1920s, Swedish and Danish builders dominated racing canoe and kayak design and construction. But in 1986, the U.S. Canoe and Kayak Team commissioned Composite Engineering Inc. in Concord, Massachusetts to design and build a new fleet of boats for the 1988 Olympic Team. In 1988 at Seoul, South Korea, Greg Barton of the United States won Olympic Gold in K-1 and teamed with Norm Bellingham for a Gold in K-2, using the newly designed Van Dusen kayaks. Since then, the Van Dusen boats have been popular throughout the world.

TOP: Finish of a Canadian Singles race at the 100th Anniversary Canadian National Championships, at Lake Banook in Dartmouth, Nova Scotia in August, 2000. Leading the race is Steve Giles (9) followed by Maxime Boillard (8). All four paddlers are using the Polish Starlight Futura model, characterized by a deeply scalloped sheerline between the widest point of the boat and the foredeck. This design innovation permits a more unimpeded stroke path by the paddler and reduces the hull surface above the waterline, which is otherwise susceptible to troublesome broadside winds.

BOTTOM: Steve Giles, Olympic Bronze Medal winner of the 1000-meter Canadian Singles, Sydney, 2000, in a Starlight Futura 2000. At the ICA Congress in November, 2000, specifications for the beam of the boat were eliminated altogether. The width of the current model of the C-1 will be as narrow as paddlers can tolerate.

FACING PAGE: Contemporary fiber-glass North canoe running rapids on the Blue Chute of the French River, 1995. Despite the resculptur-ing of the Canadian canoe at the international level, the classical shape and form survive in examples such as this simulated North Canoe.

provide international-caliber athletes with full time coaches, training camps, the expenses of international competition and the most current model of canoe or kayak in order to be competitive. Each year the big event is the World Canoe Championships and every four years it is replaced by an even bigger event, the Olympic Games.

But the Canadian Canoe Association in 2000 is more than just flatwater canoe and kayak racing. A small group of canoeists still practice the arcane sport of canoe sailing as an associated group within the CCA, and World Championships are held every two years. Two other disciplines are now part of the CCA. In the post-1945 era, with the influx of European immigrants from Central Europe, whitewater paddling developed as a distinct sport. Competitions take place in Slalom and Down River events. Whitewater Slalom has been an Olympic sport in the last three Olympic Games, after its original entry in 1972. In Slalom both men and women race against the clock through a course of hanging gates in kayak singles events, but only men race in whitewater slalom canoe singles and tandem events. More recently, the International Canoe Federation has accepted canoe water polo, an offshoot from the whitewater kayak sport, as an international sport. Canoe polo, for both men and women, takes place in short, flat, highly maneuvrable kayaks in pools or on courses laid out on open water.

Marathon canoeing, in international kayaks and open canoes, has a long tradition in North America, but not until 1980 did a national organization take form: the Canadian National Marathon Canoe Racing Association. In 1984 it entered the CCA as the third Technical Discipline, motivated largely by the acceptance of marathon canoeing as a competitive discipline at the international level in that year.

And a variety of new canoe activities take form on the margins of sport as adventure-seeking, recreational activities: dragon boat racing, whitewater rafting, whitewater "freestyle" rodeoing, kayak surfing, sea kayaking and outrigger canoe racing. What begins as recreation invariably takes on rules and structures, the accoutrements of sport, looking forward to the day when it becomes an international sport with the final act of acceptance, admission to the Olympic Games.

One hundred and eleven national canoe associations are members of the International Canoe Federation, a measure of the international popularity of canoe sports. The deep, lasting appeal of canoeing among cultures and nations whose peoples share it as a common experience holds great promise for further development and expansion of paddle activities as both recreation and sport.

PRESERVING the HISTORY of the CANOE

Tappan Adney, 1943.

For hundreds of years, some form of the canoe has served the inhabitants of North America. The Native peoples were able to adapt its basic design to many different materials and uses. The very essence of the Native canoe, however, was transitory; the biodegradable materials eventually broke down and disappeared into soil. The skills to build new craft were handed down from father to son, and new canoes were built when needed by Native craftsmen.

But with the coming of Europeans to North America, that cycle of passing skills from generation to generation was gradually broken and some of the knowledge was lost. Canoe manufacturing fell into the hands of the settlers, and the old Native ways of building weren't necessary. The motorboat took over in many places as a faster and easier means of transportation. By the 1920s it was obvious that some styles of canoes would never be made again, and the existing specimens were quietly rotting away.

The design of any canoe or kayak was determined by the people who used it and the conditions of the land around them. The study of canoes, therefore, is a vital key to understanding the people who made and used them. Historians, anthropologists and museums have devoted a substantial amount of time to the study and preservation of the canoe. In this section the focus is on two people who made valuable contributions to this growing body of knowledge: a scholar and a collector.

In the late nineteenth century, Tappan Adney, a man of considerable vision, realized that the past was slipping away and set about to preserve a record of Native and voyaging canoes by making exact models based on careful mathematical calculations. He singlehandedly preserved the memory of many vanishing birchbark canoes, kayaks and umiaks: he crafted more than one hundred and fifty models and made copious notes, on which most of our knowledge of these craft is based.

Although canoes were acquired by museums from time to time, many were lost until Kirk Wipper began making his enormous contribution to the preservation of important canoes. Over a period of about forty years, Wipper collected nearly six hundred boats. His collection formed the basis of the Canadian Canoe Museum in Peterborough, Ontario, which continues to collect and preserve important canoes, with a special emphasis on keeping the old building skills alive. In 2002 Kirk Wipper was made a Member of the Order of Canada.

The Scholar: Tappan Adney   240
JOHN JENNINGS

The Collector: Kirk Wipper   242
GWYNETH HOYLE

Kirk Wipper inside the log building of the Kanawa Museum, circa 1987, holding a Haida paddle beside the stern of the Adams Haida dugout. Above it is the elegant, sewn-plank canoe, decorated with white star and circle drawings along the thwarts, which belonged to a chief in the Solomon Islands and was used for ceremonial travel. Kirk obtained it during a sabbatical year in the South Pacific in 1981.

The scholar: TAPPAN ADNEY

JOHN JENNINGS

Tappan Adney in his home in Woodstock, New Brunswick, 1943. In the top left-hand corner of the picture is a model of an end-frame unit. Adney's contribution to the knowledge of canoe culture in North America is inestimable. He built a hundred and fifty finely crafted models of Native craft and amassed a large collection of documentation about them. After his death Howard Chapelle wrote *The Bark Canoes and Skin Boats of North America*, using Adney's notes and drawings. This remains a classic authority on the subject.

Much of our knowledge of the Native bark and skin canoes of North America would have been lost forever, except for one man, Edwin Tappan Adney. His name is little known outside the canoe world, but for those who know, he is accorded a stature given to no other. For six decades he almost single-handedly kept alive an important part of the canoe heritage of North America until others woke up to its significance. Both canoe scholars and builders acknowledge a large debt to his work.

In a way, Adney was a tragic figure. His epitaph should read, "Here lies the victim of too much talent." He would probably be largely unknown today if someone else had not written his great book for him, since he never quite got around to finishing it. The study of canoes was clearly his first passion, but it was too easy to distract him with his many other obsessions: Native languages and ethnology, photography, painting and music. Adney spoke Greek, Latin, French and Maliseet. Eighty-eight boxes of research at the Peabody and Essex Museum just north of Boston attest to the depth of his scholarship. They include material on Native linguistics and ethnology, botany, astronomy and heraldry. His illustrations were used in museum publications and in a standard bird book of the time. Pierre Berton has called his book on the Klondike gold rush the best in existence. But it was always to canoes that he returned.

Though born in the United States, in Athens, Ohio, in 1868, he eventually became a Canadian. He first came to Woodstock, New Brunswick, in 1887 at the age of nineteen, seeking out the girl he would later marry, Minnie Bell Sharp. They had met in New York, where she was studying music and he art. Through Minnie, Adney was introduced to Peter Jo, a Maliseet trapper and canoe builder who lived near Woodstock on the St. John River. The meeting would change Adney's life.

Two years later, in 1889, Adney was back, this time to spend the year with Peter Jo's family. Adney had a triple purpose; to be near Minnie, study canoe building and learn the Maliseet language. It is interesting to speculate that perhaps the greatest of all canoe scholars came to that calling because he needed an excuse to pursue a woman. But he had also watched Peter Jo building a canoe two years earlier and had caught the fever. From this tutelage came the first detailed description of bark canoe building ever written. The following year his article and drawings were published both in *Outing* and in *Harper's Young People*.

Thus, in 1887, began six decades of canoe scholarship that only ended with his death in 1950. His main interest was the bark craft of North America and he set out to find as many as he could and to talk to as many builders as possible. Already he was almost too late. In his correspondence are moments of euphoria when he found a new example of a Native craft. But these moments were rare. He found, for instance, only one example of a voyaging canoe, the big canoes used by the European fur traders, and that one was rather small and unrepresentative. All the others had settled back to earth, and no one seemed to care. Few museums thought it worth the bother to preserve one.

Adney became a Canadian in 1916 at the age of forty-eight, then joined the Canadian army and spent the rest of the war producing models of trench warfare for the training of troops. At this time he also intensified his search for the remnants of the continent's canoe culture. He began his mission to record this culture, focusing his studies on the function of the craft within the different regions and peoples. Since certain types of craft had already disappeared, his approach involved some reconstructing of canoes based on a detailed study of Native cultures and languages. Adney claimed that much of Native culture had remained remarkably unaltered by European contact, so it was possible even in the early twentieth century to make accurate speculations about types of craft that no longer existed.

Fortunately there were still a few active Native builders and some retired fur traders that he was able to track down through the Hudson's Bay Company. Adney was an excellent artist with an ability to make very precise drawings of the canoes he encountered and the ones he watched being made. He also relied heavily on early photographs, especially those of the Geological Survey of Canada, which was still using a few birchbark canoes into the twentieth century. His voluminous papers related to Native canoes and kayaks at the Mariners' Museum at Newport News, Virginia, are full of detailed interviews with both Native and white builders. When it came to the accurate representation of Native canoes in art, he expressed a general contempt. "Old drawings with the sole exception of the paintings of Paul Kane … and Mrs. E. Hopkins … are utter travesties."

At some point Adney realized that it was not enough to merely collect information and make drawings. Important categories of craft were fast disappearing and they would soon be gone from memory. So in 1925 he began to construct models of these canoes, in the belief that exact scale replicas could be built for museums. He believed that this was the only way to save this vital heritage. According to Adney, when museums finally awoke to the importance of preserving these canoes, there were few good specimens left. Most of what was left was of inferior quality. Few museum people knew the difference and because there was no published material on Native canoes to help them, many embarrassing examples ended up in well-known museums. Unlike dugout canoes, those made of bark and skin, unless carefully protected, just did not last and most of the good ones were gone.

Adney also felt a compulsion to gather his information before it was too late because he felt that much of the ancient knowledge of canoe building was disappearing in Native society. He thought that the modern world was fast eroding the old Native occupations and ways of thinking. Among the Maliseets, whom he knew so well, knowledge of canoe building was disappearing in his generation.

After some experimenting with the scale of his models, he settled on a scale of five to one and then set about to record all the important types of Native bark craft and, to a lesser degree, the skin kayaks and umiaks of the Inuit. In his papers at the Mariners' Museum he left intricate mathematical calculations for every minute detail of construction in order that his models would be accurate to the fraction of an inch, and thus be capable of being copied at full size. From then until his death, he produced about one hundred and fifty models of such exquisite detail and craftsmanship that they have been referred to by David Gidmark, one of the leading birchbark builders of Canada, as "the most valuable single resource for the interpretation of Native North American watercraft." Adney calculated that these models represented somewhat over twenty thousand hours of research and building. Seen collectively, they take one's breath away.

Adney's collection of models represents a vital part of Canadian heritage and should be in place of honor in a Canadian museum. Instead, in 1939, after he "vainly sought to place them with [a Canadian museum] at almost any terms," Adney was forced to sell them to an American institution, one that had far more foresight and appreciation of the history they represented. Adney sold 125 models to the Mariners' Museum in Newport

News, Virginia, for $1,000, the price of his loan from a museum in Montreal where the models were stored as collateral. Thus, this priceless collection of Canadiana left Canada because no one cared. The Mariners' Museum paid his debt, agreed to pay him a monthly stipend to write his canoe book, bought him a typewriter and new clothes, put electricity into the converted barn where he lived, and periodically saw to it that his larder was stocked. Adney was terribly poor, but, to the continual frustration of the Mariners' Museum, money it sent him kept being given to his Native neighbors and the "book" never materialized because he became increasingly sidetracked by his role as an advocate for the Native people of New Brunswick.

Adney died in 1950 in his converted stable in Woodstock, New Brunswick, surrounded by his birds and squirrels, his lifetime of research notes and drawings and a few of his remaining treasured models. By all accounts he could be obstinate and opinionated, but never self-important. Seemingly oblivious to his meager surroundings and, as one friend said, "tough as a pine knot" to the end, Adney single-mindedly assured that the great heritage of the bark canoe would not die.

After his death, Adney's unfinished manuscript and massive collection of notes and drawings were transformed by Howard Chapelle of the Smithsonian Institution into *The Bark Canoes and Skin Boats of North America*, published in 1964, a book that continues to this day to be the bible of both canoe scholars and builders.

Model of a Montreal canoe built by Tappan Adney, scale 5:1. The exquisite detail and craftsmanship evident in this model is typical of Adney's work. He took great pains to get each canoe exactly right and made copious notes of the detailed mathematical calculations he made to ensure accuracy down to a fraction of an inch. His intention was that his models could be copied at full size to recreate the lost canoes of the past.

RIGHT: Commanda Algonquin canoe, fourteen feet, eight inches long, thirty-four inches wide. This birchbark canoe was built by William and Mary Commanda of Maniwaki, Quebec, from a single piece of bark in the 1970s. Commanda, a renowned builder, often uses figures of wildlife that are important to the Algonquin culture to decorate his canoes. They are created by scraping away the fine outer layer of dark winter bark to reveal the figures in relief on a lighter background.

MIDDLE: Haida dugout detail. Victor Adams, a Haida of the Queen Charlotte Islands, was commissioned to carve this dugout by hand for the museum collection. It took him three years to complete. The eagle with spread wings, symbol of a chief, guides the bow of the dugout. The wings are completed at the stern. This was the first such canoe to be constructed by the Haida within living memory, the forerunner of a regenerated interest in maintaining the living tradition. See page 75.

BELOW: On their first attempt to paddle the Haida dugout, the eastern crew mistook the bow for the stern, but once that was rectified the canoe moved gracefully through the water. The Haida canoe was launched beside the Canadian naval destroyer *Haida* in the Toronto harbor, and then paddled by crews of Kandalore campers up the Trent Canal and Gull River to Minden, where it was received with a special welcoming pageant.

national personnel director of the YMCA, who, recognizing Kirk's qualities, created a challenging job for him—that of recruiting boys from street gangs in downtown Toronto to take part in organized activity at the "Y". Kirk exceeded the expectation of the director tenfold, bringing in more than two hundred youths.

An all-round varsity athlete with insatiable drive, Kirk completed his Physical Education degree in two years, took a year's job as secretary of the Central Toronto YMCA, and embarked on a degree in Social Work, majoring in Group Work. His work at the "Y" took him to Camp Pinecrest, where Kirk's love of canoes and canoeing had its real beginning. He saw the canoe as a vehicle for exploring a range of methods for leadership training as well as a way of approaching the natural world.

When Kirk completed his degree in 1950, Professor M.G. Griffiths, of the School of Physical and Health Education, insisted that he join the faculty of the University of Toronto. Kirk did so, and remained there until retirement. Meanwhile, during the summers he continued to learn and experience aspects of camp life.

In 1957, Camp Kandalore, on Lake Kabakwa in the Haliburton Highlands of central Ontario, became available and Kirk acted quickly to secure it. As a camp director, Kirk Wipper had all the qualities of an outstanding leader. He sought to involve the campers in the natural world in every possible adventurous way without making an adverse impact on their surroundings. From the beginning, artifacts relating to the pioneering aspect of the program themes found a place in the camp as a reminder of the heritage of Canadian frontier life.

Knowing Kirk's love of heritage and canoes, his friend Professor Griffiths presented him with a basswood dugout canoe he had found on the Griffiths farm near Lakefield, north of Peterborough. This plain brown canoe with sleek, modern lines was carved from a huge basswood tree by the Payne brothers, Jacob and William, in the late nineteenth century. The Mississauga people of the Lakefield area used dugouts almost exclusively rather than the birchbark canoes preferred in other areas. The dugouts were often narrow and tippy, taking their shape from the natural curve of the tree from which they were carved. The Payne brothers, with some knowledge of boats, gave their canoe a shape less trough-like and more reminiscent of the graceful birchbark canoe.

In 1959 the Payne dugout was given a place of honor in the Kandalore dining hall, the first of the myriad of self-propelled boats that would eventually form the collection of The Kanawa International Museum of Canoes, Kayaks and Rowing Craft. There was not yet any idea of

Basswood dugout, fifteen feet, nine inches long, thirty inches wide. The Payne dugout, carved from a basswood tree to a thickness of less than three-quarters of an inch, shows the craftsmanship of the Payne brothers of Warsaw, Ontario. It was one of three dugouts (all still in existence) that were produced from three trunks that grew from one root. See page 164.

a museum, but one canoe soon led to another. Within three years there were fifteen handcrafted canoes making up what came to be known as "The Charter Group," forming the basis of the Historical Canoe Collection of Camp Kandalore.

The first birchbark was acquired from M. Poirier and Sons of Maniwaki, Quebec, and the Master-level canoeists were able to experience the thrill of paddling such a responsive craft. It was part of Kirk's philosophy that a few of the canoes in the collection were to be used and experienced, as well as treasured as historical artifacts.

As Kirk's interest in canoes grew and became widely known, the pace at which new acquisitions arrived at Kandalore quickened. Canoes and information on available canoes reached him in a steady stream. In the late 1960s, along with Claude Cousineau of Ottawa, he developed the National Canoe Instructor School System with the aim of setting a national standard for teaching canoeing skills. This took Kirk to canoeing areas across the country and incidentally provided opportunities to find unique regional craft to add to the growing collection at Kandalore.

In those early years the collection grew at an amazing rate. Thirty-one canoes as well as paddles, models, tools and art pieces were added in 1973 and 1974, bringing the grand total to three hundred and fifty canoes. The acquisition of notable canoes often came with a hefty price tag, both for the craft and for transportation. The financial statements of the camp in the years of major canoe purchases show that Kandalore, by then a year-round outdoor educational center, operated at a loss. It became obvious that the camp could no longer cope with the museum's growth, and in June of 1975 the museum became a separate entity and was officially incorporated as "The Kanawa International Museum of Canoes, Kayaks and Rowing Craft."

The collection of canoes had outgrown the dining hall of Camp Kandalore and was housed in a log building built by staff and campers as part of their exposure to heritage traditions. When more space was needed for the ever-expanding collection, Kirk persuaded the noted builder, B. Allan Mackie, to hold a series of log-construction schools at the camp. Over three summers, while Kirk provided materials, food and accommodation, Mackie and his students built a

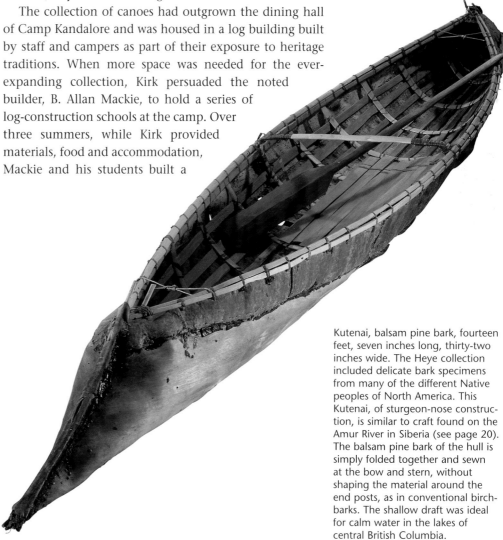

Kutenai, balsam pine bark, fourteen feet, seven inches long, thirty-two inches wide. The Heye collection included delicate bark specimens from many of the different Native peoples of North America. This Kutenai, of sturgeon-nose construction, is similar to craft found on the Amur River in Siberia (see page 20). The balsam pine bark of the hull is simply folded together and sewn at the bow and stern, without shaping the material around the end posts, as in conventional birchbarks. The shallow draft was ideal for calm water in the lakes of central British Columbia.

magnificent three-storey wing onto the original museum building to accommodate the craft.

During this time Alika Webber, a Vancouver anthropologist with a special concern for Canadian Native heritage, started working with Kirk to acquire canoes. Working as a freelance procurer of artifacts, Webber had a wide network of contacts and associates in museums and in the Aboriginal communities throughout the continent. Canoes are bulky and a problem to store in limited museum space. Through the noted anthropologist, Dr. Edmund Carpenter, it became known that the Museum of the North American Indian in New York City was having difficulty housing and maintaining the Heye Foundation's collection of rare canoes and kayaks. After intercession by Webber with the director of the museum, a period of negotiation began between Kirk and the museum that lasted eight years.

Kirk's position was that Kanawa was a specialized museum dedicated entirely to watercraft and the Heye collection consisted of mainly Canadian craft. The decision was finally put to a vote of the museum board's sixty members. It was close to midnight when Kirk was finally informed that the sale of the boats for the sum of $150,000 in American funds had been approved by a narrow margin.

With the arrival of these forty-four craft at Kanawa in 1976, the collection had not only increased in size, but had gained impressive international stature. However, the new canoes were seriously in need of conservation, which the museum in New York had not been able to afford to undertake. Part of the negotiations to acquire the collection included the commitment to bring the craft back to life, and this became the work of Richard Nash, a canoe builder already resident at Kandalore.

BELOW: Salish racing canoe, fifty-three feet, eight inches long, thirty-four inches wide. *Blue Bird* was carved by Simon Charlie in 1970 near Duncan, British Columbia, and was reputed never to have lost a race.

BOTTOM: *Blue Bird* in transit on Kirk Wipper's truck. The boat was too long to be carried by conventional means: transport truck, train or plane. The extension racks were added to the truck to balance the boat.

BLUE BIRD

Throughout the 1970s, Alika Webber ranged far and wide over the continent. She collected unique dugouts in the Pacific Northwest and found an interesting collection in San Diego that needed a new home. Among the latter was a double outrigger from the South Pacific, which inspired Kirk to take his sabbatical leave in that region in 1981. From the Pacific Islands he added ten more artifacts to the collection, including a magnificent high-prowed canoe from the Solomon Islands.

As the collection developed, canoes were occasionally exchanged with other museums for desirable items. A Canadian birchbark was sent to the Adirondack Museum in return for an original guideboat, and another birchbark went to the Mariners' Museum at Newport News. But such exchanges were rare. A different type of exchange was occasionally effected closer to home, when a used but serviceable fiberglass camp canoe bearing the Kandalore name might be exchanged for an unseaworthy historic canoe that had been stored for years in the rafters of someone's boathouse.

At times it seemed as though Kirk would go to any length to obtain a choice specimen, and length took on a double meaning in the case of the *Blue Bird,* a West Coast Salish racing canoe. The Salish, from the east coast of Vancouver Island, have a long history of canoe racing, with fierce rivalry between the villages. Each community has its own carver who directs the building of the long war canoe from a solid cedar log, usually with carved bow pieces to represent the village. Simon Charlie, a master carver and at one time chief of the Cowichan Band, has been credited with keeping the Coast Salish arts and skills alive. His carvings and totem poles can be found in galleries and museums across

Canada. When Kirk heard that the fifty-three-foot *Blue Bird,* carved by Simon Charlie and reputed never to have lost a race, was being retired and might be available for the museum, he immediately went west. The price was steep but in Wipper's eyes worth every penny. The problem would come in transporting such a long vessel three thousand miles across the country to Ontario. It was too long to be moved by conventional means: transport truck, train or plane. He had anticipated the problem in advance and fitted extension racks on his half-ton diesel truck for the drive. By careful maneuvering on and off ferry boats, and by driving through the northwestern states of the United States to avoid the tight turns

Orellana, twenty-one feet, four inches long, thirty-six inches wide. This travel-worn orange fiberglass canoe, covered with decals, made the journey from Winnipeg to the mouth of the Amazon, paddled by Don Starkell and his son Dana.

Mandan bull boat, three feet, nine inches long, four feet, nine inches wide. This perfect specimen of a Mandan bull boat was in the Heye collection. Like the Kutenai, it shares its design with craft from the other side of the world, notably the Welsh coracle and the Irish curragh. The Mandan people, a group of Sioux who lived along the lower Missouri River, constructed the oval-shaped bull boat out of the materials at hand: buffalo hide sewn onto a frame of willow saplings. They used it to cross the Missouri and other rivers in their prairie home territory.

Welsh coracle, four feet, three inches long, four feet, five inches wide. The design of this boat is very similar to the Mandan bull boat, even though it was built and used on the other side of the Atlantic Ocean. Kirk was able to add it to the museum's collection by having it brought to Canada as the centerpiece for a touring Welsh choir.

through the Canadian Rockies, the tortuous drive was completed in about three weeks. Wipper frequently slept beside the highway in his small tent at night to guard the precious load, which was too long to turn into the parking lot of most motels and restaurants.

Sometimes a relatively ordinary canoe was valued for the journey it has taken. The battered orange fiberglass canoe covered in decals and named *Orellana* in honor of the first European to descend the Amazon River was a case in point. Built in Winnipeg by Bill Brigden, it carried Don Starkell and his son Dana on an astonishing twelve-thousand-mile journey from its Manitoba home, up the Red River, down the Mississippi, around the coast of the Gulf of Mexico to the Orinoco River, and finally down the Amazon to its mouth. In the course of its travels, the canoe was battered by ocean waves and its occupants were menaced by pirates, drug-traffickers and overzealous soldiers. Kirk offered Starkell a permanent home for *Orellana* in the museum, and he was proud to donate it.

While much of the collection at Kanawa was assembled through the persistent effort of following every lead with the necessary negotiation, travel, letter-writing and phone calls, on rare occasions a desirable specimen would arrive quite spontaneously. Such was the case when the museum received the beautifully carved Sahnteeng cedar-plank canoe, manned by three carved figures, along with two carved paddles. The Hudson's Bay Company had commissioned the ceremonial craft from the Sahnteeng people living on the Winnipeg River to commemorate the centennial of the province of Manitoba, which coincided with the three-hundredth anniversary of the Company. It was carved with symbols: the beaver representing their past and the eagle showing their hopes for the future, and with panels showing the Sahnteeng way of life. The canoe was exhibited in the flagship store of the Hudson's Bay in Winnipeg throughout 1970, the centennial year, and was then donated to the Royal Ontario Museum in Toronto. When the ROM decided that it did not fit their collection policy they were pleased to pass it along to Kanawa.

For years Kirk had been performing a juggling act keeping three balls—his three full-time careers—in the air. In the beginning the museum ball was tiny, and the two balls representing his professorship at the University of Toronto and the directorship of Camp Kandalore were nicely synchronized by the seasons. When the museum ball began to grow, reaching the size of the other two, at first it was manageable. But as the growth continued unabated, it was a continuous struggle to maintain the

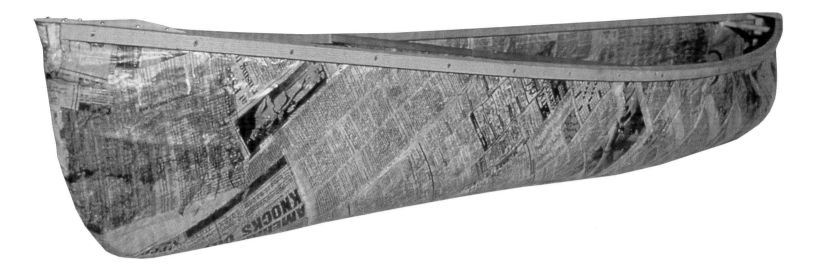

previous smooth balance. At the end of 1978 Camp Kandalore was sold to several senior members of the staff, and Kirk's role became that of an advisor. And in 1983 a Board of Directors was formed to assist in the administration of the Kanawa Museum, which had become too big to be handled by one man.

With the collection approaching six hundred craft, some of them extremely large and many of them delicate, the beautiful log buildings were no longer adequate. Security, conservation, humidity control, insurance and curatorial services were now a priority to do justice to the world-class aggregation of canoes, kayaks and other boats. After much thought and discussion, the collection was transferred to a new home in Peterborough, Ontario, with its important tradition as a center of canoe building. In 1997 the Canadian Canoe Museum opened it doors to the public with two exhibition galleries in a former office building, with the bulk of the

collection stabilized in a concrete, glass and steel manufacturing plant. Both facilities were a gift to the Museum from the Outboard Marine Corporation. Since his retirement to a country house close to Peterborough, Kirk has been able to make himself and his expertise available to the Museum staff and its army of volunteers.

In his career as a teacher Kirk Wipper touched the lives of thousands of students, and as a camp director he inspired a generation of campers, many of whom became leaders in their fields. His collection of artifacts that now forms the core of the Canadian Canoe Museum is a crowning achievement in a life filled with accomplishments and adventure. It is a legacy that will continue to tell the story of the much-loved, simple canoe, which provided access to a continent and continues to carry those who cherish wilderness into quiet and secret places of the heart.

ABOVE: Canoe made out of newspaper, ten feet, eight inches long, twenty-eight inches wide. Paper boats were made in Troy, New York, in the late 1800s by Elisha Waters and Son, who specialized in racing shells. In 1874 Nathaniel Bishop (see page 203) made a journey by canoe from Quebec down the intercoastal waterway to the Florida Keys. He used a conventional canoe until he reached Troy, where he switched to a fourteen-foot paper boat. The newspaper canoe shown here, constructed using white glue and coated in varnish, with thwarts of ash and black cherry, was made at a YMCA camp in New Jersey in 1983 to commemorate Bishop's journey.

LEFT: HBC Commemorative canoe, eighteen feet, two inches long, thirty-five inches wide, built by Max Bossi, 1970. Cedar-plank ceremonial canoe carved by the Sahnteeng people of the Winnipeg River to commemorate the centennial of the province of Manitoba and the three hundredth anniversary of the Hudson's Bay Company. The beaver in the bow represents their past; the eagle in the stern, their hopes for the future; and the carved panels on the side illustrate their way of life. The figures portray three generations: the child in the bow, the grandmother in the middle and the father in the stern.

A Living Tradition

JAMES RAFFAN

Thirty-two thousand feet above the sparkling blue Pacific, flying home from an international rivers conference in Australia, I am looking down on a constellation of white-rimmed Polynesian islands and thinking, as ever, about canoes. I imagine paddles flashing in the ocean below, propelling a Samoan dugout, perhaps with an outrigger of palmwood, marking waypoints on a voyage that once led humanity by canoe around the Pacific Rim and eventually—or so some imagine—to North America's shores.

The Australian conference has brought together from around the world scientists and engineers, artists and writers, water managers and event organizers, to discuss the centrality of rivers—of water—to the future of humankind. I have been invited to speak about Canada's rivers and the spirit of water. Because Canada is a nation of rivers, I must begin by talking about the diversity of paddlecraft, because it is the canoe that ultimately connects us to the waterways that bring life and meaning for many of us to the places we call home. Everyone at the event has in common a need for fresh water and stories about rivers in their particular corner of the world, but the canoe, as a connection to landscape, stands out as a distinctly Canadian phenomenon. No one else seems to dream about putting a boat in any river in the land and paddling to tidewater—the essential Canadian conceit. No one else has such preoccupation with canoes.

On the west coast are the baidarkas of the Aleuts and great dugouts of the Tsimshian, Haida and Nuu-chah-nulth. On the Cordilleran plateau are sturgeon-nosed bark canoes of the Kootenay region. Toward the Mackenzie Delta are the long-decked bark craft of the Dogrib and Gwich'in, often sewn together from the bark of many northern birch trees no bigger in circumference than a child's arm. Across the Arctic coast are Inuit umiaks and kayaks, each with its own distinctive form and grace. In the prairies are the unsteerable bull boats of the Mandan. And on it goes as one moves from north to west to east. The classic Algonquin canoes of the central woodlands, with lines extended to create the venerable freight canoes of the fur trade and re-echoed by many modern canoe manufacturers to make boats like the Peterborough Champlain, the Chestnut Prospector and the Old Town Morris Model A. East again, the crooked canoes of the Cree and Montagnais, the softer curves of Mi'kmaq and Maliseet craft, and on to the iconic mustache-shaped canoes of the Beothuk in Newfoundland.

These designs, and their modern descendants, speak not only of individual form, function and aesthetics, but also of particular places and distinctive people from region to region. In spite of these differences, however, the experience of living in this nation of rivers creates for the makers of these craft and for the people who paddle them a common connection to the land and to each other brought about by canoe experiences and the stories that etch them in mind and heart.

To paddle a canoe is to embark on a liminal voyage that can sweep a willing heart across thresholds of new worlds. If indeed it was in the paddlecraft of the Pacific Rim that people first inhabited North America, this may have been one of the first stories to be told about moving from one world to another in a hand-hewn canoe. But it is just one of many. In a creation story of Eastern tribes, the omnipotent character Glooscap arrived from the great beyond in a white stone canoe, as did Dekanahwideh, who brought peace to the Iroquois Confederacy. As legend would have it, the Neutral Indians of the Great Lakes region sacrificed a young woman to the Creator at harvest time by sending her over Niagara Falls in a bark canoe—the so-called Maid of the Mist. In Quebeçoise folklore, lonely lumberjacks in the *pays d'en haut* make a deal with the devil to return to their loved ones in town for a night of New Year's revelry, traveling from one world to another in, what else? A flying canoe: *La Chasse Galerie*.

Canoe experience also unites people from coast to coast to coast in its ability to cross the threshold from settled land to wilderness, as described in the journals of Lewis and Clarke, Radisson and Groseilliers and latterly by the likes of Bill Mason, Eric Morse, Kate Rice or Pierre Trudeau. Whether it is paddling across or around continents, or employing the canoe as a vessel for spiritual Odysseys closer to home, the canoe connects its paddler to new worlds, to new understandings. The look of the craft may differ from place to place, from generation to generation, across the country, as it has done since time began, but the liminal experience is there for all who put paddle in hand.

Even as this idea has remained more or less constant and underscored the progress of life in North America, the vessel itself has evolved, and continues to do so. On most northern beaches in the country, beside high-tech fiberglass and stainless steel boats one still finds canvas-covered wooden canoes being used for hunting and transportation. The basic shape—the curves of stem, sheer, gunwale and keel—first established by the stretching and bending limits of bark, skin and wood, has changed as new materials and new construction techniques have created new challenges and opportunities for designers and builders. Recurved entry lines and asymmetries not possible with conventional materials are now common in craft made from space-age fibers and resins, and lately through the revolutionary marriage of industrial plastics, adhesives and sophisticated molding techniques. It is a sign of the times that Bill Mason's son is paddling in a banana-shaped plastic "play" canoe over waterfalls he once camped beside with his dad, while his sister continues the romance of flatwater paddling in aged canvas-covered cedar canoes, both continuing to cross thresholds into emerging worlds of adventure and spiritual fulfilment, as their father did before them.

Similarly, the *idea* of canoe continues to permeate popular culture. On an interactive bulletin board, part of an art exhibit related to the canoe, many visitors to the McMichael Gallery, near Toronto, chose to tell stories or post snapshots of wedding ceremonies that included canoes. One world to another. In advertising for the Canadian marketplace, one finds canoe imagery in pitches for everything from dating services to designer paints, each image evoking a different set of values that arise from the canoeing tradition in this country: youth, vigor, health, teamwork, quality, family heritage, Aboriginal connections, national history, patriotism and, at times, a little romance, nostalgia and even self-mockery. In the latter realm, a North American competition invites teams from university civil engineering schools to design, build and race the most unlikely of vehicles: a concrete canoe. And as tongue-in-cheek as this annual event may at first glance seem, building a concrete canoe may indeed be the perfect foil for helping young novitiates cross the threshold from rank amateurs to polished professional engineers.

First Nations on the coast of British Columbia have been, for the last decade or more, reviving the tradition of great canoes, which had all but been eclipsed in the first half of the nineteenth century by other boats and combustion engines. They are using huge new dugouts and fiberglass replicas to assert and, in some cases, reclaim and rediscover their Aboriginal way of life. In this sense the canoe, which was once central to their very survival because it connected them to the waters from which their main sources of food and fur came, is now being used to cross from a modern world of trawlers and wage work back into the essence of a culture tied to the land.

And on it goes. A variety of Internet service providers across North America, in French and English media, use canoes as the central icon in their marketing campaigns. It is logical that a canoe would be an effective image to bring attention to a commercial operation whose role in life it is to transport users from the real world to the virtual world and back again. One world to another. A group of breast cancer survivors in British Columbia have embraced dragon boat racing as a way to cross the threshold from sickness back to health, an idea that has has inspired many and galvanized global interest. Without question, the canoe tradition lives on, especially in Canada, even for segments of the population who may occasionally dream about becoming canoeists but who have no intention of ever actually physically stepping into a boat.

Because the canoe so resonates with our geographical circumstance, having quite possibly arrived from elsewhere on the planet, Canadians will always be drawn to images of bark canoes, and these so-called "domesticated trees" will continue to affirm significant aspects of the distinctive natural and cultural heritage of our country. To the extent that craft made of less natural materials evoke the bark connection to the land, interest in recreational canoeing can only continue to grow, partly because of its physicality and the adventure it offers but also because of its restorative and spiritual aspects. Canoeing is good for the soul. As dragon boat racing, play boating, canoe surfing, and other avant-garde pursuits rise in popularity, the face of canoeing may in fact shift, as it has done since the first boat arrived on these shores. Samoan dugouts, dragon boats, North canoes and the latest high-tech plastic "vessel without decks"—in fact all the boats in this handsome volume—may have more in common than might at first appear. They are portable, paddleable and connect us like nothing else to Canada, to ourselves and to other worlds that help make us whole.

GLOSSARY

ADIRONDACK GUIDEBOAT Wooden boat made with flush-lapped planking. Fifteen to eighteen feet long, used in the Adirondack region of the northeastern United States.

ADZE Tool for cutting wood with a blade at right angles to the handle.

AFT Towards the stern of a boat.

AMIDSHIPS The middle of a boat.

AVASISAARTOQ **KAYAK** Kayak with sharply curved ends, largely disappeared by the beginning of the twentieth century.

BAIDARKA Russian term for decked skin-covered boats often used in reference to kayaks of the Aleut and the Pacific Eskimo.

BASTARD CANOE Thirty-foot birchbark canoe used in the fur trade, from the French *canot bâtard*.

BATEAU A flat-bottomed French work boat with pointed bow and stern, used to carry large loads during the fur trade.

BATTEN Strip of wood or metal used to cover a joint between two planks.

BEAM The maximum width of a boat.

BIFID BOW Bow divided by a slot into upper and lower projections as in the Aleut baidarka.

BILGE The inside of a boat's hull where the bottom turns into the sides, often referred to as the "turn of the bilge."

BOARD-AND-BATTEN Wooden canoe building method featuring wooden battens fitted between the ribs to cover the joint between planks. Also known as wide-board-and-batten.

BOW DRILL Drill turned by a bow, with the string of the bow twisted around the drill.

BOWLINE The curve of the bow of a boat.

BOWPIECE The wide wooden piece that forms the bow on a west coast dugout canoe.

BLOCKING-IN Cutting the rough shape of the west-coast dugout.

BUILDING BED A bed of compacted earth, usually raised, but sometimes dug into the ground, where bark is laid out and held with stakes so it can be sewn together and then lashed to the frame to make a bark canoe.

CANADIAN CANOE or **CANADIAN** General reference term for an open canoe originating in Canada. American sportsmen and Europeans used the term to distinguish this style of canoe from the decked canoe propelled with a double-blade paddle or sail.

CANOE NAIL Nail made by forming a head on a length of copper wire. Peterborough canoes with hardwood ribs are put together with copper canoe nails.

CANOT BÂTARD Thirty-foot birchbark canoe used in the fur trade, known in English as the Bastard canoe.

CANOT DU MAÎTRE Thirty-six-foot birchbark Montreal canoe, used in the fur trade.

CANOT DU NORD Twenty-six-foot birchbark North canoe, used in the fur trade.

CANT Slope or slant.

CANVAS DUCK Strong, untwilled fabric used for sails, sailors' clothing and covering canoe hulls.

CAP FINIAL A decorative shape that finishes off the top of a carved form.

CAP STRIP Thin strip of wood fitted over the gunwale of a boat, also known as a gunwale cap.

CARRYBOARD Board attached to the middle crossbar of a canoe, sometimes used with a tumpline by the Mi'kmaq and Maliseet to distribute the weight when carrying a canoe.

CARVEL PLANKING Square-edge planks that are laid flush to each other. The joint is made watertight with the use of caulking in the seam.

CEDAR-CANVAS CANOE Canoe made with canvas stretched over cedar-plank hull.

CEDAR-RIB CANOE Canoe made with tongue-and-groove-fitted transverse cedar planking.

CENTERBOARD Retractable keel on a sailboat.

CENTERLINE Line drawn down the middle of a piece of wood for guidance during construction.

CHALKLINE Line marked with chalk by stretching a piece of string covered with chalk between two points.

CHECK Crack caused when a restrained plank dries out and shrinks.

CHINE A longitudinal line of transition between hull surfaces, such as where the bottom meets the sides.

CLINKER-BUILT Boat-building style using external overlapping planks, also known as lapstrake.

COAMING A vertical trim piece used to finish off the edge of a deck or deck opening. In a kayak the coaming is used to finish off the edge of the cockpit to prevent water from entering the kayak. A typical coaming in a canoe is made of steam-bent hardwood and extends slightly above the surface of the deck.

CORACLE Small boat made of wickerwork covered with watertight material, used in Ireland and Wales.

CROOKED CANOE Birchbark canoe built by Eastern Cree with extreme rocker designed to negotiate rapids.

CROOKED KNIFE Drawknife with bent handle used by Native birchbark canoe builders.

CROSSBAR Horizontal bar between gunwales on a canoe. Also called thwart.

CURVED KAYAK Kayak from Greenland's southeast coast with stern and bow gunwales that curve up slightly to form a concave profile.

CUT TACK   Tack made by forming a head on a wedge-shaped piece of flat metal. Double-cedar and cedar-canvas canoes are built with brass cut tacks.

CUTWATER   The forward edge of a boat's bow that divides the water.

DECKED CANOE   Canoe built with long decks enclosing a cockpit.

DOGRIB CANOE   Small bark canoe built by the Dogrib people in the Northwest Territories.

DOUBLE-CEDAR CANOE   Canoe made with two continuous layers in opposing directions of thin cedar planking to achieve a smooth interior and exterior.

DOVETAIL JOINT   Locking corner joint formed with tenons in the shape of a dove's spread tail.

DOWEL   Peg of wood used to hold two pieces of wood together.

END-BLOCKS   Large wooden end-pieces added to the stern and bow of a west coast dugout.

END-HORN   Extended gunwales on a west coast dugout that serve as hand-grips and decorative additions. Sometimes used on umiaks.

FLARE   The upward and outward curve of a boat's side.

FLAT KAYAK   Shallow kayak with a flat bottom used in southern and eastern Greenland.

FLUSH BATTEN   Strip of hardwood used with wide planks to make a continuous joint on the inside surface of a canoe.

FORE   Towards the bow of a boat.

FOREFOOT   The foremost section of a boat's keel. On a kayak, the point on the bow of the kayak where the stem joins the keelson.

FORE MAST   The forward mast of a boat.

GORES   Slits pierced in building material (such as birchbark or walrus hide) so pieces can be sewn together.

GUNWALE   Rail running along the sheer line of a boat used to stiffen and protect the edge of the hull.

HALYARD   Rope used for lowering or raising a sail on a boat.

HEAD CANOE   West coast dugout canoe with exaggerated extensions at the bow and stern.

HEEL   Stern end of a boat's keel and the lower end of the sternpost, to which the keel is connected.

HULL   The body or frame of a boat.

INWALE   The inboard component of a gunwale.

JIB   Triangular sail set between the fore mast and the wire rigging in the bow of a sailboat.

KEELSON   Strip of wood that forms the back-bone of the canoe, used for longitudinal stiffness on a canoe inside the hull when an external keel is undesirable.

LAPSTRAKE   Boat-building style using external overlapping planks, also known as clinker-built.

LATH   Thin, flat strip of wood, often used in a series to form a framework.

LEEBOARD   Plank fixed to the side of a sailing boat and let down into the water to improve lateral resistance

LUG   Short term for lugsail, a quadrilateral sail that is set one-third down the mast.

MAKAH CANOE   See Nootkan canoe.

METALLIC BATTEN   Channel of light metal resembling a long row of short-legged staples used inside seams to cover a joint between two planks.

MIZZEN MAST   Mast next aft of the main mast on a sailing boat.

MONTREAL CANOE   Thirty-six-foot birchbark canoe used in the fur trade, also known as *canot du maître*.

MORTISE   Hole or notch in a piece of wood designed to receive the end of another part, such as a tenon.

MULTI-CHINE   Hull with more than the single hard chine or angle between the keel or keelson and the gunwale. If there are several chines to each side from the keel, you get a quasi-round-bottomed hull.

MUNKA CANOE   West coast dugout war canoe, with an especially wide bow that was used as a shield or cover when approaching or retreating from an enemy.

NOOTKAN CANOE   Dugout canoe with very distinctive end-blocks: a vertical stern with a rectangular, sloping cap finial and a bow with a snout-like profile. Widely used among Native peoples of the Pacific Northwest, it is also known as the Nuu-chah-nulth or Makah canoe.

NORTH CANOE   Twenty-six-foot birchbark used in the fur trade, also known as *canot du nord*.

NORTH GREENLAND KAYAK   The smallest of Greenland kayaks, with very short bow and stern tips.

NUU-CHAH-NULTH CANOE   See Nootkan canoe.

OUTWALE   Outer component of a gunwale.

PEANUT   Racing shell.

PETERBOROUGH CANOE   General term for the style of open wooden canoes that developed in the Peterborough area in the late nineteenth century.

RABBET   Groove in wood cut to receive the edge or tongue of another piece of wood.

RABBETED THWART BLOCKS   Blocks fitted to the inside of the hull to facilitate attaching the thwarts. Block is rabbeted to accept and stabilize the end of the thwart.

RIB   Piece of wood used transversely in a boat's hull.

RIGGING   The arrangement of a boat's masts, sails and ropes.

ROCKER   The curve of the bottom of the boat, seen from the side.

SCARF   Shallow, angular cut on a piece of wood to form joint.

SCOW   Open, flat-bottomed boat.

SCULL   Single rowing shell propelled with two oars.

SEALSKIN FLOAT   Complete sealskin with its openings sewed up, inflated and attached to a harpoon line to use as a float during sea mammal hunting.

SHEER   The upward curve of a boat's lines from bow to stern.

SHOVELNOSE CANOE   Dugout canoe with blunt spade-shaped ends.

SKEG   A fin or projection at the aft end of a boat's keel.

SPONSON   Air-filled bulge or attachment used on either side of a canoe to reduce risk of capsizing.

SPOON CANOE   Dugout canoe shaped like a mountain-goat-horn spoon.

SPRITSAIL   Sail held in position by a sprit, a pole that extends diagonally from the mast.

SPRUCE CANOE   West coast dugout carved in one piece, usually from spruce, with bow and stern shaped essentially the same.

STANCHION   Vertical structural member.

STEM   Upright piece of wood in the bow.

STRAIGHT-EDGE   Tool with one straight edge used for testing straightness in construction.

STRINGER   Longitudinal structural member.

SWEEP   Long oar.

TENON   Projecting piece of wood made to fit into a slot (mortise) on another piece of wood.

THWART   Structural member extending across a canoe that supports the gunwale structure.

TONGUE-AND-GROOVE   Building technique fitting strips of wood together by means of a tongue or ridge along one side and a groove or indentation along the other.

TUMBLEHOME   On a boat with a rounded hull, tumblehome refers to the inward sloping of the upper part of its sides. It is also called "falling home."

TUMPLINE   Sling for carrying a load (e.g., a canoe) on a person's back with a strap that fits around the forehead.

UMIAK   Large Inuit boat built on a wooden frame with walrus skin or sealskin used as a covering.

WAR CANOE   Large racing canoe, twenty-five to thirty-five feet long, paddled by eight to twelve people, which was particularly popular in Canadian canoe clubs.

WOOD-CANVAS CANOE   Canoe made with canvas stretched over wood hull (same as cedar-canvas canoe).

SOURCES and FURTHER READING

The following lists of sources and suggestions for further reading have been divided, where applicable, into sections that correspond with the subjects covered in the text. However, some areas of study (bark canoes) have more reference material than others (umiaks), and the lists reflect this imbalance. In the interest of the general reader, footnotes have not been included, but all quotations in the text have been sourced in the text, and the authors' primary sources are listed here. A selection of interesting books for general reading about the canoe in North America has been included at the end of this section.

THE NATIVE CRAFT

BARK CANOES

Adney, Edwin Tappan, and Howard I. Chapelle. *The Bark Canoes and Skin Boats of North America*. Washington: Smithsonian Institution Press, 1964.

Allen, Robert S. *His Majesty's Indian Allies: British Indian Policy in the Defence of Canada, 1774–1815*. Toronto: Dundurn, 1993.

Arima, Eugene. *Blackfeet and Palefaces*. Ottawa: Golden Dog Press, 1995.

Belyea, Barbara, editor. *Columbia Journals: David Thompson*. Montreal: McGill–Queen's University Press, 1994.

Biggar, H.P., editor. *The Works of Samuel de Champlain*. Toronto: Champlain Society, 1922.

Brown, Jennifer S.H. *Strangers in Blood: Fur Trade Company Families in Indian Country*. Vancouver: University of British Columbia Press, 1980.

Bumsted, J.M. *Fur Trade Wars: The Founding of Western Canada*. Winnipeg: Great Plains, 1999.

Burpee, Lawrence J., editor. *The Journals and Letters of Pierre Gaultier de Varennes de La Vérendrye and His Sons*. Toronto: Champlain Society, 1927.

Campbell, Marjorie Wilkins. *The Nor' Westers*. Toronto: Macmillan, 1974.

——. *The North West Company*. Vancouver: Douglas and McIntyre, 1983.

de Champlain, Samuel. See Biggar, H.P.

de Charlevoix, Pierre F.X. *Journal d' un Voyage Fait par Ordre du Roi dans l'Amerique Septentionale*. Louis Phelps Kellog, editor. Chicago: Caxton Club, 1923.

Chittenden, Hiram Martin. *The American Fur Trade of the American Far West*. Volumes 1 and 2. Lincoln: Bison, 1986.

Cole, Jean. *Exile in the Wilderness: The Life of Chief Factor Archibald McDonald, 1790–1853*. Toronto: Burns and MacEachern, 1979.

Creighton, Donald. *The Empire of the St. Lawrence.* Toronto: Macmillan, 1956.

Dechêne, Louise. *Habitants and Merchants in Seventeenth Century Montreal*. Montreal: McGill–Queen's University Press, 1992.

Eccles, W.J. *Canada Under Louis XIV, 1663–1701*. Toronto: McClelland and Stewart, 1964.

——. *The Canadian Frontier, 1534–1760*. Albuquerque: University of New Mexico Press, 1974.

Fisher, Robin. *Contact and Conflict*. Vancouver: University of British Columbia Press, 1978.

Franchere, Gabriel. *A Voyage to the Northwest Coast of America*. New York: Citadel Press, 1968.

Francis, Daniel. *Battle for the West: Fur Traders and the Birth of Western Canada*. Edmonton: Hurtig, 1982.

Francis, Daniel, and Toby Morantz. *Partners in Furs: A History of the Fur Trade in Eastern James Bay, 1600–1870*. Montreal: McGill–Queen's University Press, 1983.

Franquet, Col. Louis. *Voyages et Memoires sur la Canada*. Quebec: Institut Canadien de Québec, 1889.

Galbraith, J.S. *The Little Emperor*. Toronto: Macmillan, 1976.

——. *The Hudson's Bay Company as an Imperial Factor*. Toronto: University of Toronto Press, 1957.

Gilman, Carolyn. *Where Two Worlds Meet: The Great Lakes Fur Trade*. St. Paul: Minnesota Historical Society, 1982.

Gough, Barry. *First Across the Continent: Sir Alexander Mackenzie*. Toronto: McClelland and Stewart, 1997.

Hafen, LeRoy R., editor. *Mountain Men and Fur Traders of the Far West*. Lincoln: Bison, 1982.

Harmon, Daniel Williams. *Sixteen Years in Indian Country: The Journal of Daniel Williams Harmon*. Macmillan, 1957.

Hearne, Samuel. *A Journey from Prince of Wale's Fort in Hudson's Bay to the Northern Ocean, 1769, 1770, 1771, 1772*. Richard Glover, editor. Toronto: Macmillan, 1958.

Hopwood, Victor G., editor. *David Thompson: Travels in North America, 1784–1812*. Toronto: Macmillan, 1971.

Houston, C. Stuart. *To the Arctic by Canoe, 1819–1821: The Journal and Paintings of Robert Hood*. Montreal: McGill-Queen's University Press, Arctic Institute of North America, 1974.

Houston, C. Stuart, and I.S. MacLaren. *Arctic Artist: The Journal and Paintings of George Back, 1819–1822*. Montreal: McGill–Queen's University Press, 1994.

Huck, Barbara. *Exploring the Fur Trade Routes of North America*. Winnipeg: Heartland, 2000.

Hunt, George T. *The Wars of the Iroquois*. University of Wisconsin Press, 1940.

Innis, Harold A. *The Fur Trade in Canada*. Toronto: University of Toronto Press, 1930.

Jaenen, Cornelius. *Friend and Foe: Aspects of French-Amerindian Cultural Contact in the Sixteenth and*

Seventeenth Centuries. Toronto: McClelland and Stewart, 1976.

Karamanski, Theodore J. *Fur Trade and Exploration: Opening the Far Northwest, 1821–1852*. Vancouver: University of British Columbia Press, 1983.

Keegan, John. *Warpaths*. Toronto: Key Porter, 1995.

Kent, Timothy. *Birchbark Canoes of the Fur Trade*. Ossineke, Michigan: Silver Fox, 1997.

de Lahontan, Baron. *New Voyages to North America*. McClurg, 1905.

Lamb, W. Kaye, editor. *Simon Fraser: Letters and Journals, 1806–1808*. Macmillan, 1960.

Lavender, David. *Winner Takes All*. New York: McGraw-Hill, 1977.

MacGregor, J.G. *Peter Fidler, Canada's Forgotten Explorer, 1769–1822*. Calgary: Fifth House, 1966.

Mackenzie, Alexander. *Voyages from Montreal on the River St. Laurence Through the Continent of North America to the Frozen Sea and Pacific Oceans in the Years 1789 and 1793*. Edmonton: Hurtig, 1971.

Mackie, Richard S. *Trading Beyond the Mountains: The British Fur Trade on the Pacific*. Vancouver: University of British Columbia Press, 1997.

Mitchell, Elaine A. *Fort Timiskaming and the Fur Trade*. Toronto: University of Toronto Press, 1977.

Newman, Peter C. *Company of Adventurers*. Penguin, 1985.

——. *Caesars of the Wilderness*. Penguin, 1987.

Nisbet, Jack. *Sources of the River: Tracking David Thompson Across Western North America*. Seattle: Sasquatch, 1994.

Norall, Frank. *Bourgmont: Explorer of the Missouri, 1698–1725*. Edmonton: University of Alberta Press, 1988.

Nute, Grace Lee. *The Voyageurs*. St. Paul: Minnesota Historical Society, 1955.

Parker, James. *Emporium of the North: Fort Chipewyan and the Fur Trade to 1835*. Regina: Canadian Plains Research Center, 1987.

Peterson, Jacqueline, and Jennifer S.H. Brown, editors. *The New Peoples: Being and Becoming Metis in North America*. Winnipeg: University of Manitoba Press, 1985.

Quaife, Milo M., editor. *The Western Country in the Seventeenth Century, the Memoirs of Lamonthe Cadillac and Pierre Liette*. Lakeside Press, 1947.

Ray, A.J. *Indians in the Fur Trade*. Toronto: University of Toronto Press, 1974.

——. *The Canadian Fur Trade in the Industrial Age*. Toronto: University of Toronto Press, 1990.

Ray, A.J., and Donald Freeman. *"Give Us Good Measure": An Economic Analysis of Relations Between the Indians and the Hudson's Bay Company Before 1763*. Toronto: University of Toronto Press, 1978.

Rich, E.E. *The Fur Trade and the Northwest to 1857*. Toronto: McClelland and Stewart, 1967.

——. *Montreal and the Fur Trade*. Montreal: McGill University Press, 1966.

Sandoz, Maria. *The Beaver Men: Spearheads of*

Empire. New York: Hastings House, 1964.

Shackleton, Philip, and Kenneth G. Roberts. *The Canoe*. Toronto: Macmillan, 1983.

Simpson, Sir George. *Simpson's Athabasca Journal*. Toronto: Hudson's Bay Record Society, 1938.

——. *Simpson's 1828 Journey to the Columbia*. Toronto: Hudson's Bay Record Society, 1947.

Stanley, George F.G. *New France: The Last Phase, 1744–1760*. Toronto: McClelland and Stewart, 1968.

Steele, Ian K. *Warpaths*. New York: Oxford University Press, 1994.

Thompson, David. *Columbia Journals*. Barbara Belyea, editor. Montreal: McGill–Queen's University Press, 1994.

Trigger, Bruce. *The Children of Aetaentsic, A History of the Huron People to 1660*. Montreal: McGill–Queen's University Press, 1976.

Trudel, Marcel. *The Beginnings of New France, 1524–1663*. Toronto: McClelland and Stewart, 1973.

Tyrrell, J.B., editor. *David Thompson's Narrative*. Toronto: Champlain Society, 1916.

Utley, Robert M. *A Life Wild and Perilous: Mountain Men and the Paths to the Pacific*. New York: Henry Holt, 1997.

——. *The Indian Frontier of the American West, 1846–1890*. Albuquerque: University of New Mexico Press, 1984.

Van Kirk, Sylvia. *"Many Tender Ties": Women in Fur Trade Society, 1670–1870*. Watson & Dwyer, 1980.

Voorhis, Ernest. *The Historic Forts and Trading Posts of the French Regime and of the English Fur Trading Companies*. Canada: Department of the Interior, 1930.

Wallace, W. Stewart. *The Peddlers from Quebec*. Toronto: Ryerson Press, 1954.

White, Richard. *The Middle Ground*. Cambridge: Cambridge University Press, 1991.

Wishart, David J. *The Fur Trade of the American West, 1807-1840*. Lincoln: Bison, 1979.

DUGOUTS

Barnett, Homer G. *Gulf of Georgia Salish. Culture Element Distributions 9*. Berkeley: University of California Press,1939.

Black, Martha. *Out of the Mist: Treasures of the Nuu-chah-nulth Chiefs*. Victoria: Royal British Columbia Museum, 1999.

Boas, Franz. "The Kwakiutl of Vancouver Island." *Memoirs of the American Museum of Natural History*. Volume 8, Part 2: 307–515. New York, 1909.

Cook, James. *A Voyage to the Pacific Ocean*. 2nd ed. London: H. Hughs, 1785.

Drucker, Philip. *The Northwest Coast. Culture Element Distributions 26*. Berkeley: University of California Press, 1949.

——. The Northern and Central Nootkan Tribes. *Smithsonian Institution, Bureau of American Ethnology, Bulletin 144*. Washington, 1951.

——. *Indians of the Northwest Coast*. New York:

McGraw Hill,1955.

Duff, Wilson. "Thoughts on the Nootkan Canoe." *The World is as Sharp as a Knife: An Anthology in Honor of Wilson Duff*. D. Abbott, editor. Victoria: British Columbia Provincial Museum, 1981.

Durham, Bill. *Indian Canoes of the Northwest Coast*. Seattle: Copper Canoe Press, 1960.

Emmons, George T. *The Tlingit Indians*. Frederica de Laguna, editor. University of Washington Press, Seattle and London. New York: American Museum of Natural History, 1991.

Gibson, James R. *Otter Skins, Boston Ships and China Goods: The Maritime Fur Trade of the Northwest Coast, 1785–1841*. Montreal: McGill-Queen's University Press, 1992.

Holm, Bill. "The Head Canoe." *Faces, Voices, and Dreams: A Celebration of the Centennial of the Sheldon Jackson Museum*. Peter Corey, editor. Juneau: Alaska State Museum, 1987.

de Laguna, Frederica. *The Story of a Tlingit Community: A Problem in the Relationship Between Archaeological, Ethnological, and Historical Methods*. Washington, D.C.: U.S. Government Printing Office, 1960.

Lincoln, Leslie. *Coast Salish Canoes*. Seattle: Center for Wooden Boats, 1991.

Niblack, Albert P. "The Coast Indians of Southern Alaska and Northern British Columbia." *U.S. National Museum Annual Report for 1888*. 225–386. Washington, 1890.

Olson, Ronald L. "Adze, Canoe, and House types of the Northwest Coast." *University of Washington Publications in Anthropology*. Volume 2, no. 1, 1–38. Seattle, 1927.

——. "The Quinault Indians." *University of Washington Publications in Anthropology*. Volume 6, no. 1. Seattle, 1936.

Swan, James G. "The Indians of Cape Flattery, at the Entrance to the Strait of Fuca, Washington Territory." *Smithsonian Institution Contributions to Knowledge*. Volume 16, No. 220, Article 8, pp. 1–105. Washington, 1870.

Waterman, Thomas Talbot. "The Whaling Equipment of the Makah Indians." *University of Washington Publications in Anthropology*. Volume 1, no. 1. Seattle, 1920.

Waterman, Thomas Talbot, and Geraldine Coffin. *Types of Canoes on Puget Sound*. New York: Museum of the American Indian, Heye Foundation, 1920.

KAYAKS

Amundsen, Roald E.G. *The North West Passage, being the record of a voyage of exploration of the ship "Gjoa" 1903–1907*. Volume 1. London: Archibald Constable, 1908.

Arima, Eugene. *Inuit Kayaks in Canada: A Review of Historical Records and construction*. Canadian Ethnology Service Paper no. 110. Ottawa: Canadian Museum of Civilization Mercury Series, 1987.

——. "Barkless Barques." John Jennings, Bruce W. Hodgins and Doreen Small, editors. *The Canoe in Canadian Cultures*. Toronto: Natural Heritage/Natural History Inc., 1999.

Chappell, Lieutenant Edward. *Narrative of a Voyage to Hudson's Bay in His Majesty's Ship Rosamond*. London: J. Mawman, 1817.

Curtis, Edward S. *The North American Indian: being a series of volumes picturing and describing the Indians of the United States, the dominion of Canada, and Alaska. List of Large Plates Supplementing Volume Twenty*. Number 718: Noatak Kaiaks. Written, illustrated, and published by Edward S. Curtis, 1930.

Dyson, George. *Baidarka*. Edmonds, Washington: Alaska Northwest Publishing Company, 1986.

Freeman, Milton M.R. et. al. *Inuit, Whaling, and Sustainability*. Walnut Creek, California: Altamira Press, 1998.

Hawkes, Ernest W. *The Labrador Eskimo*. Geological Survey Memoir no. 91. Anthropological Series no. 14. Canada: Department of Mines, 1916.

Lisiansky, Urey. *A Voyage round the World in the Years 1803,4,5&6*. London: John Booth, 1814.

Lister, Kenneth R. "Water for the Phalarope: Kayak Design and Cultural Values Among the Tununirusirmiut." *Museum Small Craft Association Transactions 1995*. Volume 2. Mystic, Connecticut: Museum Small Craft Association, 1996.

Low, A.P. *Report of the Dominion Government Expedition to Hudson Bay and the Arctic Islands on Board The D.G.S. Neptune, 1903–1904*. Ottawa: Government Printing Bureau, 1906.

Petersen, H.C. *Skinboats of Greenland*. Roskilde: The National Museum of Denmark, The Museum of Greenland, and The Viking Ship Museum in Roskilde, 1986.

Rasmussen, Knud. "Intellectual Culture of the Iglulik Eskimos." *Report of the Fifth Thule Expedition 1921–24*. Volume 7, no. 1. Copenhagen: Gyldendalske Boghandel, Nordisk Forlag, 1929.

Wenzel, George. *Animal Rights, Human Rights: Ecology, Economy and Ideology in the Canadian Arctic*. Toronto/Buffalo: University of Toronto Press, 1991.

Whittaker, C.E. *Arctic Eskimo, a record of fifty years' experience and observation among the Eskimo*. London: Sealey, Service & Co., 1937.

Zimmerly, David W. *Qajaq: Kayaks of Siberia and Alaska*. Juneau, Alaska: Division of State Museums, 1986.

UMIAKS

Adney, Edwin Tappan, and Howard I. Chapelle. *The Bark Canoes and Skin Boats of North America*. Washington: Smithsonian Institution Press, 1964.

Arima, E.Y. "Report on an Eskimo umiak built at Ivuyivik, P.Q., in the summer of 1960." National Museum of Canada Bulletin 189. Anthropological Series 59. Ottawa: National Museum of Canada, 1963.

Bandi, Hans Georg. "Siberian Eskimos as whalers and warriors." Allen P. McCartney, editor, *Hunting the largest animals: native whaling in the western arctic and subarctic*. Studies in whaling 3. Occasional papers 36. Edmonton: Circumpolar Institute, 1995.

Boas, Franz. "The Central Eskimo." *Bureau of American Ethnology Annual Report 6 (1884–85)*, Washington: Smithsonian Institution, 1888.

Bogojavlensky, Sergei. "Imaangmiut Eskimo careers: Skinboats in Bering Strait." Ph.D. thesis, Harvard University. Cambridge, Massachusetts: thesis manuscript, 1969.

Bogoras, Waldemar. "The Chukchee." *Jesup North Pacific Expedition*. Volume 8. Part 1. Memoir American Museum of Natural History 11. Leiden and New York: American Museum of Natural History, 1904.

Braund, Stephen R. *The skin boats of Saint Lawrence Island, Alaska*. Seattle and London: University of Washington Press, 1988.

Crantz, David. *The history of Greenland*. Volume 1. Translated from High Dutch. London, 1767.

Durham, Bill. *Canoes and kayaks of Western America*. Seattle: Copper Canoe Press, 1960.

Egede, Hans. *A description of Greenland*. Translated from Danish. London, 1745.

Flaherty, Robert J. *My eskimo friends, "Nanook of the North."* Garden City, New York: Doubleday, Page & Co., 1924.

Franklin, John. *Narrative of a second expedition to the shores of the Polar Sea, in the years 1825, 1826, and 1827...* London: John Murray, 1828.

Giddings, J. Louis. *Ancient men of the Arctic*. New York: Alfred A. Knopf, 1967.

Graham, Andrew. *Andrew Graham's observations on Hudson's Bay 1767–91*. Glyndwr Williams, editor. London: Hudson's Bay Record Society, 1969.

Hornell, James. *Water transport: origin and early evolution*. Cambridge: University Press, 1946.

Jochelson, Waldemar. "The Koryak." *Jesup North Pacific Expedition*. Volume 6. Memoir, American Museum of Natural History 10. Leiden and New York: American Museum of Natural History, 1908.

——. *History, ethnology and anthropology of the Aleut*. Washington: Carnegie Institute, 1933.

Knuth, Eigil. "An outline of the archaeology of Peary Land." *Arctic* 5 (1):7–33. Ottawa, 1952.

Low, Albert P. *Cruise of the Neptune*. Ottawa: Government Printing Bureau, 1906.

Mason, Owen K. "The contest between the Ipiutak, Old Bering Sea, and Birnirk polities and the origin of whaling during the first millenium A.D. along Bering Strait." *Journal of Anthropological Archaeology* 17 (3):240–325. Ann Arbor, 1998.

Nelson, Edward W. "The Eskimo About Bering Strait." *Bureau of American Ethnology, 18th Annual report for 1896–97*. Part 1. Washington: Smithsonian Institute, 1899.

Petersen, H.C. *Skinboats of Greenland*. Roskilde: National Museum of Denmark, National Museum of Greenland and Viking Ship Museum, 1986.

Spencer, Robert F. "The North Alaskan Eskimo." *Bureau of American Ethnology Bulletin 171*. Washington: Smithsonian Institute, 1959.

THE RECREATIONAL CANOE

FROM FOREST TO FACTORY

Note: The Peterborough Centennial Museum and Archives and the Canadian Canoe Museum Archives provided invaluable information for this chapter.

Audette, Susan T., with David E. Baker. *The Old Town Canoe Company: Our First Hundred Years*. Gardiner, Maine: Tilbury House, 1998.

Bond, Hallie E. *Boats and Boating in the Adirondacks*. Blue Mountain Lake, New York: Adirondack Museum/Syracuse University Press, 1995.

Cameron, Donald. "The Peterborough Canoe Story." Unpublished paper. Peterborough: Peterborough Historical Society, 1975.

Cock, Oliver, editor. *A Short History of Canoeing in Britain*. London: British Canoe Union, 1974.

Cole, A.O.C. *A Victorian Snapshot: Denne collection of old Peterborough prints*. Peterborough Architectural Conservation Advisory Committee and the Peterborough Centennial Museum and Archives, 1992.

Delledonne, Bob, editor. *Nelson's Falls to Lakefield: a history of the village*. Lakefield: Lakefield Historical Society, 1999.

Gibbon, John. *The Romance of the Canadian Canoe*. Toronto: Ryerson, 1951.

Gray, Charlotte. *Sisters in the Wilderness: the lives of Susanna Moodie and Catherine Parr Traill*. Toronto: Viking, 1999.

Hooke, Katharine. *St. Peter's on-the-rock: seventy-five years of service*. Peterborough: St. Peter's on the Rock Anniversary Committee, 1989.

MacGregor, Roger. *When the Chestnut was in Flower: inside the Chestnut canoe*. Lansdowne: Plumsweep, 1999.

Manley, Atwood. *Rushton and His Times in American Canoeing*. Syracuse, New York: Syracuse University, 1968.

Raffan, James. *Fire in the Bones*. Toronto: HarperCollins, 1996.

——. *Bark, Skin and Cedar*. Toronto: HarperCollins, 1999.

Raffan, James, and Bert Horwood, editors. *Canexus: The Canoe in Canadian Culture*. Toronto: Betelgeuse, 1988.

Rousmaniere, John. *The Illustrated Dictionary of Boating Terms: 2000 Essential Terms for Sailors & Powerboaters*. New York: W. W. Norton & Company, 1998.

Sears, George Washington. *Canoeing the Adirondacks with Nessmuk*. Blue Mountain Lake, New York: Adirondack Museum/Syracuse University Press, 1962/1993.

Simonds, Marilyn, and Ted Moores. *Canoecraft*. Toronto: Firefly, 2000. Quote on page 179 used with the permission of the authors.

Solway, Kenneth. *The Story of the Chestnut Canoe: 150 years of Canadian Canoe Building*. Halifax: Nimbus, 1997.

Stelmok, Jerry. *Building the Maine Guide Canoe*. New York: Lyons & Burford, 1980.

Stelmok, Jerry and Rollin Thurlow. *The Wood & Canvas Canoe: A complete guide to its history, construction, restoration, and maintenance*. Camden East: Old Bridge Press, 1987.

Stephenson, Gerald F. "John Stephenson and the famous 'Peterborough Canoes'." An occasional paper published by the Peterborough Historical Society. Peterborough, 1987.

Strickland, Samuel. *Twenty-seven Years in Canada West*. Japan: Charles E. Tuttle, Inc., 1970.

Young, Gordon, editor. *Mizgiiyaakwaa-tibelh: Lakefield...a look at its heritage*. Lakefield: Lakefield Heritage, 1998.

PADDLING FOR PLEASURE IN THE NORTHEASTERN STATES

Adney, Edwin Tappan, and Howard I. Chapelle. *The Bark Canoes and Skin Boats of North America*. Washington: Smithsonian Institution, 1964.

Audette, Susan T., with David Baker. *The Old Town Canoe Company: Our First Hundred Years*. Gardiner, Maine: Tilbury House, 1998.

Bond, Hallie E. *Boats and Boating in the Adirondacks*. Blue Mountain Lake, New York, and Syracuse, New York: Adirondack Museum and Syracuse University Press, 1995.

Brenan, Dan, Hallie E. Bond, Robert Lyon and Alice Gilborn. *Canoeing the Adirondacks with Nessmuk: The Adirondack Letters of George Washington Sears*. Blue Mountain Lake, New York, and Syracuse, New York: Adirondack Museum and Syracuse University Press, 1992.

Crowley, William. *Rushton's Rowboats and Canoes: The 1903 Catalog in Perspective*. Blue Mountain Lake, New York, and Camden, Maine: Adirondack Museum and International Marine Publishing Co., 1983.

Durant, Kenneth, and Helen Durant. *The Adirondack Guide-Boat*. Blue Mountain Lake, New York: Adirondack Museum, 1980.

Fenton, William, and Ernest Stanley Dodge. "An Elm Bark Canoe in the Peabody Museum of Salem." *American Neptune* 9 (3) July, 1949.

Hammond, Samuel H. *Wild Northern Scenes; or, Sporting Adventures with the Rifle and Rod*. New York: Derby and Jackson, 1857.

Kalm, Peter. *Travels in North America By Peter Kalm, The English Version of 1770*. Volume 1. Adolph Benson, editor. New York: Dover Publications, 1966.

Manley, Atwood. *Rushton and His Times in American Canoeing*. Blue Mountain Lake, New York, and Syracuse, New York: Adirondack Museum and Syracuse University Press, 1968.

Murray, William Henry Harrison. *Adventures in the Wilderness, or, Camp-Life in the Adirondacks*. With preface by William K. Verner and introduction and notes by Warder H. Cadbury. Blue Mountain Lake, New York, and Syracuse, New York: The Adirondack Museum, and Syracuse University Press, 1970.

Stelmok, Jerry, and Rollin Thurlow. *The Wood and Canvas Canoe: A Complete Guide to its History, Construction, and Maintenance*. Gardiner, Maine: Harpswell Press, 1987.

Thorpe, Thomas Bangs. "A Visit to the John Brown's Tract," *Harper's New Monthly Magazine*, 19 (110), July, 1859.

FAST PADDLES AND FAST BOATS

Johnston, C. Fred. *Book of Champions*. Ottawa: Canadian Canoe Association, 1988.

——. "Canoe Sport in Canada: Anglo-American Hybrid?" *Canexus: The Canoe in Canadian Culture*. Bert Horwood and James Raffan, editors. Toronto: Betelgeuse Books, 1988.

——. "Paddle Power." *Horizon Canada* 7 (74), 1986.

——. "The First C.C.A., August 4, 1900." *Canoe* 1 (1) February, 1976.

MacGregor, J. *A Thousand Miles in the Rob Roy Canoe on the Rivers and Lakes of Europe*. Boston: Roberts Brothers, 1867.

Manley, Atwood. *Rushton and His Times in American Canoeing*. Syracuse, New York: Syracuse University Press, 1968.

Moodie, Susanna. *Roughing it in the Bush*. Toronto: McClelland and Stewart, 1962.

Paschke, Werner S. *The World of Marathon Racing*. Florence, Italy: International Canoe Federation, 1987.

Toro, Andras. *Canoeing: An Olympic Sport*. San Francisco: Olympian Graphics Printer, 1986.

Vaux, Boyer. "History of American Canoeing." *Outing Magazine* 10 (5) August, 1887.

Vesper, Hans Egon. *50 Years of the International Canoe Federation*. Florence: International Canoe Federation, 1974.

——. *The International Canoe Federation in its Sixth Decade*. Belgrade: International Canoe Federation, 1984.

GENERAL READING

Benidickson, Jamie. *Idleness, Water and the Canoe: Reflections on Paddling for Pleasure*. Toronto: University of Toronto Press, 1997.

Bringhurst, Robert. *The Black Canoe: Bill Reid and the Spirit of the Haida Gwaii*. Vancouver: Douglas and McIntyre, 1991.

Brody, Hugh. *The Other Side of Eden: Hunters, Farmers and the Shaping of the World*. Vancouver: Douglas and McIntyre, 2000.

Dickason, Olive. *Canada's First Nations*. Toronto: McClelland and Stewart, 1992.

Dyson, George. *Baidarka, the Kayak*. Anchorage: Northwest Books, 1986.

Gidmark, David. *Birchbark Canoe: Living among the Algonquin*. Toronto: Firefly, 1997.

Hodgins, Bruce W., and Margaret Hobbs. *Nastawagan: The Canadian North by Canoe and Snowshoe*. Toronto: Betelgeuse, 1985.

Hodgins, Bruce W., and Gwyneth Hoyle. *Canoeing North into the Unknown: A Record of River Travel, 1874–1974*. Toronto: Natural Heritage, 1994.

Jennings, John, Bruce W. Hodgins and Doreen Small, editors. *The Canoe in Canadian Cultures*. Toronto: Natural Heritage, 1999.

McPhee, John. *The Survival of the Bark Canoe*. New York: Farrar, Straus and Giroux, 1975.

Morrison, R. Bruce, and C. Roderick Wilson. *Native Peoples: The Canadian Experience*. Toronto: McClelland and Stewart, 1986.

Neimi, Judeth, and Barbara Waiser, Editors. *River Running Free: Stories of Adventurous Women*. Minneapolis: Bergamot Books, 1987.

Noel, Lynn, editor. *Voyages: Canada's Heritage Rivers*. St. John's: Breakwater, 1995.

Pope, Richard. *Superior Illusions*. Toronto: Natural Heritage, 1998.

Raffan, James. *Bark, Skin and Cedar: Exploring the Canoe in the Canadian Experience*. Toronto: Harper Collins, 1999.

——. *Fire in the Bones: Bill Mason and the Canadian Canoeing Tradition*. Toronto: Harper Collins, 1996.

Raffan, James, and Bert Horwood, editors. *Canexus: The Canoe in Canadian Culture*. Toronto: Betelgeuse, 1988.

Ray, Arthur J. *I Have Lived Here Since the World Began*. Toronto: Key Porter, 1996.

Roberts, Kenneth G., and Philip Shackleton. *The Canoe*. Toronto: Macmillan, 1983.

Snaith, Skip. *Umiak: An Illustrated Guide*. Eastsound, Washington: Walrose and Hyde, 1997.

CONTRIBUTORS

Eugene Arima

Eugene Arima is a civil servant who specializes in kayak and canoe reconstruction and history. He has participated in reconstruction of Caribou Eskimo kayaks and whaling canoes and construction of Kwakwaka'wakw canoes. He has taken freighter canoe trips up the Thelon River to hunt caribou and gather driftwood for his projects. He has been associated with the National Museum of Canada and has contributed to and written many books, including *Eskimo Stories Illustrated with Soapstone Carvings from PovunLnituk, P.Q., Between Ports Alberni and Renfrew, Inuit Kayaks in Canada* and *The Whaling Indians*, as well as working on a contextual study of the Cavilan Eskimo kayaks and making contributions to Kayak Studies. His favorite kayak is a Passant.

Hallie E. Bond

Since 1986 Hallie E. Bond has been the curator of the boat collection at the Adirondack Museum in Blue Mountain Lake, New York, considered the finest collection of inland, non-powered pleasure craft in the United States. With an undergraduate degree in history, and one post-graduate degree in medieval studies and another one in American history, she has brought her love of history and boats to several books about canoeing in the northeastern United States, including *Boats and Boating in the Adirondacks* (1995); the introduction to *Canoeing the Adirondacks With Nessmuk: The Adirondack Letters of George Washington Sears (1992)* and a chapter for *Fishing in the North Woods: Winslow Homer*. She contributes to *WoodenBoat, Maritime Life and Traditions* and the *Material History Review*.

A member and past officer of the Museum Small Craft Association, Hallie received a special citation in 2000 from the Traditional Small Craft Association on the occasion of the tenth annual No-Octane Regatta. She has paddled the West Branch of the Penobscot along much of Thoreau's route and made numerous shorter trips in the Adirondacks. She lives in a 1920 farmhouse at the head of Long Lake, where she enjoys paddling her family canoe, an eighteen-and-a-half-foot E.M. White guide model built by Jerry Stelmok of Atkinson, Maine, which she bought with her husband in 1987.

Steven C. Brown

Steven C. Brown went from being the canoeing instructor at a Boy Scout camp in Washington State as a teenager to carving twelve Northwest Coast canoes of different sizes and styles by the age of forty-eight. Steve has conducted canoe-making workshops and apprenticeships with Native artists in Northwest Coast communities from Neah Bay, Washington, to Metlakatla, Ketchikan, Wrangell and Hoonah, Alaska. Steve has led the work on canoes that range in size from a sixteen-foot elaborately painted Northern-style canoe in the year 2000, to a thirty-two-foot Nootkan-style whaling canoe in the Makah Cultural and Research Center in Neah Bay in 1978, and a forty-four-foot (unfinished) Head canoe at the Daybreak Star Arts Center in Seattle. From 1990 – 2000, Steve served as the Curator of Native American Art at the Seattle Art Museum, where he published numerous articles and two major books on Northwest Coast art, *The Spirit Within* and *Native Visions,* both of which include important sections on canoe making and canoe history in the Northwest.

Steve has traveled by canoe, sailboat and other vessels to many parts of the coast, and has participated in both short and long voyages in the fishing, sealing and whaling canoes he carved with Makah apprentices between 1975 and 1978 at Neah Bay. One of these was a 1976 trip to Port Renfrew, undertaken with four Makah carvers, to visit the elder canoe maker Chief Charlie Jones of Pacheenaht village, Vancouver Island. After more than seven years of living aboard their forty-four-foot motorsailer, *Tsawayoos,* Steve and his wife Irma have recently moved ashore near Port Orchard, Washington, where he continues to carve and write about the Northwest Coast art traditions.

David Finch

David Finch is a consulting historian with a specialization in Western Canadian history. He holds a master's degree in post-confederation Canadian history and has written several books on the history of the Canadian west, including *R.M. Patterson: A Life of Great Adventure*, published in 2000. He has been associated with the Royal British Columbia Museum in Victoria, the Glenbow Museum in Calgary and the Canadian Museum of Civilization in Hull, Quebec. David has built cedar-strip canoes and restored cedar-canvas canoes. He lives in Calgary with his wife, his daughter and twelve canoes, including a treasured Commanda birchbark. He regularly canoes on rivers in the Canadian west, and has special feelings for the Kootenay. One of his most memorable canoe trips was down the South Nahanni River in the Northwest Territories.

Don Gardner

Don Gardner builds birchbark canoes, skin kayaks and a wide range of traditional tools and weapons: harpoons, sinew-backed bows and flint tools. His company, Oldways Inc., supplies museums and private collectors. He facilitates canoe and kayak building projects in schools in northern communities, including Tuktoyaktuk, Inuvik and Yellowknife. Don also plans trails for cross-country skiing, hiking and biking, ranging from wilderness trails to paved city trails. His trails were used for the 1988 Winter Olympics cross-country skiing and he has been involved in the preliminary trail layout for the Vancouver Winter Olympics in 2010. An avid cross-country skier and climber, Don has climbed in the Himalayas, solo-skied from Calgary to Squamish on the coast of British Columbia (a twenty-eight-day trip), and spent five weeks trekking across Ellesmere Island pulling a heavy sled.

Don did his undergraduate degree in archaeology, focusing on the Arctic. His particular interest is a form of experimental archaeology where old things like boats, bows, and tools are replicated and used to better understand the material culture of the past. He is the author of several reports about kayak and umiak remains found in the north.

Primarily a builder, Don enjoys paddling his boats for a few minutes to test and know them, but they are often shipped out the day they are completed. The building is the point for him and his pleasure is found in the act of creating the boats. This past year Don has completed two birchbark canoes for collectors, two kayak frames for the Canadian Canoe Museum and one kayak frame for the museum in Yellowknife, plus harpoons, paddles, darts, bows and other tools for various museums. Don lives and works by a lake (good for soaking hides and bark) outside Calgary.

Gwyneth Hoyle

Gwyneth Hoyle is a writer doing independent research on subjects related to northern travel and the fur trade, following her retirement from Trent University as College Librarian. With Bruce Hodgins as co-author she wrote *Canoeing North into the Unknown: a record of travel on northern rivers from 1874 to 1974*. Her most recent book is *Flowers in the Snow*, the biography of a Scottish woman botanist who made remarkable journeys alone across the Arctic in the 1930s. Gwyneth has also contributed numerous articles to canoe and fur-trade related books and journals. On the Board of Directors of the Canadian Canoe Museum since 1992, she is a regular volunteer at the front desk, as well as writing text for display panels or cleaning craft as needed. She has canoed across the Northwest Territories on the Thelon River, in Quebec on the Noire, and in the Temagami region of Ontario, with many short trips in the North Kawarthas near her home in Peterborough. She spends summers by the ocean, using a small kayak to explore the bay between New Brunswick and Nova Scotia.

John Jennings

John Jennings is an associate professor of history at Trent University, Peterborough, specializing in the frontier history of the Canadian-American west. He is also the Vice Chair of the Canadian Canoe Museum. John has written a number of canoe-related historical articles and recently co-edited *The Canoe in Canadian Cultures* with Bruce Hodgins. He is currently completing a manuscript on the Canadian-American ranching frontier, and is starting work on a book with photographer John Pemberton about Tappan Adney's canoe models, sponsored by the Mariners' Museum in Newport News, Virginia. John has been very active in the Canadian Canoe Museum since 1980. He received the Award of Merit for lifetime service from the Ontario Museum Association, where he is a member of the Council.

A former member of the Canadian Equestrian Team, John rode for Canada in the 1967 Pan American Games. He has canoed a number of wilderness rivers, many of them with his wife Nicola, including the Nahanni, Thelon and the Blackstone-Peel in the Northwest Territories, Canada. He lives in an 1850s mill house near Peterborough on the Indian River, which is the first river he paddles each spring. His favorite canoe is a Lakefield canoe made in 1978 by Walter Walker on a nineteenth-century Thomas Gordon form.

C. Fred Johnston

C. Fred Johnston is a retired associate professor of education at Queen's University in Kingston, Ontario. He was a competitive paddler in sprint racing and fours events in national and North American competitions from 1950 to 1962. Fred has been active in many local canoe clubs over the years, as well as Canoe Ontario (President), the Canadian Canoe Association (Commodore, Chair High Performance) and the International Canoe Federation. Since the 1970s he has been the Chair of the History and Archives Committee and the Archivist of the Canadian Canoe Association. Fred was a founder and organizer of the First Canexus Conference on the Canoe in Canadian Culture, with James Raffan, Bert Horwood and Bill Peruniak in 1988.

He has contributed to and written books about the canoe and canoe racing, including *Book of Champions of the Canadian Canoe Association*, *The Canadian Encyclopedia*, *Sport Canadiana* and *Canexus: The Canoe in Canadian Culture*. His articles have appeared in several magazines, among them: *Canoe International*, *Horizon Canada* and *Canoe*. In 1986 he presented a paper to the Royal Society of Naval Architecture Small Boat Symposium at the National Maritime Museum in Greenwich, England, called *In Search of the Canadian Canoe. The Columbian Canoe: Its place in the evolution of the Canadian Canoe*. Fred is currently updating *The Book of Champions* to *100 Years of Canadian Canoeing 1900–2000* and working on a book about canoe racing in Canada tentatively called *Paddles Up: The Origins and Development of Canoe Racing in Canada*.

Fred has enjoyed canoe tripping with his family and friends since the 1960s and now lives in Kingston with a cottage on North Buck Lake, where he maintains a modest fleet of canoes and kayaks including a very weighty 1967 sixteen-foot Chestnut fiberglass canoe for family tripping, a 1964 Kevlar racing kayak for early morning "training" sessions, a 1970s mini-kayak for his kids and grandkids, a 1970s whitewater slalom kayak, and a "very early" fourteen-foot canvas canoe that needs a great deal of loving care prior to paddling. He is looking for a very light sixteen-foot Kevlar canoe to add to his collection.

Kenneth R. Lister

Kenneth R. Lister has been on the staff of the Royal Ontario Museum, Toronto, since 1978 and he is currently head of the Department of Anthropology and curator of the Arctic, Subarctic, Northwest Coast, Paul Kane and watercraft collections. He holds a Master of Arts degree in Anthropology from McMaster University, Hamilton, and has conducted archaeological research in the Hudson Bay Lowland of northern Ontario and ethnographic research among the Cree of northern Ontario and the Inuit of northern Baffin Island.

Based upon his Arctic research, Ken curated the exhibition "In the Time of the Kayak: Hunting in the Eastern Canadian Arctic," which was the inaugural exhibition in the Royal Ontario Museum's "Gallery of Indigenous Peoples." In addition, he was invited by the Canadian Canoe Museum in Peterborough to curate an exhibition based upon their kayak collection, and he has curated and co-curated four exhibitions devoted to the work of Canadian artist Paul Kane. Ken has lectured widely for both university and public audiences on topics of traditional material culture. In addition to lectures, publications, radio and television interviews, and curating exhibitions, he has produced two videos devoted to the construction and role of the kayak in traditional Inuit culture.

Ken spends his time between Port Credit, Lake Ontario, and an island off the western shore of the Bruce Peninsula, Lake Huron. At Port Credit he lives on a forty-two-foot trawler and on Lake Huron he has two canoes: a Norwest eighteen-foot cedar-strip freight canoe and a fifteen-foot cedar-strip Chestnut Prospector.

Ted Moores

Ted Moores and his partner, Joan Barrett, own the Bear Mountain Boat Shop, a family business. The company specializes in providing the highest quality information, products and services to those interested in wooden canoe and kayak building and preserving the spirit of Canada's small craft building heritage. Ted's fascination with canoes and heritage craft began in 1972 when he pioneered an effective system for building wood-strip/epoxy canoes. Since that time the company has built or restored numerous mahogany runabouts, vintage canoes and small watercraft, from elegant one-off designs to the fastest sprint racing canoes on the water, the C4 and C15. Sprint racing is one of the oldest organized sports in Canada, and Ted is the only builder who makes these two boats, carrying on a tradition that has spanned more than 125 years of building and racing in Canada. Each year, Ted is on the road teaching canoe and kayak building classes in several locations in North America, including the San Francisco Maritime Museum, the Mariners' Museum in Newport News, Virginia, and the WoodenBoat School in Brooklin, Maine.

Ted has written two books about building boats: *Canoecraft* and *KayakCraft*, and contributed a how-to chapter article for *Build-A-Boat*, published by *Wooden Boat Magazine*. He belongs to the Wooden Canoe Heritage Association and the Museum Small Craft Association, and regularly volunteers at the Canadian Canoe Museum, where he has assisted in relocating the small-craft collection to Peterborough, developed a woodworking shop and provided graphics and historical information for displays.

Ted's most exciting recent building experience was in December 2000 in Belize, where he worked with a group of Belizians and designer Steve Killing on a cooperative project. They built a racing canoe for the annual La Ruta Maya canoe race that takes place over four days through 180 miles of jungle, from the Guatemalan border to the coast at Belize City. The boats ranged from traditional dugouts, ABS Old Towns, locally made fiberglass and Bear Mountain's version of the dugout: Spanish cedar, epoxy and a lot of varnish. The three paddlers who helped build *Young Ting* were very proud of their boat and led the race for the entire last day into Belize City, with thousands of people cheering them on. They came in third place out of seventy canoes. Ted and Steve intend to go back next year to build a faster, less conservative canoe.

Ted and Joan have just moved to a century home outside Peterborough, with a workshop for Bear Mountain and a stunning view of the Otonabee valley. Ted's favorite boats are a birchbark built by Rick Nash in 1982, a Rob Roy solo canoe Ted built in 1987, an Endeavour kayak he built in 1998, and a twenty-three-foot William Garden–designed motor sailor, in which he enjoys cruising the Trent River system.

Rick Nash

Rick Nash became a canoe builder in 1972 when, as a professional photographer, he went to do a feature on Henri Vaillancourt, the famous bark canoe builder living in New Hampshire. Nash and Vaillancourt collaborated in the next few years and made a number of research trips together documenting Native bark canoe building. In 1977 he became the curator of the Kanawa Museum, which was the precursor of the Canadian Canoe Museum. From 1977 to 1983 he conserved the Museum's boats and built many of his own. Altogether he has built about sixty bark boats, representing Native craft across the continent.

James Raffan

James Raffan is one of Canada's foremost authorities on canoeing and wilderness river experience. He has written for television and numerous periodicals and is author of best selling books *Bark, Skin, & Cedar, Fire in the Bones* and *Tumblehome*, as well as *Wildwaters* (editor), *Canexus* (co-editor) and *Summer North of Sixty*. With degrees in biology, education and geography, James was for eighteen years a professor of outdoor and experiential education at Queen's University, Ontario. Since 1999, his time is divided between writing, speaking and contracts with agencies including the Canadian Canoe Museum in Peterborough, Ontario. In a volunteer capacity, he currently serves as a fellow and governor of the Royal Canadian Geographical Society and as past chair of the Arctic Institute of North America.

James has received several awards for promoting outdoor education and canoeing, including the Dorothy Walter Award and the Robin Dennis Award from the Council of Outdoor Educators of Ontario, and the Award of Merit from the Canadian Recreational Canoeing Association. In 1968, he was given a Canadian Governor General's Award for Gallantry for involvement in a river rescue.

James continues with an active speaking schedule. Recent presentations include "Water: The spirit of celebration and event design" at the International River Festival in Brisbane, Australia, "Wet Wellies and Frozen Drawers" at the 70th Anniversary Conference of the Federation of Ontario Naturalists, and "Canadian Wilderness Waterscapes" given at the 2001 International Conference on Underground Infrastructure Research. His next book, *Deep Water: Courage, Character and the Tragedy of Lake Timiskaming*, will be published in early 2002. James Raffan lives with his family in Eastern Ontario, where his favorite trail-worn green Old Town tripper awaits its next adventure.

PICTURE CREDITS

FRONT COVER

T Corbis; B CCM 980.21.
Photo by Michael Cullen.

FRONT MATTER

1 CCM 977.51. Photo by Michael Cullen. 2 Toni Harting, Toronto. 6 © R. Gehman/Corbis/Magma.

THE NATIVE CRAFT

10T CCM 980.70. Photo by Michael Cullen. 10MT CCM 977.1. Photo by Michael Cullen. 10MB ROM HC 4353. Gift of J.W. McKee. Photo by Michael Cullen. 10B CCM 984.131.1. Photo by Michael Cullen.

THE REALM OF THE BIRCHBARK CANOE

14T Corbis. 14B Based on a map created by Virginia Smith, Sir Sanford Fleming College, Peterborough. 15 CCM 977.51. Photo by Michael Cullen. 16 Alex Henderson, NAC, PA-149753. 17T Collection of the History Section, Nova Scotia Museum, P179/59.60.1/N-14,495. 17B Bob Wilcox, Toronto. 18T Thomas Mower Martin, *Encampment of Woodland Indians*, 1880, Collection of Glenbow Museum, Calgary, Canada. PN: 134, CN: 58.6. 18B Glenbow Archives NA-1700-619. 19 QUA. 20 Adney Collection, The Mariners' Museum, MP118. 21 CCM, 977.38. Photo by Michael Cullen. 22T CMC, 20362. 22B Glenbow Archives NA-1255-44. 23 CCM, 977.24, Photo by Michael Cullen. 24–25 Based on a map created by Virginia Smith, Sir Sanford Fleming College, Peterborough.

THE CANOE FRONTIER

26 Toni Harting, Toronto. 27 CCM 980.21. Photo by Michael Cullen. 28T NAC C-011013/TC-000577. 28B NAC C-142560. 29T National Gallery of Canada, Ottawa. Purchased 1990. Acc. 30490. 29B NAC C-010512. 30T Louis Nicholas, *Codex Canadiensis*, p. 17, from the collection of Gilcrease Museum, Tulsa, Oklahoma. 30B Centre des Archives d'outre-mer, Aix-en-Provence. Archives nationales, France. All rights reserved. Fonds des Colonies, série C11A, vol. 19, fol. 43–43v. 31T National Library of Canada NL 18197. 31B Adney Collection, The Mariners' Museum, MP133. 32T Musée des Augustines de L'Hôtel-Dieu de Québec. 32M Archives nationales du Québec E53. 33T NAC C-002774. 33B CCM 977.27. Photo by Michael Cullen. 34T A.P. Low. NAC PA-038139. 34B Adney Collection, The Mariners' Museum, MP82. 35T Neil Broadfoot. "The Perseverance Coat of Arms" courtesy of Old Fort William Historical Park, Thunder Bay, Canada. 35B Franklin Arbuckle. Hudson's Bay Company Archives, Provincial Archives of Manitoba. HBCA Documentary Art P-412. 36T Centre des Archives d'outre-mer, Aix-en-Provence. Archives nationales, France. All rights reserved. Fonds des Colonies, série C11A, vol. 7, fol. 131. 36M © Canada Post Corporation, (1851), reproduced with permission. NAC POS-002250. 37 NAC C-001229. 38 NAC PA-059517. 39T NAC C-002773. 39M Neil Broadfoot. With permission of Hudson's Bay Company. 40 NAC C-002771. 41T NAC C-016442. 41B Glenbow Archives NA-2597-29. 42 G.M. Kelley. NAC PA-123355. 43T Archives of Ontario C120-2, S 5079. 43B NAC C-110917. 44–45 F.A. Hopkins, *Canoes in a Fog, Lake Superior*, 1869, Collection of Glenbow Museum, Calgary, Canada. PN: 468, CN: 55.8.1.

BUILDING BIRCHBARK CANOES

46 Toni Harting, Toronto. 47 National Gallery of Canada, Ottawa. Purchased 1957. Acc. 6663. 48T CCM 977.42.1. Photo by Michael Cullen. 48B CCM 977.44.1. Photo by Michael Cullen. 49 Adney Collection, The Mariners' Museum, MP135. 50 Photo by T.W. Ingersoll, Minnesota Historical Society, E97.35/P18. 51 QUA. 52 Rick Nash. 53 NAC PA-42083. 54–55 CMC 5663. 55 CCM 980.70. Photo by Michael Cullen. 56 QUA. 57T QUA. 57B Adney Collection, The Mariners' Museum, MP51. 58 Rick Nash. 59–63 Rick Nash.

LIGHT CRAFT FROM THE GREAT NORTHWEST

64 Photo © Wayne Lynch, Alberta. 65T CCM 977.49. Photo by Michael Cullen. 65B Alaska State Library, Alaska Purchase Centennial Commission PCA 20–51. 66T CMC 26072. 66B CCM 977.22. Photo by Michael Cullen. 67 NWT Archives N-1992-212:0085. 68 CMC 52334. 69 CMC 26142. 70–73 D. Gardner/NWT Archives.

VESSELS OF LIFE

74 Ken Powell. **75TL** Hat, Charles Edenshaw, 1850–1900, ME928.57.3. McCord Museum of Canadian History, Montreal. **75TR** CMC S93-4766. **75B** CCM 977.1. Photo by Michael Cullen. **76** Alaska State Library, Winter and Pond Collection, PCA 87-90. **77T** With permission of the Royal Ontario Museum © ROM. 912.1.91. **77B** CMC S89-838. **78T, M, B** Steven C. Brown. **79L** Courtesy of Steven C. Brown. **75TR** CMC S97-14784. **75MR** CMC S97-14507. **75BR** CMC S97-16898. **80M** E/1207, photo by Steven C. Brown, courtesy the Library, American Museum of Natural History. **80B** Joe David. Courtesy of Maltwood Art Museum and Gallery U990.14.474. **81** CCM 980.130. Photo by Michael Cullen. **82T** CMC S96-24172. **82B** From the Collection of the Jefferson County Historical Society, Port Townsend, Washington, 14:12. **83** CCM 977.205. Photo by Michael Cullen. **84** MSCUA, University of Washington Libraries, NA680. **86** CMC S96-24345. **87** CCM 977.11. Photo by Michael Cullen. **88T** CCM 980.6. Photo by Michael Cullen. **88B** CCM 977.5. Photo by Michael Cullen. **89T** CMC S96-24324. **89B** Courtesy of the Royal British Columbia Museum, Victoria, B.C., PN 1583. **90** Glenbow Archives NA-1807-10. **91** Courtesy of the Phoebe Apperson Hearst Museum of Anthropology and the Regents of the University of California, photographed by Steven C. Brown, 2-4677. **92** Photo by H.H. Brodeck. Courtesy of Richard A. Wood. **93T** Roby Littlefield. **93B** Dorica Jackson. **94–95** MSCUA, University of Washington Libraries, NA684.

BUILDING DUGOUTS

96 © J.A. Kraulis/Wonderfile. **97** Ulli Steltzer, from *The Black Canoe* by Ulli Steltzer and Robert Bringhurst, Douglas & McIntyre, Vancouver, B.C. **98T** CMC S97-14642. **98–99** Courtesy of the Royal British Columbia Museum, Victoria, B.C., cat. no. 6600. **99T** CP Picture Archive (Elaine Thompson). **100** Sitka National Historical Park. **101T** The Seattle Art Museum. Gift of John H. Hauberg. 91.1.87. Photo by Paul Macapia. **101B** Hilary Stewart. **102** Photo by J.L. Gijssen, April 12, 1986. Collection of UBC Museum of Anthropology. **103T** E. Arima. **103B** Courtesy of the Royal British Columbia Museum, Victoria, B.C., PN 5409. **104T** The Burke Museum of Natural History and Culture. Lines taken off by Bill Holm; drawn by Leslie Lincoln, 1989. Courtesy of CWB. **104M** Vancouver Centennial Museum, Vancouver, B.C. Lines taken off by Duane Pasco and Leslie Lincoln; drawn by Leslie Lincoln, 1988. Courtesy of CWB. **104–105** Lines taken off and drawn by Leslie Lincoln, 1988. Courtesy of CWB. **105T** Lines taken off and drawn by Bill Durham, 1965. Courtesy of CWB. **105M** National Forest Service, Darrington. Lines taken off and drawn by Leslie Lincoln, 1988. Courtesy of

CWB. **106** Courtesy of E. Arima. **107T, B** Courtesy of E. Arima. **108T** Hilary Stewart. **108B** Neg. no. 128023. Courtesy of the Library, American Museum of Natural History. **109** Jun Hoshikawa. **110T, B** E. Arima. **111** E. Arima. **112** E. Arima. **113** BC Archives C-08103. **114** CMC 46922. **115** Hilary Stewart. **116** Hilary Stewart. **117** Photo by J.M. Blankenburg, Courtesy Allan Lobb. **118T** Emily Carr, 1871–1945; *Cumshewa* 1912; watercolor with graphite and gouache on paper, laid down on cardboard. Collection of Alan Wilkinson. Photo by Michael Cullen. **118B** Catalogue No. 639, Department of Anthropology, Smithsonian Institution. **119** Jun Hoshikawa.

THE KAYAK AND THE WALRUS

120 Corbis. **121** ROM 991.239.1. Drawing by Marianne Collins. **122T, M** ROM. Photos by Kenneth R. Lister. **122B** CCM 977.180. Photo by Michael Cullen. **123T, M** ROM. Drawings by Marianne Collins. **123B** George Simpson McTavish. NAC C-008160. **124TL, TR** CCM 990.6.1. Photos courtesy of OSC. **124B** CCM 982.42. Photo by Michael Cullen. **125TL, TR, BL, BR** CCM 990.6.1. Photos courtesy of OSC. **126L** ROM 992x3.2. Photo by Michael Cullen. **126TR, MR** ROM HC 2363b. Gift of Sir William MacKenzie. Collected by Robert Flaherty. Photos by Michael Cullen. **126B** ROM 992x3.2. Lines taken off by Kenneth R. Lister; drawn by Kenneth R. Lister and Eric Siegrist. **127T** Private collection of James Houston. Photo courtesy of CMC S99-11239. **127M** ROM HC 2363a. Gift of Sir William MacKenzie. Collected by Robert Flaherty. Photo by Michael Cullen. **127B** ROM HC 2363a. Lines taken off by Kenneth R. Lister; drawn by Kenneth R. Lister and Eric Siegrist. **128T** OSC NH 76.34.1. Lines taken off by Kenneth R. Lister; drawn by Kenneth R. Lister and Eric Siegrist. **128TM** CMC IV-C-4094. Lines taken off by Kenneth R. Lister; drawn by Kenneth R. Lister and Eric Siegrist. **128BM** ROM 989.104.1.1. Gift of Mr. T.H.U. Bayly. Lines taken off by Kenneth R. Lister; drawn by Kenneth R. Lister and Eric Siegrist. **128B** Detail. J.J. O'Neill. NAC C-086440. **129T** ROM 989.104.1.1. Photo by Michael Cullen. **129M** CCM 980.19. Photo by Michael Cullen. **129B** Detail. A.A. Chesterfield. Hudson's Bay Company Archives, Provincial Archives of Manitoba. HBC Archives Photographs 1987/363-E-392/40 (N82-331). **130T** National Anthropological Archives, Smithsonian Institution, 38,108. **130M** ROM HC 4353. Gift of J.W. McKee. Photo by Michael Cullen. **130B** ROM HC 4362. Gift of J.W. McKee. Photo by Michael Cullen. **131** Library of Congress, Prints and Photographs Division, LC-USZ62-99663. **132T** Glenbow Archives NC-1-482(c). **132M** ROM HC 2363a. Photo by Michael Cullen. **132B** ROM HC 4353. Photo by Michael Cullen. **133** Catalogue No. 160415, Department of Anthropology, Smithsonian

Institution. **134TL, TR** Jette Bang Phot./Polar Photos. **134B** ROM 997.22.61.1-9. Dr. Jon A. and Mrs. Muriel Bildfell Collection. Gift of Donald Ross. Photo by Michael Cullen. **135L** ROM 971.166.415. Gift of the Anglican Diocese of Toronto Women. Photo by Michael Cullen. **135R** ROM HC 2164b. Gift of Reverend A.L. Fleming. Photo by Michael Cullen. **136** ROM 953.110.2c. Gift of Lorna Durst. Photo by Robert Flaherty. **137T, B** ROM 985.205.6. Gift of John Moore. Photos by Michael Cullen.

BUILDING UMIAKS

138 Jette Bang Phot./Polar Photos. **139** CMC S90-5947. **140T** H.C. Petersen. **140B** Photo by Stephen R. Braund, Anchorage, Alaska. From *The Skin Boats of Saint Lawrence Island, Alaska,* University of Washington Press, 1973. **141T** Adney Collection, The Mariners' Museum, fig. 169, p. 186. **141B** Adney Collection, The Mariners' Museum, fig. 171, p. 187. **142T, B** H.C. Petersen. **143T** Photo by Stephen R. Braund, Anchorage, Alaska. From *The Skin Boats of Saint Lawrence Island, Alaska,* University of Washington Press, 1973. **143M** H.C. Petersen. **143B** H.C. Gulløv. **144T** The Otto Geist Collection, Acc. no. 676, Archives and Manuscripts, Alaska and Polar Regions Department, University of Alaska Fairbanks. **144B** CMC S91-943. **145TL** The Mariners' Museum. **145TR** Photo by Stephen R. Braund, Anchorage, Alaska. **145B** Collins, Henry B. Dr./NGS Image Collection. **146** E. Arima. **147** Private Collection. Photo by Michael Cullen. **148T** CCM 984.131.1. Photo by Michael Cullen. **148B** CCM 984.131.1. Photo by Michael Cullen. **149** Provincial Archives of Alberta, Ernest Brown Collection B9959. **150** Glenbow Archives NC-1-1314(b). **151** Glenbow Archives NC-1-880. **152** Adney Collection, The Mariners' Museum, MP175. **153** Glenbow Archives NC-1-273. **154T** Jette Bang Phot./Polar Photos. **154–155** Catalogue No. 36935, Department of Anthropology, Smithsonian Institution. **155R** Glenbow Archives ND-1-35. **156** Morten Gøthche. **157T, B** H.C. Petersen.

THE RECREATIONAL CANOE

158T ADK 67.209. Photo by Erik Borg. **158B** Michael Cullen. On loan to CCM from Ralph and Nancy Andrews. **159** Gordon McKendrick. **160** Map of the Trent Canal and Navigation Route. Department of Railways and Canals Canada: Ottawa 1933. Courtesy of Trent University Archives. **161** Michelle Walker

FROM FOREST TO FACTORY

162 Toni Harting, Toronto. **163** CCM 986.27. Photo by Michael Cullen. **164, 165T** CCM 977.12. Photos by Michael Cullen. **165B** City Archives/ Peterborough Centennial Museum and Archives. **166T** Detail. NAC C-074863. **166B** CCM. Photo by Michael Cullen. **167T, B** City Archives/

Peterborough Centennial Museum and Archives. **168** CCM 977.109. Photo by Michael Cullen. **169** CIPO. **170T** City Archives/Peterborough Centennial Museum and Archives, PG 5-4a. **170M** Photo courtesy of the Canada Science and Technology Museum, Ottawa. **171, 172** CIPO. **173T** CCM. **173M** City Archives/Peterborough Centennial Museum and Archives. **174T, B** CCM 986.27. Photos by Michael Cullen. **175T** Glenbow Archives NA-3235-32. **175B** City Archives/Peterborough Centennial Museum and Archives, PG 5-4d. **176T, M** Jennifer Moores. **176B** CCM. Photo by Don Rankin. **177** Courtesy of Bill Twist, Christ Church Community Museum, Lakefield, Ontario. **178** City Archives/Peterborough Centennial Museum and Archives. **179T, B** On loan to CCM from Ralph and Nancy Andrews. Photos by Michael Cullen. **180L, R** Jennifer Moores. **181T** CIPO. **181L, R** Jennifer Moores. **182** Courtesy of Ken Brown. **183** Glenbow Archives NA-949-24. **184T** CCM 999.16.1. Photo by Michael Cullen. **184B** CIPO. **185** Tom Thomson, Canadian 1877–1917, *The Canoe* 1914, oil on canvas, 14.4 x 25.3 cm. Art Gallery of Ontario, Toronto. Gift from the J.S. McLean Collection, Toronto, 1969. Donated by the Ontario Heritage Foundation, 1988. Acc. # L69.48. Photo by Carlo Catenazzi. **186** NAC C-030786. **187** From the Gray Family Collection, Old Town Canoe Company. **188** CCM. **189** A.C.Fine Art. **190, 191, 192** CCM. Photos by Don Rankin. **193TL, TR, BL** CCM. Photos by Don Rankin. **193BR** Ted Moores.

PADDLING FOR PLEASURE IN THE NORTHEASTERN STATES

194 Corbis. **195L** ADK. Drawing by Sam Manning after a 1949 description. **195R** Peabody Essex Museum. Salem, Mass. E928. Photo by Jeffrey Dykes. **196T** ADK P.7751. **196M** ADK 71.135.1. Photo by Erik Borg. **196B** ADK 58.350.1. Photo by Erik Borg. **197** ADK. Photo by Richard Walker. **198T** ADK. Drawing by Sam Manning. **198B** ADK. Photo by Richard Walker. **199T** ADK. **199M** ADK 73.113.1. Photo by Erik Borg. **199B** ADK 67.209. Photo by Erik Borg. **200** ADK P.19986. **201T** ADK. Photo by Richard Walker. **201B** Benton Library Board of Trustees. Photo courtesy of Frederic Remington Art Museum, Ogdensburg, NY. **202T** ADK P.47654. **202B** ADK. Photo by Richard Walker. **203T** ADK. **203B** From *Rushton and His Times in American Canoeing* by Atwood Manley, The Adirondack Museum and Syracuse University Press, Syracuse, New York, 1968. **204T** ADK Library. **204B** ADK P.30083. **205T** ADK. Drawing by Sam Manning. **205B** From the Gray Family Collection, Old Town Canoe Company. **206T** ADK. Photo by Richard Walker. **206B** ADK. **207** ADK P.13330. **208T, M** Courtesy of the Smithsonian Institution, NMAH/Transportation. Photos by Richard Walker. **208B** ADK. Photo by Richard Walker. **209, 210**

From the Gray Family Collection, Old Town Canoe Company. **211** ADK.

FAST PADDLES AND FAST BOATS

212–13 NAC C-013285. **214–15** NAC PA-112273. **214B** Royal Canoe Club Archives. **215T** British Canoe Union. **215B** Royal Canoe Club Archives. **216T** By permission of the British Library, Halifax N.S. vol 16 1881 PG 376. **216B** C. Fred Johnston. **217** ADK. Photo by S. Stoddard. 845P 15453. **218T** New York State Historical Association Library, Cooperstown. **218B** New York State Historical Association Library, Cooperstown. **219** Toronto Reference Library (TPL): T12123. **220** New York State Historical Association Library, Cooperstown. **221** American Canoe Association. **222** CCAC. **223** J. Ross Robertson Collection, Toronto. **225** New York State Historical Association Library, Cooperstown. **226T** John N. MacKendrick Collection, CCAA. **226B** Gordon McKendrick. **227** Aubry Ireland Sr. Collection, CCAA. **228** NAC PA-122156. **229** Brockville Museum Archives 999A47.01. **230** NAC PA-32333. **231** City of Ottawa Archives, Britannia Yacht Club Collection, CA-1832. **232T** Olympic Spiele, Berlin, 1936. Zurich: Verkehrsverlag. A.G. 1936. **232B** Mary Amyot, CCAC. **234** CCM, Sailing Canoe. Photo by Michael Cullen. **235** Photo F. Scott Grant, CCAC. **236T** Steve Giles. **236B** Steve Giles. **237** Toni Harting, Toronto.

PRESERVING THE HISTORY OF THE CANOE

238 Adney Collection, The Mariners' Museum, PP444. **239** Kirk Wipper.

THE SCHOLAR: TAPPAN ADNEY

240 Adney Collection, The Mariners' Museum, PP444. **241** Adney Collection, The Mariners' Museum, MP84.

THE COLLECTOR: KIRK WIPPER

242 Rick Nash. **243** CCM. Photo by Michael Cullen. **244T** CCM 980.21. Photo by Michael Cullen. **244M** CCM 977.1. Photo by Michael Cullen. **244B** Kirk Wipper. **245T** CCM 977.12. Photo by Michael Cullen. **245B** CCM 977.47. Photo by Michael Cullen. **246T** CCM 986.16. Photo by Michael Cullen. **246B** Kirk Wipper. **247T** Don Starkell. **247B** CCM *Orellana*. Photo by Michael Cullen. **248T** CCM 980.2. Photo by Skip Dean. **248B** CCM Welsh coracle. Photo by Skip Dean. **249T** CCM 984.135. Photo by Skip Dean. **249B** CCM WP 983.1a. Photo by Michael Cullen.

BACK COVER

T Glenbow Archives NC-1-273. M CCM 977.1. Photo by Michael Cullen. BM ROM HC 4353. Gift of J.W. McKee.Photo by Michael Cullen. B ADK. Photo by Richard Walter.

INDEX

Numbers in italics refer to illustrations, photos and caption text.

A

Abenaki, *13*, 20, 21, 53
ACA. *See* American Canoe Association
Adair, 224–25
Adams, Victor, *75*, *239*, *244*
Adirondack guideboats, 198, *198*, 199, *199*, *200*, 205
Adirondack region, *161*, 195, 196, 197, 198, *202*, 205
    and Nessmuk, 207, *208*
Adney, Edwin Tappan, 19, 20, 43, 68, *240*, 240–41
    models by, *31*, *34*, *49*, *57*, *152*, *241*
adornment. *See* decoration
adze, 48, 98, *108*, 113, 114
Alaskan kayak styles, 131–32
Alden, W.L., 202, 204
Aleut canoes, *23*, *25*, *33*, 42, 53–55, *58*, *244*
Aleut kayaks, 131–32. *See also* baidarkas
Aleut *nigilax*, 149, 153, 155
Aleut peoples, *12*, 133
Algonquin canoes, *23*, *25*, *33*, 43, 53–55
Algonquin peoples, *13*, 21, 25, *31*, 43, 53
Allegra, *199*
all-wood canoes, 179, 183, 187. *See also* wooden canoes
aluminum canoes, 188, 210
American Canoe Association (ACA), *21*, 178, 179, *203*, 204, *217*, 219–31
    Canadians and, 203–204, 220, 226, 232, 233
    formation, 203, 219
American Canoeist, The, 218, 221, 222
American west, 33–35
Amur Valley canoes, 20, *20*, 23, 69
Amyot, Frank, *232*, 234
angyapik, 140, *143*, *144*. *See also* umiaks
animal fat, 43, 62
animal hides, 58, 66, 67, 125, 126. *See also* names of individual animals
animal hunting. *See* hunting
animals, Inuit relationship with, 136–37
aquatic sports, 216, 217. *See also* canoe sport; names of individual sports
Arctic Bay kayak, *121*, 121–22, *123*, 124–25
Arima, Eugene, 127
Armstrong, William, *29*
artifacts, 126, 127, 154, 198, 243, 246, 247

Peary Land umiak (1440 CE), 142, 143, 155
Athapaskan canoes, 20, *65*, 68–69
Atlantic Labrador kayaks, *126*, 130
Attikamek, 53
Avasisaartoq kayak, 128
awl, 61, 53, 59, 71
axe, 47, 71, 98, 112, 113, 114

B

baidarkas, *130*, 131–32, *133*, 133
baleen, 123, 142
Band canoes, 103, *110*, *118*, *119*
bark, 23, *23*, 44, 60, 70, 71. *See also* birchbark; elm bark; spruce bark
bark canoes, 19–20, *22*, 23, *30*, 198, 241. *See also* birchbark canoes
Bark Canoes and Skin Boats of North America, The, 19, *240*, 241
basswood, 164, 168, 176
basswood canoe, 190–93
basswood dugout, Payne, *164*, *165*, 244, *245*
Bastard canoes, 40, *41*, *42*, 43
bâtard canoes. *See* Bastard canoes
bateaux, 198, 199, 205. *See also* Adirondack guideboats
battens, 175, 193
beaver, 36. *See also* fur trade
Beaver peoples, *12*, 22, 68
Bell of Peterborough, 165
Bellingham, Norm, *235*
Bering Sea kayak, 131
Bering Strait kayaks and umiaks, *130*, 155, 156
bifid bow, *130*, 131–32, *133*, 154
bilge, 51
Birch, George, 188
birch trees, *14*, 16, 19, 47, 60, 197
birchbark, 23, 49, 57, 67, 197, 205
    qualities of, 15–16, 69, 180
birchbark canoes, 15–23, *31*, 47–63, 197, 219. *See also* names of individual canoes; names of individual canoe types
    Algonquin, Abenaki and Attikamek, 53–55
    building, 47–58. *See also* construction sequences
    Cree, 56–58
    Mi'kmaq and Maliseet, 49–53
    origins and evolution, 47
    scarcity of today, 23, 47, *243*
    sizes, *41*, 43, 50, 51, 56

Birchbark Canoes of the Fur Trade, 45
bird spear, 133, 135
Bishop, Nathaniel Holmes, 201, 203, *217*, 219, 220, 227, *249*
Black, Annie, 70, *70*
Black, Martha, 81
Black, Nick, 70, *70*, *71*, *72*, *73*
Blackburn, Robert C., 233
blocking-in, 109, *110*, 111
blocks, 57
Blue Bird, *246*, 247
board-and-batten canoes, 169, 172, 174. *See also* wide-board-and-batten canoes
boats. *See* names of individual boat types
Bohemian Club, 231, 233
Boillard, Maxime, *236*
Bonnie, 225
Bossi, Max, *249*
bow drill handle, 144, *144*
bows, bifid. *See* bifid bow
Braund, Stephen, 147, 153
Britannia Boat House Club, 231, *231*, 232, 233
British, contribution to canoe sport, 214–15
British Nautilus Canoe Club, 215
British North America, 36, 40
Britton, Ralph, *223*
Broadfoot, Neil, *35*, *39*
Brockville Evening Recorder, The, 232, 233
Brockville Rowing Club, *229*, 231, 232
Brody, Hugh, 18
Brown Bear canoe, 80, *90*, 90
Brown Boat Company, *163*, *174*
Brown, Frank, 95
Brown, John G., *163*, *174*
Brownscombe, Felix, *175*, 177, 187
Buffalo Yacht Club, 52, *243*
building canoes, 47–58. *See also* building dugouts; construction sequences
    Algonquin, Abenaki and Attikamek, 53–55
    Cree, 56–58
    decline, 86, 93, 94
    mass production, 166–68, 174–76
    Mi'kmaq and Maliseet, 49–53
    revival, 67, 86, *93*, 99
    voyaging fur trade, 42–45
building dugouts, 97–118
    acquiring log, 101–103
    carving shape, 103, 109, 111–13
    fittings and finishing, 117–18
    hollowing and patching, 113–15
    spreading, 115–17

building umiaks, 139–57
  covering, 145–49
  framework construction, 140, 142–45
building bed, 57
building forms, *166*, 166–67
building frames, 57, 59, 60
Burchard, R.B., 204
Burkhart, Will, *93*
Bush Garden, The, 23
Butler, Paul, *223*

C

Camp Kandalore, 243, 244, 245, 248, 249
Camp Pinecrest, 244
camps, summer 209, *225*
Canada, 18, 39, 42, 163
  agriculture, 16–17
Canadian Shield, 16, 163
  canoe sport, 216–17, 235–36
  fur trade, *24–25*, 35–40
    mapping, 38. *See also* Geological
      Survey of Canada
    northwest, 65–69
Canadian Canoe Association (CCA), 204,
  230, 231, 232–34, 235, 236
Canadian Canoe Company, *170*, *175*,
  177, 187, 230
Canadian Canoe Museum, *75,* 124, *148*,
  176, 216, 233, 249
Canadian canoes, 177, 204, 221, 226,
  235. *See also* open canoes
  and ACA, 227–28, 229
  modern, 216, 217–18
Canadian Museum of Civilization, 91,
  144
Canadian turn, *230*
Canadian Watercraft Limited, 186–87,
  188
canoe bailers, *91*, *98*
canoe birch. *See* white birch trees
canoe frontier, *24–25,* 27–45
Canoe in Canadian Cultures, The, 127
Canoe Islands, *217*
Canoe Lake, *185*
canoe liveries, 207, 209, 210
canoe-making tools, 102, *112. See also*
  names of individual tools
Canoe Manned by Voyageurs Passing a
  Waterfall, 40
canoe nails, 170
Canoe or the Flying Proa, or, Cheap
  Cruising and Safe Sailing, The, 202
canoe-pullers, 95
canoe routes, map, *24–25*

canoe scholarship. *See* Adney, Edwin
  Tappan
canoe sport, 212–36
  American Canoe Association, 219–31
  British contribution, 214–15
  in Canada, emergence, 216–17
  Canadian Canoe Association, build-
    ing, 232–34
  golden years (1919–39), 234
  modern Canadian canoe and, 217–18
  post–Second World War, 235–36
  Second World War, 235
canoe tents, 202, *202*
Canoe, The, 185
Canoecraft, 179
canoedling, *179*
Canoes, 30
canoes. *See also* dugouts; names of indi-
    vidual canoes; names of individual
    canoe types
  building, 47–58. *See also* construction
    sequences
  costs, 100, 103, 210
  decoration, 69, *76*, 89, 90, 118, *205,*
    244
  demise of, 45
  living tradition, 250–51
  mass production, 166–68, 174–76
  sizes, 20, 55, 57, 69, 84, 85, *106*
  study and preservation. *See* Adney,
    Edwin Tappan
  synthetic materials for, 210–11
  transporting, 210
  value of to Native societies, 15, 78–80
Canoes in a Fog, Lake Superior, 45
canot bâtard. See Bastard canoes
canot du maître, 41. See also Montreal
    canoes
canot du nord, 243. See also North canoes
Canuck, 226
canvas, 45, 180, 205, 206
canvas-covered canoes, 187, 206. *See also*
    wood-canvas canoes
cap finial, 83
cap strip, 117, 118
Capital Boat Works, 230
carbon fiber, 235
cargo canoes, 22, 69
caribou hide, 58, 67, 126
caribou hunting, *128, 129,* 131, 134–35,
    151
Caribou Inuit kayak, 131
Carleton, Guy, 180, 182, 205
Carleton Place Canoe Club, 232
Carpenter, Dr. Edmund, 246

carpentered canoes, 16
Carr, Emily, *118*
cars, 210
Cartier, Jacques, 17, 28
carvel planking, 218
carving dugout shape, 103, 109, 111–13
Catholic religion, 29, 45
caulking, 43, 102, 190
cedar, 49, 58, 59, 60, 91, 168. *See also*
    names of individual types of cedar
cedar branch rope, 115, 117
cedar-canvas canoes, *169, 170,* 178–83,
    184, 186
cedar-plank canoes, 248, *249*
cedar-rib canoes, 171–73, 174, *188, 234*
cedar-strip canoes, 100, 172, 173, 174,
    176
Cedar Strip Cruiser No. 44, *179*
cedar-strip outboard runabouts, 187, 188
center rot, 102, *103,* 109, 115
centerboard, *201*
centerline, 109
Century Magazine, The, 222
ceremonial canoes, *89,* 90–91, *102, 249*
chainsaws, 71, *108,* 111
de Champlain, Samuel, 17, 25, *31*
Chapelle, Howard, 19, *240,* 241
Charlie, Simon, 247
Charter Group, The, 245
Charters, Harvey, 234
Chebucto Canoe Club, 216
Chestnut and Sons, R. *See* R. Chestnut
    and Sons
Chestnut Canoe Company, 20, 182,
    183–87, 188, 189
Chestnut canoes, 184, *184, 189*
Chestnut, Harry, 186
Chestnut, Robert, 183
Chestnut, William G., *181,* 184, *184,* 186
children, role in building Native craft,
    43, 98
chine, 140
chine stringers, 143, *143*
Chinook canoes, 83, *214*
Chinook peoples, *12,* 75
Chipewyan canoes, *15,* 22, *50,* 68
Chipewyan peoples *12,* 22. *See also*
    Ojibwa peoples
Chukchi umiaks, 155, 156
Cincinnati Canoe Club, *217*
Civilian Conservation Corps, 91
claws, *176*
Clipper canoes, 100
Clipper Northern Dancer, 100
clipper ships, 85

clothing, Native, *75, 134, 135*
club canoes, 224, 229, *232*
clubs, 217, 218. *See also* names of indi-
    vidual clubs
coamings, 125, *130, 132*
Coast Salish canoes, 86–88, *88,* 94–95,
    104, 105
Coast Salish peoples, *12,* 75, *82,* 86, 87
cockpits, 121, 122, *130,* 131, 132
Coleman Company, 210
collecting canoes. *See* Wipper, Kirk
Colville, Alex, *189*
Comet, 218
Commanda Algonquin canoe, *244*
Commanda, Mary and William, *25, 244*
Commercial Advertiser, The, 231
Composite Engineering Inc., *235*
Connecticut River, 195, 200
Conover, Alexandra and Garrett, 211
construction. *See* building canoes; build-
    ing dugouts; building umiaks
construction sequences
  Arctic Bay kayak, 124–25
  birchbark canoe, 59–63
  Dogrib canoe, 70–73
  wide-board-and-batten basswood
    canoe, 190–93
coracles, 152–53, 154, 155, *248*
cottonwood, 76, 91
Coulonge river system, 55
Cousineau, Claude, 245
covering umiaks, 145–49
coverings, 125, 126, 145–49, 180
Cowichan Band, 247
Craigie, John, 166
Cranmer, Doug, 100
Cree canoes, *51,* 55, 56–58, 180
Cree peoples, *18, 19,* 21, 44, 53, *54, 175*
Creighton, Donald, 17, 28
Crichlow, Renn, 235
crooked canoes, *19, 30,* 56, *56,* 57, *57*
crooked knife, *51,* 59, 71
crossbars, 54, 58, 59, 60
crosspiece, *83*
Cruising Canoeist, A, 201
cruising canoes, 195, *201,* 204, 222
Cumberland House, 44
Cumshewa, 118
Currier and Ives, 198
Curtis, Edward S., *18, 131*
Curved kayak, 128
cut tacks, 170
cutting gauge, 175
Cutty Sark, 85
cutwater, *87,* 88, *106,* 113, 118

265

D

D-adze, *79*, *98*
Dalhousie, Earl of, 216
Dalton, George, Sr., 91
Darling, J., 180, 205
David, Joe, *80*
Davidson, Alfred, 91
Davidson, Robert Sr., 91
Dean, Walter, 176, *182*
deck caps, 193
decked canoes, 174, *201*, 215, 222
    cruising, 195, 204
    sailing, *223*, *234*
decks, 69, *124*, 192
decoration, 69, *76*, 89, 90, 118, *205*, *244*
DeKay, Charles, 222
deLaguna, Frederica, 92
Dene canoes, *69*
Dey, Joseph, *233*
Diana, *202*
Dogrib canoes, 22, *66*, 67, *69*, 70–73
Dogrib Divisional Board of Education, 70
Dogrib peoples, *12*, 22, 68
Dorset Culture, 152
Dorval Juniors, 231
double-blade paddles, *126*, *136*, 215, *218*, *219*, 221, 233
double-cedar canoe, 169–70, 172
Douglas, Campbell Mellis, *216*, 221–22
Douglas, George, *216*, 221
Douglas, Lionel, *216*
dowels, 113, 114
driftwood, 123, 140
du Guay, Antoine, 42
dubbing irons, *176*
duck boats, 174
Duff, Wilson, 85, *98*
dugouts, 23, *196*. *See also* names of individual dugout types
    building, 97–118
    design influence, 80–81
    in the twentieth century, 93–95
    Northwest Coast styles, 75–95
    Payne, *164*, *165*, 244, *245*
    value of to Native societies, 78–80
Durant, William West, *208*

E

Earl of Dalhousie, 216
East Arctic umiaks, 155
East Hudson Bay kayaks, *124*, 130
East Hudson Bay umiaks, 156, 157

Eastern Canadian Arctic kayaks, 123, *124*, 128, *128*, 130–31, *136*
Eastern Hudson Bay kayak, *123*, *128*, *129*
Eastmure, Beatrice, *227*
Eastmure, Evelyn, *227*
Eckford, Henry, 222
Edenshaw, Charles and Isabella, *75*
Edwards, Elihu Burril (E.B.), *217*, 220, 221, 222
Elisha Waters and Son, *249*
elk antler chisel, 102
elk hide, 115
Elliott Bay, *84*
Elliott, Orville, 233
elm bark, *31*, 22, 197
elm bark canoes, 22, *30*, *31*, 32, 45, *195*
E.M. White Company, 211
Emmons, George T. (G.T.), 86, 89, *90*, 92
end-blades, 113
end-blocks, 91, *93*
end-fins, 92
end-pieces, 84, 89
English Canoe Company, 225
English, James, 168
English, Samuel W., 168
English, William, 168
"Eskimo About Bering Strait, The," 149, 150, 152, 156
Etchinelle, Gabe, *67*
European boats, *35*, 136
Europeans, 18, 43, 47, 67, 126, 136
Everson, James, 203
Evinrude Detachable Engine, 185
Expo '86 , 91, *102*

F

Faces, Voices, and Dreams, 88
Fahey, Mick, 211
Farnham, Charles, 195, 198
felling trees, 101, 102
Femmes cousant les peaux de l'umiaq, 147
Fenimore, James, 203
fiberglass, 100, 235
fiberglass canoes, 188, 210, *236*, *237*
fiberglass kayak, *211*
Fidler, Peter, 66
Field Magazine, The, 215
finishes, for wooden canoes, 176
finishing dugouts, 118
fins, 92
fire, use of, 102
fires, at canoe companies, 176, *177*, 177, 186, 187

firearms, 86, 136
First Manitoba Lone Scouts, 243
First World War, 185, *186*, 18, 233, 234
first-class canoes, 215
fishing boats, 94
Fisk, Homer, 187
fittings, 117–18
fixed coaming, *132*
Flaherty, Robert, *127*
flares, 88, 89, 91, 92, *95*, *100*
Flat kayak, 128
flat models, 98
Fleming, Sanford, *36*
flush batten, 178
flush-lap planking, *198*
Flying Cloud, 165
folding canoes, 174
Forbes, H.C., *183*
forefoot, *121*, 122, *128*, *129*
Forest and Stream, 202, *207*, 215, 217
    on canoe sport, 225, 226, 227, 228, 229, 231
Fort Anne, 197
Fort Chipewyan, as a trading post, *36*
Fort Duquesne, 34
Fort Frontenac, 33
Fort George, *19*
Fort McPherson, 40
Fort Norman, 65, *68*
Fort Ouiatenon, 34
Fort Rae, *66*, *69*
Fort Rouille, 34
Fort William, *29*, 43, 44
Fort Yukon, 40
forts, map, *24–25*
François, Claude, *32*
Frank, Randy, *110*
Fraser, Simon, 38
Freeman, Milton, 136
freighter canoes, *53*, *175*, *183*
French, in North America, 25, 29, 30, *32*, 33–35, 36, 42
French River, *46*
Friede, Leo, *223*
frontier, canoe. *See* canoe frontier
Frye, Northrop, 23
Full Circle journeys, 95
fur seal hunting, 85
fur trade, 22, *24–25*, 29, *32*, *36*, *45*, 65
    Canadian, 35–40
    voyaging canoes of, 42–45
Fur Traders at Montreal, The, *28*

G

Gananoque Club, 235
Gardner, Don, 67
Garrish, Evan (Eve) H., 182, 208
gas engines, 94
gasboats, 85
Gatineau region, 23, 54, 55
gatwaat, 152–53
gauge, cutting, 175
Geological Survey of Canada, *34*, 38, 40, *41*, 135, *183*
Gibson, Robert W., 224, 228
Gidmark, David, 241
Giles, Steve, *236*
gillnet fishing boats, 94
Gitk'san, 76, 89
Glwa canoe, 95
Going Out: Deer Hunting in the Adirondacks, *199*
gold rushes, 40, 87, *182*
Googoozenia, 229
Gordon Canoe Co., 174, *177*
Gordon, Gilbert, 168
Gordon, Thomas, 166, *166*, 167–68, *174*, 177, 218
gores, 58, 60
Gores Landing, 168, *170*
Governor General of Canada, 216, 220
Grahamdale, 243
grain, of wood, 15, 49, 102, 112
Grand Portage, 43
Grand Trunk Boating Club, 217, 232
Grant, H.D., *199*
Gray, George, 183, 208
Gray, Herbert, 208
Gray Hardware, 183
Great Canoe Meet at Stony Lake, 221
Great Canoes, The, 95
Great Peace of 1701, *30*, 32
Great Whale River, 56
Greenland jacket, *134*
Greenland kayaks, *122*, 127, 128
Greenland umiaks, 157
Griffiths, Professor M.G., 244
Grindstone Island, 222, 224
Grumman Aircraft Engineering Corporation, 188, 210
Grumman, Leroy, 210
Grunau River, *233*
guideboats. *See* Adirondack guideboats
guideboat-style planking, 199
guides, 183, 205
gum, spruce. *See* spruce gum
gumming, 58

gunwales, *47*, 90, *124*, 144
gutskin jacket, *134*
Gwich'in canoes, *66*, 68
Gwich'in peoples, *12*, 22

H

Haida canoes, *89*, *102*, *106*, *118*
Haida dugouts, *239*, *244*
Haida Gwaii, 90, *102*
Haida peoples, *12*, 76, 89, 90
half-lap joint, 173
Halifax Harbour, 216
Hammond, Samuel H., 199, 200
Han, 22
hand tools, 112, 113. *See also* names of
 individual tools
handholds, *130*, 131
Hare canoes, 68
Hare peoples, *12*, 22
Harmony, 222
harp seal, 145
Harper's Young People, 240
harpooning, 139–40
harpoons, 84, 133, 135, *136*, 136
Harvard University, Peabody Museum, 93
Hauthaway, Bart, *211*
Hawkes, Ernest, 135
Hay Island, 230
HBC. *See* Hudson's Bay Company
head block, *111*
Head canoes, 89, 92–93, *110*, *112*
headboards, 68, 143
headdress frontlet, *77*
Hearne, Samuel, 66
Heiltsuk canoe, 80, 89, 90
Heiltsuk peoples, *12*, 76
Herald Canoe Company, 168
Herald Patent Canoe, 169–70
Herald, Dan, 168, *168*, 169–70, *170*, 218,
 220
Herald's Boat and Canoe Mould, 169,
 169
heritage, Native, 246
Heye collection, *245*, 246, *248*
hides. *See* animal hides; names of indi-
 vidual animals
high kneel position, *226*
hiking boards, 204
hiking seat, sliding, *223*
Hillcrest, 222
Hinckley, E.L., 183
Hoffman, William J., 210
hog, 51

hogging, 69
hollowing dugouts, 113–15
Holm, Bill, 88, 91
Homer, Winslow, 198
hooded seal, 145
hook scarf, *142*
Hoonah, 91, *92*
Hopkins, Edward, 39, *45*
Hopkins, Frances Anne, *33*, 39, *39*, *40*,
 43, *45*
Hornell, James, 152
hounding, *200*
Hudson Bay, 126
Hudson–James Bay system, 16
Hudson River, 196, 200, *211*
Hudson River Gorge, 195
Hudson Strait kayaks, *127*, 130
Hudson Strait umiaks, 146, 156, 157
Hudson's Bay Company, 36, 38–40, *39*,
 44, 65, 185, 240
Hudson's Bay Company canoes, *43*, *249*
Hudson's Bay Store, Fort William, *29*
Hudson–Mohawk system, 33
hull spreading, 115–17
hulls, *76*, 80, 101, *126*, 130, 131
Hummingbird, *99*
Hunt, Chief Calvin, *110*, 111, *112*, *118*
Hunt, Tony, 97
hunter-gatherer peoples, map, *17*
hunting, 133, 134. *See also* names of
 individual animals
 canoes and, 78
 clothing, *134*, *135*
 equipment for, *129*, 133, 135
 kayaks and, 121–22, 127, 132–37
 umiaks and, 139–40
Huron peoples, 17, 22, 45
hybrid canoes, 54, 57

I

In the Land of the Head-Hunters, 93
In the Land of the War Canoes, 94
Indian Encampment, Fort William, *29*
Indian Frontier of the American West, The,
 30
Indian Old Town Canoe Company. *See*
 Old Town Canoe Company
Indigenous Games, *118*
Industrial Development Bank, 188
Industrial Journal, The, 180
innovators, canoe mass production,
 167–71
Innu peoples, *13*, 21

Intellectual Culture of the Iglulik Eskimos,
 126
International Canoe Federation, 231, 236
International Sailing Challenge Cup, *223*
Inuit-animal relationship, 136–37
Inuit art, *127*, *134*, *137*, *147*
Inuit culture, 121, 136
Inuit hunting, 134, 136
Inuit kayaks, 20, 123–26, 127
Inuit, Whaling and Sustainability, 136
Inukpuk, Charlie, *147*
Inuvialuit kayak, 131
Inuvialuit peoples, *12*, 133
Invincible, 223
inwale, 72
irons, dubbing, *176*
Iroquois canoes, 28, 30, 31, 32, 45
Iroquois Defeat at Lake Champlain, *31*
Iroquois peoples, *13*, 17, 22, *30*, 45, 197,
 216
Isabel, photo of, *220*
Island Amateur Aquatic Association
 Regatta, *227*
Ivaluardjuk, 136
Ivuyivik, 146

J

Jackson Creek, 168
Jackson, Nathan, *93*
James Bay, 19, 44
J.C. Risteen Co., 184
Jenness, Diamond, *128*
Jerome, Noel, *23*
Jersey Blue, 219
Jessup's Neck, *219*, 224, 226
Jo, Peter, 240
Johnston, Fisk, 220, 221, 222, 223,
 224–25, 226, 227
joints, 84, 142, 173
Jones, Ford, 226
Juniper Island, 221

K

Kahnawake, 45, 216
Kaigani Haida, 76, *76*
Kalm, Peter, 197
Kanawa International Museum, *239*, 243,
 244, 245, 246, 249
Kane, Paul, *77*, 86
Kanesatake, 45, 216
Kasaan village, *89*
kayak-type canoes, 22, 68–69
kayaks, 20, 65, 66, 68, 69, 121–37, 139

 See also baidarkas; names of indi-
 vidual kayaks; names of individual
 kayak types
 Alaska, 131–32
 Curved, 128
 of eastern Canada, 128, 130, 131
 Flat, 128
 geographic range of use, 139
 Greenland, 128
 hunting and, 121–22, 132–37
 sporting events, *227*, *235*, 235, 236
 walrus and, 136–37
keel, 128, 140, *142*, 142, 192
keelson, 122, 172, 173
Kéet Yakw., 90
Kelly, George, 233
Kennebec River, 20, 195
Kennedy, Senator Robert, *211*
Kent, Timothy (Tim), 43, 45
Kevlar, 100, 211
Killer Whale canoe, 90–91. *See also* cere-
 monial canoes
King Island vessels, *130*, *141*, 153
Kingston Yacht Club, 231, 232
Klanie, Archie, 91
Klondike gold rush, 40, *182*
Knappe, E.C., 225, 226
Ko-ko-ko-ho, 224, 229
Koryak umiak, 152–53, 154
Kotzbue Sound umiaks, 156
Kutenai canoes, *20*, 23, 69, *245*
Kutenai peoples, 20
Kwakiutl canoes and dugouts, *110*, 111,
 118, *119*
Kwakiutl peoples 76, 88. *See also*
 Kwakwaka'wakw peoples
Kwakwaka'wakw canoe, *109*
Kwakwaka'wakw peoples, *12*, 76, 86, 88

L

L'Hirondelle, *234*
Lac St.-Jean, *55*
Lachine, *35*, 39, 45
Lachine Boat and Canoe Club, 217, 232
Lachine Regatta, 217
de Lahontan, Baron, *28*
Lake Banook, 216, *236*
Lake Champlain, 196, 223, 226
Lake George, 196, 203, *217*, 219, *220*,
 220, 225
Lake of the Woods, *15*, *21*
Lake St. John, 56, 57
Lakefield, 163, 217

Lakefield Canoe Building and
    Manufacturing Company, 175,
    177, *177*, 178, *182*, *216*
Lakefield Regatta, 165
lances, *217*, 133, 135
Langley, Maud, *227*
lapstrake canoes, 184
lapstrake planking, 198, *198*,
lapstrake skiffs, 174
lard, 62, 73
lashing, 53, 58, 61, 114–15, *122*, 122,
    123
Laughlin, William, 153
laws, against Native traditions, 86
Laws, Jack, 233
leeboard
Lightning, 218
Little Whale River, 56, 57
liveries, canoe, 207, 210
Lock-Wood Limited, 188
logs, 101–103, *103*, 109, 111, 112–13
Longworth, Judge Nicholas, *217*
Lootaas, 91, *102*, 103
Lord Dufferin, 220
Lorna Island, *217*
Lowell, 205
Loyalists, 207
lumber, 117, 140
Lumbermen's Regatta, 212, 213
Lyle, Morley, *175*, 187

M

M. Poirier and Sons, 245
MacGregor, John, 200, 202, *202*, 214,
    215, 215, 219
MacGregor's Line, 202
machined edge, 172
MacKendrick, Harry F., *226*, 226, 227
MacKendrick, James, 226
MacKendrick, John N., 226, 228
MacKendrick, William (Will), 226, 228,
    229, 231, 232
Mackenzie, Alexander, 38, 66
MacKenzie, Alister M., 233, 234
Mackenzie Delta kayaks and umiaks, 131,
    149, 155
Mackenzie, George, *70*
Mackenzie Inuit umiaks, 142
Mackenzie, Joe, 70, *70*, *71*, *72*
Mackenzie, Julie, 70
Mackie, B. Allan, 245
Macrae, Maida, *227*
Maggie, 222
Main Channel, *24*, *25*

Maine bateaux, 198. *See also* bateaux
Maine canoe production, 178–83, 206,
    208
Maine guides, 183, 205
de Maître, Louis, 42
Makah peoples, 75, 77, 82
    and canoes, 77, 82–86, 87, *99*
Maliseet canoes, *48*, 49–53
Maliseet peoples, *13*, 20, 50
    Tappan Adney and, 240, 241
Mallory, Michael, 188
Mamie, 222
Mandan peoples, *12*, *248*
Manley, Atwood, 224
maple, 118, 164
maps
    Adirondack Waterways, *161*
    Growing Area of the Birch Tree, *14*
    Native peoples, *12–13*
    Fur Trade Frontier, *24–25*
    Northeast Coast of North America,
        160
    Northeastern United States and
        Canada, *161*
    Peterborough, Ontario and
        Surrounding Area, *160*
    Territory of the Hunter-Gatherer
        Peoples, *17*
Maranda, Patrick, *23*, *243*
Mariners' Museum, 240, 241, 247
Martin, Joe, *99*
Martin, T. Mower, *18*
mass production, canoe, 163–89
Matilpe, Alfie, *110*
McLain, Bill, 180, 205
McNaughton, C.A., 232
McNeil, E.R., 232
McNichol, A., 233
Memorial Canoe #2, *80*
men, role in building Native craft, 43,
    71, 124
metallic batten canoes, *163*, *174*, 174–76
metallic battens, *174*, 175
Metis, *29*, 29, 40
Mi'kmaq canoes, *48*, *49*, 49–53, 58
Mi'kmaq peoples, *13*, *17*, 20
Milligan, S.J., 234
Mississauga peoples, 164, 244
Mississauga River, 15, *162*
models, 98, *98–99*, *101*, *118*, 126, *133*.
    See also Adney, Edwin Tappan
Mohawk River, and Iroquois territory, 22
Mohican, 229
molds, 57, 167, 178. *See also* solid build-
    ing form

Montagnais canoes, *31*, 57
Montagnais peoples, *16*
Montagnais/Cree canoes, *22*, *51*, 56
Montagnais/Naskapi, 53, 56
Montreal, 42
Montreal canoes, *29*, *33*, *34*, 43, 45, 212,
    241
Moore, Jack J., 183, 184
moose hide boat, *67*, *68*
moose hides, 66, 67
Morris, B.N., 208
mortises, 121
MotorBoat magazine, 209
motors, outboard, 149, 209
mouth slit, *88*
Munka canoes, 86, *110*. *See also* war
    canoes
Muntz, R.H., *227*
Museum of the North American Indian,
    246
museums. *See* names of individual
    museums
Muskoka Lake, 232

N

Nanook of the North, *127*
Nanya.aayí clan, 90
*Narrative of a Voyage to Hudson's Bay in
    His Majesty's Ship Rosamond*, 123
Nash, Rick (Richard), *58*, 246
Naskapi, 21, 57
Naskapi canoes, *55*, 57
Naskapi/Montagnais, 53, 56
National Championship of Canada, *227*,
    233, 234, 235
Native canoe races, *214*, 216, 217, *228*
Native canoes, 16, 20, 47, *54*, *197*, 241.
    See also names of individual types
    of canoes
Native clans, 90
Native division of labor, 71, 124
Native heritage, Canadian, 246
Native peoples, *12–13*, 18, 22, 29, 30, 43,
    196–97. *See also* names of individ-
    ual bands
Native traditions, 70, 85, 86
Nautilus 5 and *6*, 219
Nawashish, Cesar, *33*
Neel, David, 95
Nelson, Edward, 149, 150, 152, 156
Nessmuk (canoe), 207
Nessmuk (George Washington Sears),
    207, 207, *208*
Netsilingmiut, *12*, 134

Netsilingmiut kayak, *128*, *129*, 131
New Brunswick Government, 188, 189
New France, 28, 29, *30*, 32, 35, 42
New North West Company, 36
New Voyages to North America, 1703, *28*
New York City, 224, 246
New York State. *See* Adirondack region
New York Times, The, 220
newspaper canoe, *249*
Nicolas, Abbé Louis, *30*
Nishga'a, *12*, 76, 89
No. 3 Nautilus, 219
Nootka, 76. *See also* Nuu-chah-nulth
    peoples
Nootkan canoes, *82*, *83*, 82–86, 87, 103,
    105, 111, 115
    decorative painting, 118
    influence of umiak on, *98*
    voyaging canoe, *117*
Nootkan sealer, *106*, *107*
Nor'Westers, 36, 38
North Alaska kayaks and umiaks, 131,
    141, 155, 156
North Alaskan Eskimo, 139
North America, 15, 16, 17, 23, 240
    frontiers, 25, 28
    hunting cultures, 18–19
    maps, *12–13*, *14*, *24–25*, *160*, *161*
North American Indian, The, *131*
North American Indigenous Games, 109,
    110
North Baffin Island kayak, 130–31
North canoes, *29*, *33*, *42*, 45
    fiberglass, *236*, *237*
    photos of, *52*, *242*
    size of, *41*, 43
North Greenland kayak, 128
North West Company, *29*, 32, 44, 45, 65,
    216
    and Canadian fur trade, *35*, 36, 38, 39
North West Mounted Police, 32, *183*
North Woods, 198
North-Alaskan-style kayak, *131*
northeast coast of North America, map,
    161
northeastern states, 196–97, 205
Northern Baffin Island kayak, *128*
Northern canoes, 76, 88–90, *89*, 100,
    103, *104*, 111, 115, 213
    decorative painting, 118
    influence of Coast Salish canoe, 87
    photos of, *75*, *93*, *100*, *111*, *113*, *114*,
        116
    replacement of Head canoes, 92
    vs. other canoes, 88, 89, 91, 92

Northern ceremonial canoes, *89*, 90–91
Northern Forest, *196*, 196
northwest Canada, light craft of, 65–69
Northwest Coast dugouts, 74–96
    design influence, 81–82
    styles of, 81–95
    value of to Native societies, 78–80
Northwest Coast Native peoples, 75–76, 78, 79, 80
Northwest Territories, and canoe building rediscovery, 67
Norton Sound umiaks, 156
Nunivak Island kayak, *133*
Nuu-chah-nulth peoples, *12*, 75–76, 79, 82, 87
    and Nootkan canoes, 82–86
Nuxalk canoes, 82, 89, *114*
Nuxalk peoples, *12*, 76
Nuytten, Phil, 100

O

O'Neill, John J., *128*
oak, 121, 164
oars, 118, *154*, 174, *198*. See also paddles
ocean-going canoes, 20, 87
Odawa peoples, 17, 21
Ohio Valley, 34, 35
Ojibwa birchbark canoe, *21*
Ojibwa Encampment, *18*
Ojibwa peoples, *13*, 21, *22*, 43, 56
Okanagan Valley, British Columbia, *230*
Old Town (Maine), 180, 183, 184, 205
Old Town Canoe Company, 183, 184, *187*, 208, 210
Olympics, *233*, 234, *235*, *236*, 236
Ontario Canoe Company, *173*, 174, 176, 177, 224, *225*, *234*
Oowekeno, 76, 89
open canoes, 177, 204, *219*, 229, 230, 236. See also Canadian canoes
Orellana, *247*, 248
Ottawa Canoe Club, 231
Ottawa River, 212, 213
otter, *92*, 133
Out of the Mist: Treasures of the Nuu-chah-nulth Chiefs, 81
Outboard Marine Corporation, 249
outboard motors, 149, 209
outboard runabouts, 187, 188
Outing Magazine, 204, 222, 240
outwales, 192
Oyukuluk, Andrew, 121, *122*
Ozette village, 77, 79

P

Pacific Eskimo kayak, 131–32
Paddle to Seattle event, 95
paddles, *126*, *219*, 227, *239*
    double-blade paddles, *126*, *136*, 215, *218*, *219*, 221, 233
    single-blade paddles, *130*, *218*, *219*, 221, 227, 228
paddling,
    competitive, in Canada, 185, 186
    positions for, 225, *226*, 227
    whitewater, 236
paddling canoes, 219, 223
paddling races, 225, 226, 227. See also canoe sport
paper birch trees. See birch trees
paper canoe, 203
Passamaquoddy canoes, *48*, 51
Passamaquoddy peoples, 20, 49
patching, 113–15, 126
patent drawings, *169*, *181*, *184*
patents, 169, *171*, 172, 184
Path of the Paddle, 184
Payne dugout, *164*, *165*, 244, *245*
Payne, Jacob, 244
Payne, William Alfred, *164*, *165*, 244
Peabody and Essex Museum, 240
peace treaties, *30*, 32, 35
peanuts, 225, 231
Pearl, 219
Peary Land umiak, 155, *156*, *157*
Pecowsic, 224
Pellissey, George, *67*
Penobscot River, 20, 180, 195, 205, 211
Perdita I and II, 216
Peterborough, 19, 163, 218
Peterborough Boating Club, *217*, 220
Peterborough Canoe Company, 168, *173*, *175*, 177, *178*, 185, 188
    and Canadian Watercraft, 186–87
    cedar-canvas canoe, *180–81*
patent infringement, 184
Peterborough canoes, *165*, 169, *171*, 178, *179*, 183, 222
Peterborough Examiner, The, 177
Peterborough Regatta, 165
Peterson, H.C., *127*, 140, 146, 150, 151, 157
petroglyphs, *17*
Phillips, Walter, *43*
pine bark, 23, 69
Pine Bluff camp, 183
pinned oars, *198*
pitching, 58, 73

planked boats, 94
planking, 52, 58, 68, 191, 198, *198*
    plank-on-frame boats, 195, 198
poling, 50
Polish Starlight Futura model, *236*
polyethylene canoe, 210
Pontiac, 32–33, 40
Port Hardy High School, *110*
portaging, *41*, *43*, 50, 53, 213
potlatches, 85, 91
Pov, Joni, *127*
power tools, 97, 111, 113, 114, 115
Powers, Cecil, 235
Price, Wayne, *93*
Prince Albert Edward, 45, *52*, 165, 212, *243*
Prince Andrew, *188*
Prince Charles, *188*
Prince of Wales Northern Heritage Centre, *67*, 67, 70
Princess canoe, photo of, *202*
Princess Diana, *188*
Princess Elizabeth, *188*
Prospector canoe, *184*
Puget Sound Salish, 75, 87
Punuk Culture, 151
put-put, 97

Q

Qajaq: Kayaks of Siberia and Alaska, 126, 127
Qamanirq, Simon, 121, *122*
Quatsino, *103*, *111*
Quatsino Band canoe, *110*
Quebec, *52*
Quebec, fur traders after 1760, 35
Queen Charlotte Islands, *74*, 76, *244*. See also Haida Gwaii
Queen Mary, *188*

R

R. Chestnut and Sons, 183, 184, 185, 186. See also Chestnut Canoe Company
Rabesca, Elizabeth, 70
Rabesca, Paul, 70, *73*
races,
    singles, 226, *227*, 227, 230, 233, 235, *236*
    for decked canoes, 230
    fours, *227*, 226, 233, 235
    paddling, 225, 226, 227, 230
    tandem, 227, 230, 233, 235

kayak, 235
umiak, 149
war canoe, *225*, *228*, 231, 233
    racing, 235. See also canoe sport
canoes, 94–95, 98, *104–105*, 211, *246*
    dugouts, 165
    stroke, "high kneel" position, *226*
    effect on canoe design, 204
    war canoes, *229*, *230*, *231*
racing canoes, 227
Radix centerboard, *201*, 234
Rae-Edzo, 70
railway, 40, *43*, 45, 204
Rapid Lake canoe, *23*
Rasmussen, Knud, 126, 136, 137
Record Trophy, 226
recreational canoeing, 183, 185, *186*, 187, 195–211
red cedar, 76, 91, 101, 117
Red Feather canoes, *174*
redwood, 101
regattas, *165*, 165, 212, 213, 216, 217, 218
Reid, Bill, 91, *97*, 103, *106*
Reid, George Agnew, *28*
reindeer. See caribou
religion, 18, 23, 29, 73, 214
Remington, Frederic, *201*
reservation lands, 93
Return of the War Party, 77
rib shaping, St. Francis canoes, 54
rib-and-batten, *53*, 218
rib-and-plank construction, 47, 51, 52, 53, 54, 57, 58
ribs, 51, 63, 128, *142*
Rice Lake (Ontario), 164, *170*, 220
Rice Lake Indian Band, 165
Rice Lake Regatta, *165*, 165
Rice Laker, 219
Richardson, Harold, 188
Rideau Canoe Club, *235*
Riel, Louis, 40
rigging, 118
River canoes, 82, *82*, 111, 113
river systems in North America, 16, *24–25*, 28
Riverin, Denis, 45
Rob Roy, 200, 204, *214*, 214, 215, 219
Rob Roy Number Five, 215
Rob Roy On The Jordan, 215
Robertson, J.R., 208
Rockefeller, Anne and Avery, *197*
rockers, *51*, 56, *57*, 57, 113, *142*
Rogers, James Zacheus (J.Z), *173*, 173–74, 177

rolling logs, 112–13
root-and-batten, 53, 58
roots, 71, 140. *See also* spruce roots
rope, 115, 117, *123*
rot, center, *103*, 109
roughing-in, 112
routes, canoe, 43
rowboats, 94
rowing, 216, 217. *See also* canoe sport
rowlocks, *88*
Royal British Columbia Museum, 90
Royal Canoe Club, 215, 216, 221, 223
royal canoes, *188*, *243*
Royal Ontario Museum, 121, *122*, 248
rudders, 118
Ruggles, George, 203
runabouts, cedar-strip outboard, 187, 188
Rupert Fort, 44
Rushton, Henry, 224
Rushton, J.H, 198, *201*, *203*, 203, *204*
    canoes of, *201*, *202*, 204, *206*, 207,
    208, 209, 210

S

safety line, 109
Saguenay River area, *22*, 56
Sahnteeng canoe, 248, *249*
sailing canoes, 174, 204, 219, 223
Sailing Trophy Race, 224, 226
sails, 118, 174
Sairy Gamp, 208
Saker, Warren, 234
Salish. *See also* Coast Salish
Salish canoes, 23, *104–105*, 111, 118, *246*
Salish peoples, 247
Salish racing canoe, *246*
Salish water bucket, *75*
Salteaux, 21, *243*. *See also* Ojibwa peoples
sampan style, 156
sandpapers, 115
Saqqaq Culture site, 127
Sauvé, Michel, 226
scarfs, *83*, *84*, *142*
Scots, 36
Scribner's Monthly, 195
sculptures, Inuit, *127*
sea-going canoes, 20, 75, 91
sea mammal hunting, *123*, *128*, *133*, 135
seal (animal), 92, 145, 146
seal (stamp) of the *Conseil souverain*, *32*
seal-hunting canoes, 85, *106*, *107*
seal oil, 151
sealskin, 67, 125, 146
    clothing, *134*, *135*

coverings, 126, 145
    floats, 85, *123*, 135, *136*
    rope, *122*, 122, *123*
seams, 58, 73
Searle & Sons, 215
Sears, George Washington ("Nessmuk"),
    207, 207
Seattle, *84*
Second World War, 187–89, 210, 234,
    235
sectional canoe, *182*
seine boats, 94
Seine River, 91
semi-lunar knife, 125, 147
settler dugouts, 164
sewing, 53, 125, 147
sewn-plank canoe, *239*
Shadow, 219
Shadow canoe model, 195
Shakes, Chief, 80, *90*
Sharp, Minnie Bell, 240
sheathing, 51, 54, 58, 62, 68, 69, 72
sheer, 109, 111
sheer line, 128
Sheldon Museum, 91
shell, *219*. *See also* peanuts
shiplap joint, 173
Shooting Star, 165
Shooting the Rapids, 33
Shovelnose canoes, *105*
Siglit umiaks, 142, 144
Simonds, Merilyn, *179*
Simpson, Sir George, 39, 45, *45*
sinew, 115
single-blade events, *227*, 230, 233
single-blade paddles, *130*, *218*, *219*, 221,
    227, 228
single-strake canoes, 215, 222
Sioux, 22, *248*
Sitka National Park, *93*
Sitka spruce, 76, 91, *96*, *97*, 101, 111
*Skin Boats of Saint Lawrence Island, Alaska,
    The*, 147, 153
Skinboats of Greenland, 127, 140, 146,
    150, 151, 157
skins. *See* animal hides; names of indi-
    vidual animals
Slavey canoes, 22, *65*
Slavey peoples, *12*, 22, 68
sliding seat, *223*, 224
slope. *See* cant
Smithsonian Institution, 19, 80, *90*, 208,
    241
snout, on Munka and Nootkan canoes,
    83, 86

solid building form, *166*, 166–67, 179,
    180–81, 206
Sonaxaat, Chief, *89*
Song of the Paddle, 184
South Alaska umiak, 154
South Pacific, double outrigger, 247
Southern canoes, 103, *106*, 111, 112. *See
    also* Nootkan canoes
Spanish cedar, 176, 226
Spencer, Robert F., 139
Spirit of Haida Gwaii, The, 97
splash guards, 68
splints, 60, 62
split bow. *See* bifid bow
sponsons, *184*, 208
Spoon canoe, *81*, 82, 111
Sport Canada, 235
sports (tourists), 182, 183, 198, *199*, 200
sports, canoe. *See* canoe sport
Sprague, Herbert M., 203
spreader sticks, 115, 116
spreading, 109, 115–17
spritsails *117*, 118, *150*
spruce, 49, 58, 71, *79*, 91. *See also* Sitka
    spruce
spruce bark, 21–22, 23, 69, 197
spruce bark boats and canoes, 22, 197
Spruce canoe, 91, 92. *See also* Head canoe
spruce gum, 63, 73
spruce roots, 43, 58, 61, 62, 63, 68
St. Croix River, 195
St. Francis canoes, 54–55
St. Francis people (Abenaki), *13*, 20, 21,
    53
St. Lambert Boating Club, 234
St. Lawrence–Great Lakes, 16, 29
St. Lawrence Island umiaks, 147, 155
St. Lawrence River, 28, 196
St. Lawrence Valley, 17, 43, 45
St. Louis Club, *228*
St.-Jean Boat Club, 217
stanchions, 121, 123
Starkell, Dana, *247*, 248
Starkell, Don, *247*, 248
Starlight Futura 2000, *236*
Stave Island, 224, 226
steaming, 76, *79*, 80, 115, *116*, 116–17,
    206
Steele, Ian K., 33
stem-pieces, 63, 69
stems, 52, 58, 68, 190, 192, *199*
Stephens, W.P., 201, 202, 203, 204, 229,
    230
Stephenson and Craigie planing mill,
    168

Stephenson, John, 165, 166, *167*, 168,
    171–73, 178, 218
Stephenson's Longitudinal Rib Canoe,
    172, 172
Stephenson's Rib Boat, *171*
stern-block, of Arctic Bay kayak frame,
    122
stitching, 58, 61, 125. *See also* sewing
Stoddard, Seneca Ray, 201, *204*
Stony Lake, 185, 221
Story of a Tlingit Community, The, 92
Strickland, George, 164, 165, 168, 177,
    217
Strickland, Henry Thomas, 165, 218
Strickland, Robert A., 177, 217
Strickland, Sam, 164, 165, *167*, 217
stringers, 68, 73, *140*, *143*, 143
sturgeon-nosed canoes, 20, 23, 69, *245*
Sugar Island, 233
Sunnyside Beach, 176
Sunnyside Cruiser, 175
Sunock River umiak, *152*
support blocks, 111
Suttles, Wayne, 86

T

Tait, Arthur Fitzwilliam (A.F.),198, *199*
Talon, Jean, *32*
Tanana peoples, 22, 68
tandem events, 230, 233
Taseralik, 151
Tebb, Arthur, *175*, 177
tenon, 142
test hole, *101*
Tête de Boule, 21, 43
Thompson, David, 38
Thomson, Tom, *185*
Thoreau, Henry David, 50, 51
Thorpe, Thomas Bangs, 199
Thousand Islands, 204
*Thousand Miles in the Rob Roy Canoe on
    Rivers and Lakes of Europe, A*, 200,
    215
throwing board, 135
Thule Culture, 144, 150, 152
Thunderbird, 114
thwarts, 62, *66*, 73, 117
thwarts pairs, 54
Tilikum, 85
Tlingit canoes and dugouts, *87*, 89, 90,
    91, 92, *110*, *112*
Tlingit Indians, The, 86, 89
Tlingit peoples, *12*, 76, 86, 90
tongue-and-groove, 173

tools, 59, 73, 97, 98, *103*, 111, *112. See also* names of individual tools
top rail, in Mi'kmaq canoe construction, 53
Toronto, 176, 216
Toronto Balmy Beach Club, 234
Toronto Canoe Club, *219*, 220, *220*, *222*, 224, 231, 233
Toronto Canoe Company, 226
Toronto Islands, 176, *227*
Toronto Mail, The, 220, 221
Torrance, Alexander, 226
toy canoes, 21
trade, 17, 29, 39, 42, 49, 66. *See also* fur trade
trade bark, *23*, 44
trading posts, *36*, 42, 44
Travels in North America, 197
Travels through the States of North America, 45
Treaty of Utrecht, 39
trees, 79, *101. See also* names of individual trees
Tribal Journey voyages, *109*, 100, *110*, 118
Trois Rivières, 42, 45
Tsimshian canoes, 89, *115, 116*
Tsimshian peoples, *12*, 90
tumblehome, *49*, 50, 51, 53, *113*
tumpline, 54
Tyson, Robert, *220*, 220, 221, 222

U

Ugwamalis, 118, 119
ulu, 125, 147
umiaks, *98*, 139–57, 241
    angyapik, 140, *143, 144*
    building, 139–57
    covering, 66, 145–49
    development of, 152–57
    framework construction, 140, 142–45
    and hunting, 139–40
    Peary Land, 142, 143, 155
    performance and use, 149–52
    sizes, 139, 156, 157
United States. *See also* Adirondacks, northeastern states
    American West, 33–35
    fur trade, *24–25*, 35
    northeastern states, 196–97, 205
    Olympic Games and, *235*
Unk-ta-hee, 224, *225*, 229

V

Valois Boating Club regatta medal, *222*
Van Dusen Eagle II, *235*
Van Norstrand, James, 100
Vancouver, Captain George, 79
Vaux, Boyer, 222
de Véniard, Etienne, 35
Venturesome Voyages of Captain Voss, The, 85
Vesper, 224
Vesper Canoe Club, *223*
Vesper model decked canoe, *201*
Vickers, Roy, 100
Victoria Island, 212
Voss, Captain John Claus, 85
Voyage of the Paper Canoe, From Quebec to the Gulf, The, 201
Voyage round the World in the Years 1803, 4, 5 & 6, A, 133
voyageurs, 35, *38*, 212, 213
    Iroquois, 45, 216
    life and work of, 38, *39, 41*
Voyageurs at Dawn, 39
voyaging canoes, *38, 40, 41, 43*, 42–45, *117*

W

Walker, Walter, *176, 188*, 190, *190–193*
Wallace, Thomas Henry, 203, 220
walnut, 164
walrus hide, 67, 145, 147–48
walrus, kayaks and, 136–37
Wamiss, Stan, *103, 111*
War Canoe League, 232
war canoes, *77*, 86, 204, *225. See also* Munka canoes
    races and racing, *227, 228, 229*, 231, 233
War of 1812, 33
warfare, 32, 34–35, 151–52
Warpaths, 32, 33
water, 15, 16, 17
Water Transport: Origin and Early Evolution, 152
waterline, 87, 89, *106*
waterproof stitching 125
waterproofing canvas, 206
water-pushers, 85
Waterwalker, 184
Wave Eater (Lootaas), 91, *102*, 103
weapons, hunting, *123, 129*, 135
Webber, Alika, 246, 247
wedges, 48, *79*

Wee Lassie, 208
Weld, Isaac, 45
Weller, H.B., 220
Weller, J.L., 222, 223
Wendat Nation, 45
West Alaska umiak, *148*, 155
West Coast canoe, model, *98–99*
West Greenland kayak, *122*
West Greenland umiaks, *154*, 157
Western Canoeing Inc., 100
western Cree, 20, 56
whale hunting, 84–85, 133–34, 135, 139–40
    canoes and, 84, *106*
    dugouts and, 23
    materials for, *123*
    as a sacred affair, 136–37
    umiaks and, 139, 151, 154
whaling. *See* whale hunting
whaling canoes, *99*
whaling umiaks, *141*, 156
white birch trees, 16, 47, 60, 197. *See also* birch trees
white birchbark. *See* birchbark
white cedar, 48, 52, 57, 58
White, E.M., 183, 209
White Mountains, New Hampshire, 195
White, Richard, 30
whitewater sports, 236
Wickett, Alfred E., 183, 208
wide-board canoes, *163, 174*, 175, 177
wide-board-and-batten canoes, 168, *170*, 170, 190–93
Willsborough Point, 226
Wilson, Robert F., 234
Winnipeg River, 248, *249*
Wipper, Kirk, *239, 243*, 243–49
Woman Carrying Canoe, 189
women
    and canoe sport, 236, *227*
    role in building Native craft, 43, 71, 124
women's boat. *See* umiak
wood, 123, 126. *See also* names of individual types of wood
wood, green 71, 72
wood-canvas canoes, 178, 182, 205, *206*, 206, 210
wooden canoes, 168, *176*, 176–78, *183*, 218
wooden canoes, rib-and-batten, 218
Woodstock (New Brunswick), 240
work boats, 97, 179, 186
World Canoe Championships, 216, *235*, 236

World Wars. *See* First World War, Second World War
Wrangell canoes, 90, 91
Wrangell Museum, 91
Wulsin, Lucien, *217*

X

<u>X</u>*oots Yakw, 90*, 90
XY Company, 36, 45

Y

yachting, 216
Yakutat canoe, *106, 107*
Yellowknife peoples, *12*, 22
yew, *79*, 118
YMCA, 243, 244, *249*
Yonkers Canoe Club, 224
York boats, *43*, 44, 45, *68*
Young, Matt, 217

Z

Zimmerly, David, 126, 132
Zoe, John B., 67